Stewards of Democracy

New Perspectives on Law, Culture, and Society

ROBERT W. GORDON AND MARGARET JANE RADIN, SERIES EDITORS

Stewards of Democracy

Law as a Public Profession

PAUL D. CARRINGTON

Westview Press
A Member of the Perseus Books Group

Photo Credits
Thomas Cooley: Courtesy of Bentley Historical Library, University of Michigan
Louis D. Brandeis: Courtesy of Princeton University Press
Ernst Freund: Courtesy of University of Chicago
Learned Hand: Courtesy of the Hand Family
Byron White: Courtesy of AP World Wide Photos

New Perspectives on Law, Culture, and Society

Published in 1999 in the United States of America by Westview Press, 5500 Central Avenue, Boulder, Colorado 80301-2877, and in the United Kingdom by Westview Press, 12 Hid's Copse Road, Cumnor Hill, Oxford OX2 9JJ

Find us on the World Wide Web at www.westviewpress.com

Library of Congress Cataloging-in-Publication Data
Carrington, Paul D., 1931–
    Stewards of democracy : law as a public profession / Paul D. Carrington.
        p. cm. — (New perspectives on law, culture, and society)
    Includes bibliographical references and index.
    ISBN 0-8133-6832-4
    1. Law—United States—History.   2. Lawyers—United States—
Biography.   I. Title.   II. Series.
KF352.C33   1999
349.73—dc21   99-20269
                                                                          CIP

The paper used in this publication meets the requirements of the American National Standard for Permanence of Paper for Printed Library Materials Z39.48-1984.

10   9   8   7   6   5   4   3   2   1

For Bessie
My partner in a More Perfect Union,
Who Insures Domestic Tranquility,
Promotes the General Welfare,
and Secures Blessings to Our Posterity

Contents

Preface and Acknowledgments

For some time, I have been recording in diverse articles the history of university legal education in America. While lawyers have at times been admired for their ability to think about a thing to the exclusion of other things to which the object of their attention is inextricably related, I have been unable to keep the focus on university law schools to the exclusion of the professional context in which they function. Law schools are not only parts of universities, but also of the legal profession that they share with courts and other institutions of government, which, in turn, are parts of a larger social and political order. Accordingly, my work in this field has inevitably expanded to become an account of the role of lawyers in American political history, with special attention given to those who have participated in the education of novitiates. Thus, in my articles, I have recorded many stories of the political roles and adventures of law teachers, judges, and other lawyers.

This book was generated by that larger enterprise. It expresses a theme revealed to me by some of the stories I have been recounting, a theme that I find inspiring even if controversial. It is presented to judges, law teachers, lawyers, and especially to students envisioning careers in law whom I hope to infect with my enthusiasm for ideas not presently in vogue.

The larger enterprise, which may some day be completed, has been supported by the Simon Guggenheim Foundation. It has also been supported by the E. T. Bost Fund of Cannon Trust III and the Duke University School of Law. An early draft of part of this work was prepared under the roof of the Rockefeller Foundation. I am grateful to Guggenheim and Rockefeller, as well as the Duke University School of Law and its Bost Fund, for that support. Also, lectureships at the law schools of the Universities of Alabama and Kansas afforded stimulating opportunities to bring together some of the material in the later chapters, and I am grateful to those institutions for their help.

This work is also a secondary product of earlier efforts sustained by other benefactors. My earliest work on legal education during 1969–1971 was done under the auspices of the Association of American Law Schools and was funded by the Ford Foundation; traces of that work abide in chapter 19. My earliest work on the federal judiciary during 1966–1968 was funded by the American Bar Foundation; ideas formed then reappear in chapters 6 and 17. Other benefactors and supporters of my work on that subject include the Cook Fund of the University of Michigan Law School, the United States Law Enforcement Assistance Administration, and the Walter E. Meyer Fund of Columbia University.

In addition, I also owe a debt to the voters of Ann Arbor, Michigan, who kindly afforded me clinical experience in local government during 1970–1973 as an elected trustee of their public schools and to the Trustees of Duke University, who afforded me pertinent experience as the dean of their law school (1978–1988). In that vein, I should also thank the hundreds of judges, lawyers, and law professors with whom it has been my privilege to work over the last forty years. Despite the misgivings expressed here about our collective direction, my acquaintance with them has ever been an inspiration.

Some of the material in this book has been published in the *American Journal of Legal History, Law and Social Inquiry,* and the *Alabama, Duke, Iowa, Kansas,* and *Stanford Law Reviews.* I am indebted to those publications for editorial assistance and for permission to use my own material here. Related articles have appeared in the *Cardozo, Florida, Kansas, Mercer, Northwestern, Pittsburgh, Toledo,* and *Utah Law Reviews, Constitutional Commentary,* and the *Journal of Legal Education.* I am indebted to each of these publications for editorial assistance indirectly reflected in this work.

Two professional historians who kindly encouraged my amateurism in their field were Alan Jones and the late Willard Hurst. Robert Gordon and John Henry Schlegel, also real historians, made especially heavy and helpful comments on an earlier draft. I am also grateful to Roger Cramton, David Currie, Dan Farber, Paul Haagen, Jeff O'Connell, Sallyanne Payton, Jeff Powell, Terry Sandalow, and the late Preble Stolz for other helpful comments on partial earlier drafts. The Duke and Michigan law library staffs have been very helpful, especially Margaret Leary and Janet Sinder, as were the staff of the Bentley Library in Ann Arbor. Clare Fried Drake, Laura Kelley, Erika King, Traci Jones, Paul Rozelle, Terry Ryan, John Shepherd, and James Vaughan helped with the references and provided editorial assistance. Indispensable secretarial services were provided by Sandi Perkins, June Hubbard, and Ann McCloskey.

Paul D. Carrington
Durham, North Carolina

Thomas Cooley, c. 1886

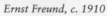

Louis D. Brandeis, c. 1910   *Ernst Freund, c. 1910*   *Learned Hand, c. 1910*

Byron White, c. 1946

Stewards of Democracy

1

An Embattled Faith

This work is an affirmation. Like the farmer affirming to a skeptic his faith in Holy Baptism, I not only believe in democratic law, I have seen it done. My faith is redeemed when lawyers and judges subordinate their own political preferences to those expressed by the institutions of representative self-government. Although the precise demands of this professional duty are often difficult to discern with confidence, frequently even more difficult to perform, and sometimes thankless, the duty is not illusory. I have seen it performed.

My vision of the role of the profession was expressed metaphorically by Alexis de Tocqueville when he proclaimed a resemblance between the American legal profession and a feudal aristocracy.[1] When he made that comparison, he was speaking not of lawyers' status or entitlements, but of their role in mediating between the ruling democratic majority and the monied class or other minorities who may at times be found in opposition to the majority. Like the aristocracy, the democratic legal profession served to stabilize an otherwise fragile social order.

De Tocqueville's conception of the profession, if not the comparison he made, was widely shared among members of the revolutionary generation, some of whom created higher education in law in early American colleges in the hope of nurturing lawyers who would be aware of that public responsibility. George Wythe (1720–1803), the founder of higher education in law (and law teacher to Thomas Jefferson, John Marshall, and Henry Clay), is only the clearest example.[2]

The professional role the early legal educators strove to establish was analyzed and elaborated in the 1830s by Francis Lieber (1798–1872),[3] de Tocqueville's principal American informant. He published his *Political Ethics* in 1837 and his *Legal and Political Hermeneutics* in 1838; together, these works elaborate the professional morality that is the theme of this book. Lieber encapsulated his teaching in the phrase: "No rights, no duties; no duties, no rights."[4] My purpose in writing this book is to illustrate the performance by later exemplars of the role earlier exemplified by Wythe, then defined by de Tocqueville, and elaborated by Lieber.

Among Lieber's many readers was Thomas McIntyre Cooley (1824–1898), an exemplary "aristocrat" in the sense in which de Tocqueville meant that term. Much of this book is devoted to an examination of his career, because it has four dimensions and so elegantly links early American law judging, legal scholarship, and teaching about law to the twentieth century. I also briefly examine the careers of four twentieth-century exemplars.

As a judge and legal scholar, Cooley regarded the Republic as a client whose instructions, given in the form of legislation enacted by elected representatives, ought be obeyed as best they could be understood, even if ill-advised, unless they were in conflict with express constitutional protections of private or group interests interpreted to conform to the common understanding of their meanings. In short, he strove to facilitate constitutional *self*-government even if that might require him to perpetuate policies with which he disagreed. He thus, with few lapses, practiced the political and legal ethics professed by Lieber. Also featured in this account are Louis Brandeis (1856–1941), Ernst Freund (1864–1932), Learned Hand (1872–1961), and Byron White (b. 1917). All were persons such as Felix Frankfurter described: "depositories of law, who by their disciplined training and character and by withdrawal from the usual temptations of private interest [could] reasonably be expected [by citizens] to be as free, impartial, and independent as the lot of humanity will admit."[5]

All were, in the senses enumerated by Anthony Kronman, Aristotelians:[6] They deemed experience, not reason or arcane learning, to be the source of legal and political wisdom; they did not aspire to geometric precision in their professional discipline; and the attainments to which they aspired were those of character more than intellect. Indeed, as judges, they were "independent" in the sense that they were invulnerable to bribery or intimidation, but never "independent" in the sense that they were free to act in disregard of legal texts and traditions. One of the temptations of private interest from which Frankfurter's "depositories of law" must withdraw is the temptation to impose their own moral and political preferences on their fellow citizens.

These men's deference was not animated by any maudlin belief in the wisdom of the common folk or those whom the voters select to make their law. Along with most of those to whom this work is addressed, they did not expect elected lawmakers to get things right and they despaired of direct democracy. But they were equally skeptical that those putting themselves forward as a decision-making class (a group that included themselves) possessed superior wisdom with respect to the large moral questions underlying many important legal issues touching the lives of citizens. Like the Founders, they perceived that representative government, for all its limitations, would over time best "insure domestic tranquility," "promote the general welfare," and "secure the blessings of liberty to ourselves and our posterity."[7]

There have, of course, long been American lawyers who claimed the prerogatives of aristocrats in the traditional sense not intended by de Tocqueville, were preoccupied with their status and entitlements, supposed that their moral judgment was superior to that of the unwashed, and regarded the public will merely as a thing to be overcome. Typical of such lawyers, Governeur Morris, a Founder, explained that the aim of the Constitution and the function of the judiciary and the profession of which it is a part was and should be "[t]o save the people from their most dangerous enemy: to save them from themselves."[8]

Among my exemplars, Cooley, Brandeis, and White were the products and voices of an agrarian society. Cooley was in his own time regarded as the most important American lawyer of the nineteenth century, save for John Marshall; Brandeis in the early decades of this century was equally esteemed. Despite their agrarian origins, these men adapted many of their democratic ideas and values to an industrial age and urged their co-professionals to do the same. Those ideas and values were shared by Freund, perhaps the most progressive of legal academics in the Progressive Era, and by Hand, perhaps the most esteemed American judge in the mid-twentieth century until his apparent apostasy in 1958 at the age of eighty-six. All of them professed democratic law as an instrument of mediation between those with much power over their fellow citizens and those with little.

The responsibilities of stewardship these professionals performed are in opposition to some tendencies of our post-industrial age. The opposing spirit of Governeur Morris abides and flourishes, not only among partners in the giant law firms of our day and among their clients, but also in the minds of many judges and professors, and in the commercial media that now dominate so much of our public discourse.

This opposition between the commitments of lawyers such as Cooley or Brandeis and those of many contemporary lawyers is manifested in at least three ways. First, there is endemic tension between the profession's democratic tradition represented by Cooley and the status and role of its most elevated members, the life-tenured federal judiciary. As Governeur Morris stated, the Supreme Court of the United States was conceived as a brake on self-government. Having scant accountability to citizens, almost since its creation it has gone beyond its role to obstruct policies made by those elected to express the popular will, often invoking one form or another of natural (i.e., unenacted) law that its members have found to be implied in the text of the Constitution. Until 1937, when the Court went beyond its role, it did so to protect the monied class. Since that time, its transgressions have been of a more heroic sort, but have been no less indifferent to the values of self-government.

Second, there is rising tension between the profession's democratic tradition, of which Cooley and his successors were a part, and the technocratic pretensions of a profession adorned in the increasingly costly academic credentials that became ascendant after 1890. The origin of that tension is illustrated here by contrasting Cooley with his close contemporary, Christopher Columbus Langdell (1826–1906), the Harvard Law School dean and prophet of pseudo-scientific formalism and credentialization in law. As legal education becomes ever more expensive and more responsive to the self-preoccupied demands of consumers, the distance between law schools and their democratic origin is extended.[9]

Third, there is rising tension between the profession's democratic tradition and the more extravagant intellectual pretensions of academic law emerging after 1900. The origin of that tension is presented here by contrasting Cooley with Oliver Wendell Holmes Jr. (1841–1935). While Holmes shared Cooley's estimate of the importance of judicial self-restraint, and was not an academic, but rather a man much engaged in the events of his time, he was, in his Olympian scorn of fellow citizens and his belief in the possibility of legal genius, a prophet of intellectual arrogance characteristic of the most elevated academic thought. That Olympian perspective is widely shared by postmodern judges, lawyers, and legal academics. It is manifested most clearly in the literary efforts of utopian legal theorists. Today, the most elegant academic work is increasingly written to be read only by other academics. Any hope of consequentiality for such work lies in the prospect of ambitious constitutional adjudication in courts having no accountability to the people, thus circumnavigating noisome democratic politics.

This book suggests a connection among these three tensions. The increasingly costly and pretentious structure of the contemporary university law school, the immodesty of much legal academic literature, and the indifference of the judiciary to the product of democratic political institutions may tend to reinforce one another. Their combined effect has been that American law in the last half-century has been increasingly disdainful of the expressed wishes and expectations of the citizens it purports to serve.

This observation about American law is consistent with the broader observations of modern American historians. Robert Wiebe, for example, has identified World War II as marking the general ascendancy to controlling power of what he denotes as the "national class," a ruling class including many lawyers and most judges and law teachers, and, of course, much of the media.[10] The "national class" of lawyers identifies itself by credentials, mostly academic credentials. Its members tend to lack connections to and sympathy for an increasingly alienated underclass who have ceased to see themselves as participants in government. Members of this "national class" are prone to disdain the messy moral compromises of elective politics, perhaps especially local politics, and hence envision constitutional adjudication as the appropriate means of resolving conflicts of moral import.

Thus, in our moment of prosperity and world domination, while we insist on the virtues of self-government in every corner of the globe, we are forgetting its value to ourselves. As perceptive foreign observers writing for *The Economist* in 1998 could see, American lawyers, judges, and even politicians are increasingly given to "ramming down the throats of voters policies which they have not endorsed,"[11] at the very moment that other Americans are wisely demanding the right to self-government for people in such distant places as Kosovo, Malaysia, and Iraq.[12] We are in too many respects, as Mary Ann Glendon has put it, a nation *under* lawyers.[13]

The reader will already have noted that all my primary exemplars are white males. The chief reason for this is that I am tracing a tradition antedating the prominence of women lawyers or lawyers of color. Among the thousands of lawyers who have performed the role of which I write, there are surely numerous women and persons of color, but none whose writings and biographies are sufficiently visible to sustain confidence that they belong in this account. I depend on the investigative work of others and make no claim to be "doing history" as a professional historian might.[14]

There are of course lawyers, some of whom are women or persons of color, who choose to regard themselves as "Outsiders," disowning the role assigned lawyers by de Tocqueville. Some Outsiders may describe themselves as "Cause Lawyers," devoting their careers to the advancement of a particular group or interest in opposition to majoritarian self-government.[15] They may, whether or not they wish to, be serving the public interest more effectively than most "Insiders" who profess the faith. But if they are not careful to avoid the moral arrogance so often associated with zealotry, they may be destructive of both the common interest and the special one they seek to advance. I have elsewhere suggested that Charles Sumner, the passionate abolitionist, may, in contrast to Lincoln, be an example of the counterproductive kind of Cause Lawyer.[16]

But this book is not about Cause Lawyers or Outsiders. It is addressed to those who presently think of themselves as Insiders, or those who aspire to that status. It would be gratification enough to attract a few of them to the professional role identified by my exemplars, to cause them to share the faith that democratic self-government is possible if those responsible for the Republic's law can acquire and maintain the requisite traits of character.

My faith is embattled, perhaps especially among Insiders. Given the advent of pollsters, electronic media, sound bites, and the resulting elevation of the manipulative arts, it is ever more difficult to believe that citizens have minds of their own, or for citizens to take their political responsibilities seriously. Moreover, in a time of self-absorption, and one of deepening class lines, the civic virtues extolled by Pericles seem ever more difficult to find and nurture. Yet in a world in which erratic absolutism and brutal chaos are the viable alternatives to self-government, a great deal depends on our ability to make government *by* the people work, and that is a mission for lawyers who are *of* the people, not over them.

2

A Celebration

Harvard celebrated its 250th anniversary in November 1886. It was therefore a time for self-praise in Cambridge.[1] Among the events fitting the occasion was the award of an honorary doctorate to Thomas McIntyre Cooley of Ann Arbor, Michigan.[2] Cooley was then the most respected lawyer in America and was among the most widely respected persons in American public life. Indeed, given that John Marshall had many critics, Cooley was perhaps the nineteenth-century American lawyer most esteemed by his contemporaries. Nothing could have been more appropriate than that he would be invited to honor Harvard with a ceremonial utterance.

Cooley had two years earlier retired from a quarter-century of service as the founding dean, esteemed teacher, and intellectual leader of a university law school in Ann Arbor that had for a time far surpassed Harvard in its ability to attract students.[3] His former students were so active in public life that they might also have surpassed Harvard's alumni in their service to the Republic.

In addition to his role as an educator, Cooley in 1865 had been elected to the Supreme Court of Michigan and had served that court for twenty years, many of them as Chief Justice, often as the court's intellectual leader.[4] His court had been regarded in the 1870s as possibly the ablest appellate court in America.[5] Its decisions were closely read even in Boston.[6] Many lawyers had favored, and some had sought, his appointment to the Supreme Court of the United States; on one occasion, a leading legal publication, the *Central Law Journal* of St. Louis, spoke of his qualifications for the Court as "transcendent."[7] The appointment was withheld, apparently because he was viewed by the barons of his Republican party as too independent.[8] In 1885 his judicial career had come to an end when he was defeated for re-election in a tide of Democratic votes.

Despite the distinction of his teaching and judicial careers, it was Cooley's professional legal writing that had won him the greatest fame. In 1868, he had published his *Constitutional Limitations*, a work recounting and comparing the interpretations of the constitutions of the states and of those few provisions of the antebellum federal constitution applicable to state governments. That work was still, in 1886, the most scholarly and most widely used American law book; it was then in its fifth edition. It was said that no other work had "been cited more freely or with a greater measure of commendation";[9] one reviewer may have expressed the prevailing opinion when he went so far as to say that

> it is impossible to exaggerate its merits. It is an ideal treatise, and not only a standard authority, but almost exclusively sovereign in its sphere. It is cited in every argument and opinion on the subjects of which it treats, and not only is the book authoritative as a digest of the law, but its author's opinions are regarded as almost conclusive.[10]

Cooley had also published, in 1873, a new edition of Joseph Story's *Commentaries on the Constitution of the United States*, adding to that dated but popular work an account of then-recent post-war amendments imposing new restraints on the powers of state governments.[11] In 1876, he had published a useful treatise on taxation[12] which, like its predecessors, analyzed judicial interpretations of constitutional provisions. He had published yet another treatise in 1879, on torts, a field then emerging from the interstices of common law pleading, a work in which he aptly described the role of an American common law court. And in 1880, he had published a short text, *The General Principles of Constitutional Law*, which by 1886 was required reading at the Harvard Law School for students enrolled in James Bradley Thayer's course in constitutional law.[13] While several of these works would be the object of later editions prepared by other hands, when he came to Cambridge Cooley had ceased his endeavors as a legal writer.[14]

Although after 1886 Cooley would no longer judge, teach, or (with one exception[15]) write law, his career as a lawyer was not at an end. He remained in demand as a speaker and as an author of articles in popular periodicals on public issues of the day having legal dimensions. He served as a neutral in the resolution of several disputes involving the railroad industry, then America's largest and most complex business. When the Interstate Commerce Act was approved in 1887, there was great concern over the selection of the commissioners to exercise the modest powers over railroads conferred on the new Interstate Commerce Commission. The aged Cooley had no interest in the appointment, but was importuned by President Cleveland to chair the Commission. Cleveland believed him to be perhaps the one person in America sufficiently disinterested to be trusted on all sides to give the embattled Commission a chance of useful service. Illness forced Cooley to leave the Commission in 1891, but his early leadership of that body provided significant guidance for the national, independent administrative agencies established in the decades to follow.

In 1893, the American Bar Association graced itself by electing Cooley its president. Over the course of the next century, the Supreme Court of the United States cited Cooley's writings frequently, almost certainly more than those of any other legal writer. But these later events only underscored the eminence that Cooley had already achieved by 1886, an eminence that Harvard was bound to acknowledge.

The award, appropriate though it was, caused a moment of tension. That tension signified changes in the American legal profession occurring at that moment. Those present honored both the declining agrarian-democratic aspirations or homely pretensions of nineteenth-century American law represented by Cooley and the rising technocratic aspirations or pretensions of the profession most clearly reflected in the emerging character of the Harvard Law School.

The year 1886 was a time when the resolution of the enduring conflict between democracy and professionalism was being re-ordered by the secondary and tertiary effects of industrialization. The resolution effected at that time seemingly fit the needs, or at least the tastes, of an industrializing society. The outcome was academization, an ardent embrace by the profession of academic credentials and the idea of intellectual meritocracy.

When receiving his degree, Cooley acknowledged this tension. He spoke briefly at a dinner in Hemenway Gymnasium, along with Justice Holmes, then of the Supreme Judicial Court of Massachusetts, and Dean Langdell. With appropriate modesty, Cooley saluted the Harvard Law School as an institution that had rendered great service to the nation and promised greater service in the future. But he spoke in terms unsettling to those present:

> [W]e fail to appreciate the dignity of our profession if we look for it either in profundity of learning or in forensic triumphs. Its reason for being must be found in the effective aid it renders to justice and in the sense that it gives of public security through its steady support of public order. These are commonplaces, but the strength of law lies in its commonplace character; and it becomes feeble and untrustworthy when it expresses something different from the common thoughts of men.[16]

That utterance stated a guiding premise of Cooley's career, a premise shaping the conduct of his law school, the character of his scholarship, his judicial behavior, his public comments on the political issues of his day, and his future leadership of the Interstate Commerce Commission. That premise was an axiom of American public law to many of those who professed and practiced it in the half-century preceding 1886.[17] Nevertheless, its assertion at Harvard almost surely offended his host, Christopher Columbus Langdell, whose novel case-method teaching had been celebrated earlier that day[18] and was on the verge of becoming a standard of a new professional class. In the hands of Langdell, the case method was the emblem of a technocratized profession, one committed primarily to the conduct of private affairs and the management of private relations through the use of expert knowledge of increasingly complex legal texts presumed to be incomprehensible to laypersons.

Cooley's remark also struck Justice Holmes with sufficient force that he was moved to respond to Cooley on another celebratory occasion at Northwestern University in 1902, four years after Cooley's death. On that occasion, Holmes called forth "the lightning of genius" to correct the failings of the "common thoughts of men."[19] In 1886, Holmes was known to those present not only as a local judge, but also as the author of *The Common Law*. He was destined for elevation to the Supreme Court of the United States, but remained relatively obscure until his canonization in the 1920s by some of the leaders of the newly emerging legal academy.[20] Then he came to overshadow Cooley and others as the most memorable lawyer of his time and as the intellectual patron of the newly emerging subprofession of academic law, a subprofession that over the following century drew its inspiration less from its public responsibility and more from its academic status.

Cooley spoke at Harvard not only as a late Jacksonian, but also as an early Progressive. His words not only were in keeping with the antecedent tradition established in the eighteenth century, but also foretold many of the thoughts and aspirations of a generation of twentieth-century reformers who inherited his professional morality. Thus, in the first half of the twentieth century, Langdell's reforms were in part appropriated by those sharing Cooley's perception that the primary mission of the legal profession is to provide stewardship for the institutions of democratic self-government. Cooley's professional morality was perpetuated in the careers of Progressive lawyers and judges such as Louis Brandeis, Ernst Freund, and Learned Hand, and would abide in the later careers of others such as Byron White.

3

The Brahmin Hosts

The differences between Cooley and those he met in Cambridge in November 1886 were, of course, not all attributable to the fact that Cooley's conception of his roles as teacher, judge, and scholar were formed in a pre-industrial society. There were large subcultural differences resulting from geographical distance as well as time. Cooley's remark was not only unsettling to his audience in Hemenway Gymnasium, but would have been so to many of their forebears who had given rise and impetus to Harvard University, its law school, the leadership of Dean Langdell, and the judicial career of Justice Holmes.

Harvard was then still a regional institution. It had been founded to train Puritan-Congregationalist ministers for the Massachusetts Bay colony and that purpose had been its defining mission into the nineteenth century.[1] Central to that Puritan faith was the dour Calvinist belief that most souls are doomed at birth. In the eighteenth century, the colony was still among the least tolerant places on Earth; Quakers were not allowed to set foot there and Baptists were driven into Rhode Island.[2] Some Puritans became merchants and ship owners; it was they who settled on Boston's Beacon Hill and lent support to Harvard.

Harvard's Puritan roots may account in some part for the fact that it was the one established college in America that did not in the years after the Revolution commence teaching law as moral preparation for public life; moral education was, to a true Puritan, unpromising, for no mere school could be expected to alter God's plan. Such moral teaching had, however, been established at William and Mary in 1779 and thereafter at Yale, Columbia, Princeton, Dartmouth, and numerous other institutions.[3] But when at last Harvard opened its Law School in 1817, it was not presented as a service to the people or the Republic, but as a program useful to students preparing themselves gainfully to serve private clients.

That initial venture failed to attract an adequate paying clientele and, in 1829, Harvard Law School was reorganized around the teaching of Joseph

Story, then a justice of the Supreme Court of the United States. It then pursued the vision of service to the national law pressed upon it by a Unitarian benefactor, Nathan Dane.[4] Story's "Dane Law School" was more in keeping with programs of legal education at other colleges established by such lawyers as Jefferson, Hamilton, Madison, and Clay and sustained by such teacher-judges as George Wythe, St. George Tucker, George Robertson, and Timothy Walker.

In Story's time, Harvard began to attract students from the South, but it was not until the arrival of Roscoe Pound in 1910[5] that the Law School appointed and retained a law teacher who was not native to New England. Until then, everyone having an enduring association with the Harvard Law School was decidedly a New Englander. The Puritanical Calvinism had been muted and secularized, but it was still a current running deep in the veins of the institution.

The muting had occurred in the first half of the nineteenth century. Beacon Hill and Harvard then became centers of an intellectual community of admirable richness and depth. In 1815, in something like a coup, the governing board of Harvard was taken over by Unitarians; the university then participated fully in the "flowering of New England." But New *England* it remained, and therefore it was not altogether American. In 1814, Massachusetts had refused to supply troops for "Mr. Madison's War" against England; Harvard honored Isaac Parker, the judge who had opined that the governor had no legal duty to respond to President Madison's call for help (and later appointed him Royall Professor of Law).[6] There was also in 1815 a convention at Hartford, Connecticut, attended by representatives of Massachusetts, some of whom wanted to discuss the possibility of a New England secession.[7] It may have been Emerson who observed that Europe still extended to the Alleghenies, for even in the middle of the nineteenth century, Boston was about as British as Edinburgh.

The relative isolation of Boston from the rest of America was in part a consequence of economic forces. The building of canals in the early decades of the nineteenth century had tied the West (the region beyond the Allegheny Mountains) to the ports of New York, Philadelphia, and Baltimore, leaving Boston, like Charleston, on an economic island, limited in its ability to participate in the spreading national economy and assured that its residents would be less inclined to share in the national identity forming chiefly in the West and in the major port cities. While New England's textile mills flourished, the movement of people, goods, and ideas across America was so latitudinal that its economy shrank in relation to those in the mid-Atlantic and western sections of the nation.

Perhaps the economic isolation stimulated, or at least sheltered, the haughty self-assurance of New Englanders. Even well-informed Bostonians were disinclined to notice events west of the Connecticut River. Their claim to cultural superiority was undoubted. Emerson put the matter bluntly. "I do not speak with any fondness," he said, "but the language of coldest history when I say that Boston commands attention as the town which was appointed in the destiny of nations to lead the civilization of North America."[8]

This self-assurance had a large moral dimension suited to the Puritan tradition of severe moral judgment such as that suffered by Nathaniel Hawthorne's memorable Hester Prynne. It seemed to be especially easy for Bostonians to detect the moral failings of others. This was most evident in the emergence of the abolition movement in Boston in antebellum years. There were emancipationists and abolitionists in the western states, too, and active underground railways as well. But there was an exceptional moral arrogance in the expressions of abolitionist sentiment by Bostonians such as Wendell Phillips, Lloyd Garrison, and Charles Sumner that was seldom equaled outside of Boston. Although residents of Beacon Hill had benefited unblushingly from the slave trade, many of the descendants of their slave-trading culture felt no compassion for the moral plight of Southern slaveowners; making no distinction between sin and sinners, they denounced a whole population as among the most morally degraded persons on earth, a feeling that was of course reciprocated. Harriet Martineau, an English visitor in the 1830s, was appalled by the livid hatred between these two groups of countrymen.[9]

This secular Calvinism had other dimensions than the demonization of the South; its success in the Civil War led its adherents to other reformist efforts premised on their moral and intellectual superiority. In the years following the Civil War, Boston became the center of the American Social Science Association.[10] Founded by former abolitionists, it became an organization of "gentry intellectuals" who aimed to employ social science as an engine of social reform. They would make America "an earthly paradise" by reforming our prisons, animating the poor to take better care of themselves, eliminating prostitution and intemperance, causing the construction of libraries and savings banks, and achieving a score of other triumphs of comparable dimension over the degraded persons populating the lower classes and the lesser regions of the nation. That association was near its zenith in 1886.

Moreover, the traditional smugness of Boston was reinforced by a secondary effect of industrialization on American society. Academic credentials, which had been of little value in antebellum America, were by 1886 in growing demand. The idea of division of labor seemed to promise the satisfaction of all human wants. Persons of talent and ambition sought to have their competencies certified, partly for economic reasons and partly for reasons of social status. Soon, that demand would give rise to a boom in higher education as universities became the factories of human capitalism.

Old professions would compete for academic ornamentation, and new ones would be established to meet the demand for professional status. No institution was better situated to respond to this demand than Harvard; not only was it the oldest college in North America, but it was draped in the "old-money" pretensions of Beacon Hill. On that account, Harvard was the ready center of the technocracy emerging in the legal profession in 1886.

Thus, when Cooley received his degree, Boston and Harvard were as self-assured as ever; their puritanism had been secularized, but it was alive and well, and even prospering. Their claim to status rested not on predestined moral worth, or on great fortunes such as those being amassed elsewhere, but on their intellectual desserts. Their superiority was in at least some measure real, for Emerson's hyperbole contained a kernel of truth. An exceptional number of highly literate and prudent persons resided on Beacon Hill and in its environs. The institution of slavery they despised, if not every individual caught in its web, merited their odium. The American Social Science Association had admirable aims and some useful, if still half-baked, ideas. And Boston was a hub, not only of New England, but of the flowering of higher education in America.

Langdell and Holmes manifested that flowering in different ways, and each can be contrasted with Cooley. Cooley can be seen as the prophet of Civic Virtue, of service to the Republic. Langdell may be seen as the prophet of Professional Competence and thus of credentialism in American legal education, soon to become the instrument of social and economic pretensions in the American bar. Holmes, in this locution, can be seen as the prophet of Philosophical Truth and thus of the intellectual pretensions of the emerging legal academy. Langdell and Holmes were not in these roles in league with one another; indeed, there was perhaps as much personal tension between Holmes and Langdell as between either of them and Cooley. It is fair to say that as Langdell was not given to philosophy, so Holmes was not given to legal technicality. What Cooley represented was a profession that consciously sought to express the moral values and emerging aspirations of a classless, self-governing people. In this, he and those who followed him embraced an utterance of Emerson, who was no less a New Englander than Langdell or Holmes: "I ask not for the great, the remote, the romantic; I embrace the common; I sit at the feet of the familiar, and low."[11] A profession with such a commitment was not a congenial venue for either Langdell or Holmes.

4

The Barnburner Persuasion

The culture from which Thomas Cooley emerged was in important respects a negative of Beacon Hill. He had come a long way to stand at the rostrum of honor in Hemenway Gymnasium that fall evening.

Four Cooley brothers left their father's Massachusetts farm in 1800 for the Genesee region of New York, an area that had been until a short time before that populated predominantly by Iroquois.[1] The Cooleys were among many immigrants to New York from New England. In 1808, Mortimer Cooley laid out his farm on a hill southwest of the town of Rochester, near the village of Attica. There, he was able to provide subsistence, but little more of material value, for his very large family. Thomas Cooley later recorded the lives of such pioneer farmers:

> A rude log cabin for a home and the bare necessaries of life for their families contented them while they were clearing with their hands; and the lessons of industry and economy would have been forced upon them by the situation even if they had not learned them before, as the most of them had. . . . [H]ard labor and the chills of fever incident to the clearing of a new country gave them sallow complexions and made them prematurely old; but in coming [west] they had calculated not so much upon their own immediate advantage as upon giving their children an opportunity "to grow up with the country;" and they accomplished all they had counted on if they could see that year by year their possessions increased in value and could rely with confidence upon giving their children the rudiments of education and a fair start in the world, and on being independent in their circumstances in their old age. Even though they could not supply their wants from their farms, they contracted few debts, but postponed purchases when they had nothing to barter for the articles they desired.[2]

Despite all this personal sacrifice, the social order created by men like Mortimer Cooley was reviled by socially elevated observers from the settled, Puritan realm east of the Hudson River, who perceived moral and religious degradation almost everywhere in western New York. While here and there he found a village resembling admirable old New England,[3] James

Kent, the chancellor of New York, "pronounced whole communities immoral."[4] Yale President Timothy Dwight toured the state and concluded:

> Together with a collection of discreet and virtuous people, there is sometimes [in upstate New York] an unhappy proportion of loose, lazy, shiftless, and unprincipled inhabitants. . . . Too ignorant . . . to discern in what the real respectability . . . consists, and too vicious willingly to adopt what is excellent . . . , they employ themselves in copying the fashions, follies, and vices of cities. To be first and excessive in fashions; to make a parade in the midst of poverty; to be pert; to gamble; to haunt taverns; to drink; to swear; to read newspapers; to talk on political subjects; to manage the affairs of the nation and neglect their own; to profess themselves infidels; to seem to know everything and plainly to care nothing about religion; to array themselves against its ministers, its friends, and its interests and to be *wiser in their own conceit than seven men who can render a reason* are strong features of the character of such men (italics in original).[5]

Even the more tolerant adherents of Thomas Jefferson found cause for objection in what they saw. The most popular American novel in the years when Mortimer Cooley was first breaking sod in Western New York was written in neighboring Pittsburgh by Hugh Henry Brackenridge, an ardently Jeffersonian lawyer and judge, and former Presbyterian minister, who had been among the early settlers in western Pennsylvania. His *Modern Chivalry*[6] was a satire ridiculing the ignorance and venality of his fellow pioneers. His antihero was a greedy, unlettered Irish immigrant who sought and received from the frontier citizenry unmerited advancements resulting inevitably in disgrace for himself or misery for the public. The idea that ordinary citizens unguided by wiser heads are capable of governing themselves and one another was depicted as quixotic.

A few years later, another Jeffersonian novelist, James Fenimore Cooper, returned home to upstate New York after an extended sojourn in Europe, where he had been boasting about the Republic,[7] to find cause for deep concern about its fate. Pleading with fellow citizens to regain the public virtue that had been manifest in the War for Independence,[8] Cooper's fiction depicted lawyers as self-seeking and cunning pettifoggers.[9] The antihero of his *Home as Found* was a status-hungry lawyer who is proud to be American, but has no idea of any obligations that this status might entail. In that work, Cooper expressed the fear that America was crashing[10] and decried the leveling process that was displacing the rules of social propriety.[11]

Perhaps in manifestation of the social conditions observed by Kent, Dwight, Brackenridge, and Cooper, upstate New York in the early decades of the nineteenth century was a center for religious revivalism. Mormonism emerged not far from Attica,[12] as did a dozen Protestant denominations now forgotten. A likely cause of this religious activity was a reaction of citizens against the moral and intellectual arrogance of the traditional Congregational and Presbyterian clergies, an arrogance reflected in the observations of Dwight and Brackenridge, both of whom were former ministers of those traditional Calvinist faiths. The Anti-Masonic movement also had its origins near Attica;[13] although associated with Whig rather than Democratic politics, it revealed a related hostility to a different form of moral pretension.

Among the most influential new faiths was the modified Puritanism of a revivalist, Charles Grandison Finney of Utica,[14] who in "plain and pungent" language[15] taught that damnation was not so predestined as traditional Puritans supposed, but could be avoided by firm acts of will resulting in a morally correct life.[16] Each soul, he taught, was responsible for his or her own moral fate, a religious doctrine closely fitting the politics of antislavery,[17] and bearing some resemblance to the teaching of Immanuel Kant[18] then in vogue on the continent of Europe, but unavailable in frontier New York. This spiritual independence was a logical extension of Protestant resistance to clerical dictates. And it was a better fit with the political sentiments of those who had experienced war waged in the name of the principles expressed in the Declaration of Independence than was the fatalism of Puritan New England.

The settlers of upstate New York were among the first to identify themselves as citizens of a nation as well as a state. People crossing the mountains, unlike those who remained in Massachusetts, mingled together with Irish and Germans and others to form a different consciousness. They expected their children to marry spouses of differing ancestries and move farther west. So it was that the Cooley brothers forsook their fealty to Massachusetts and replaced it with a sense of belonging to a much larger space, one of continental dimension.

Among the distinctive features of the settlers' emergent national culture was a widely shared preoccupation with law and politics that was a striking departure from antecedent Puritan traditions, a preoccupation persons such as Timothy Dwight found repugnant. The novelty of self-government called many to politics, while the unique bonding of politics to law effected by the Philadelphia Convention of 1787 elevated the visibility of legal institutions, all of them new or newly recognized as belonging to the people. The observations of such European travelers as Alexis de Tocqueville[19] and Harriet Martineau[20] merely confirmed the locals in their shared sense of themselves as a people devoted to law and politics. Thus, a joke of the time depicted two thirsty Americans meeting by chance in the Sahara; they promptly held an election. This preoccupation with politics did not reflect unbounded trust in the wisdom of the masses. Although, as de Tocqueville observed, their politicians, like those of later times, were fawning sycophants more given to groveling to the electorate than were the oiliest courtiers in Europe in their submission to monarchs,[21] democracy in America was political

Protestantism. It was favored less out of regard for the popular or conventional wisdom than out of disregard for the wisdom of those putting themselves forward as political or intellectual leaders or as religious or moral guardians.

There was thus a political and legal subtext to the revivalism celebrating everyman's responsibility for his own fate. Suspicion of the pretensions of "learned" professions was widespread among these citizen-revivalists. The causes of temperance, pacifism, extension of suffrage, prison reform, and women's rights, and especially opposition to slavery, which were keen among the struggling farmers of upstate New York, all gained support. Not many were prepared to follow William Lloyd Garrison[22] and dissolve the federal union to rid themselves of co-citizenship with despised slaveowners, nor were many yet prepared to wage a war over the issue, but absolute was their intention to rid their new Republic of the moral blight. Daniel Webster, although unmistakably a Whig serving the interests of bankers and industrialists, was in the 1830s and 1840s the premier spokesman for the views of these western agrarians on the issue of slavery.[23]

The political manifestation of this culture was first led by Governor, later President, Martin Van Buren; its adherents were sometimes known as Barnburners because it was said that they were willing to burn their barns to kill the rats residing in them.* Their favorite political writer was the editorialist William Leggett.[24] Leggett had been a seaman and poet before becoming theater critic and editorialist for the *Evening Post*, a newspaper he owned with the poet William Cullen Bryant. It was Leggett who stated the doctrine of Equal Rights as one requiring "free labor, free schools, free trade, and free speech." Free speech in this context centered on freedom of religious expression. Leggett resisted all forms of religious intolerance, perhaps especially anti-Catholicism, which was at that time and place the most common form of intolerance, being a reaction to Irish immigration.[25]

The Barnburners' views on matters of political economy were simple. Leggett voiced the position that government is inevitably and shamelessly committed to "charter-mongers and money-changers who choose to live in idleness by their wits rather than earn an honest livelihood."[26] Barnburners

---

*They called themselves the Equal Rights Party, a term I avoid as misleading to contemporary readers. The Whig press of the day referred to them as Locofocos. That term, also used to refer to recently invented friction matches, called attention to the sometimes riotous character of their meetings, which were on occasions calmed by turning off the gas lights. Although now often used by historians, I find it less agreeable and surely less descriptive to contemporary readers than "Barnburner," a term that appeared later but was applied to substantially the same people who constituted the Equal Rights Party. Schlesinger, *Age of Jackson*, 398; and see Rifkin, *William Leggett*.

often cited Jefferson's dictum that government should leave men "free to regulate their own pursuits of industry and improvement, and shall not take from the mouth of labor the bread that it has earned."[27] They placed second only to the Declaration of Independence[28] the 1830 message of Andrew Jackson accompanying his veto of the renewal of the charter of the Bank of the United States:

> It is to be regretted that the rich and powerful too often bend the acts of government to their selfish purposes. . . . [W]hen the laws undertake to add to [their] natural and just advantages artificial distinctions, to grant titles, gratuities and exclusive privileges, to make the rich richer and the potent more powerful, the humbler members of society—the farmers, mechanics, and laborers—who have neither the time nor the means of securing like favors to themselves, have a right to complain of the injustice of their government. There are not necessary evils in government. Its evils exist only in its abuses. If it would confine itself to equal protection, and as heaven does its rain, shower its favours alike on the high and the low, the rich and the poor, it would be an unqualified blessing.[29]

For Barnburners, mistrust of government intervention was a reaction against eighteenth-century mercantilism, vestiges of whose economic regulation remained in place in much of antebellum America, reflected in a thousand local laws regulating trade to the advantage of men established in commerce.[30] Their economic beliefs[31] resembled those of Adam Smith,[32] who likewise reacted against the same English mercantilism. They united in opposition to the protective tariff raising the price of textiles and farm implements that subsistence farmers required, a tariff central to the economic policy that their Whig rivals denoted as "The American System."[33] As Jacksonian Democrats, they sternly opposed public facilitation of the aggregation of private wealth through monopolies, charters, licenses, and other privileges granted to corporations by governments practicing mercantilist economic theories. In its more extreme forms voiced by Leggett, this position resisted public asylums for the insane and pensions for Revolutionary War veterans and favored the privatization of West Point and state prisons.[34] These convictions were reinforced when the depression of 1837–1843 triggered a bank panic. That event was regarded as the just and inevitable consequence of government intervention supporting the efforts of some citizens to gain wealth quickly and easily.[35]

William Leggett expressed the related feelings of Barnburners about so-called learned professions:

> Take a hundred ploughmen promiscuously from their fields, and a hundred merchants from their desks, and what man, regarding the true dignity of his nature, could hesitate to give the award of superior excellence, in every main

intellectual, physical, and moral respect to the band of hardy rustics, over that of the lank and sallow accountants, worn out with the sordid anxieties of traffic and the calculations of gain?[36]

In accord with this premise, wherever Barnburners gained power, they dismantled the ramparts of privilege, and often first among the privileged regulatory protections stripped away were licensing requirements in medicine[37] and law.[38]

In most states, they succeeded in eliminating apprenticeship requirements for admission to the bar. Such requirements had been imposed as necessary to assure the quality of professional services in a world regulated by law of arcane complexity. In the English tradition brought to America, as Lord Coke had expressed it:

> [C]auses which concern the Life, or Inheritance, or Goods, or Fortunes of his Subjects were not to be decided by natural Reason, but by the artificial Reason and Judgment of Law which requires long Study and Experience before . . . a man can attain the cognizance of it.[39]

The Jacksonian view was that such entry requirements erecting a structure of "artificial Reason" disadvantaged the working poor. For this reason, the Indiana Constitution of 1850 guaranteed to every citizen of good moral character the right to practice law.[40] Despite their own lack of organization, a condition generally deplored by Whigs,[41] the bar of New York managed for a time to maintain control of admission to the profession.[42] Only Massachusetts required a longer period of apprenticeship.[43] But the Jacksonians in New York, led by David Dudley Field, achieved success in 1846 when the new constitution drafted by them deprived the professions of the power to control admission of their members and conferred that prerogative on the state legislature.[44]

A related political reform advocated by Barnburners was the election of judges. This reform was in part a reaction against the arrogance of colonial and post-colonial Federalist judges.[45] Their stated purpose in electing judges was to strengthen the courts as a constitutional bulwark against the abuse of power by legislatures and governors. Elected judges were presumed to be independent *of the other branches* and thus to have a stronger claim to political status than mere appointees.[46] Moreover, accountability to the electorate was thought both an inducement to responsible performance of public duty and an assurance that the courts would interpret legal texts to reflect the values of the people, not their own eccentric preferences or those of a professional class. This reform was first adopted for all its judges by Mississippi in 1832; New York followed in 1846,[47] and by 1860 most American states had adopted or amended their constitutions to provide for the election of judges.[48]

Although sometimes accused of kinship with the Jacobins who authored the reign of terror in France, these advocates of Equal Rights were not Marxists resentful of economic class distinctions.[49] They did not object to the honest accumulation of wealth by means of private initiative and made no claim to wealth so produced in enterprises unsubsidized by public revenue or exactions on the working poor. Their economic views paralleled their religious beliefs as neo-Calvinists in placing responsibility on each man for the welfare of himself and his family. In this, they shared the sentiment of their contemporary, the Victorian Carlyle, that work, almost any work, is morally redemptive: "Know thy work and do it"[50] was the injunction they asked all to obey. Mob violence could on no account be justified.

This was the environment in which Thomas Cooley was raised as the tenth of fifteen children on a subsistence farm. His mother singled him out as the one of her brood who should be sent to school despite the all-but-prohibitive cost, and so he had the benefit of three years of formal instruction at the Attica Academy. He then spent a year as an apprentice in the law office of the Jacksonian congressman representing his district.[51]

Upstate New York had been tied to the opening West by 1818, when steamboats appeared on Lake Erie. Children of the first settlers of western New York were soon laying out farms in northern Ohio. The Erie Canal was completed in 1825, when Thomas Cooley was a year old. The Canal made New York a world-class city, and set Rochester and Buffalo on the path to becoming metropolitan centers. It also powerfully stimulated the stream of migrants to northern Ohio and southern Michigan. They were joined by nineteen-year-old Cooley, who arrived in the village of Adrian to commence his career in 1843. Cooley came equipped with the democratic politics of a Barnburner, a politics shared by his neighbors in that newly settled agrarian community.

Michigan in 1843 was in its sixth year of statehood. It was a rustic place. The native Wyandotte occupying the lower peninsula when settlers began to arrive were a remnant of the Huron who had been greatly diminished in a genocidal war waged against them in 1649 by the Iroquois. As settlers arrived in number, the sparse native population receded north and west. Roads were slowly cut through the thick forest; Cooley later described Michigan as a state that was "almost lost in the woods."[52] However, a road west from Detroit to Chicago was opened in 1832, and an encyclopedia first published in Edinburgh in that year described to its Scottish readers the prospects of emigrants to Michigan in glowing terms. It reported the account of one farmer, Ferguson, who bought 160 acres for $240 and *netted* a profit on his first year's harvest of $1000,[53] then added:

Detroit, the capital of Michigan, is the embryo Constantinople of the inland seas of North America. It is situated in a narrow channel, which connects the lower lakes, Ontario and Erie, with the three upper, Huron, Michigan, and Superior. Having access in every direction to countries of more fertile soil than those of Greece or Asia, and possessed of an equally favorable climate, it begins its career with political institutions far more propitious to human welfare than were possessed by the celebrated city we have mentioned; and it promises one day to be the abode of a more numerous as well as happier population.[54]

Although there were, of course, Whigs in Michigan, Jacksonian Barnburners were dominant. The state constitution was replaced in 1850 with a new one bearing a marked resemblance to the New York Barnburners' Constitution of 1846. Cooley fit readily into the politics of those who drafted and secured the ratification of that text.

In 1848, Cooley married Mary Horton, an event he declared to be the most important of his life. Together, they raised five children, one of whom became a noted scholar. When she died, Cooley wrote that "for forty five years my wife and I have been inseparable. Nothing has in any way come between us, even in thought or desire."[55] All the available evidence tends to confirm that this was so.

Slow to develop a law practice, Cooley first borrowed money from his widowed mother to buy law books. Later, he also bought and read the bulk of the available English and American literature. Among his own published works are numerous poems; a few lines of his "Austria," a comment on the Revolution of 1848, serve to illustrate the modest level of his talent:

> Austria is but the world's great moral teacher,
> A grim and haggard relic of the past,
> That lives to prove by daily illustration,
> How slow our progress which we think so fast.
>
> If she could make, without a pang of sorrow,
> Her brother Christian's land a land of blood,
> And hear, unmoved, the children she had orphaned,
> The homeless, friendless children cry for food, –
>
> 'Tis but to lift the veil that hid her features,
> And show them in their brazen boldness plain,
> That all may see who thought the world grew better
> The race still lives that bears the mark of Cain!
> Austria is but the world's great moral teacher,
> To prove to all who thought the proof was vain,
> That those exist who bear with less compunction
> The scorn of all their fellows, than did Cain![56]

Cooley's biographer accurately describes much of his poetry as Emersonian in its preoccupation with the dignity of "the near, the low, and the common."[57] Although there is a religious subtext to much of his poetry, Cooley did not join a church. Yet he regularly attended Congregationalist services with his wife, and took an active part in the affairs of her church. He was also active in the temperance movement, advocated pacifism in international relations, and was an outspoken opponent of capital punishment. In all of these respects, Cooley was one of the worthy yeomen whom Jefferson foresaw as the rightful heirs of the American continent.

5

Legal Education for
the People

The law school led by Thomas Cooley at the University of Michigan from 1858 to 1883 was quite different from Langdell's Harvard Law School, as different perhaps as Attica or Adrian from Beacon Hill.

Many Jacksonians imbued with the spirit of Equal Rights had opposed public support for higher education as yet another form of government aid to the rich; some justified their anti-intellectualism as implicit in the democratic ideals of the Republic. Thus, Hugh Henry Brackenridge, in his satire, depicted frontiersmen feeling deep shame if suspected of reading a book.[1] Kentucky's Governor Desha, in that spirit, eliminated the small state subsidy to Transylvania University, protesting that the state had "lavished her money for the benefit of the rich to the exclusion of the poor; the only result is to add to the aristocracy of wealth the advantage of superior knowledge."[2] In 1834, the Indiana legislature proposed that both faculty and students at Indiana University be required to engage in manual labor, such as tree cutting (then the chief pastime in the state), to correct for their patrician leanings. Four decades later, the same legislature abolished the university's law and medical schools, reporting that it was "no duty of the people to help men into these easy professions."[3]

Nevertheless, hostility to higher education was not an essential feature of Equal Rights politics. Some New York Barnburners were engaged in developing colleges and universities, and even law schools. Law departments at New York University, Hamilton College, Oberlin College, and the University of Michigan were Jacksonian in their origins. Many state universities, in Wisconsin,[4] Kansas,[5] and other states west of the Mississippi, would be established on the Michigan model. So would the Cornell Law School.[6]

This Jacksonian tradition in higher education seems to have originated in 1829, when a distinguished group of New York City Democrats[7] gathered to establish the institution that became New York University. The group was dissatisfied with the classical, patrician, and Episcopal bents of Columbia College. They were mindful of the establishment, in 1828, of the University of London,[8] which aimed to provide useful instruction for young men of the emerging English middle class,[9] and of the rising standards of German universities.[10] Even more, perhaps, they were attentive to the 1828 election of President Jackson, an event demonstrating that political power in the United States had passed from the social elite that had formed the base for Federalist and Jeffersonian politics.

The ideas these New Yorkers had about education were not far different from those of Jefferson and other revolutionaries responsible for the creation of other colleges, with law departments envisioned as capstones to systems of public schools preparing citizens to exercise their franchise. As one New Yorker explained, it appeared "impossible to preserve our democratic institutions and the right of universal suffrage unless we could raise the standard of general education and the mind of the laboring classes nearer to a level with those born under more favorable circumstances."[11] Together, the group acknowledged "that the diffusion of knowledge among the people is essential to the purity and stability of a republican form of government."[12]

The group accordingly ordained that there should be a professorship on "The Law of Nations and Constitutional Law" at their new university. They requested and received from the state supreme court a ruling reducing by two years the apprenticeship requirement for those regularly attending its law lectures.[13] Benjamin F. Butler[14] was identified as the person to establish the law program. Butler was not only a Jacksonian and a Democrat, but also a close adviser and ally of Governor Van Buren,[15] in whose law office Butler had served his clerkship.[16] The opening of the law school was postponed for several years while Butler served as attorney general of the United States in the administration of President Jackson. After it opened, Butler's program survived only one year. In addition to a financial convulsion of the university resulting in part from the Panic of 1837, there was probably some disappointment in the number of students attracted.[17] In any case, the Law Department subsided for a time.[18]

A similar, and for a time more enduring, effort was pursued upstate at Hamilton College in Clinton, not far from Utica, the center of Finney's religious revivalism. Hamilton had been established as an Indian mission in 1789 by Samuel Kirkland, a traditional Congregationalist minister.[19] A Jacksonian member of the state senate died in the cholera epidemic of 1832 and left his estate to endow a law professorship in the college.[20] In 1835, John Hiram Lathrop was appointed the first Maynard Professor of Law, History, Civil Polity and Political Economy.[21] While little is recorded of Lathrop's teaching at Hamilton, we know that he was a Barnburner adhering to Leggett's doctrine of free speech, free schools, free labor, and free trade. He was especially outspoken on the issue of freedom of religion. He urged his students to be "too Christian to be sectarian" and, although regular in his attendance at divine services, he, like Cooley, long refused to join a church. He was also an advocate of women's rights to higher education and vocational opportunity.

In 1841, Lathrop moved west to become the founding president of the University of Missouri,[22] and law at Hamilton became the work of Theodore Dwight. Dwight was another native of upstate New York[23] whose law teaching won much favor. In 1858 he forsook Hamilton College for the Columbia Law School.

Among the early converts to Reverend Finney's modified Puritanism was John Jay Shipherd, who organized Oberlin College in 1833, stating the object to be "the education of gospel ministers and pious school teachers."[24] Oberlin was not a college of choice for young patricians. A part of the Oberlin environment was daily, hard, physical work for every student—the sort that the Indiana legislature sought to impose on both teachers and students. No amenities were provided at Oberlin and no entertainments were permitted. The college was not only open to African-American students,[25] but through the Finney churches it actively recruited them long before any other college was recruiting students of any color or class. It soon merged with the neighboring female academy, also established by Shipherd, to become the world's first coeducational college as well. Oberlin was in the pre-Civil War years one of the largest colleges in America. It was an academic manifestation of the Barnburning culture of Equal Rights.

In 1838, Edward Wade, a Cleveland lawyer, was appointed professor of law at Oberlin, a position he held for a decade. Not much is known of his teaching,[26] but we are told that at the outset "the young men who attended cross-questioned him so mercilessly that he concluded that his preparation was, for the time at least, inadequate."[27] He taught for a decade, but his program did not purport to be complete preparation for professional work. At least two Oberlin students in his time were among the first African-American lawyers, but both also "read law" with other mentors.[28]

While Butler, Lathrop, and Wade were embarking on their law-teaching efforts in New York and Ohio, Michigan achieved statehood. As early as 1817, the Jeffersonian chief justice of the territory of Michigan had argued for the establishment of a law department like that at William and Mary,[29] one that would educate republican leaders for the territory of Michigan. Reflecting the same impulse, the first state constitution directed the legislature to establish a university that would, among other things, teach law to the youth of the new state.[30] The governing board first sought to employ as its president George Bancroft of Harvard,[31] one of the few New Englanders who publicly supported the Jacksonian reforms.[32] Bancroft declined and recommended Henry Philip Tappan, who was appointed.

Tappan was yet another native of upstate New York, who had served on the faculty of New York University.[33] His ideas about education were essentially those of Jefferson and Bentham. Under Tappan's leadership, the University of Michigan moved away from the rigidly classical model of Harvard and Yale and favored studies having more direct application to the lives being led by nineteenth-century graduates.

In 1859, President Tappan opened a law department that would soon become an ornament to the university. No tuition was charged; literacy "and evidence of good moral character" were the only admission requirements.[34] Cooley was the youngest of the three faculty members. The faculty was selected by a committee of the governing board who had consulted with members of the Supreme Court of Michigan in making their selections. Cooley was the only one willing to move to Ann Arbor, and so he assumed administrative responsibility.

The department quickly attracted students from most of the states of the old Northwest Territory, and then from states west of the Mississippi. When the Civil War ended in 1865, the law school enrolled 385 students, making it at the time the largest law department or school in America,[35] and perhaps the world. For its first quarter-century, it would bear the flags of both Jeffersonian conceptions of republican leadership and Jacksonian populism.

The differences between that law department and the law school administered by Langdell were numerous. Cooley was admired for the clarity of his lectures and his courtesy to students; Daniel Coit Gilman, the founding president of Johns Hopkins University and perhaps the most celebrated educator of the age, acclaimed Cooley as the most lucid lecturer he had ever heard.[36] Langdell, in contrast, was reviled by most of his students for his obstinate refusal to supply them with answers to the many annoying and challenging questions he posed for them.[37] Cooley taught constitutional law, a subject that Langdell did not regard as law at all and would have preferred to exclude from his curriculum of professional training.[38] In all that he taught, Cooley emphasized the historical and cultural origins of law and the social and political aims it is shaped to serve. Langdell taught his students that American private law (like Lord Coke's) is an internally complete discipline, often rather like chess,[39] and is formed and best understood without regard for its secondary social, economic, and political consequences.[40] Cooley's law school took pride in being open to all persons literate in English (including over eighty subjects of the Emperor of Japan, who were sent to Ann Arbor as a part of the opening of that empire to external influence). Academic failure was unknown; the curriculum extended over only two short academic years; students learned what they thought they needed to know and then moved on, often to careers of public service.

One may doubt whether the enthusiasm of Cooley's students was fully warranted. The lucidity of his lectures was almost surely purchased at some cost of oversimplification. And the absence of academic failure confirms that Cooley and his colleagues did not do all that might have been done to foster intellectual discipline and professional standards. Nineteenth-century Michigan students were passive vessels into which some useful information about law was poured. Students generally find that role gratifying and seldom complain about it, but the enduring value of the experience must have been modest. While Cooley and his colleagues were suitable role models for those training to become members of the public profession, those who made themselves into sound members of the profession must have brought most of the requisite qualities with them when they embarked on formal training.

Whatever the true worth of a Michigan legal education in Cooley's time, there is little doubt that Harvard students misjudged the worth of Langdell's teaching. If he withheld gratification from his students, Langdell nevertheless prodded many of them to acquire a measure of intellectual self-reliance they would not otherwise have achieved. Those who survived the rigors of the Langdell program gained a measure of confidence that a program such as Cooley's could not have provided.

Neither Michigan nor Harvard ever denied admission to a student because of his race, and both graduated African-American lawyers soon after the Civil War,[41] but Michigan was also a leader in educating women in law, and was said in 1890 to have by far the largest number of law alumnae.[42] The Equity Club, a national organization of women lawyers, was founded in Ann Arbor at that time.[43] Langdell's law school increasingly aspired to be exclusive, its curriculum was extended to three years, academic failure was common, and admission standards were being steadily elevated.[44] Accordingly, Langdell's students were early exemplars of human capitalism; they were making a heavy investment from which they expected a suitable return.

Cooley lectured occasionally at Johns Hopkins[45] and Yale,[46] but never regularly taught elsewhere than at Michigan. Yet his teaching of law students was not limited to those who enrolled in his school. In 1871, he edited for contemporary readers William Blackstone's *Commentaries on English Law.* Blackstone had been through many previous American editions, the first and most important having been prepared in 1803 by St. George Tucker, Wythe's successor at William and Mary.[47] More even than the work of James Kent,[48] Blackstone had served as the first book in law for most Americans entering the legal profession in the nineteenth century. Indeed, more than a few American lawyers (albeit no sound ones) may very well have read little else.[49] A glancing knowledge of that book might, in 1870, suffice to enable personable applicants to secure licenses to practice law in many, and perhaps most, states. With his edition, Cooley helped perpetuate that tradition of an open profession, an action that would have endeared him to William Leggett and the advocates of Equal Rights. In introducing his work, he gave conventional advice on professional ethics and intellectual self-development to young men and women who proposed to enter the legal profession without academic training in law.[50] Those novices were an object of contempt for Langdell, and it is unimaginable that he would have encouraged them as Cooley did. Cooley also encouraged them to study politics and American history, something Langdell would not have been likely to do.

The differences between Cooley and Langdell as law teachers reflected other differences between them. Langdell, although of rural origins, secured an elaborate education, at Phillips Exeter Academy, Harvard College, and Harvard Law School.[51] He remained at the law school an additional year to assist Professor Parsons in completing his text on the law of contracts and was twenty-seven when at last he commenced law practice in New York in 1853. He saw himself as a member of an elite social class. In contrast, Cooley, it may be recalled, had but three years of formal schooling. He saw himself as a member of a classless society. He had little regard for wealth, social status, or intellectual pretension as insignia of moral worth; while he relished the affection and respect of his students and colleagues, he did not put himself forward as a person entitled to extraordinary regard.

Both Cooley and Langdell had as young men suffered the disability of shyness, and neither was very successful in attracting a professional clientele. Langdell practiced for fourteen years in New York as a reclusive lawyer's lawyer. Cooley partially overcame his shyness by throwing himself into a wide range of social and political activities. By 1851, not yet thirty, Cooley was a sometime orator at public celebrations. He was also a sometime political journalist, and a leader in the literary society of his village. He was an omnivorous reader. Langdell, debilitated by poor sight, apparently read only law, and mostly English law at that. He also seems to have had little or no experience as a public speaker before returning to Harvard to teach.

Not surprisingly, the politics of the two men were opposed. It was said that Langdell longed for the time of the Plantagenet royalty[52] and had no interest in political events occurring after 1850.[53] He seems to have been among those few taking no more than moderate interest in the progress of the Civil War that raged around him. Despite his rural origins, his only visible interest in the welfare of farmers was that of an occasional mortgage lender. Even less was he concerned about industrial workers and their families. When asked in 1871 to join the reformist American Social Science Association, he declined, explaining that he had too little interest in changing the law to assume the obligations of membership.[54] He was, however, induced to participate in the work of that organization when it interested itself in raising the standards of the professions so as to exclude the ignorant and the unwashed. In seeking an American label for the politics of Langdell, one is attracted to the term "Federalist," the label worn by the party of Alexander Hamilton, a group that was openly oligarchic.[55]

Cooley left the Democratic party of his family and friends in the 1850s to join the Free Soil movement, and followed Lincoln into the Republican Party. Like Lincoln, whom he came to revere, he was committed both to emancipation and the preservation of the union. He identified the interests of farmers and other working poor as the central concern and responsibility of democratic government, but, along with Leggett, supposed that those interests would generally be favored by governmental passivity, fearing that government involvement usually resulted in preferential treatment of the rich and powerful.

Cooley was appointed by the Republican legislature in 1857 to compile Michigan's statutes. He excelled at that work. On that account and because of his careful advocacy in cases argued to the court, he earned appointment in 1858 as reporter of the decisions of the Supreme Court of Michigan. He held that position when, a year later, he was appointed to the university faculty and made responsible for the development of a program of legal education to serve the people. From the very beginning, Cooley's department enjoyed enormous popularity. Indeed, the enthusiasm of the students resulted in the practice of cheering teachers upon their arrival in the classroom, a practice continued at Michigan for at least a quarter-century, but one that never caught on elsewhere.

Langdell was picked for his position by Charles Eliot, the president of Harvard. Eliot was one of the persons most perceptive about the emerging role of higher education in an industrialized America and it was his vision that Langdell's program sought to implement. In 1875, Eliot explained Langdell's mission:

> An institution which has any legal prestige and power will make a money profit by raising its standard, and that either at once or in a very short time. Its demand for greater attainments on the part of its students will be quickly responded to, and this improved class of students will in a marvelously short time so increase the reputation and influence of the institution as to make its privileges and its rewards more valued and more valuable. [56]

Responding to Eliot's leadership, Langdell invented the casebook,[57] grilled his students on their reading of cases, set written examinations, extended the length of his program to three academic years, and raised admission standards to require a baccalaureate degree. All of these reforms were designed to elevate the professional status of Harvard Law graduates, and they had precisely that effect.

Associated with Langdell's reforms was an intellectual framework (one cannot denote it a philosophy of law) resting on astonishing assumptions. Among these were the notions that American law is an empirical science accessible only by means of prolonged study; the common law is the same in all states; the law can be discerned by a careful reading of selected English, Massachusetts, and New York decisions and making the correct inductions from those cases; what intellectually challenged legislators and judges say or think is not law; and the Constitution of the United States and the constitutions of the states are not law, but mere politics.[58] Langdell's fullest statement of his theory was presented to Cooley's audience in the Hemenway Gymnasium in 1886; most memorable among his remarks that day was his statement that "printed books are the ultimate source of all legal knowledge."[59] Accordingly, he asserted, "[w]hat qualifies a person, therefore, to teach law is not experience in the work of a lawyer's office, not experience in dealing with men, not experience in the trial or argument of causes,—not experience, in short, in using the law, but experience in learning law."[60]

These notions had two notable features: They conformed comfortably to the secularized Puritanism of the Beacon Hill intellectual community and they served to rationalize the academic credentialization of the American legal profession. They were, however, never fully accepted by many, even at Harvard.[61] Langdell's colleague, John Chipman Gray, privately noted to Eliot that Langdell's "intellectual arrogance and contempt is astonishing" and "his detachment from reality a cause for despair about the future of the school."[62] Holmes, who for a brief time was also Langdell's academic colleague, was in private equally contemptuous of Langdell's thinking. He ridiculed the claim that the law is empirical science, and compared Langdell's teaching to that of a biology teacher "who would give one of his pupils a sea urchin and tell him to find all about it he could." He condemned Langdell's casebook on contracts as a "misspent piece of marvelous ingenuity" that served the "powers of darkness"[63] and dismissed Langdell as a "legal theologian."[64] Nevertheless, on that commemorative occasion in 1886, Holmes managed some kind words about the case method, if not about the theory offered by Langdell to justify it.

Despite the hopeless frailty of its intellectual premises, Langdell's program became in its second decade a huge success. Eliot's prophecy was fulfilled. By 1886, the University of Michigan had begun to see the light and had begun lengthening its program, raising admission standards, and adopting the case method. Cooley did not oppose these changes; indeed, he fostered the extension of the academic calendar at Michigan.[65] But he found the implementation of these changes an occasion for terminating his own teaching, because they were dissonant with his own aims as a teacher. And it was likely his discomfort with what Eliot and Langdell were doing that prompted his remark at the rostrum of honor that sound democratic law must reflect the commonplace ideas of the people, a remark that was surely intended to impose at least minor discomfort on his hosts.

6

Law and the Lightning of Genius

Holmes took issue with Cooley's words at Harvard on quite different grounds than those dividing Cooley from Langdell. He was perhaps the first American to gain status in the legal profession as an intellectual and a theorist. In his talk at Northwestern in 1902,[1] Holmes conceded that there was some truth in Cooley's observations that the law is and ought to be rooted in commonplace morality. Cooley would have agreed with much that Holmes said on that occasion, especially that law is not unchanging, but "an eternal pursuit." But when Holmes went on to characterize law as "a field for the lightning of genius," or to say that from law "may fly sparks that shall set free in some genius his explosive message," Cooley might have risen from his seat to protest.

While Cooley and Holmes agreed on much, the difference revealed in the Northwestern address goes to the heart of the mission of the legal profession in a democratic society. Is the law an expression of the popular will and moral judgment, or is it an opportunity for a higher class of intellect to impose benign government on a passive people? Langdell and Holmes, despite many differences, shared disdain for the moral judgment of the people whom Cooley aimed to serve: Langdell as a paradigmatic technocrat facilitating the affairs of the monied class and Holmes as a paradigmatic theorist inspiring the ambitions of an intellectual class to make decisions controlling the lives of the unwashed. While Holmes deserves neither credit nor blame for the merit or demerit of the explosive messages of later professionals regarding themselves as geniuses of the law, he was in a sense the herald of twentieth-century lawyers and judges who would see themselves as agents of the politics and morality of a new ruling class.

Cooley, unlike Holmes, was genuinely modest in his intellectual pretensions. He believed and taught that a great mind cannot by its own exertions create new principles of morality or law. On another occasion, he insisted that "no one can think the thoughts of law with its reasons, unless he is in sympathy with the morality and truth which underlies it."[2] In response to Holmes, he might, as he did on other occasions, have quoted Cicero to the effect that "the fruits of speculative genius in government are of little value."[3] Cooley in this respect sided with Thucydides, who was perhaps the first to record the opinion that

> [o]n the whole it is the more ordinary men, in contrast to the more intelligent, who run cities better. The intelligentsia want to appear wiser than the laws, and to outdo whoever is currently speaking in public, supposing that there is no better way of showing their good judgment; and by this kind of behavior they usually bring disaster on their cities. But those who distrust their own intelligence acknowledge that they are more ignorant than the laws and less able than an accomplished speaker to find fault with what is said; being impartial judges, rather than competitors, they are for the most part successful. We must follow that model, and must not be excited by cleverness and intellectual rivalry into giving advice to you, the citizen body, contrary to [y]our own beliefs.[4]

Robert Wiebe has observed that the idea of popular self-rule central to Cooley's thought began to lose its hold on the American mind at the turn of the century as a "national class" emerged that would gain ascendancy and dominance as a result of World War II.[5] Perhaps "national class" is a euphemism for "elite," an elite asserting entitlements based on their technical competence and the worth of their services as measured by national and global markets. Cooley, as much as Holmes, was a precursor of that national class, especially in his role at the Interstate Commerce Commission, a role examined below.

Cooley's conception of self-rule survived at least into the Progressive Era, for it was voiced by none other than Herbert Croly, the intellectual centerpiece of the movement undertaking radical transformation of American law in the first fifteen years of the twentieth century. Croly, in the midst of his call for radical reform, observed that

> [t]he ... [Supreme] Court has been, on the whole, one of the great successes of the American political system, because the lawyers, whom it represented, were themselves representative of the ideas and interests of the bulk of their fellow countrymen; and if for any reason they become less representative, a dangerous division would be created between the body of American public opinion and its official and final legal expositors. If the lawyers have any reason to misinterpret a serious political problem, the difficulty of dealing therewith is much increased, because in addition to the ordinary risks of political therapeutics there will be added that of a false diagnosis by the family doctor. The adequacy of the lawyers' training, the disinterestedness of their political motives, the fairness of their mental outlook, and the closeness of their contact with the national public opinion—all become matters of grave public concern.[6]

Holmes never questioned the substance of Croly's observation but, in his delphic complexity, he spoke for those who did not share the concern. He thought of himself as a sort of legal genius, yet Thucydides could have been assured that Holmes was far from rash in his judicial behavior. Holmes was not one to "overrule every proposition brought forward," and was hardly one to ruin a country by dramatic exhibitions of his wit in crafting novel solutions to public problems. On the other hand, he did possess some of the characteristics of judges whom Thucydides urged us not to imitate: He was in some ways given to "intellectual rivalry," he seldom mistrusted his own cleverness, and he was not "content to be less learned" than the law. And those traits would be manifested by those coming later who would celebrate his genius.

Antonin Scalia has made the arresting suggestion that the tendency of twentieth-century American lawyers to admire genius in law is a result of Langdell's case method, which emphasized the creative dimension of the role of the common law judge. The first year of law school is exhilarating, he suggests, "because it consists of playing common-law judge, which in turn consists of playing king—devising, out of the brilliance of one's own mind, those laws that ought to govern mankind."[7] He likens the celebrated judge to a broken field runner who stiff-arms precedents on all sides to reach "the best rule of law for the case at hand."[8]

To his discredit, Holmes deployed his own genius to strip democratic law of its moral content when, in a celebrated essay,[9] he fixed attention on the bad man's prediction of judicial action as being the essence of law and decried the use of "words of moral significance." That was nonsense,[10] as Cooley would have been quick to observe, for it is the reassurance law gives to conventional, responsible men and women, and the direction it gives to those who are confused or uncertain, that makes law so useful that it is universal among human societies. As Alan Alschuler has noted, it is the sheriff, not the judge, who is the concern of the truly bad man, and maybe the sheriff can be bribed. Paraphrasing Lincoln's youthful encomium to law, Alschuler affirmed that

> [o]ne cannot revere predictions of what the courts will do in fact; patriots have never pledged their lives, their property, or their sacred honor to the prediction of judicial decisions; and no mothers have told their babies to predict and honor whatever the courts will do.[11]

Holmes did not himself as a judge "wash the law with cynical acid," but he lent his repute to generations of lawyers and scholars who would. He may therefore bear some responsibility for such antic thoughts as those, who, smitten with economics, are willing to put a price on the right to engage in harmful conduct,[12] or, who, smitten with hermeneutics, invoke the revelation that legal texts are sometimes indeterminate to commission the judiciary to remake the social order according to their hopes.[13]

While Holmes has sometimes been regarded as a prophet of pragmatism,[14] he was in truth little concerned with practical politics. Perhaps he could better be described as a theoretician of amoral pragmatism. When accepting his appointment to the Harvard Law faculty, he had requested that his title be "professor of jurisprudence," to signify his aim to be a theoretician.[15] As full an expression as any of the spirit of academic purity and isolation from the realities of public life was Holmes's assertion that there may be no

> more exalted form of life than that of a great abstract thinker, wrapt in the successful study of problems to which he devotes himself, for an end which is neither unselfish or selfish in the common sense of those words, but is simply to feel the deepest hunger and to use the greatest gifts of the soul.[16]

Despite this adulation of the life of the mind, Holmes discarded that life in favor of active involvement. When he soon resigned his faculty position at the Harvard Law School, he gave as the reason that "the field for generalization inside the body of the law was small, that the day would soon come when I felt that the only remaining problems were of detail and that as a philosopher [I] must go over into other fields."[17] This suggests that it was perhaps not legal theory that Holmes had in mind when at Northwestern he proclaimed law to be ripe for the "lightning of genius."

On another occasion, Holmes foretold that the lawyer of the future would be the "man of statistics and the master of economics"[18] and thus an expert on policy whose opinions might be justifiably imposed on passive citizens mindful of their own incompetence in statistics and economics. This thought reflected the shared belief of an industrializing society in the advantages of expertise. "The people ought to be masters," John Stuart Mill wrote, "but they are masters who must employ servants more skillful than themselves."[19]

An important source of difference between the Cooley and Holmes visions of law was their relationship to the democratic electorate. Massachusetts is among the very few states that has never elected a judge. It is difficult to imagine Holmes as a candidate for public office. To secure election, he would have needed to forsake his Olympian manner, and the adaptation would likely have influenced his appreciation of the office and its role in the constitutional scheme. As a judge holding life tenure, he was seldom required for his own welfare to consider the "common thoughts of men."

It is today the conventional wisdom among the "national class" that electing judges is a bad idea, that judges ought to hold tenure for life, as federal judges do.[20] The reason generally given for this view is, of course, that judges enforcing individual rights provided in constitutions must inhibit, and should not be intimidated by, but must be independent of, majoritarian politics. In this view, the Supreme Court of the United States is a paradigm of political virtue because it is structurally indifferent to the moral judgment of any democratic electorate.

Contrary to this now-conventional view, Cooley to the end defended the practice of electing judges.[21] Many have agreed with him that judges exercising constitutional power to review legislation should themselves be limited. Despite the almost universal emulation of the idea of a constitutional republic, almost nowhere else have judges of a constitutional court been given life tenure. Of the scores of constitutions written for American jurisdictions since 1840, or the hundreds written in the twentieth century for foreign countries emulating our constitutional democracy, American Samoa's may be the only other constitution to allow judges exercising the power of judicial review of legislation to retain their offices for life.[22] Most American states hold judicial elections in some form. The explanation for this almost universal opposition to life tenure may be widespread agreement with another insight of Mill that

> [t]he disposition of mankind, whether as rulers or as fellow citizens, to impose their own opinions and inclinations as a rule of conduct for others, is so energetically supported by some of the best and some of the worst feelings incident to human nature, that it is hardly ever kept under restraint by anything but want of power.[23]

Holmes fully understood the risk of judicial arrogance to democratic law. He himself made no use of natural or "eternal" law and placed a high value on legal certainty.[24] While extolling legal genius, he urged that judges confine themselves to "molecular motions."[25] He praised Lemuel Shaw, his predecessor on the Supreme Judicial Court of Massachusetts, as a great judge because he possessed an "accurate appreciation of the community whose officer he was."[26] However, Holmes was limited in his own appreciation of the community he served by his patrician instincts. He was "alienated from his people and his culture" and was "playing a role, serving the Republic that in many ways he had come to disdain."[27] It was that disdain that made him attractive to many of those denoted by Wiebe as the "national class," who have disdained the "common thoughts of men" while lionizing the memory of Holmes, the cosmologist.

Cooley's appreciation of the community he served seems to have come naturally. He does not appear to have reflected deeply on the question, How does the judge know what "the people" think?[28] Relying largely on his own instincts, he was apparently correct in his belief that his sternly Protestant, Jacksonian, and egalitarian values were shared by most of his constituents. He was "of the people" to a degree that Holmes was not and never could have been.[29]

On the other hand, Cooley understood that widely unpopular decisions were required when public opinion is uninformed or formed in haste or passion, resulting in harm to constitutionally protected rights, and he fully accepted the dictum of *The Federalist* that respect for the citizenry does "not require an unqualified complaisance to every sudden breeze of passion, or to every transient impulse which the people may receive from the arts of men who flatter their prejudices or betray their interests."[30] But he doubted not only his own independent wisdom, but also that of others occupying high judicial office, and therefore favored both judicial deference and accountability to the majority.

Paradoxically, Holmes, the Brahmin, earned a reputation for being deferential to the will of democratic legislatures, while Cooley has been identified with the intrusive arrogance of the Supreme Court in the *Lochner*[31] era. Holmes's reputation as a wise judge is in some measure attributable to the fact that he generally adhered to Cooley's dictum and refrained from aggressive exercise of the power of judicial review in an era when many of his colleagues on the Court were less restrained. Especially celebrated has been his dissent in *Lochner*,[32] in which he summarily dismissed the majority's fidelity to "Herbert Spencer's Social Statics," a brutally Darwinian ideology not far different from his own. In such cases, he prudently suppressed his own "spark of genius" and adhered to the modesty favored by Cooley.

It bears emphasis that Holmes and Cooley thus came to similar positions on judicial self-restraint in constitutional matters, but from very different premises regarding the political substance of the law to be administered. Holmes's professional restraint as a judge was fortified by his indifference, in maturity, to political issues. Seemingly embittered by his military experience, he was more dour even than most eighteenth-century Puritans in his distrust of humanity and its capacity for self-improvement. As an eminent biographer reported:

> [Holmes] was an unreconstructed social Darwinist on economic issues, believing in competition but also in combination as the logical end of competition. He was not at all interested in the humanitarian dimensions of work in an industrialized society. He did not think redistributive legislation had any meaningful effect, believing that consumption was the major pressure point of economic activity and that economic regulation only shifted the "bill" from one sector of the consuming public to another. . . . He was not interested in social assimilation or the breaking down of class barriers, did not believe the future was an improvement on the past, and did not favor the state as an omnipresent policymaking force.[33]

Holmes later complained of the many hopeful authors who "make me wonder whether I live on a lower plane than is attainable by man, or whether, of course, as I maintain, they are churning the void in the hope of making cheese."[34]

Cooley, in contrast, cared a great deal about many public issues. He, too, was generally pessimistic about the possible benefits of legislated solutions, and he came to ratify Gibbon's doleful dictum "that the united reigns of the Antonines were possibly the only period in history in which the happiness of a great people was the sole object of government."[35] But he was not overcome by despair. He continued to see law at its best as "an educating force"[36] that, prudently conceived and administered, can help the citizenry elevate their behavior better to reflect their own republican values of social equality, political self-restraint, tolerance, and mutual respect.

"[I]n the last resort," Holmes said, "a man rightly prefers his own interest to that of his neighbors. And this is as true in legislation as in any other forms of corporate action."[37] Cooley, in contrast, believed that there is a common good measured by common values. For him, the common good centered on the interests and values of farmers and laborers and their spouses who did the world's work and raised the next generation of good citizens, whom he served as a fiduciary. Cooley prefigured the view more recently expressed by Bruce Ackerman that "most people have a rough and ready grasp of the animating constitutional ideals of American democracy,"[38] and he sought to embrace those ideals as guides to the public good he strove to serve. Like all good Jacksonians, he fully appreciated the core of truth in public choice theory[39]—legislatures and courts are often deflected from pursuing the common good by their own self-interests—but he maintained a base of optimism that professionals committed to serving the common good can enjoy some success. He would not have disagreed with the communitarian aims of contemporary civic republicans such as Frank Michelman,[40] although he might well have lost patience with the efforts of theorists such as Ackerman and Michelman to distinguish themselves from one another or to rationalize the politics of a ruling class as expressions of democratic values.

Cooley would surely have endorsed with enthusiasm Marc Galanter's assertion, perhaps the central insight of those committed to an empirical approach to law, that "what appears [in law] to be top down is really bottom up, that it is the unconscious, the folkways, the proletariat that are the dwelling place of the forces that move (or should move) and shape the social world."[41] As did Galanter, Cooley saw "the less formal, the less organized, the less respectable . . . not as mere material to be ruled, shaped, tamed, but as another, perhaps principal, source of value and meaning." When Holmes encouraged the use of economics and statistics, he did not see the reality to which Galanter calls attention, a reality precluding the advent of a legal genius.

Given these differences between Cooley and Holmes, there is some irony in this century's conventional contrast between the estimates of these two judges. Cooley, the man of the people, has been scouted as reactionary, an estimate based largely on the uses to which his scholarship was put by other judges making decisions years after Cooley's death and decades after he had ceased writing legal scholarship.[42] Holmes, on the other hand, the Boston Brahmin, has been acclaimed a "heroic liberal judge,"[43] a characterization resting on a handful of the thousands of opinions he wrote.

The contrast in the political reputations of Holmes and Cooley affords an opportunity to consider the meaning of standard political labels. Holmes may have been more "liberal" than Cooley in the diction of political theorists who contrast the contractarian and imputedly "liberal" ideology of John Locke and other authors of the Enlightenment with the mercantilist or Whig and imputedly "conservative" ideology of Edmund Burke.[44] Holmes was more Lockean and less Burkean than Cooley. Yet the Locke/Burke distinction is often at odds with the understanding of less learned persons, who might regard Locke's conception of individual rights as protective of vested interests, and thus conservative, while seeing Burke's conception of duties to society as an imposition on vested rights, and thus liberal. In that popular locution, Holmes was no liberal, but Cooley was.

Indeed, the contrast between the Cooley and Holmes illustrates the deeply contextual meanings of such political ascriptions as "conservative" and "liberal" so popular with contemporary journalists. It is equally instructive that each term was applied by different biographers to Francis Lieber,[45] whose relation to Cooley is described in a later chapter. Even John Rawls, as careful a thinker as any contemporary American, has exhibited imprecision in elaborating in the name of "liberalism" a political theory rooted in his egalitarian conceptions of justice.[46] Nowhere in his tightly reasoned work does he explain his use of the term "liberal" to describe his theory.[47] He acknowledges the historical origins of his theory to be in the Reformation and thus related to what Judith Shklar described as "the liberalism of fear."[48] Such "liberalism" is a commitment to tolerance as a preventive of mutual destruction. Burke, it seems clear, was a premier example of a "liberal of fear" deeply influenced by the French Revolution, and there is no reason to suppose that he would have contested Rawls's abstractions. We could expect that Rawls and Burke would reach different conclusions with respect to specific problems, but one could not accurately forecast those differences on the basis of their commitments to abstract theory, and certainly not on the basis of labeling one liberal and the other conservative. Indeed, the differences between Burke and Locke may be largely contextual. It is not clear that Locke would have written as he did had he been doing so at the time of the French Revolution, nor that Burke would have written as he did had he been writing during the reign of an absolute monarch. In some respects, the differences between Holmes and Cooley are likewise contextual.

Cooley thought of himself as a conservative in the Burkean sense. But his conservatism was that of one who admired democratic institutions and conceived of the judicial task as the protection of those institutions. "Here," James Fenimore Cooper wrote in describing the culture from which Cooley emerged, "the democrat is the conservative, and, thank God, he has something worth preserving."[49] This conservatism was communitarian; it was communitarian duty that Cooley had in mind when he told his students, "[t]he lawyer is and should be conservative."[50] He articulated his conservatism in 1878 to an audience at Johns Hopkins University. "There are," he said

> two senses in which one may be in advance of his age; the one useful, the other mischievous. The man who fully appreciating what the world is now and his competency to enlighten and benefit it, devotes himself to the task of doing so and waits patiently for the germination of the seed he sows, content that others shall reap the harvest which no hotbed forcing would ripen for his own enjoyment—this man may justly be called in advance of his age and praised for his labors as such, for by such labors may great reform be wisely and safely brought about. But the man more commonly praised as being in advance of his age is of a different sort. He is the man who, scorning the slow process of preparation, will insist upon forcing upon the world now what only a patient training of generations can fit it for; who sees in every people a present adaptability to his ideal, and who scoffs at all experience that does not conform to his preconceived notions as to what, under the circumstances, should have taken place. Such a man naturally ventures upon any experiment in government with no misgivings respecting the result, and if it proves calamitous, it is enough for his self complacency that he can say it was because he was too greatly in advance of his age. If he suffers with those who blindly followed his leading, he looks for and will think he deserves the martyr's crown as one who has given himself for the good of the world. But as all premature experiments in government are likely to have reactionary influence, we shall believe the world seldom wrong in withholding its praise from such persons. To usefully lead an age as statesman one must be of it, must recognize its prevailing ideas and sentiments and take note of and respect such obstacles as these present to any great and sudden change. If the age is not yet prepared for his ideal, he will content himself with what is practical and attainable instead of forcing upon it something which could be better only if voluntarily accepted.[51]

As a judge, Cooley was conservative in just the sense he defined. When he exercised constitutional prerogatives, it was (with one arguable exception) not to author "experiments in government" envisioned by a legal genius. But he not infrequently encouraged political leaders to do "what was practical and attainable" to serve, perhaps "liberally," the needs of the farmers, workers, and mothers on whom, in his view, the fate of the Republic rested. Thus, he also addressed less cautious words to legislators:

> "The Constitution as it is and the Union as it was" can no longer be the motto and the watchword of any political party. We may preserve the constitution in its every phrase and every letter, but only with such modification as was found essential for the uprooting of slavery; but the Union as it was has given way to a new Union with some new and grand features, but also with some engrafted evils which only time and the patient and persevering labors of statesmen and patriots will suffice to eradicate.[52]

In the same vein, Cooley counseled the North Dakota Constitutional Convention of 1889 against drafting a text that would too tightly confine the state's legislature and disable it from regulating "engrafted evils."[53]

Holmes saw little that was "new and grand" in the "new Union" and doubted that even "the patient and persevering labors of statesmen and patriots" could eradicate evil. Yet he would have agreed with Cooley (and with Lieber before him) that in drafting constitutional texts, "tight will tear, wide will wear"[54] and that judges cannot wisely assert themselves on matters of grave interest and dispute except under the protective legitimation of an explicit legal text as generally understood by those bound to accept their decision.

So which of the two was more "liberal," Cooley or Holmes? The question has no answer, because the terms "liberal" and "conservative" are useless to communicate the differences between such men, or to depict a position on the role of law or courts in the social order. A reason for this paradox is that those identifying Holmes as a liberal have often been partisans of an academized "liberalism," sharing his Olympian detachment and disdain for the moral conventions of the "community whose officers they are." In his posthumous work, *The Revolt of the Elites*,[55] Christopher Lasch wrote of a syndrome of withdrawal centered in the American academy and the media that scorns the populist and communitarian instincts voiced by Cooley and his co-professionals seeking to conserve democratic institutions.

Lasch describes this revolt as a "betrayal of democracy." This observation may be no more than a confirmation of Wiebe's sighting of a "national class" gaining dominance during World War II and having little regard for local politics and government. Members of that class seem to prefer constitutional adjudication to democratic legislation as the means to address important political issues. Holmes did not share that preference, but he expressed and symbolized the intellectual arrogance and class bias that sustains it. Constitutional adjudication is a forum in which legal genius can be heard and where its "lightning" can strike. It is also a mode of government bearing the risks of which Thucydides and Cicero wrote. It is a venue for Olympian "liberals" ready "to impose their own opinions and inclinations as a rule of conduct for others," and "to venture upon experiments in government" without "misgivings respecting the result," who, if the results "prove calamitous" will be satisfied with the thought that they were "too greatly in advance of their age."

7

The Supreme Court in Jacksonian Perspective

Cooley's affirmation that law should reflect the "common thoughts of men," when uttered at Harvard, was a reaction to Langdell and a provocation to Holmes. It was, however, also an expression of the Jacksonian tradition of which he was a part, a tradition that was to some extent a reaction to earlier experience with the Supreme Court of the United States, an institution that had given ample evidence that self-acclaimed geniuses in judicial robes, exercising constitutional powers and shielded by life tenure from accountability for their political acts, can by their "explosive messages" create grave hazards for the Republic. Dissatisfaction with the Court, and the profession it represented, was one reason for the popular demand that state constitutions require that judges serve limited terms and stand for elections.

The terms of employment of federal judges were not debated in the Constitutional Convention at Philadelphia. It was assumed without discussion that any judges would be appointed for the period of their "good behavior" and removed through the impeachment process for bad behavior. The term "good behavior" derived from an Act of Parliament in 1700 conferring effective life tenure on judges in the royal courts.[1] Prior to that date, judges on the royal courts were subject to removal by order of the Crown. The royal judges on whom employment security was conferred were members of a small, socially elite profession of modest technical competence.[2] Although they were much involved in politics as advisors to the Crown and Parliament,[3] it was not imagined in England in 1700 that such a group would exercise the political role conferred by written constitutions on American judges.

Colonial judges were appointed by the British Crown on the same terms. Many were despised by their colonial subjects. Especially resented was their presumption that they, as heirs of the English Court of Chancery, were entitled to deploy the contempt power to coerce reluctant subjects to obey their commands even outside the courtroom, a power not generally available to ordinary judges in other legal systems.[4] Most of the royal judges left the colonies during the Revolutionary War, and many were replaced by persons of dubious professional competence. Some of the replacements were appointed by governors and some elected by legislators. In 1777, Vermont became the first state (although it was then a territory) to elect judges by popular vote.[5] John Dudley, a farmer, was elected to the Supreme Court of New Hampshire in 1785 and proudly promised that he would never read Coke or Blackstone, but would do justice "by common sense and common honesty as between man and man."[6]

Most early American judges, however selected, enjoyed the same terms of employment as their English predecessors.[7] When the proposed Constitution authorized Congress to create "inferior" federal courts, misgivings were rampant; antifederalists imagined that the federal judges would have class biases similar to the departed and unregretted Royalists. The amendment to the Constitution most ardently demanded by antifederalists at the time of ratification was the right to jury trial in civil cases.[8] Its purpose was to constrain the predicted class bias of the federal judiciary.[9] Little attention was given to the prospect that life-tenured judges would invalidate legislation. It seems likely that the antifederalists would have made much of the issue had they fully understood what was in store.[10]

The behavior of Federalist judges appointed by Presidents Washington and Adams did little to disarm their antifederalist critics. Some Federalist judges deployed their powers to impede the advent of Jefferson, especially in their administration of the Alien and Sedition Acts of 1798.[11] Justice Samuel Chase, for example, announced that "he would teach the lawyers in Virginia the difference between liberty and the licentiousness of the press" and refused to seat any but Federalists as jurors in sedition cases tried in his circuit.[12] When Jeffersonians came to power in 1801, they hoped to even the score with Chase and his like, whom they deemed "partial, vindictive, and cruel."[13] Also on their political agenda was the removal of Chief Justice John Marshall and other last minute, "midnight," appointments by President Adams.[14] Their first step was to withhold commissions from some of the other judges appointed at midnight by President Adams, an action leading to the celebrated case of *Marbury v. Madison*.[15] However, the Senate could not muster the votes to convict Chase.[16] President Jefferson concluded that the impeachment process was a "mere scarecrow."[17] The scheme to cleanse the federal judiciary of Federalists was aborted, and the political autonomy of the federal judiciary was reinforced.

Marshall's first act as chief justice was to employ a novel device, the opinion of the Court, to replace the seriatim opinions of individual judges theretofore known to English practice.[18] This device greatly enlarged the political role of the Court because it enabled it, through Marshall's opinions, to utter legal texts of its own, something no English court had previously done. In 1810, after leaving the presidency, Jefferson wrote that "[w]e have long enough suffered under the base prostitution of law to party passions in one judge." "In [Marshall's] hands," Jefferson said, "the law is nothing more than an ambiguous text, to be explained by his sophistry into any meaning which may subserve his personal malice."[19] He proposed term limits for federal judges.[20]

McCulloch v. Maryland,[21] decided in 1819, aroused Marshall's critics more than any other decision in which he participated. Maryland had sued a cashier of the Baltimore branch of the Bank of the United States to collect a tax imposed by its legislature on all banks doing business in the state. The Bank resisted the tax on the ground that, as a federal instrumentality, it was immune to state taxation. Marshall, writing for a unanimous Court, published a thirty-seven page opinion not only confirming the position of the Bank, but also laying a political foundation for the relationship between the nation and the states by reading the Necessary and Proper Clause expansively and by declaring the Constitution to be an instrument created by the People and not by the governments of the states who had initiated the process producing it.[22]

Marshall's political theory proved to be sound, at least to those of us who value the cohesion of the federal union. The nature of the relations of the states to the Constitution expressed in his opinion of the Court was the one later invoked by Daniel Webster,[23] President Jackson,[24] and Joseph Story[25] in the nullification controversy with South Carolina,[26] and underlay the argument advanced by Lincoln[27] in his debates with Senator Douglas.[28]

McCulloch was, however, a troubling case for those claiming the right of self-government. There was no unavoidable conflict between the interest of the people of Maryland and the power of the federal government. The Court could have sustained both the Bank and the Maryland tax, leaving the state's taxing power to be resolved when and if Congress explicitly provided the Bank with immunity from state taxation. The expansive opinion of the Court denying Maryland's power to tax a commercial enterprise because it held a federal charter needlessly trespassed on the political rights of the citizens of Maryland to tax and regulate banks and contributed to the demise of the Bank.

Criticism of *McCulloch* was stringent. Marshall responded in a journalistic exchange with his Richmond neighbor, Spencer Roane,[29] an ardent Jeffersonian. Even more incensed at Marshall than Jefferson or Roane was John Taylor, who in 1820 published *Construction Construed and Constitutions Vindicated*,[30] a work portraying Marshall and his brethren as an arrogant lot who had abused the political power of the federal judiciary. Unknown to Marshall's critics was a fact Marshall took pains to conceal: He had a substantial personal financial investment in the Bank that was enhanced by his Court's decision.[31]

A secondary effect of *McCulloch* was to strengthen the position of President Jackson when he vetoed the renewal of the Bank's charter. Had the Bank been paying taxes like other banks, it is at least possible that its charter would not have been vetoed and the Bank might have been functioning still in Cooley's time.

In the same year in which *McCulloch* was decided, the Court also decided *Dartmouth College v. Woodward*.[32] Article I of the Constitution forbade states to make laws "impairing the Obligation of Contracts."[33] The language was an adaptation of a clause in the Northwest Ordinance of 1776 and was explained by Madison (its draftsman) as a restraint on the states' practices of making depreciated paper legal tender for the payment of debts.[34]

In *Dartmouth College*, the Court applied this provision to bar New Hampshire from revoking the corporate charter of the college. This required an impressive stretch of the constitutional text. The charter had been issued by the British Crown. Because donors had made gifts to the college in reliance on its charter, Marshall was able to find a contractual duty of New Hampshire to continue the institution in accordance with its original charter, on which the donors had relied. And in dicta he went further, stating that

> [t]he object[s] for which a corporation is created are universally such as the government wishes to promote. They are deemed beneficial to the country; and this benefit constitutes the consideration, and in most cases, the sole consideration of the grant.

In short, because corporations are "universally" benign institutions, the state that charters them is barred from changing its mind, whatever the popular will. While one might later have distinguished *Dartmouth College* as a case involving a non-profit corporation, it was soon extended, without discussion, to purely commercial firms.[35] On the other hand, Marshall indicated that his holding would not apply to corporations chartered to exercise political power.[36] Thus, the state retained power to dissolve local governments without regard for the wishes or interests of local residents who may have relied upon the existence of their municipal charter when settling where they did.[37]

Swift v. Tyson,[38] although less a subject of political resentment at the time it was decided, was another notable transgression by the Court. Acting on the initiative of Justice Story, it attempted a grand misappropriation of the common law. Although the holding was limited in its application to cases within the federal judicial jurisdiction because of the diversity of the parties' citizenships, Justice Story seems to have envisioned that the states' highest courts would adhere to his utterances in all cases requiring application of an American common law. His declaration that in diversity cases the controlling common law is federal in character was achieved by a dubious reading of the Judiciary Act. John Chipman Gray, a man of preeminent wisdom and modesty,[39] attributed the decision to Justice Story's arrogance. As Gray explained:

> [Story] was then by far the oldest judge in commission on the bench; he was a man of great learning, and of reputation for learning greater even than the learning itself; he was occupied at the time in writing a book on bills of exchange, which would, of itself, lead him to dogmatize on the subject; he had had great success in extending the jurisdiction in Admiralty; he was fond of glittering generalities; and he was possessed of a restless vanity. All these things conspired to produce the result.[40]

Given that Maine case law was scant at the time of the decision, there may have been some wisdom in Story's opinion disregarding it, but, as Gray forcefully demonstrated, *Swift*, in the breadth of its sweep, was intellectually and politically indefensible. Indeed, the Court in overruling *Swift* in 1938 went so far as to denounce the decision as a transgression against the Constitution, because it converted the Judiciary Act into an instrument subverting law made by state courts.[41]

The premier example of the abuse of political power by the Supreme Court was its notorious decision in *Dred Scott*.[42] That 1857 decision denied the power of territories to prohibit slavery and declared that the Constitution of the United States conferred no rights whatever on Negro citizens. The decision, rendered at the private request of President-elect John Buchanan,[43] was without foundation in the text or the tradition from which it emerged.[44] The Court seemingly hoped to save the Union by finding in the Constitution all the rights desired by Southern slaveowners. That hope proved to be as unfounded as the decision itself, which provided the material for the Lincoln-Douglas debates and thus became a central cause of Lincoln's election to the presidency[45] and a precipitant of the Civil War itself. On the occasion of his first inaugural, Lincoln commented on the decision:

> [I]f the policy of the Government upon vital questions affecting the whole people is irrevocably fixed by decisions of the Supreme Court . . . the people will have ceased to be their own rulers, having to that extent practically resigned their Government into the hands of that eminent tribunal.[46]

Dred Scott illustrated the hazards of foreclosing the political resolution of divisive issues, and was also a superior example of the impotence of the Court to influence the moral sentiments prevailing in the Republic. No one was convinced by the Court's opinion. Because it was contrary to "the common thoughts of men," it served instead to inflame an alarmed opposition to the incipient spread of slavery by purporting to foreclose the normal avenues of democratic political debate and legislative resolution, where compromise might have been effected. It may also have had the malign effect of reinforcing the belief of the ruling class in the slave states that their claims were rooted in constitutional rights. The Court's decision was, in Cooley's term, "feeble" in its intended effect.

President Lincoln, not without cause, mistrusted the Court that had authored that misdeed, and feared that it would deploy its power to impede the military effort he led to save the Union. On one occasion, he defied a writ issued by Chief Justice Taney for the release of a congressman held for inciting draft evasion, and even considered arresting the chief justice.[47] To prevent the Court from other mischief, he persuaded Congress to enlarge the Court to ten members, permitting him to appoint Stephen Field, a reliable Unionist, to its membership.[48]

These events were almost certainly in Cooley's mind when he spoke in 1886. More recent misadventures of the Court may have been as well. As he spoke, the federal judiciary was aligning itself solidly on the side of "capital" against "labor," and, under the intellectual leadership of Stephen Field, was beginning to invalidate, as contrary to natural law embodied in the Fourteenth Amendment, state laws enacted to protect workers and consumers from predation by those who had amassed economic power.[49] Ironically, Field's leadership would reflect Field's own Jacksonian origins, resting, as it did, on a suspicion that any governmental regulation of the economy would likely disserve the public interest.[50] It was Field who in 1895 led the Court in invalidating the federal income tax, which he denounced as the commencement of class war.[51] That decision rested on the opaque clause of the Constitution prohibiting Congress from levying a "direct tax," a provision apparently understood at the time of ratification to apply to taxes on property.[52] The holding would have to be overruled by ratification of the Sixteenth Amendment.

As a member of the Court, Holmes would later resist the impulse of Justice Field and his brethren to read the Fourteenth Amendment as an enactment of their political preferences. Cooley, as we shall see, had parted company with co-Jacksonians such as Field to favor regulation rooted in "the common thoughts of men," who felt themselves oppressed and abused by concentrated wealth. While retaining his Jacksonian commitment to democratic institutions, his agrarian instincts yielded to the Progressive insight that many citizens needed the protection of government.

Thus, long before 1886, Cooley and other Americans favoring self-rule had experienced numerous dramatic occasions on which the Court and the profession it represented had usurped powers claimed by the people themselves. At least in the instances named, the nation had paid a substantial price for misrule resulting from chronic failures of political judgment by the Supreme Court. There was ample reason to believe that the collective judgment of the electorate was no more imprudent than that of a pretentious profession and an arrogant Court.

8

Deference to Democracy:
A Barnburning Court

The Jacksonian politics and jurisprudence subsiding in November 1886 was illustrated by Cooley's work in his two decades on the Supreme Court of Michigan. What remains of Cooley's unpublished papers does not illuminate his judicial decisions, but his many judicial opinions reveal that the "common thoughts" he celebrated were conventional in the Jacksonian social order. He employed his power with cautious regard for the prerogatives and responsibilities of groups elected to legislate. Only once in his twenty years on the bench did he render a decision that could be reasonably regarded as idiosyncratic and intrusive, and even it was much admired by many co-Jacksonians.

Frederick Grimke suggested as one reason for the election of judges that elected judges are more courteous than appointed ones.[1] So it may be. Soon after his election to the court in 1865, Cooley became known to the Michigan bar as an exceptionally attentive listener, one who would in his opinions respond forthrightly to the arguments advanced by losing counsel.[2] He was re-elected in 1869 and 1877, but failed to be re-elected in 1885.[3]

Cooley's twenty years on the bench occurred in a time denoted by Robert Wiebe as a "search for order."[4] America was responding to the destabilizing effects of an epic war in which a million young men, constituting at least a fifth of those of military age, had been killed or maimed. The popular hope for restored stability in the social order was reflected in a desire, widely shared among lawyers, for predictability in the law.[5] Cooley understood and shared in this anxiety, and it was likely a factor in his preference for "safe" judges. Several years after his defeat at the polls and retirement as a judge, Cooley found occasion to reassure the electorate and the bar that the legal process in his time on the bench had been predictable in its results.[6]

Nevertheless, Cooley was always conscious that his judicial office was a political one and did not recoil from giving political reasons for judicial decisions.[7] When he expressed political values, they were often those of the Equal Rights doctrine embodied in the culture brought to Michigan from western New York, values that he shared with most of the people of Michigan. His behavior was controlled by a professional discipline requiring scrupulous attention to the mandates of legislation and to the text of the 1850 Michigan Constitution, as understood by his political constituents. Cooley read both constitutional and statutory texts in light of the cultural context from which they arose and viewed their ratification or enactment as events in the social history of Michigan. He did not deny the possibility that constitutional language might over time experience a change of meaning, but his historicism and professional self-restraint dictated that such changes originate in cultural change already reflected in the values and moral aspirations of the people. Genuine cultural change ought, in this view, be reflected in the understandings of a broadly representative legal profession, not merely in a change in the personnel of the court or the personal ambitions of judges to effect cultural change reflective of their idiosyncratic, subcultural or class preferences.

One of Cooley's first judicial opinions in 1865 seemed admirably professional to his constituents. He held the state's election laws to be in violation of the Michigan constitution's requirement that voters be resident in the state.[8] The law his court invalidated was enacted to permit voting by soldiers on military duty outside the state, a purpose warmly approved by the people of Michigan, and also by Cooley and the other members of his court, all of whom were committed to the Union cause. Because the absentee soldiers were predominantly Republicans, the decision was especially unwelcome to those who had supported Cooley's election to the court. As a result of the decision, some Republican legislators lost offices to which they had been elected by votes cast by servicemen.

Cooley explained that the text of the constitution was clear, and to disobey it "in times like these" would loosen "the anchor of our safety." The judiciary, he said, should do nothing to "bend the meaning of words to meet unexpected exigencies."[9] "Plain meanings" of constitutional dictates must be obeyed. "Times like these" required the court to give no one occasion to question its fidelity to law.[10]

Cooley did not add that he was constrained not to bend the meaning of words to advance his own interests or the obvious interests of his political allies, for that was the difficulty he faced. His political adversaries, not without reason, would have identified a holding for the military voters as a self-serving manipulation. He was aware that many Americans had in the past been offended by seemingly partisan judicial decisions, such as *McCulloch*, *Dartmouth College*, and *Dred Scott*.[11] There could be no Michigan judges wholly disinterested in the outcome of the case, because all had political allegiances of one stripe or another. Possibly an appointed judge having no political constituents might have reached a different result, because he could have done so without fear that his decision would be regarded as self-serving. While the constitution limited the franchise to those in residence in Michigan, a disinterested judge might well have concluded that soldiers performing their public duty to the state of Michigan by serving in its militia were "present" in Michigan within the "plain meaning" of the constitutional text.

Cooley's strict fidelity to text in this circumstance proved to be good politics. The decision led the Democrats in 1869 to give serious consideration to supporting his re-election; even though it caused Republicans to complain that while they did the electing, the Democrats got the decisions,[12] many may have taken special pride in the integrity of their court.

While the voting rights decision exemplified Justice Cooley's obedience to "plain meaning" even when it yielded personally unwelcome results, he was not committed to strict adherence to "original intent"[13] as the source of constitutional meaning. He was quite willing to project the constitutional purpose of 1850 to unforeseen circumstances and thus to accommodate the constitutional text to discernible contemporary mores, where in his judgment the text admitted of such accommodation, at least in circumstances different from those bearing on the voting rights case.

For example, the 1850 Michigan Constitution had authorized the state to provide for "primary schools." In 1874, the question was presented whether a school district created by the legislature was authorized to collect taxes to support a high school teaching adolescents non-elementary subjects such as Latin. Cooley held that it was. In his opinion for the court, he reviewed the history of public education in Michigan and praised the foresight of the founders of 1850 in authorizing the state to furnish "the poorest boy of the state" with instruction as good "as the rich man can furnish for his children with all his wealth."[14] He found in the constitution no restriction on "primary schools," with respect to "the branches of knowledge which their officers may cause to be taught, or the grade of instruction [that] may be given, if their voters consent in regular form to bear the expense and raise the taxes for the purposes."[15] It was pertinent that the constitution required the legislature to create and support a public university; the founders of 1850 would have been irrational to authorize and even require elementary and higher education while forbidding the use of public revenue to support interconnecting secondary education.

Although this case contrasts with the voting rights case in its method of interpreting constitutional texts, an important difference lay in the fact that Cooley and his political allies had no stake in the secondary schools case. There being no risk that his decision would be seen as self-dealing or self-indulgent, Cooley was more free to interpret the text without artificial formal rigidity. This was, indeed, an easy case; it is hard to imagine an American court reaching a contrary result. The two cases together serve as a good example of the inadequacy of "plain meaning" or "original intent" as overriding principles of interpretation.

Other examples of Cooley's interpretative art exhibit his commitment to democratic politics as the appropriate source of the moral values informing his judgments. He believed in local government as the best outlet for the expression of popular morality. He explained this preference to his audience at Johns Hopkins University in 1878, advancing the idea of constitutional home rule to protect local government as Burkean conservatism. His proposal was then an idea of some novelty, and ran contrary to the dictum of John Marshall in *Dartmouth College*, but was reflective of thought expressed by Francis Lieber in 1852.[16] The idea would become an article of faith for twentieth-century Progressives.[17] In presenting it, Cooley was "in advance of his age," but his aim was, as Cooper put it, to "conserve democracy" and the institutions of popular self-government.

As a judge, Cooley assumed that the Michigan legislature shared his predisposition favoring local self-government. While this supposition may have been unwarranted, he was careful not to insist on his position, but left it open to the legislature to reject it. An illustrative case is *People v. Hurlbut*.[18] The 1850 Constitution in pertinent part provided that "[j]udicial officers of cities and villages shall be elected; and all other officers shall be elected or appointed as the legislature may direct."[19] The Common Council of Detroit had designated sewer and water commissioners, of whom Hurlbut was one. The legislature had thereafter created a Board of Public Works for Detroit, with powers formerly exercised by Hurlbut, and it designated other persons to serve on that board. Pursuant to that enactment, an action was brought by the attorney general of Michigan to remove Hurlbut from his now disabled office. Cooley's court held for the attorney general and removed Hurlbut, but interpreted the statute in question as one making only provisional appointments to the Board of Public Works, thus leaving the Common Council free to make permanent appointments to that Board, perhaps even of Hurlbut himself.

This decision embodied an aggressive interpretation of the controlling legislation, one that could be said to have twisted its apparent meaning. The statutory text expressed rather clearly a legislative purpose to displace the officers appointed by the Common Council. What the Cooley court did was to return the issue to the legislature, with a cautionary expression of concern that the legislature had perhaps overlooked public values of constitutional import.[20] If the legislature were to revise the Board of Public Works legislation to make it explicit that the responsibility for appointment of its members had been taken away from the Common Council, then the court would, Cooley noted, be forced to decide an issue that it had evaded by its strained interpretation of the statute.

If forced by explicit legislative re-enactment to reconsider, the later court might defer to the superior political station of two legislatures. It could then rely on the most obvious meaning of the constitutional text quoted above, that is, that the mode of selection of the members of the Board is a matter for unfettered legislative choice. But Cooley's opinion also left open the possibility of a different decision by a later court that would give force to a different principle.

This technique may be usefully contrasted to a technique sometimes employed by judges who are less deferential to the legislature. I refer to the "constitutional flare."[21] A flare is dictum not necessary to decide a case before a court that utters it, and may appear in a concurring opinion. It is a caution to the legislature that, while the present case does not require judicial intervention, there is something amiss in a statute to which the legislature's attention is called. While this device is not without its utility, it is not one to be employed by a deferential court seeking to perform its role with minimum intrusion on the legislative role.

The different principle that Cooley had found in the interstices of the Constitution of 1850, and that he was calling to the legislature's attention in the *Hurlbut* case, was a general constitutional preference for local government. He argued that it was implicit in the constitutional language quoted that the officers of a local board of public works should be either elected or appointed, as the legislature might choose, but only by local voters or their locally elected representatives. They could not, he suggested, be appointed by a potentate in distant Lansing or elected by the voters of some larger region such as the state as a whole.[22] It might thus be unconstitutional for the voters of the state to presume to elect a mayor of Detroit.

In justifying this inference, Cooley did not rely on case law, but on the whole range of literature asserting self-government to be an essential element of the English and especially the American legal tradition. In particular, he relied upon Jefferson, de Tocqueville, and Lieber. Lieber, no Jacksonian, had emphasized in his work on comparative constitutional law[23] the importance to republican government of decentralization facilitating participation by citizens in public decisions most affecting their own interests. The right to jury trial was viewed as part of the same fabric woven to assure every man an equal voice in government. Cooley wrote in Lieber's terms:

> When the state reaches out and draws to itself and appropriates the powers which from time immemorial have been locally possessed and exercised, and introduces into its legislation the centralizing ideas of continental Europe, . . . we seem forced back upon and compelled to take up and defend the plainest and most primary axioms of free government, as if even in Anglican liberty, which has been gained step by step, through extorted charters and bills of rights, the punishment of kings and the overthrow of dynasties, nothing was settled and nothing established.[24]

"Some things," Cooley said, weakening in his resistance to natural law, "are too plain to be written." Breathlessly, he elaborated:

> If this charter of state government we call a constitution were all there was of constitutional command; if the usages, the customs, the maxims, that have sprung from the habits of life, modes of thought, methods of trying facts by the neighborhood, and mutual responsibility in neighborhood interests, the precepts which have come from the revolutions which overturned tyrannies, the sentiments of manly independence and self-control which impelled our ancestors to summon the local community to redress local evils, instead of relying upon King or legislature at a distance to do so, if a recognition of all these were to be stricken from the body of our constitutional law, a lifeless skeleton might remain, but the living spirit, that which gives force and attraction, which makes it valuable and draws it to the affections of the people, that which distinguishes it from the numberless constitutions, so called, which in Europe have been set up and thrown down in the last one hundred years, many of which in their expressions have seemed equally fair and to possess equal promise with ours, and have only been wanting in support and vitality which these alone can give, this living and breathing spirit, which supplies the interpretation of the words of the written charter, would be utterly lost and gone.[25]

One might guess from the shrill tone of this opinion that the judge was on thin legal ice, as indeed he was. The conventional view, expressed by Marshall in *Dartmouth College* and acknowledged by Cooley in his treatise,[26] was that local government is the mere creature of the state, having no status independent of the legislature, in the absence of explicit constitutional provisions conferring "home rule" powers. Nevertheless, the Michigan legislature was apparently for the moment persuaded by the court; it revised the statute to provide that members of the Board of Public Works should be appointed by the Detroit Common Council.[27]

Cooley performed a similar interpretation of another statute imposing state control on local matters. The legislature had created a Park Commission for Detroit as part of the state government. The Commission identified land suitable for an urban park and sought to compel the Common Council elected by the people of Detroit to buy and improve it at local expense.[28] The Supreme Court of Michigan upheld the Council's right to refuse the "unfunded mandate," interpreting the statute to avoid conflict with the constitutional values of local self-government. The same principle of construction was later invoked to shield local communities from the efforts of a state-appointed regional drain commissioner to require them to build drains at local expense to serve neighboring communities.[29] In none of these cases was there a conflict between local government and an office of state government having statewide jurisdiction and thus the full political backing of the legislature. Justice Cooley, for the court, reasoned that in such matters, "the motive for outside interference [by the state] will very likely be something besides a desire to do good to a community in which the parties interfering have no personal interest."[30] The legislature, he concluded, should be presumed (in the absence of the most explicit language expressing a statewide policy or establishing a statewide program) to respect the right of a local community to control local affairs.

In these matters of local self-government, Cooley likely succeeded in expressing the prevailing values of the people of Michigan, and perhaps also those of the legal profession of Michigan, although this is less clear. Cooley and his court were also anticipating, by only a few years, the Home Rule movement that inserted into many state constitutions explicit provisions limiting the powers of state legislatures to regulate or burden local communities. That movement first surfaced in Missouri in 1875, and was fostered in the early years of this century by Progressives.[31] The Supreme Court of the United States would hold that institutions of local government are not protected from the state by the federal Constitution,[32] but the Court would recognize local self-government as having constitutional value bearing in other respects on the application of the Fourteenth Amendment.[33]

Cooley also employed his interpretative art to protect other values favored by the Barnburners' principle of Equal Rights that he found embedded in the interstices of the Michigan Constitution. For example, the technique of interpreting legislation to avoid a constitutional issue was also employed in an early school segregation case. In 1869, Cooley's court ordered the elected Detroit Board of Education to reverse its decision and admit African-American children to schools previously restricted to white children.

Public schools in Detroit had been segregated from an early time when African-American children first began to appear in the community. The legislation creating the Detroit schools and governing their operation was silent on matters of attendance. There was, however, an 1867 amendment to the laws generally governing schools in the state that provided, somewhat enigmatically, that local schools should be open "to residents of any district therein." For other purposes, the general school laws had been regarded as inapplicable to the Detroit schools because those schools were the subject of a separate body of legislation. Justice Campbell argued that the clause quoted was (like the rest of the general school code) inapplicable to Detroit schools and did not, in any case, address issues of racial assignment. But the majority, led by Cooley, rejected Campbell's interpretation of the statutes and held that the Detroit practice violated the new state law.[34]

Cooley also slyly noted that inasmuch as the statute applied, "it does not become important to consider what would otherwise have been the law,"[35] thus implying the possibility that the practice of the Detroit schools was constitutionally proscribed. He refrained from quoting his own recently published text elaborating on his statement of a general doctrine of state

constitutional law that "[e]quality of rights, privileges, and capacities unquestionably should be the aim of the law."[36] Nor did he refer to the
"Equal Protection Clause" of the recently adopted Fourteenth Amendment
to the Constitution of the United States. Had he, even in dicta, pursued the
avoided constitutional issue, his court's decision could have been a precedent of some weight favoring the dissent in the 1896 decision of the
Supreme Court of the United States in *Plessy v. Ferguson*.[37] And he might
thus have enshrined his name in the history of the civil rights movement.

The constitutional issue that Cooley avoided in so deciding the school
segregation case was not raised by any explicit provision of the Michigan
constitution. Cooley had, however, in his treatise stated it to be settled law
under diverse state constitutions that legislatures cannot lawfully enact
"unequal or partial" legislation. "Equality of rights, privileges, and legal
capacities should be the aim of the law," he wrote. And, "[t]he State, it is to
be presumed, has no favors to bestow, and designs to inflict no arbitrary
deprivation of rights."[38] These are among the few statements in the treatise
that are not heavily documented. Perhaps this gloss was warranted, but
Cooley's opinion confirms that he was not always a close textualist.

Another Cooley interpretation favored freedom of expression, another
Barnburner icon. Perhaps most prescient of Cooley's constitutional opinions was his dissent in *Atkinson v. The Detroit Free Press*.[39] Atkinson had
been a member of the Detroit Board of Trade. The *Free Press* reported that
Atkinson, as a member of the Board, was engaged in activity that it not un-
reasonably deemed fraudulent. Atkinson sued the publisher and recovered
a judgment for libel that was affirmed by the Supreme Court of Michigan
with an opinion by Justice Campbell. Cooley filed a long dissent, arguing
that a newspaper commenting on the conduct of a public figure should be
held liable for defamation only on proof of malice. His position was supported by an inference from provisions of the Michigan Constitution protecting freedom of expression, but prefigured the 1964 decision of the
Supreme Court of the United States in *New York Times v. Sullivan*.[40] He
emphasized the need for integrity on the Board of Trade and the duty of the
press to expose moral shortfalls in the performance of duty by its members.[41] He concluded:

> If such a discussion of a matter of public interest were prima facie an unlawful
> act, and the author were obliged to justify every statement by evidence of its
> literal truth, the liberty of public discussion would be unworthy of being
> named a privilege of value. It would be better to restore the censorship of a
> despotism than to assume to give a liberty which can only be accepted under a
> responsibility that is always threatening and may at any time be ruinous. . . .
> [E]very man of common discernment who observes what is taking place
> around him and what influences public opinion, cannot fail to know that rep-
> utation is best protected when the press is free.[42]

Although prescient, Cooley's reasoning in *Atkinson* can be questioned. His suggestion that prior restraint might be less objectionable than the imposition of tort liability for defamation has been roundly rejected by the Supreme Court of the United States.[43] And one "who observes what is taking place around him and what influences public opinion" in 1999 might possibly fail to recognize that "reputation is best protected when the press is free of any accountability for purveying falsehoods about participants in our public life." Had Cooley encountered modern media and the transmogrification of our politics by their means he might have wondered whether media free of the restraint imposed by defamation law is the best protection either of honest reputation or of public discussion. When politics are conducted through false and misleading advertisements ornamented with professional art and music, inserted into spots within commercial entertainment when large and inadvertent audiences can be filled with disinformation, Cooley's dictum seems out of touch with reality. Perhaps had he decided *Atkinson* a century later, he would have led the way in an opposite, or at least a different, direction. Illustratively, his court (and the Supreme Court in *Sullivan*) could have imposed liability for proven special damages on publishers who cannot show a sound basis for their allegations, limiting only the liability for general or punitive damages. This would have afforded public officials a forum in which to challenge statements made about them without the severe chilling effect that concerned Cooley. In any case, Cooley's decision again reflected his willingness to interpret the constitutional text as an expression of Jacksonian Barnburner values.

Only once did Cooley's court frontally challenge the Michigan legislature so as to provoke serious controversy. This was yet another occasion when his Jacksonian premises were detected in the interstices of the constitutional text. The case involved public financial assistance to privately owned railroads. Cooley's decision was widely heralded by the people of Michigan, even as it deeply distressed railroads and investment bankers. The decision was perhaps more quaint than prescient, although a postmodern generation chafing over the expenditure of hundreds of billions of tax dollars to repay individuals for improvident investments made through excessively insured savings and loan institutions might see the issue in a light favorable to Cooley.[44] So might those who have lost their jobs as a result of plant closings caused by subsidies paid by distant state and local governments to employers as inducements to relocate,[45] or taxpayers whose taxes are used for the benefit of private profit-seekers such as the operators of major league franchises, or fans whose teams are moved to secure the benefits of a public subsidy provided in a different venue.

The signal case involved the town of Salem, Michigan, which had pledged its credit to aid construction of the Detroit & Howell Railroad in consideration of a promise by the railroad to provide service to the town; the railroad was constructed in reliance upon that and other such pledges. Many towns in Michigan, indeed thousands in the United States, had made such pledges under the duress that their failure to make the commitment would result in a denial of rail service and the almost certain atrophy of the local economy. In 1864 the legislature, at the insistence of the railroads and after a sustained dispute signaling widespread popular opposition,[46] had authorized municipalities such as Salem to levy taxes to aid railroads. In 1870, the Detroit & Howell Railroad sued the town of Salem to compel it to honor its promise of support by issuing bonds to be retired from the town's future tax revenues. The Supreme Court of Michigan denied relief, holding the 1864 legislation unconstitutional because any payment of interest or principal on such bonds would entail the use of public revenue for a private purpose; because the municipalities were unable to pay interest or principal, it would be fraudulent to issue bonds as demanded by the railroad.[47]

The opinion of the court first distinguished public subsidies from the exercise of the power of eminent domain. "It is true," Justice Cooley wrote,

> that a railroad in the hands of a private corporation is often spoken of as a public highway, and that it has been recognized as so far a public object as to justify the appropriation of private property for its construction; but this fact does not conclusively determine the right to employ taxation in aid of the road in the like case. Reasoning by analogy from one of the sovereign powers of the government to another, is exceedingly liable to deceive and mislead. An object may be *public* in one sense and for one purpose, when in a general sense and for other purposes, it would be idle and misleading to apply the same term. All governmental powers exist for public purposes, but they are not necessarily to be exercised under the same conditions of public interest. . . .
>
> [The railroads'] resemblance to the highways which belong to the public, which the people make and keep in repair, and which are open to the whole public to be used at will, and with such means of locomotion as taste, pleasure, or convenience may dictate, is rather fanciful. . . . [Railroads] are not, when in private hands, the *people's highways*; but they are private property, whose owners make it their business to transport persons and merchandise in their own carriages, over their own land, for such pecuniary compensation as may be stipulated. . . . [Their] business . . . has indeed its public aspect inasmuch as it accommodates a public want. . . . But it is not such a purpose [so different from] the opening of a hotel, the establishment of a line of stages, or the putting into operation of a grist mill.[48]

The court then proceeded, with restraint, to give expression to the received doctrine of Equal Rights embodied in the Michigan Constitution of 1850:

> We concede . . . that religion is essential . . . yet we prohibit the state from burdening the citizen with its support. . . . Certain professions and occupations in

life are also essential, but we have no authority to employ the public moneys to induce persons to enter them. . . . [49]

However great the need in the direction of any particular calling, the interference of the Government is not tolerated because, though it may be supplying a public want, it is considered as invading the domain that belongs exclusively to private inclination and enterprise.[50] . . .

[T]he discrimination between different classes or occupations, and the favoring of one at the expense of the rest, whether that one be farming, or banking, or merchandising, or milling, or printing, or railroading is not legitimate legislation, and is a violation of that equality of right which is a maxim of state government. . . . [W]hen the state once enters upon the business of subsidies, we shall not fail to discover that the strong and the powerful interests are those most likely to control the legislation, and that the weaker will be taxed to enhance the profits of the stronger.[51]

This decision was "the great news of the summer" of 1870.[52] The governor heatedly reported that it destroyed the value of millions of dollars of bonds already issued by Michigan towns other than Salem, some of them in the hands of third parties, and asked the legislature to do something to protect the innocent investors. Railroad men were apoplectic. The decision was criticized as contrary to the great weight of precedent,[53] which it was, and lacking footing in any explicit constitutional text, which it was,[54] but defended as a prudent application of established principle to restrain the savaging of the public fisc by titans of industry extorting payments of public money as a precondition to the provision of a private service to private citizens. The decision proved to be popular among Michigan voters, and every member of the court rendering it was considered a candidate for higher public office.[55]

There is no reason to doubt that Cooley knew precisely how shocking the decision would be, and that he intended it as a rallying cry against what he regarded as widespread knavery. The *New York World* crowed:

[I]t is a pleasing reflection that, mocked and disregarded as it has been as effete, illiberal, and unprogressive, [the old doctrine's] sound sense and old fashioned honesty are bringing it once more into prominence, approved and vindicated. . . . [I]f now reaffirmed in other courts . . . and maintained in the press and in the ballot box, many spoliations may be averted.[56]

But too few rallied to the cry for it to have had its intended consequence. While the railroads never succeeded in effecting any change in the Michigan law to reverse the holding of the Cooley court, they did succeed in preventing the spread of the doctrine so damaging to their interests.[57] Had Cooley's doctrine been federal law in the 1980s, the Supreme Court might have forbidden the use of federal tax revenues to bail out failed banking institutions and their depositors, and state supreme courts might have forbidden cities and states to compete in giving public funds to private investors in the expectation of creating new jobs stimulating to their local economies, or of attracting major league franchises away from other cities.

That the *Salem* case was singular merits emphasis. More characteristic was Cooley's dictum in *State of Michigan v. Iron Cliffs Company*.[58] Iron Cliffs in that case challenged the powers of the Tax Commission established by the legislature in 1882; Cooley responded for the court:

> If the demurrer is sustained the law will be defeated, and we shall have decided that the Legislature has assumed to exercise authority which does not belong to it. In cases heretofore presented for our examination we have indicated certain rules of propriety and caution which should be observed by us when thus invited to declare void the action of a coordinate department of the government, and to those rules we should be inexcusable if we did not strictly adhere. One of these is that we must enter upon an examination of a constitutional question like this assuming that the Legislature has been guilty of no usurpation. We are to remember also that we have no supervisory power in respect to legislation; that the lawmaking power is not responsible to the judiciary for the wisdom of its acts, and that however unwise or impolitic their acts may appear, they must stand as law unless the Legislature has plainly overstepped its constitutional authority, or lost jurisdiction in the attempt to exercise it, by failing to observe some express constitutional direction. And the case must be clear: a mere doubt on our part of the validity of what the lawmaking department of the government has undertaken to enact is no ground for annulling it. These are commonplaces in constitutional law; they have often been declared by us, and still more often by other courts. . . . [I]t is to be feared that courts sometimes, without perhaps being conscious of the fact, proceed in the examination of questions concerning the constitutionality of legislation as if they were at liberty to consider the questions as questions of policy merely. . . .
>
> But every such case is mischievous in its tendency, for it shows that courts lay down proper rules for the government of their own conduct, and then fail to observe them. It is not less important that a court keep carefully within its proper jurisdiction than that the Legislature should observe the limits set by the Constitution to its powers. [59]

Whether Cooley was faithful to his own dictum in all the cases described above is a question the reader may well consider. Perhaps *Salem* merely confirms that even Cooley was imperfect in his own self-restraint. To the extent that Cooley imparted his own personal values to constitutional texts, he exhibited the failing against which he protested in *Iron Cliffs*. On the other hand, it is not unlikely that Cooley was right in believing that his Jacksonian premises were the "common thoughts of men" in Michigan in his time.

The reader may wonder how a judge so solicitous of "the common thoughts of men" failed to gain re-election in 1885. His defeat seems to have had little to do with public reaction to his professional work. Some of his court's decisions on employer liability for work-related injuries had drawn criticism from some engaged in the labor movement. It was likely more significant that he had in non-judicial writing been a critic of Republican Presidents Grant[60] and Hayes,[61] but this was more an explanation for his failure to be appointed to the Supreme Court of the United States than for the weakness of Republican support for his re-election. Moreover, it was known that he had supported Grover Cleveland, a Democrat, for president in 1884 against the candidacy of William Blaine, a Republican senator widely known for his elastic public morals.[62] Indeed, Cleveland's campaign slogan, "A public office is a public trust," was known to be Cooley's expression. He lacked the support of Detroit newspapers for more personal reasons. The owner of *The Free Press* had been an aggressive member of the Board of Regents who had attacked the president of the university, whom Cooley had publicly and effectively defended. The other major paper, *The Evening News,* was one against whom Cooley's court had recently rendered an unfavorable decision in a libel case,[63] leading its editorialist to describe him as an "ingenious sophist" who "covered up with the ermine of the highest tribunal in the commonwealth the shameful record of fraud and corruption" that it had sought to reveal.[64] It might have been a factor that he also accepted the nomination of the Prohibition Party; temperance, it may be recalled, was another Barnburner tradition, but did not attract universal support among Michiganians. All these causes of his political weakness may have been inconsequential, because the voters recorded a "Democratic Deluge"[65] in which all Michigan Republican candidates lost.

9

A Nineteenth-Century Classic

It was Cooley's scholarship, particularly *Constitutional Limitations*, that brought him into disfavor in this century. Much of the disapproval of Cooley's work could have been more appropriately directed at the uses to which it was put decades after he ceased to be involved in its editing. Those who misused Cooley as an authority and those who later disparaged his work shared the failing that they ignored the social and political context in which he wrote. His book was a remarkably faithful account of the law as it stood at the time of writing in 1868.

Read in context, Cooley's great book was conventional in the values informing its interpretations, which is precisely what he intended it to be. He was as a text-writer, as he was as a judge and teacher, seeking to express "the common thoughts of men" as reflected in the texts of the constitutions of the states and in those few portions of the federal Constitution limiting the powers of the states and embodied in the judicial decisions of the highest state courts.

To understand Cooley as a scholar and the reasons for his high repute among his contemporaries, it is necessary to understand what he was trying to do and how his efforts were informed by the world around him. While not invulnerable to the attractions of instrumental interpretation of legal texts, Cooley strove to resist those attractions and to be a "safe" writer, much as he strove to be a "safe" judge. In the preface to the *Taxation* treatise, he explained his purpose:

> The preparation of any treatise on taxation necessarily involves the presentation of disputed points, and the expression of opinions upon them. This has been done in the following pages. It has not been the purpose, however, to take any positions which it was not believed the authorities would justify; and if this has been done in any instance, the references which are made to authorities will doubtless enable the reader to detect the error. [1]

In some other legal cultures, especially those based on Roman traditions, text writers have long assumed a larger responsibility to guide judges to principles and results deemed most desirable by the text writers.[2] That tradition can be found alive and well in modern and postmodern legal scholarship, but academic work in America, at least when addressed to great social and political issues, is seldom read by those exercising power, for the reason that they are under no professional obligation to regard academic authority and are prone to rely on their own opinions as informed by those of other judges. Cooley, unlike many modern and postmodern academic authors, accepted the subordinate status of a "secondary" authority; his words were written to have influence only to the extent that they accurately reflected the judgments of those having "primary" authority, that is, sitting judges.[3]

In their misperception of the modest aims of *Constitutional Limitations*, historians and others may have been misled by the style of judicial opinions.[4] Most opinions of a court are written defensively. They tend to disavow personal responsibility for the political consequences of the decisions they defend. One need not be a judge to recognize the prudence of attributing one's unwelcome decisions to others, preferably some abstract other, such as "the law" or "the rules" or "management." Moreover, this style of disavowal serves to remind judges that they have professional duties to restrain their personal impulses, that indeed the law is not theirs to shape to their own desires. To the author of an opinion of the court, the most attractive citation is to a previous decision of the same court, then to decisions of other high courts, then to a text synthesizing such decisions, and only thereafter to non-judicial literature.

But deference to literary authority seldom if ever so beguiles an American judge that he or she would heed the advice of a mere treatise writer on a politically sensitive question such as the constitutional validity of state legislation. Beneath the veneer of deference to authority are found in most American judges the strong wills of politically active persons. They are almost without exception persons with ideas of their own about the merits of significant legislation and about the appropriate measure of the judicial role in imposing constitutional limitations.[5] Even a fellow judge as eminent as Cooley, as a mere text writer having no vote in the collegium, is unlikely to have significant influence on the resolution of particular issues having substantial political content. To be cited by a court on an issue laden with political implications is not to have influence, but to be used.

An error not uncommon among those reviewing legal texts from a distance in time is to assume that the writer was recording his or her personal views of what the law ought to be, that is, that his or her purpose in writing was largely instrumental. As a "safe" or conventional man of his time, Cooley must generally have shared the values and the impulses of the judges whose opinions he synthesized in his texts. But he wrote chiefly to assist his fellow judges in discerning patterns in their collective work, not to persuade them, and it was because they and other readers could detect his integrity and self-discipline in this respect that he was held in such esteem as a legal writer by his contemporaries. When Cooley reported the law in his texts, he was generally describing the actual conduct of judges; his report was therefore generally an accurate account of what other judges had done and would do with like cases, at least in the near future.

Constitutional Limitations was the text of Cooley's lectures to law students. He modestly supposed that it might be of some use to clerks and minor officials.[6] He was astonished when it was quickly recognized as a masterpiece of its kind and occupied its field to the virtual exclusion of other authors.[7] Lawrence Friedman has acknowledged it to be the most important law book "for its own generation."[8] Andrew McLaughlin went further, depicting the work as "the chiefest American law book."[9]

Constitutional Limitations was necessarily a political tract, but its politics, like the opinions of the Marshall Court, were mostly a politics of first principles, emphasizing the linkage between reported judicial decisions and the core of the national political culture embodied in the constitutional texts they were enforcing. Perhaps the book played a minor role in more deeply imprinting on American culture the prevailing ideas that constitutions limit government and are thus law as well as politics.[10] The political reality to which the author called attention was that state supreme courts had been, at least since the decision of the Supreme Court in *Marbury v. Madison*,[11] invalidating state legislation found to be in violation of their state constitutions. Because those constitutions shared many common provisions, there were themes to be discerned in the cases interpreting them. Such themes provided the substance of *Constitutional Limitations*.

Most of the themes and first principles expressed in *Constitutional Limitations* can also be found in the utterances of the Marshall Court or in the work of Francis Lieber. Lieber had emigrated from Prussia after two periods of imprisonment, where he had been held on suspicion of political unreliability, despite being twice wounded in the Napoleonic Wars and holding a doctorate from the university at Halle.[12] He arrived on American shores in 1827 to take up employment as a swimming instructor in Boston. When the president of the United States came to swim in his gym, Lieber quickly became known to an astonishing number of the intellectual elite and political leaders.[13] He became the person in America most frequently consulted by Alexis de Tocqueville in preparing his luminous work on American politics.[14] He was a professor of politics at the University of South Carolina from 1833 to 1857 and while there had produced a body of literature that won him international fame, and even an invitation to return to Prussia as counsel to the king,[15] an invitation he declined, deciding to remain in South Carolina.

As noted, Lieber's first major work was his *Manual of Political Ethics*, published in 1837.[16] A companion volume, *Legal and Political Hermeneutics*, followed in 1838.[17] These works comprised the first comprehensive statement of the role of lawyers in a constitutional democracy. *Political Ethics* drew heavily on classical and medieval sources describing the trait of civic virtue. *Hermeneutics* drew in part on the work of German Protestant theologians struggling to identify the true teachings of the scriptures without the authority of a Pope. Equally important to Cooley was the book published by Lieber in 1852, *Civil Liberty and Self-Government*.[18] This was a work of comparative law extolling the "Anglican" traditions Lieber detected in the Constitution of the United States and deploring the "Gallican" tradition of centralized authority to which comparison was made. Although an admirer of Alexander Hamilton and a political follower of Henry Clay, Lieber praised local government and the right to jury trial, and even found merit in the election of judges.[19] The book emphasized the cultural origins of legal institutions and ideas and established a school of scholarship appearing in Germany as well as the United States, a school to which the present work could be said, in some respects, to belong. All of these works would be revived in the decade after Lieber's death in 1872,[20] seemingly in reaction to the technocratic approach to law advanced by Langdell.[21]

We do not know when Cooley first read Lieber's work. But two of his closest colleagues in Ann Arbor were Andrew Dickson White[22] and Charles Kendall Adams,[23] both political historians who had trained in Germany and who were intellectual acolytes of Lieber. With Lieber, White and Adams were in 1865 among the founders of the American Social Science Association, the reformist group centered in Boston that hoped to deploy the crafts of social science to eradicate crime, poverty, ill health, and injustice.[24] Given the close connection between Cooley and White and Adams, it is unsurprising that much of the thought expressed by Lieber, derived by him from classical and continental sources, found its way into Cooley's work

Although cautious in its representations, *Constitutional Limitations* was nevertheless intellectually ambitious. It revealed close study of the Constitution of the United States as well as the constitutions of many states. In its comparative dimension, it resembled Lieber's *Civil Liberty*, to which numerous references were made. Cooley contrasted the enumerated and more limited powers of Congress with those of state legislatures that shared with the British Parliament absolute power subject only to those constraints explicitly imposed upon them by constitutional texts. He was chiefly concerned with state constitutions because, at the time he wrote, these were the source of most limitations on the powers of state legislatures, which, in turn, were the source of most important legislation. Cooley could not have been writing in 1868 about the Fourteenth Amendment to the Constitution of the United States, which was being ratified while he wrote. That was a subject he left for another time.

Cooley acknowledged in the preface that he wrote "in full sympathy with all those restraints which the caution of the fathers has imposed upon the exercise of the powers of government."[25] Hostile twentieth-century readers have attached significance to that comment as evidence of a desire on Cooley's part to manipulate his judicial readers in favor of weak regulation of economic predators.[26] But the constitutions of the states about which he chiefly wrote had seldom been invoked to constrain legislators striving to restrain predation. Constitutional law was not then in play to shield industry from progressive legislation. He was therefore affirming little more than that he accepted the premise, expressed in *Marbury v. Madison*, that the government and its officers are bound by the law. So far as appears, no contemporary of Cooley read the prefatory comment as a revelation of any political partisanship.

In an early chapter, Cooley dealt with problems of construction and interpretation,[27] summarizing some of the analysis supplied in Lieber's *Hermeneutics* and another earlier work by Theodore Sedgwick,[28] Cooley's fellow Barnburner. As did Lieber, Cooley distinguished construction from interpretation,[29] and offered maxims to be employed in the performance of those judicial tasks.[30] These were for the most part cautions against self-aggrandizement. He quoted as representative the statements of Chief Justice Bronson of New York:

> It is highly probable that inconvenience will result from following the Constitution as it is written. But that consideration can have no force with me. It is not for us, but for those who make the instrument, to supply its defects.[31]

Although not denying, as he had said, that "some things are too plain to be written,"[32] he insisted that there is no principle of natural law or "spirit" in a constitution to justify extravagant constructions not founded in any text set forth in the instrument;[33] for this abnegation of natural law as constitutional law, he cited abundant authority.[34] His tenor is captured in his treatment of constitutional doubt:

> But when all legitimate lights for ascertaining the meaning of the Constitution have been made use of, it may still happen that the construction remains in doubt. In such a case, it seems clear that every one called upon to act where, in his opinion, the proposed action would be of doubtful constitutionality, is bound upon that doubt alone to abstain from acting. Whoever derives power from the Constitution to perform any public function, is disloyal to that instrument, and grossly derelict in duty, if he does that which he is not reasonably satisfied the Constitution permits. Whether the power be legislative, executive, or *judicial*, there is manifest disregard of constitutional and moral obligation by one who, having taken an oath to observe that instrument, takes

part in an action which he cannot say he believes to be no violation of its provisions. . . . [35] [emphasis supplied]

This was, it seems apparent, a bold statement with which many legislators would not agree. It follows that, although Cooley favored federal antitrust legislation, he presumably disfavored the decision of its draftsmen to extend the law without explicit limits, leaving the courts to establish in constitutional litigation the parameters of its application to interstate commerce.[36]

Cooley also devoted a lengthy chapter to "the circumstances under which a legislative enactment may be declared unconstitutional,"[37] again emphasizing throughout the chapter the importance of judicial self-restraint. He found no occasion to discuss *Dred Scott*,[38] but his contemporary readers must surely have had that decision in mind when considering his injunction against judicial overreaching. He observed that courts were prudently disinclined to proclaim constitutional limitations unless required to do so by a case presented to them for decision. He identified as firmly established several principles that were later elaborated, as we shall see, in the judicial opinions of Learned Hand and Louis Brandeis, two later practitioners and advocates of judicial self-restraint. A second time, he emphasized that legislation cannot be invalid merely because it offends "the spirit" but not the text of a constitution[39] and that judicial doubts must be resolved in favor of sustaining legislation of questionable validity.[40]

This part of the treatise was the forebear of a celebrated article published a quarter-century later by Cooley's junior contemporary, James Bradley Thayer. Cooley and Thayer wrote at different times and in different contexts, and there may have been significant differences of degree between them. Thayer's oft-quoted dictum was that a court can invalidate legislation only

> when those who have the right to make laws have not merely made a mistake, but have made a very clear one—so clear that it is not open to rational question. . . . This rule recognizes that, having regard to the great, complex, ever-unfolding exigencies of government, much which will seem unconstitutional to one man, or body of men, may reasonably not seem so to another; that the constitution often admits of different interpretations; that there is often a range of choice and judgment; that in such cases the constitution does not impose upon the legislature any one specific opinion, but leaves open this range of choice: that whatever choice is rational is constitutional.[41]

This "clear error" test may go further than did Cooley's text in the advocacy of judicial restraint. [42]

Nevertheless, Cooley and Thayer both expressed the widely shared judgment of the American judiciary of the nineteenth century,[43] for them tested and proved by the counterexample of *Dred Scott*, that courts should venture to employ their constitutional powers only when on solid ground in the text *and* in the moral precepts of the national political culture.[44] For sharing in this observation of reality, Thayer, too, has been identified as an uncaring reactionary,[45] an identification, like that of Cooley, based on little evidence[46] and inaccurate. Thayer was active in several political causes separating him from hardened reaction. He was, for example, especially active in efforts to secure justice and protection for Native Americans.[47] In any case, even as late as Thayer's time, there was no competing view. No one defended *Dred Scott* as an appropriate exercise of judicial power, and no one contended that courts could responsibly employ their constitutional powers to correct apparent oversights or even perceived injustices in the constitutions they were charged to enforce.[48]

Many of the state constitutions of which Cooley wrote in 1868 were readily and often amended. Indeed, New York in 1846 and Michigan in 1850, and other states as well, had entirely replaced their constitutions. It was therefore, in Justice Bronson's words, possible to "remedy their defect." The relative difficulty of amending the federal Constitution[49] may be seen to affect the degree of judicial self-restraint appropriate to its construction. One might, for example, imaginably approve a speculative decision such as *Roe v. Wade*[50] yet disapprove the same interpretation of the more readily amendable constitutions of New York or Michigan. The appropriate degree of restraint might also be reasonably thought to be qualified by the terms of employment of the particular court; judges subject to reelection might be thought to have a commission to exercise broader powers than those enjoying tenure for "good behavior."[51] On that account, one might imaginably disapprove the decision of the Supreme Court of the United States in *Roe*, but not if rendered by an elected court such as most of those of which Cooley wrote. These differences in constitutional context may account for such differences as may have existed between Cooley and Thayer. Cooley was chiefly concerned with the enforcement of amendable state constitutions by elected judges, whereas Thayer was addressing only the federal Constitution.

In a chapter following his treatment of constitutional interpretation and the role of the judiciary, Cooley addressed the constitutional status of local government. As we have seen, Cooley, as a judge, was in the forefront of those upholding the prerogatives of local government.[52] As a "safe" textwriter, however, he acknowledged that the powers of municipal corporations depend upon the sufferance of state legislatures:

> They have no inherent jurisdiction to make laws or adopt regulations of government; they are governments of enumerated powers, acting by a delegated authority; so that while the State legislature may exercise such powers of gov-

ernment coming within the designation of legislative power as are not expressly or impliedly prohibited, the local authorities can exercise those only which are expressly or impliedly conferred.

The creation of municipal corporations, and the conferring upon them of certain powers and subjecting them to corresponding duties, does not deprive the legislature of the State of that complete control over their citizens which was before possessed. It still has authority to amend their charters, enlarge or diminish their powers, extend their boundaries, consolidate two or more into one, overrule their action whenever it is deemed unwise, impolitic, or unjust, and even abolish them altogether in the legislative discretion.[53]

Nevertheless, Cooley asserted, local government in America preceded the erection of state government, and the premise of our constitutions "is one of complete decentralization."[54] Conceding that the "general disposition of the courts" had been to construe municipal charters strictly,[55] he affirmed that limited local power and autonomy could be acquired by usage.[56]

In his preference for localism, Cooley followed Lieber, who contended that civil liberty was dependent on active self-government, and that active self-government is a local phenomenon.[57] Centralized power, Lieber observed, tends to be vulnerable to despotism and the loss of civil liberty, while local authority tends to resist despotism and thus to secure civil liberty. This observation rested on the belief that citizens who often participate in government are, over time, more likely to respect one another's rights than are those who do not. Or, in other words, those who do not participate in a government will not in time of stress support it. Local government affords more opportunities for participation and to reward those who participated with a greater sense of control over their lives and communities. Neither Lieber nor Cooley called attention to the deficiencies of local governments as protectors of minorities, deficiencies that became extremely visible after 1876, when Reconstruction came to an end and local governments in the South were "redeemed" by the same white families who had created the Confederacy.

Although closer to recognizing Cooley's aims than many who have written about him in this century, Joan Williams mistook his support for local self-government.[58] She, with others,[59] contrasted with respect to the Home Rule issue Cooley and John Forrest Dillon,[60] a judge and professor in Iowa who was the contemporary author of a respected treatise on *Municipal Corporations*.[61] The contrast is apt, for Cooley's politics were very different from Dillon's. Yet their differences are not very visible in their analyses of the cases bearing on the powers of municipal governments. Cooley favored local empowerment and Dillon did not, but they read the cases in the same ways. Dillon's treatise, like Cooley's, was for decades widely cited because it was a complete and accurate account of what was happening.

Williams, however, employing the dark arts of deconstruction, finds Dillon's real purpose to be protection of railroads and industrialists from socialist town governments[62] and Cooley's real purpose to be the denial of power to state legislatures, and "only secondarily an attempt to empower localities."[63] While Williams is not wrong that Cooley mistrusted state legislatures, he also in some measure mistrusted local governments, whom he did not suppose would often govern wisely or well. But Cooley found in state constitutions a purpose to diffuse power; with Lieber, he perceived it to be the aim of constitutions to limit the possibilities for catastrophic abuses of power and enlarge the chances that civil liberties would be protected over time. It appears not to have been within Williams's range of consideration that Cooley and Dillon as text writers shared a common purpose: to provide their readers with an accurate account of what other judges were in fact doing. Like many late twentieth-century observers, Williams could not believe Cooley when he said that he was trying to avoid having any position other than those "the authorities would justify." There must be, she assumed, some ulterior purpose to the words of such a writer.

Constitutional Limitations is, it is true, most suspect in its treatment of local government. Outside his role as text writer, Cooley, as we have seen, was an early advocate of Home Rule, a principle embraced by the Progressives of the next generation.[64] And as a member of the Supreme Court of Michigan, he not only interpreted the state constitution as one favoring local authority, but also supported his interpretation with words of exceptional passion.

The 1868 chapter on local government prefigured Cooley's own 1870 decision in *People v. Salem*[65] in affirming that local tax revenues must be applied to a public, not a private, purpose.[66] In his usual straightforward style, he noted cases authorizing municipal corporations to engage in public works outside their territorial limits and to become stockholders in private corporations, but judged that such cases have "gone to the very limits of constitutional power." Surely, he speculated, a legislature could not require such a use of local tax revenues. No significant modification of his treatise was made in later editions to reflect his own court's decision in the *Salem* case,[67] presumably because he and later editors recognized his own decision as outside the general pattern.

It would in a way have been heartening to Cooley to foresee that David Barron could in 1999 find traces in recent opinions of the Supreme Court of the United States of Cooley's presumption favoring local discretion.[68] On the other hand, it seems unlikely that Cooley would join in federal court decisions limiting the power of states to subject local governments to severe limitation of their powers. However ill-advised a state's suppression of local government, Cooley would have regarded it as beyond the power and responsibility of the federal judiciary to intervene, save to enforce an explicit and clearly applicable provision of the federal Constitution.

Cooley devoted a substantial chapter to protections of personal liberty, chiefly rights arising in the enforcement of criminal law. Characteristic is his comment on the right to counsel. After reviewing the shortcoming of English law denying the right, he proclaimed:

> With us, it is a universal principle of constitutional law that the prisoner shall be allowed a defense by counsel. The humanity of the law has generally provided that, when the prisoner is unable to employ counsel the court may designate someone to defend him, who shall be paid by the government; but when no such provision is made, it is a duty which counsel so designated owes to his profession, to the court engaged in the trial, and to the cause of justice, not to withhold his best exertions in the defense of one who has the double misfortune to be stricken by poverty and accused of crime. No one is at liberty to decline such an appointment, and it is to be hoped that few would be disposed to do so.[69]

Cooley thus stopped short of declaring a constitutional right not then existing, but he foretold a series of twentieth century decisions of the United States Supreme Court that would do so.[70]

Following the chapter on the protection of personal liberty was one on the protection of property. Cooley opened that chapter with a reference to the Magna Carta and its promise not to impose forfeitures of rights in land; he noted that such royal pledges are not needed here in light of the universality of due process clauses in American constitutions.[71] He validated with citations the conclusion of Justice Johnson that "due process" is "intended to secure the individual from the arbitrary exercise of the powers of government, unrestrained by the established principles of private rights and distributive justice."[72] He was then at pains to distinguish between those vested rights that are entitled to the protections of due process from those interests that are too ephemeral to merit such protection. The distinction he made, it seems fair to say, is not a crisp one to the eye of a late twentieth-century reader, entailing as it does further distinctions between property and speculative interests, and between rights and remedies, that are not always readily apparent. Yet it is not certain that the distinction has been greatly clarified in the 130 years since Cooley's publication.[73]

In this setting, Cooley included a section on "Unequal and Partial Legislation" that some later historians supposed he included for the ulterior purpose of lending aid and comfort to rich industrialists preying on the poor.[74] In this section, he relied less on judicial authority. He quoted Locke's preference for "established laws, not to be varied in particular cases, but to have one rule for rich and poor, for the favorite at court and the countryman at plough," and declared it a "maxim in the law, by which may be tested the authority and binding force of legislative enactments."[75] Oft-quoted was his affirmation that

> Equality of rights, privileges, and legal capacities should be the aim of the law. . . . The State, it is to be presumed, has no favors to bestow, and designs to inflict no arbitrary deprivation of rights. Special privileges are obnoxious, and discriminations against persons and classes are still more so, and as a rule of construction are always to be leaned against as probably not contemplated or designed.[76]

This passage is a succinct statement of the idea expressed by President Jackson in his bank veto message. It is a statement of the position of most American courts of the time, for they generally disfavored as iniquitous the practice of issuing special charters and licenses. It is also a statement of the rule expressed by a unanimous Court in *Clinton v. Jones*[77] in its 1997 decision withholding special status to a president defending a civil action. It was presumed by Cooley that government intervention would almost certainly serve the interests of the monied class. It was hardly imaginable to him in 1868 that government might be used to restrain the predations of "arrogant wealth," or that his words would be invoked to invalidate legislative efforts to impose such restraints.

One reading Cooley's text on unequal legislation in 1999 is moved to wonder how Jacksonian dogma might apply to the law of intellectual property, which can reasonably be viewed as a bestowal of favors by the federal government. It seems likely that Cooley would have deemed the entire field of patent and copyright law as replete with obnoxious special privileges of questionable constitutional status.

Cooley, as well as virtually all his contemporaries and antecedents, accepted without question gender distinctions to protect women.[78] Nancy Erickson italicized Cooley's few words on this subject to emphasize their influence in support of such legislation, which she, a century later, deemed to have been repressive of women.[79] As we shall see, one of Louis Brandeis's most notable victories was to sustain just such a law,[80] and few if any Americans of either gender, even in the Progressive Era, would have questioned Cooley's judgment, or that of other nineteenth-century judges who accepted the need for laws protecting women.

Cooley then turned to liberty of speech and of the press,[81] noting that a counterpart to the First Amendment of the United States Constitution existed in every state. The protections, he observed, include the right intemperately to criticize the government and its officers. Other topics treated with care, and with exhaustive citation of cases, were religious liberty, the power of taxation, and the power of eminent domain.

In a penultimate chapter, Cooley addressed "The Police Power of the States," that is, their power to regulate the conduct of citizens. He supported the statement of Chief Justice Shaw of Massachusetts that all property is subject to general regulations necessary to the common good and general welfare, there being no "vested right to do wrong."[82] He observed that the courts also had extended this limitation to charters and contracts.[83] More than once, he weakened in his self-restraint to criticize the *Dartmouth College*[84] case for its tendency to entrench contract rights so as to forestall legislation needed to prevent antisocial consequences of corporate behavior. In a footnote in the second edition, he allowed himself to protest that

> It is under the protection of [that] decision that the most enormous and threatening powers in our country have been created; some of the great and wealthy corporations having greater influence in the country at large, and upon the legislation of the country, than the states to which they owe their corporate existence. Every privilege granted or conferred—no matter by what means or by what pretense—being made inviolable by the Constitution, the government is frequently found stripped of its authority in very important particulars, by unwise, careless, or corrupt legislation; and a clause of the Federal Constitution, whose purpose was to preclude the repudiation of debts and just contracts, protects and perpetuates the evil.[85]

While he noted a requirement that police regulations serve the general welfare, not merely private interests, Cooley did not reiterate his earlier comments on the right to equality as a source of restraint on the police power. One could nevertheless infer, as some later readers did, that legislatures making arbitrary distinctions in the application of the lash of the police power could be restrained if they failed to meet the requirements of equality and impartiality stated in the earlier chapter.

Constitutional Limitations was not only widely admired, it was also widely cited, thousands of times by highest state courts and hundreds of times by the Supreme Court of the United States. To some extent, the text he wrote in 1868 would, like the judicial rhetoric he faithfully recorded, take on different meaning with the passage of time and the interposition of new social and political relationships. The industrialization of America proceeded apace[86] as small workshops were replaced by factories, deflation crushed many small businesses, railroads charged rates disadvantageous and even ruinous to some farmers and businesses (and sometimes to one another), industries ravaged natural resources, patent owners collected royalties on such simple and necessary products as barbed wire, and manufacturers learned to make and sell glitzy products that were ineffective or even harmful to users. Such consequences of industrialization accelerated through the last quarter of the nineteenth century,[87] creating many needs for regulation to protect the health and safety of citizens and especially to protect landless workers subjected to working conditions that were dangerous, not only to themselves and their families, but also to the public interest, by whatever measure that interest might be accounted.

In the decades following publication of *Constitutional Limitations*, many exercises of "the police power" to afford protections of the weak against exploitation by the strong were upheld by courts against constitutional challenges. The constitutional limitations on the police power became, however, a major political battleground between capitalists and those who sought to regulate them. The ratification of the Fourteenth Amendment to the federal Constitution broadened the encounter by providing a new constitutional text from which those seeking to limit legislative power could derive support. In revising his treatise, Cooley faithfully reported these developments, but made no major changes in the structure of his presentation. Perhaps the most important difference between the editions was their increasing girth as more and more citations were added to support and illustrate the text. He did not extend *Constitutional Limitations* to comment on the law emerging under the federal Constitution, and many important police power cases were decided by the Supreme Court without reference to that work.[88] Yet, although the treatise did not speak to the Fourteenth Amendment, some federal courts nevertheless invoked it as a source of legitimacy for their Fourteenth Amendment decisions.[89]

Cooley's treatise was hardly the cause of Supreme Court decisions in which it was cited. He did not, for example influence Justice Stephen Field,[90] but was used by him. Stephen Johnson Field was the younger brother of David Dudley, and in his youth, with his brother, an ardent advocate of the Jacksonian doctrine of Equal Rights. He had moved to California in the Gold Rush of 1849, gained election to the Supreme Court of California, and been appointed by President Lincoln in 1864 to the Supreme Court of the United States. Perhaps as much as any other justice, Field was responsible for enlarging the Fourteenth Amendment restraint on the state police power. Field had served in the rustic California legislature of the 1850s and was keenly aware of the ignorance and venality sometimes controlling the actions of such bodies. Moreover, he served on the Court for over three decades, an experience that did not diminish his confidence that his political and moral wisdom was superior to that of almost any legislature. And he had experienced many years of verbal abuse (possibly merited abuse) from members of "the public," leading one biographer to conclude that he felt little sympathy for the masses, whom he regarded as an ugly mob.[91] He was for these reasons increasingly quick to conclude that legislation was so violative of the principle of Equal Rights as to be vulnerable to challenge under the Fourteenth Amendment.

10

The Civil War
Amendments

From the perspective of the late twentieth century, the most significant law-making event of the nineteenth century was the ratification of the Fourteenth Amendment in 1868, the year of publication of Cooley's *Constitutional Limitations*. At the time, there was much criticism of that fateful text. Charles Sumner, the most outspoken champion of radical Reconstruction, was so disappointed that he spoke in opposition to it.[1] Feminists were also bitterly disappointed. Of course, those who had formed the ruling class in the Confederate states were even more bitterly opposed, but powerless to resist. And there were others, not only those in the former slave states, who were concerned that the text went too far in nationalizing matters appropriately left to the state constitutions.

Although *Constitutional Limitations* was a work on state constitutions written for the purpose of assisting state courts and lawyers appearing before them, its author might have been expected to write about the new provisions in the federal Constitution, and he did. In 1873, five years after publication of *Constitutional Limitations*, Cooley produced an edition of Joseph Story's *Commentaries on the Constitution of the United States*. His was the fourth edition of a work first published in 1833.[2] It was then the sole comprehensive book on the federal Constitution and was widely used for access to precedents interpreting that instrument. As editor, Cooley added references to cases decided in the previous fifteen years, thus bringing the work up to date. While the Story treatise remained in use and went through several later editions, it has seldom, if ever, been suggested that Cooley's editing of Story's work reflected a purpose to assure constitutional protections of laissez-faire economic policies.

Cooley added three chapters to Story's work, one each for the Thirteenth, Fourteenth, and Fifteenth amendments. Explaining these additions, he wrote:

In preparing them, the editor has not been ambitious to enter upon original discussions, or to advance peculiar views; and he has contented himself with a brief commentary on the provisions and purposes of the amendments, aiming as far as possible to keep in harmony with the opinions and sentiments under the inspiration of which they were accepted as ratified in the several States.[3]

Indeed there was little that was "original" or "peculiar" in these chapters. They are of interest as revelations of Cooley's role as text writer and of his understanding of the aims of those amendments. Of particular interest is Cooley's understanding of the relationship between the state constitutional provisions of which he wrote in *Constitutional Limitations*, and the provisions of the new Fourteenth Amendment.

With respect to the Thirteenth Amendment, Cooley was very brief and gloating:

Nothing by way of comment can make its provisions plainer; the boast of English lawyers and philanthropists after *Somerville's* case[4] that "a slave cannot breathe in Britain, but the moment he sets foot upon her soil he becomes free," is equally or even more strictly true in America.[5]

Regarding the Fifteenth Amendment, Cooley explained that continued discrimination at the polls perpetuated a feeling of degradation and put African-Americans "at a serious disadvantage" in competition with others. A penultimate passage was so optimistic that it merits quoting at length:

This . . . amendment crowns the edifice of national liberty. Freedom is no longer sectional or partial. There are no longer privileged classes; the laws have ceased to be invidious, and all classes of citizens who are to be governed by them are admitted also to participate in their administration.

   The question may indeed be raised, whether it be not possible that we have plunged into new dangers in laying thus broadly the basis of responsible citizenship. There are those who foresee only evil, and who prophesy only calamity. But evil is always prophesied when concession is made to democracy; when kings are set aside, when hereditary privileges are abolished or restricted, when the press is unmuzzled, when the conscience is set free. It was prophesied in England when toleration was extended to dissenters from the established church, and again when Catholics were emancipated, and again when political rights were extended to the Jews. Every step in that country towards making the parliament a truly representative body of the whole nation, every disenfranchisement of decayed or corrupt boroughs, and every extension of the franchise to the people, has been earnestly opposed as fraught with danger to the state. Every step in America in the same direction has met with the like opposition. The rulers, whether they be kings or lords or privileged classes, always believe they rule by right divine. Power is safe in their hands, but it would be dangerous in the hands of the people at large: this is the assumption always where the demands of new classes for a voice in the government are to be resisted. The American people have assumed that that which is most just is also the wisest and safest, and they trust to time and experience to justify their confidence. It is beyond question that many unfit persons will demand and exercise the right of suffrage, but no test that could be prescribed—whether of education, property, experience, race or color—could be completely effectual in separating out the fit from the unfit, the virtuous from the vicious, the patriotic and public-spirited from the selfish, mercenary and mean.[6]

The author of these words did not foresee the redemption of the former Confederate states only a few years after his writing. Cooley plainly assumed that the Fifteenth Amendment would be judicially enforced. But the Supreme Court, contrary to Cooley's assumption, declined to enforce the right to vote without additional legislation by Congress, thereby clearing the way for "Redemption" and the enactment of segregation laws.[7] While the amendment was later enforced against blatant discrimination,[8] various evasions were tolerated, notably the whites-only primary.[9]

The Court's decision not to enforce the Fifteenth Amendment was not publicly criticized by Cooley, but he was not given to such criticism and was at the time a sitting judge. Moreover, the decision reflected the moral fatigue of the nation which, in 1876, was ready to believe the worst about Reconstruction and anxious to heal the relationship with former Confederates. Yet, it bears note that, if Cooley's understanding of the amendment had been confirmed by the Court, it would have been much harder to enact segregation laws and much easier to dismantle them when the time came to do so.

It is equally significant that Cooley's account of the Fourteenth Amendment was written in 1872, when Reconstruction of the South was still in full flower.[10] Reflecting his pacific impulses, it begins with courtesies to the "great, brave but unsuccessful army now broken up and remanded to civil life."[11] He affirmed that the amendment responded to the need to protect the rights of freemen in the highly disturbed conditions then existing in the former Confederate states and also to meet or fulfill the desire of those supporting the Union clearly to impose on citizens in Southern states the duty to share in repaying the nation's war debts.[12] In protecting the rights of freemen, the amendment explicitly overruled the despised decision in *Dred Scott*.[13]

Cooley examined separately three operative clauses of the amendment. First, he turned to the clause providing that "No state shall make or enforce any law which shall abridge the privileges and immunities of citizens of the United States." Cooley conceded that the "privileges or immunities" that states are forbidden to abridge cannot be satisfactorily enumerated. He explained the aim of that clause as an assurance to freemen that they would be protected by "equal and impartial laws which govern the whole community."[14] He emphasized that the privileges to be protected are those of the

citizens of the United States.[15] In this assertion, he drew on a widely accepted opinion of Justice Bushrod Washington in an 1823 case[16] interpreting the phrase "privileges and immunities" that citizens are assured by Article IV of the Constitution that "The Citizens of each State shall be entitled
to all Privileges and Immunities of Citizens in the several States." Possibly
the language of the amendment could have sustained a broader interpretation of protected privileges than Justice Washington had given to the same
language as it appeared in Article IV.

But, as the decisions of Justice Field would soon demonstrate, such an interpretation would have been employed to the substantial disadvantage of
states seeking to regulate harsh working conditions and other unwelcome
consequences of industrialization. In any case, the Court read the provision
as Cooley did, but without citing him.[17]

Justice Field preferred to find the textual basis for limiting the power of
state legislatures not in the Due Process Clause, but in the Privileges and
Immunities Clause.[18] Field also invoked the Declaration of Independence in
support of his view that the natural law right to the "pursuit of happiness"
included the right to pursue any lawful business or vocation.[19] While Field's
broad interpretation of the Privileges and Immunities Clause did not prevail, he was surely much more influential than Cooley in moving his
brethren in the direction of what today might be described as strict scrutiny
of economic regulation by the states. It is incorrect to suppose that Stephen
Field was in any degree subject to the influence of Thomas Cooley.

As Philip Paludan has observed,[20] Cooley's restrained reading of the Privileges and Immunities Clause treated the amendment more as a promise
kept than as a promise made. Yet, citing Story and Lieber, Cooley quoted at
length from the abolitionist Senator Charles Sumner's hopeful assessment
of the aim of the Fourteenth Amendment, which Sumner had earlier opposed as too conservative:

> Here is the great charter of every human being drawing vital breath upon this
> soil, whatever may be his condition and whoever may be his parents. He may
> be poor, weak, humble, or black . . . but before the Constitution all these dis-
> tinctions disappear . . . he is a MAN, the equal of all his fellow-men. He is one
> of the children of the state, which, like an impartial parent, regards all its off-
> spring with equal care. . . . The state, imitating the divine justice, is no re-
> specter of persons.[21]

Turning to the prohibition against deprivations without due process of
law, Cooley first noted the purpose of protecting freemen from paternalis-
tic deprivations ostensibly made for their own protection. Such, it was
feared, would "keep the colored race for a time at least in [a] condition of
pupilage and dependence" and perpetuate their degradation.[22] He ob-

served that due process of law imposed on the states the duty to protect all citizens against arbitrary procedures or arbitrary legislative enactments. The latter obligation he likened to that imposed on the English crown by the twenty-ninth chapter of the Magna Carta: There must be one "law of the land," the same for all.[23] Thus, he concluded that the Due Process Clause merely federalized what was already the law of all states, commissioning the federal courts to enforce those pre-existing public duties he had enumerated in *Constitutional Limitations*.[24] That conclusion was shared by others at the time[25] and was soon unanimously ratified by the Supreme Court.[26]

But, Cooley cautioned, it followed that:

> All the property and vested rights of individuals are subject to such regulations of police as the legislature may establish with a view to protect the community and its several members against such use or employment thereof as would be injurious to society or unjust toward other individuals.[27]

As an example of a proper use of the police power, he affirmed the authority of the states to prohibit the sale of intoxicating liquors and even to destroy such beverages if kept for sale in violation of the law.[28]

Cooley did not suggest that the Due Process Clause incorporates the Bill of Rights expressed in the first ten amendments to the Constitution to make all the restraints on the power of the federal government applicable to the states as well.[29] Although he did, as we have seen, regard "some things as too plain to be said," he was generally disinclined to favor the natural law theories advocated by some abolitionists[30] because they empowered judges to disregard positive law made democratically. If narrowly construed to include such entitlements as the right to make a political speech or engage in religious worship, his commentary would have allowed federal enforcement of provisions common to state constitutions as "the law of the land." But there is nothing in his text to support the more extravagant readings of the Fourteenth Amendment to prohibit states from regulating pornography, sexual mores, commercial advertising, symbolic speech, or campaign finance that would later be adopted by the Supreme Court and imposed on the states and on local governments.

To Cooley, the provision requiring the states to assure equal protection of the law "would not seem to call for much remark."[31] He regarded this clause merely as a formal declaration of a principle pervading the whole "spirit" of the Constitution, that all are equal before the law, a term adapted from the English Magna Carta, and the central conviction of Jacksonian democrats. Here he cited the opinion of Chief Justice Shaw in *Roberts v. City of Boston*,[32] the 1850 Massachusetts decision declining to desegregate public schools and observed with satisfaction:

And now that it has become a settled rule of constitutional law that color or race is no badge of inferiority, we doubt if any distinction whatever either in right or in privilege, which has color or race for its sole basis, can either be established in the law or enforced where it had previously been established.[33]

As in his enthusiasm for the Fifteenth Amendment, Cooley thus failed to foresee the enactment of repressive black codes in the South, an event that did not begin to occur until after 1876.[34] As we have seen, Cooley's court was responsible for the desegregation of the Detroit Public Schools in 1868,[35] but Cooley had then found it unnecessary to consider the constitutional status of racial segregation. He seems, in 1873, to have taken for granted its unconstitutionality under the new Equal Protection Clause.

Section 5 of the Fourteenth Amendment empowered Congress to enforce its provisions. Cooley explained the need for this provision as arising from the possibility that equal protection of the laws might be impaired other than by direct denial by the state. He explicitly approved of the civil rights legislation of 1871 as a proper use of Section 5.[36]

Cooley's final conclusion about the scope of the Fourteenth Amendment demonstrates that he was not the mystic seer some later presumed him to be:

Important as [its provisions] unquestionably are, it is nevertheless to be observed that they have not been agreed upon for the purpose of enlarging the sphere of the powers of the general government or of taking from the states any of those just powers of government which in the original Constitution were "reserved to the States respectively." The existing division of sovereignty which had been found equal to the preservation of our liberties, not only in time of peace and general harmony but in the trials of a most desperate civil strife, is not disturbed by it[.] ... The states, in adopting it, have not struck blindly and fatally at their reserved powers; they have rather given security that in certain important particulars they will not pervert or abuse them.[37]

Cooley did not foresee what Holmes observed in 1930:

I have not yet adequately expressed the more than anxiety that I feel at the ever increasing scope given to the Fourteenth Amendment in cutting down what I believe to be the constitutional rights of the states. ... I see hardly any limit but the sky to the invalidating of those rights if they happen to strike a majority of this Court as for any reason undesirable.[38]

Perhaps the pivotal event in the evolution that excited Holmes's "more than anxiety" was the decision of the Supreme Court in *Lochner v. New York*.[39] *Lochner* was decided in 1905, thirty-seven years after the publication of *Constitutional Limitations* and seven years after the death of its author.[40] The New York legislature had amended its labor code to forbid bakeries (but not other employers) to employ bakers (but not other employees) for more than ten hours a day or sixty hours a week (a work week much closer to the average American's work week than readers in the late twentieth century can readily imagine). Lochner, the owner of a bakery shop, was convicted of working his bakers an excessive number of hours. Lochner's lawyers cited numerous decisions of the Supreme Court, as well as Cooley and other legal writers, for the proposition that the Court was obligated to decide whether there really is something significantly different about bakers who work in bakeries that would justify a special rule limiting their hours of employment, but no one else's.[41] They emphasized that the law applied only to bakers in bakeries and not those working in hotels or other places where bread is made, many of which provided their workers with more unhealthy work environments than did bakeries, who were regulated by other provisions of the same statute to assure a reasonably healthy workplace. New York argued in defense of its law that Lochner had not carried the burden of persuasion that the statute was irrational. The state supplied the Court with no history or data justifying the regulation of hours of work or justifying a difference between bakers in bakeries and bakers in hotels, or non-bakers working in bakeries, but merely asked the Court to take notice that New York legislators are presumptively reasonable folk.

A majority of the Court found that there was nothing special about bakeries, and held that the New York law was therefore "class legislation" violating the principle of equality in legislation and therefore proscribed by the Fourteenth Amendment. They emphasized that "[t]here is no contention that bakers as a class are not equal in intelligence and capacity to men in other trades or manual occupations. . . . They are in no sense wards of the state."[42] Finding that the law regulated labor and not health, the Court compared it to state laws forbidding the shoeing of horses without a license, a form of legislation recently invalidated by courts in New York[43] and Illinois.[44] They concluded that the public interest was "not in the slightest degree affected"[45] by the bakers' hours of work.

Justice Harlan's dissent proceeded from the same legal premise as the majority but perceived its application to bakers in a different light. One justice joining in this dissent was Justice Day, Cooley's former student and intimate friend.[46] This dissent took judicial notice of the uncited history of bakers' ill health and of literature reporting the dangers of prolonged inhalation of flour.[47] While conceding that the legislation might have been initiated with an illicit legislative purpose, the dissent presumed that the legislature had determined "upon the fullest available information, and for the common good" that too many hours in a dusty bakery are especially harmful to bakers.[48]

Some commentators thought the decision correct.[49] Roscoe Pound, however, forcefully criticized the majority opinion for its ignorance of the facts

and took it as an occasion to advance his argument for what he denoted as
sociological jurisprudence, that is, the making of law on the basis of knowledge of law's social consequences.[50] Critical of the Court, but perhaps
somewhat ambivalent, was Andrew McLaughlin, another distinguished
former student of Cooley who coincidentally was his son-in-law.[51]
McLaughlin, stating views that Cooley would have been likely to share, observed that

> We have outgrown in business activity and in social sentiment the conditions
> of individualism that were dominant in the early days of the Republic and for
> decades thereafter; we are face to face with the fact that society has duties and
> responsibilities and that any principles which set up isolated and individual
> right as over against community interest are at least fraught with danger, if
> they are not pure anachronism.[52]

Nevertheless,

> [i]f a law to limit the hours of bakeries, like that of New York recently passed
> on by the courts, has for its purpose, not the uplifting and protection of the
> health and well-being of the community, but the giving of advantage to a cer-
> tain class of workers without regard for the rights and desires of the rest, or if
> it is merely an attack on an employer's right of contract, it can hardly be sup-
> ported as an exercise of the police power.[53]

Ernst Freund of the University of Chicago Law School, who was cited
along with Cooley by the lawyers for the state of New York, commented
adversely on the decision, but made a concession to the principle of equality in legislation similar to that made by McLaughlin. He criticized the majority's blindness to the reality of working conditions in bakeries[54] and emphasized that the issue raised by an application of the principle of equality
in legislation is often one of fact, not law. The majority had ignored the evidence on the central issue, that is, whether there is something especially
dangerous about working long hours in bakeries. Freund hoped that the
Court, when better informed, would reach the opposite conclusion. Indeed,
it was a very short time before Louis Brandeis, Freund's political ally,
would as an advocate persuade the Court to sustain a regulation of working conditions for women by presenting in his brief a surfeit of detailed social data as justification of the legislation under attack.[55]

Whether a thorough "Brandeis brief" could have turned the Court in
Lochner is uncertain. In any case, as Pound, McLaughlin, Freund, and
Brandeis recognized, the outcome depended very little on the verbal formulation of the legal principle applied (the only part of the decision in any way
connected with the Cooley treatise) and rested very much on what the justices knew, or thought they knew, about bakeries. The majority opinion in

Lochner would be cited in a series of cases in which the Supreme Court found progressive state legislation unconstitutional,[56] but eventually the Court came to sustain most exercises of the police power upon a minimal showing of real effects on health and safety justifying the enactments.[57]

Justice Holmes's *Lochner* dissent was almost casual;[58] he refused to entertain the issue of whether there is or is not something special about bakeries and simply dismissed the majority as unduly preoccupied with a deductive methodology that proceeded from a false premise. He accused the Court of deciding the case "upon an economic theory which a large part of the country does not entertain." The theory he attributed to the majority was laissez-faire economics derived from the social Darwinism of Herbert Spencer.[59] Holmes may have been the member of the *Lochner* Court most sympathetic with the tenets of social Darwinism,[60] so his opinion can be taken as a strong application of the principle of judicial restraint set forth in *Constitutional Limitations*. Curiously, Roscoe Pound found in Holmes's brief opinion "the best exposition . . . of sociological jurisprudence" despite Holmes's seeming indifference to the sociological facts at issue.[61]

There is assuredly no reason to believe that Cooley, had he been alive and on the Court, would have joined the majority in *Lochner*. His adherence as a judge to the principles of self-restraint alone would have assured his deference to the New York legislature on such a matter. Moreover, Cooley was an advocate of health and safety law. Not only in *Constitutional Limitations*,[62] and again in his chapter on the Fourteenth Amendment, but also in his more popular writing, he asserted the need to subordinate property and contract rights to the protection of public health and safety. He did not hesitate to support stringent quarantine and environmental laws to restrict the exercise of individual rights that endangered others.[63] He also favored stronger regulation of enterprise to protect the land, deploring the savaging of timber resources by American pioneers. And in his edition of Story's *Commentaries*, as we have seen, he supported the constitutionality of prohibitions of intoxicating liquors, perhaps the most extreme form of public health paternalism then practiced.

Cooley would not, on the other hand, have joined in the opinion of Justice Holmes.[64] Cooley believed that the principle Holmes was prepared to ignore was the essence not only of the Equal Protection Clause of the Fourteenth Amendment, but also of the pre-existing state constitutions embodying the Jacksonian doctrine of Equal Rights. That doctrine imposed on the Court a solemn duty to prevent the New York legislature from succumbing to the blandishments of the rich and the powerful or the well-organized bakers, seeking advantage over those lacking influence in the corridors of power, such as unorganized bakery owners, or perhaps of hotels and restaurants seeking an advantage over bakeries. He could not have joined in Holmes's washing-of-hands, but would have joined Justice Harlan in requiring a showing that New York had reasons that could withstand scrutiny in the light of day.

Cooley's writing on the Fourteenth Amendment has drawn a second line of criticism seemingly at war with the assertions of those blaming him for the intrusiveness of the Supreme Court in limiting the police power of the states. The competing criticism is that Cooley bears some responsibility for the failure of Reconstruction.[65] Philip Paludan, for example, contended that Cooley's view of the role of the Court in interpreting the Privileges and Immunities and Equal Protection clauses of the Fourteenth Amendment was unduly narrow. Paludan's criticism comes not from the generation enamored with the wisdom and humanity of the New Deal, but from a later generation viewing Cooley's writing from the perspective of *Brown v. Board of Education*.[66] Paludan contends that Cooley failed to recognize that the Civil War had not merely saved the Union, but had transformed it, resulting in the empowerment of the Supreme Court of the United States to impose its notions of equality on the state governments, especially those in the South.

But, as we have seen, Cooley supposed that the Fifteenth Amendment would continue to be effectively imposed on the South. And in his cautious reading of the Fourteenth Amendment, Cooley spoke for his time. The Fourteenth Amendment would never have been ratified if it had been presented to the generation who so reviled *Dred Scott* as a new commission to the Court to impose on legislatures its doubtful wisdom on a wide range of social and economic issues. The amendment was presented to the people in the only way that it could have won approval, as an instrument declaratory of rights already existing in state constitutions.[67] Had it been presented as an affirmation of natural law to be interpreted by judges holding office for life, it would not have been ratified by a single state. No honest legal writer of Cooley's time could have described the effect of the amendment in terms less modest than those Cooley employed.

In any event, Cooley's edition of Story was not frequently cited as a source legitimating decisions applying the Fourteenth Amendment. Although *Constitutional Limitations* did not speak to that amendment, it was, as the New York brief in *Lochner* illustrates, a work that was perceived to be pertinent.

Meanwhile, other authors addressed the law limiting the police power of the states and gave close attention to the Fourteenth Amendment and interpretative decisions rendered after 1880, when Cooley ceased to write on the subject. Two of the later authors bear notice here. In 1886, eighteen years after Cooley published *Constitutional Limitations*, Christopher Tiedeman, then at the University of Missouri, published a 600-page account of the limits, both state and federal, on the police power of the states.[68] Tiedeman may in fact have been the social Darwinist[69] that some later historians presumed Cooley to have been. His preface concluded in libertarian fervor:

> If the author succeeds in any measure in his attempt to awaken the public mind to a full appreciation of the power of constitutional limitations to protect private rights against the radical experimentations of social reformers, he will feel that he has been amply requited for his labors in the cause of social order and personal liberty.[70]

Unlike Cooley, Tiedeman argued that courts should review legislation to prevent manifest injustice and to assure legislative fidelity to the social contract,[71] but regretfully acknowledged that it was settled American law that a court cannot nullify legislation simply because it conflicts with natural right.[72] Tiedeman, again unlike Cooley, found no need to include a section on "unequal" legislation. He repeatedly emphasized, even more strongly than Cooley, the requirement that valid police regulation must have a legitimating public purpose and cannot rest on legislative impulses that are irrational or intended to serve a private purpose.[73] Showing his contemporaries how far he was willing to take his point, Tiedeman argued that the state had no legitimate purpose in preventing miscegenation.

Tiedeman was thus indifferent to Cooley's extended caution about the dangers of judicial usurpation. Indeed, it is possible to perceive James Bradley Thayer's 1893 essay on those dangers[74] as a response to Tiedeman's advocacy of firm judicial control over unruly legislatures controlled by unwashed voters.

Another eighteen years after the appearance of Tiedeman's book, yet another exhaustive work on the police power appeared,[75] written by Ernst Freund of the University of Chicago. Freund's politics were far removed from those of Tiedeman; among his sometime allies were Jane Addams,[76] Eugene Debs,[77] Clarence Darrow,[78] and Louis Brandeis, all of whom were regarded by many of their contemporaries as leftist radicals.

Freund, the subject of a later chapter of this book, was in important respects an intellectual heir of Francis Lieber, and therefore intellectual kin to Cooley. Freund's *The Police Power: Public Policy and Constitutional Rights* reported many recent developments, acknowledging that most of the law on the limits of the police power had developed since the publication of Cooley's first edition and was even yet in a formative stage.[79] Freund defined for a generation the limits of states' power to regulate the conduct of firms and citizens. His work was cited, along with Cooley's, by the state of New York in its brief in *Lochner*, but also by many courts as a welcome corrective for the misuses to which Cooley's work had been employed to justify judicial restraints on legislative enactments applying the lash of the law to correct various forms of predatory conduct.

Cooley's understanding that the Fourteenth Amendment was declaratory of existing law and a reinforcement of that law by placing in the federal Constitution the restraints previously expressed in most of the constitutions of the states was amply supported by Freund. He described the principle of substantive due process in terms redolent of antebellum state law reported in 1868 by Cooley and observed the national law to be that

> [w]here a restraint is confined to a special class of acts or occupations, that class must present the danger dealt with in a more marked and uniform degree than the classes omitted, and where the restraint is general, with certain exceptions, the excepted classes must either be entirely free from the danger, or the exception must tend to reduce the general danger, or a distinct and legitimate public policy must favor the toleration of the evil under circumstances where it is outweighed by great benefits.[80]

Freund, even more than Cooley, was preoccupied with the principle of equality, devoting the final third part of his work to it.[81] He accepted the doctrine stated by Cooley forbidding "class legislation" and devoted his efforts to analyzing what that broadly stated restraint might mean in particular circumstances. He drew on Cooley's language favoring "equal rights" in praising judicial intervention to limit the growing practices of racial discrimination by law, which he found to be irreconcilable with the Constitution.[82] And he was among the first to contend that the equal protection clause implied an obligation of the state to assure women of equal pay for equal work.[83] Writing in 1941, William Seagle appraised Freund's book as "the constitutional classic of [its] period."[84] That Freund, a lawyer unmistakably committed to the welfare of industrial workers, reported in such a work that the law was much as Cooley had described it further confirms the integrity of Cooley's work.

11

Industrialization

Thomas Cooley was sixty-three in 1887, when he embarked on a fourth public career. He was no longer the Cooley who had moved from Adrian to Ann Arbor in 1858 to assume his new duties at the University of Michigan. Advanced in years, he had substantially modified the political views motivating his earlier careers.

As ideological change so often is, this drift away from the politics of his youth appears to have been caused more by Cooley's reactions to events than by any intellectual influence of others. He had lived since 1858 in the academic community of Ann Arbor. Since 1865, he had been in the public domain as a judge and celebrated author. He had read as well as written much. He had formed close friendships with intellectuals such as Andrew Dickson White and Charles Kendall Adams and had acquired newer friends of a younger generation.

But in addition to these influences, Cooley by 1880 had become increasingly concerned, and even alarmed, about industrial relations in the United States. While problems between capital and labor had not been uncommon in earlier times, it was not until the 1870s that they aroused his concern. In 1873, a sharp depression had hit, and for the ensuing two decades and more, violent strikes were chronic. This turmoil provided the background from which federal administrative law emerged in 1887.

In 1875, as much as a fifth of the nation's industrial workers were completely unemployed and without means; many others were reduced to part-time employment. Textile workers and miners tried to strike, but their strikes were quickly broken and their wages were cut.[1] That year, the Pinkerton Company won a reputation for strike breaking by its private police; a tactic sometimes employed was to secure the convictions of labor leaders on false evidence of violent misconduct.[2] Miners thus deprived of leadership were dolefully singing, "We've been beaten, beaten all to smash."[3] Railroad workers were also subjected to wage cuts.

In 1877, there was an insurrection against the Baltimore & Ohio Railroad when its brakemen and firemen struck.[4] They seized the depot at Martinsburg, West Virginia, and stopped all trains. President Hayes dispatched troops. The leaders of the strike were arrested, but the insurrection spread, often with broad public support, because many Americans had reason to revile the managements of railroads. The workers of the Pennsylvania Railroad went out on strike, and then those of the Erie. Some railroads rescinded wage cuts, but the protest extended, soon reaching to California. When the militia was sent out, they often fraternized with the strikers. But here and there were pitched battles between workers and police. Chicago exploded in violence; cavalry charged one crowd, killing twelve. Soldiers who had been fighting Sioux on the frontier were brought to Chicago as reinforcements and scores more citizens were killed or wounded. A United States district judge in Indianapolis declared that "society was disintegrating if it had not dissolved."[5]

In San Francisco, a meeting called to express support for railroad workers broke up in a race riot that stormed Chinatown and demolished Chinese laundries in the not irrational belief that the low wages of the Chinese were causing low wages for others.[6] The hoodlums were suppressed by a "pick-handle brigade." One of the vigilante brigade's members was Denis Kearney, an Irish drayman who had acquired some wealth by uncertain means. After helping to suppress one mob, he decided to pursue a future at the head of another. He organized the Workingmen's Party in California, a group given to Marxist rhetoric. Punished for breach of the peace, Kearney proclaimed himself "the voice of the people" and used his own hoodlums to abuse workers who failed to support him enthusiastically. The Party succeeded in electing a mayor of Sacramento, but soon disintegrated amid allegations of racketeering.[7]

The disorders of 1877 produced predictable reactions. One was the advent of social Darwinism.[8] In 1874, three years before the outbreaks, Herbert Spencer had published in England his *Study of Sociology*, contending that wealth and poverty merely reflected the relative moral worth of individuals; his work was destined to sell well to prosperous Americans. Workers were said by his followers to deserve their poverty because they were lazy, thriftless, substance-abusing folk who engaged in "excessive reproduction, sexually." And if they did not deserve their fates, they were at best victims of a tragic destiny that none could prevent because it was biologically predetermined. Exponents of this view in America found support in the fatalism of two celebrated economists, William Graham Sumner of Yale[9] and Simon Newcomb of Johns Hopkins.[10] Some social Darwinists took up residency among the founders of the academic discipline of economics emerging after 1870.[11]

This truly "dismal science" in turn evoked reaction among public lawyers and other members of the rising academic profession. Cooley, for one, recognized as legitimate the grievances of workers forced to compete with Chinese workers imported in gangs from the rice paddies of Asia, but as an old Jacksonian, he was also prone to blame the riots on the profligate subsidies given to western railroads, which had called forth the invective of "sand lot orators," able to contrast what the government had done for bondholders with what it was allowing their representatives to do to laborers.[12] He explicitly rejected the social Darwinist argument that low wages are the result of iron laws of political economy. It was not labor that needed awakening to the inevitability of economics, but capital that needed awakening to the moral duties accompanying citizenship in a republic.[13] Cooley knew by 1879 the plight of the urban workers:

> In the great cities arrogant wealth is here side by side with abject poverty; and here honest industry wages its desperate warfare with want, perpetually doubtful of the result, and in many cases having the rewards of its hard labor doled out grudgingly as if it were a gratuity.[14]

He regarded capitalists who insisted on their legal rights to pay low wages and maintain dangerous or unhealthy working conditions as short-sighted pursuers of quick gain at the cost of long-term injury to self-interest as well as the public interest. "Peace," he said, could "never come from the triumph" of capital over labor.[15]

Cooley did not oppose legislation to protect labor from capital, nor, as we have seen, did he envision the Constitution as an impediment to legislative efforts reasonably designed to protect those having no economic leverage with which to bargain for a living wage. Writing in 1884, he cautioned general readers that traditional constitutional protection of property from government could not be sustained, else

> the benefit of this protection is reaped by those who have possessions, [and] the Constitution itself may come to be regarded by considerable classes as an instrument whose office is to protect the rich in the advantages they have secured over the poor, and one that should be hated for that reason.[16]

Searching for moral or religious constraints on the conduct of employers that would be more effective than legislation, Cooley in the 1880s came to admire the preaching of Washington Gladden, a Protestant minister whose Social Gospel movement was arrayed against the greed and materialism of industrial America. Cooley sought to recruit Gladden for his wife's church.[17] At the same time, Cooley refused to address a large audience of Michigan capitalists whose anti-labor program he described as "absurd."[18]

In the 1880s, the Knights of Labor were in the forefront of the struggle to reverse the allegedly predetermined effects on workers.[19] At times, they proved so adept at using the boycott as an economic weapon that they were able to cause saloons to refuse to serve beer to strikebreakers, and one worker in New Jersey lost his job at their behest because he lived with a brother who was deemed a strikebreaker.[20] In 1885, the Knights won an epic struggle with the Missouri Pacific Railroad, forcing it to cancel wage cuts. This was followed by another victory in a Michigan lumber strike and, for the moment, the Knights surged in power and membership.[21]

In 1886, the summer after Cooley's canonization at Harvard, Chicago again erupted in labor violence. McCormick Harvester locked out 1,400 workers. When they protested, police killed four. When thousands gathered in Haymarket Square to protest the killings, the police opened fire again. Someone threw a bomb, killing a police officer. Eight labor organizers were tried for the bombing; they were convicted, not on any evidence that one of them had thrown the bomb, but on evidence that they had made inflammatory speeches inspiring the bomber. The jurors rendering the verdict had been specially selected by a bailiff designated by the prosecutor; all of them were foremen in large factories. Judge Joseph E. Gary sentenced seven of the eight to hang.[22]

Those in the labor movement protested vehemently, with the support of many leaders of the bar. Leonard Swett, a former partner of Abraham Lincoln, signed the petition seeking review in the Supreme Court of the United States, but it was denied. Lyman Trumbull, a former United States senator and sometime political ally of Lincoln, and Stephen Gregory, later a president of the American Bar Association, joined in an unsuccessful effort to secure clemency. But there was widespread support for Judge Gary's action.[23] Four of the accused were hanged, and a fifth either committed suicide in jail or was killed by his jailers.

The Knights nevertheless extended their brief period of strength and influence. Their ritual hymn concluded in a rousing chorus: "Storm the fort, ye Knights of Labor, Battle for your cause; Equal rights for every neighbor, Down with tyrant laws!" Among the principles advocated by the Knights was equal pay for equal work by women. They recruited African-American members even in the South, where the Knights' recruiters were threatened with lynching.[24] In 1886, while Chicago was in eruption, they boldly held a convention in Richmond, Virginia; many districts sent their African-American members to represent them.[25] Yet at the same time the Knights favored the exclusion of Chinese workers from the continent of North America.[26]

The labor movement gained the support of some members of the academic profession; among them were the emerging "new school" or "ethical" economists who opposed the "old school" of social Darwinists. The "new school" of economics was first led by Richard Ely, then at Johns

Hopkins University, who in 1884 attacked the existing dogma in economics as English, hypothetical, inductive, and fatalistic. Ely proposed a new economics that would be German, realistic, deductive, and a service to suffering mankind.[27] Ely came under fire in 1885 as an unreliable radical and soon thereafter moved to the University of Wisconsin, but he was supported by a distinguished group that included Andrew Dickson White and Cooley, to whom Ely thereafter gave allegiance.[28]

Among Ely's allies was Henry Carter Adams, then a young economist holding appointments at both Cornell and Michigan. While critical of Ely's professionalism,[29] Adams joined the effort to transform economics into a reformist ideology.[30] Together Ely and Adams organized the American Economics Association in 1885. Among those invited to join was Washington Gladden, the leader of the Social Gospel movement. Among those not invited were the social Darwinists Simon Newcomb and William Sumner.

At Michigan, Henry Carter Adams was closely associated with Cooley. He was in the early 1880s a Marxist, but he was also a pacifist who rejected confrontation and violence as the means to his social ends. His pacifism was shared by Cooley, who, despite his anger at employers for their failure to perform their moral duties, was among those who assumed that the Haymarket defendants were violent anarchists as well as bombers and approved their convictions, if not their executions.[31]

Henry Carter Adams was a strident supporter of the Knights. Indeed, his defense of the radical Knights of Labor marked him as so unreliable that he was fired in 1886 by Cornell University, then led by Cooley's friend and former colleague, Charles Kendall Adams.[32] Despite his political leanings and his misadventure at Cornell, Henry Carter Adams was tenured at Michigan, partly on account of Cooley's support.[33] The aged Cooley and young Adams became frequent dinner companions, and it seems likely that this relationship intensified Cooley's strong disapproval of the contemporary business morality favoring the reduction of costs by driving workers to the wall.

In 1886, Cooley disagreed with Adams about the Knights, whom Cooley dismissed as demagogues willing to disturb the peace for their own advantage, but unlikely to gain benefits for their followers.[34] He published an article for general readers urgently recommending arbitration as the method for avoiding dangerous confrontations.[35] He also differed with Adams on the role of government, being less optimistic that the government could effectively diminish the suffering of the working poor. As a Jacksonian, he continued to suspect that the rich or powerful would subvert almost any state intervention that well-intentioned, ethical economists might devise.

While Cooley shared many ideas with Richard Ely, Henry Carter Adams, and Washington Gladden, it was likely his faith in traditional democratic values that led him to change his mind about the role of law and government in economic matters. The agrarian world in which the dogma of Jefferson and Jackson had been framed, and in which Cooley had matured, had given way to industrialization that greatly increased the opportunities for predation and diminished the ability of less resourceful citizens to protect themselves.

The cataclysm foretold by Marx was thus increasingly visible on the horizon. That perception was an important stimulus to Progressive politics, a "liberalism of fear" beginning to germinate in the last years of the century. It was also a signal to those obliged to perform the duty of the public profession of law to mediate class conflict and thus sustain the Republic, a signal that a time had come to lead the Republic in a less dangerous direction. It was on account of this confluence of Progressive politics with professional duty that Cooley was not only among the last Jacksonians, but also among the first Progressives.

12

Rails

While Cooley was expressing concern about the legal status of labor in America, he was also acquiring a professional interest in the nation's railroad industry, in which so many workers were employed and which was destined to become the nation's first and premier regulated industry. In 1882, he became personally involved in railroad regulation, writing the chair of the Senate Committee on Interstate Commerce that "[s]omebody ought to write a paper on The Overlooked Moral Considerations Involved in the Railroad Problem."[1] And he increased his own activity in that field after 1884, when he retired from the law school and turned his legal treatises over to other writers.

It is not easy today to comprehend the role that railroads played in the American economy, politics, and culture in 1882. Robert Wiebe described the erosion of the "sovereignty" of "island communities" that occurred during Cooley's lifetime.[2] Regionalization and then nationalization of markets caused by the railroads deprived the small, familiar villages of their identities; local leaders were reduced in significance as their communities were made to seem provincial and even backward in the minds of their own citizens. Thomas Haskell was describing Cooley and his generation when he observed that "individuals were deprived of the sense of boundless self-sufficiency characteristic of Jacksonian America and were encouraged to construe their own and other people's lives as a product of external circumstance."[3] This was especially evident with respect to law and politics, because the communities giving rise to Jacksonian beliefs were impotent to regulate the influences or to limit the predations coming to them behind the iron horse.

In 1882, about a tenth of the nation's wealth was invested in railroads, but much of the other nine-tenths was at least partly attributable to what has been fairly described as a transportation revolution occasioned by the laying of rails.[4] At the time of Cooley's birth, goods or produce could be moved by wagon for about fifteen cents per ton-mile; water transport, where available, was a bit less than half the cost of surface transport, or still less if a steamboat had the benefit of a downstream run. By 1882, goods and produce were moved on rails for about a penny per ton-mile; wagons and steamboats had almost disappeared.[5]

The availability and price of rail service were then crucial to the welfare of virtually every business and every community,[6] as the people of Salem, Michigan, had recognized when they reluctantly agreed to finance the construction of a railroad to their town. In the early years, when the competition was horse-drawn, profits achieved monopolistic heights on almost every railroad. Competition gradually materialized on longer carriages of goods that could be routed over alternate lines, because it mattered little to most shippers whether their goods went from St. Louis to Chicago by way of St. Paul or by way of Louisville, and the costs of providing services between those two points were about the same, whichever of many routes was taken. This competition could be ruinous, with rates falling in some places to the level of marginal costs, yielding no revenue with which to repay the sometimes heavy indebtedness incurred in the building of the railroads. On this account, some railroads were doomed to fail.

A central and defining problem for railroads was that most of their costs were fixed capital costs, that is, not variable with service delivered. In other words, most of the cost of moving a boxcar of grain from one point to another was incurred before the first boxcar was loaded. Not only were fixed costs high, but much of the costs represented an immovable investment permanently locked into whatever market conditions might prevail on the line's routes. Moreover, the marginal cost of hauling the grain a longer rather than a shorter distance was very slight because there was little fuel expense incurred by adding more cars to a freight train moving along a preordained route. Therefore, when it appeared that a load would otherwise be moved by a train on another railroad and hence provide no revenue to a carrier, incentives were strong for each competitor to take whatever return it could achieve by cutting prices below the level needed to provide sufficient revenue to pay returns on the capital invested in incurring the fixed costs. Competition was especially severe for railroads whose competitors had become insolvent and were in receivership,[7] because the latter no longer had to pay a return on their fixed costs; such railroads were therefore quite free to lower their rates to cover only their variable costs, a situation replicated by airline competition a century later.

Ruined railroads posed in turn a serious problem not only for their workers, but for farmers and other shippers when service was limited or discontinued. Some knowledgeable observers believed that the American railroad system was overbuilt; most recognized that there was what is now described as a market failure making competition inherently inefficient.[8] The railroads were "either filthy rich or perpetually broke."[9] It was for such reasons that railroads had been nationalized in most countries, including many that were not otherwise given to governmental ownership of enterprise.[10] Nationalization of the rails was advocated by the Populist Party that won support in western farm states in the 1890s. That party was given to strong statements; their 1892 platform protested: "From the prolific womb of governmental injustice, we breed two great classes—tramps and millionaires."[11] But their idea about railroad ownership gained little support among the electorate in more settled regions.

The American railroads struggled to survive such feast-or-famine competition. One means of survival was differential pricing disfavoring shorter hauls where the marginal costs (of loading and unloading) were proportionally higher and where often a monopoly price could be charged. This practice enraged short haul shippers, many of whom were farmers. Another survival technique was the pooling of revenues, a form of cartel to reduce the vigor of price competition, but one that proved to be generally unstable because it depended on mutual trust between railroads. Yet a third method of survival was the merger of competitors to facilitate monopoly pricing.

Every freight pricing practice had secondary consequences for competition among shippers. Thus, the railroads' ability to ship grain long distances enlarged the farmer's market, but also brought competing grain into his market. New York merchants, like western farmers, favored a standard price per ton-mile because long-haul discounts enabled inland merchants to compete with them in ways previously impossible.[12] Everywhere, shippers favored lower rates for themselves and higher rates for their competitors and maintained relatively little interest in the absolute level of rates that could be passed on to consumers. There was no single solution attractive to all; no conception of fair pricing could gain general assent.[13] Nor could there be agreement on the role of courts in any regulatory scheme: "Depending on whether the particular interest group perceived the agency as attuned to its concerns, the group either favored or opposed substantial judicial review, political independence of the commissioners and so forth."[14]

Few public issues have aroused so widespread a demand for governmental intervention or have allowed for so little agreement on what the substance of that intervention ought to be. As with many issues of great public concern, what was one man's justice was another's denial of due process. As is often the case, there was simply not enough justice to supply the demand for it.

By 1880, the rates of most railroads were regulated by the states, but only with respect to the intrastate carriage of goods and passengers,[15] because the states were held constitutionally powerless to regulate interstate carriage.[16] At least some of this state regulation favored the interests of local users of railroads, with external consequences disadvantageous to users in other states whose interests were of little concern to local regulators.[17]

Cooley's first assignment as a railroad man was to serve as one of the arbitrators to resolve disputes between railroads and shippers over trunk-line rate differentials to the major port cities of New York, Philadelphia, and Baltimore. His 1882 report touched on all these aspects of the railroad problem[18] and acknowledged that there was no rate structure that would be satisfactory to all the legitimate interests concerned. His balanced report was well received by all of the many sides of the controversy.

In 1883, Cooley published an article reviewing the work of state railroad commissions as a response to abuses by wealthy owners "who are arrogant, overbearing, and reckless of the rights of others."[19] He agreed with Charles Francis Adams[20] that a regulatory commission should seek to lead by moral suasion and publicity.[21] In another article, he contended that rate regulation could be justified only in the absence of competition to restrain the abuse of monopoly power. He also explained to the public a constitutional obstacle faced by nineteenth-century railroad regulation:

> What is a fatal impediment to [the railroad's] control by law is that the States and the nation have, in respect to it, a divided power; and while it is for the interest of the nation at large to encourage the competition which favors long hauls, it is for the interest of localities to make competition most active in short hauls. A State is therefore likely to favor legislation which compels proportional charges, or something near such charges, for all distances; but this, if it should be adopted and enforced, would preclude the great through lines of New York and Pennsylvania from competing at Chicago, St. Paul and St. Louis in the grain-carrying trade of the Northwest, and would reduce such links as are wholly within a State, to the condition of mere local roads, compelled to impose high charges or go into bankruptcy.[22]

The next year, he wrote a technical piece explaining the business reasons for traffic pooling as a response to ruinous competition.[23]

By 1885, the political pressure on Congress to regulate railroads was becoming irresistible. A committee of the Senate of the United States sought Cooley's advice. He urged caution, noting that the public had earlier been all too eager to favor railroads with unwarranted concessions and might now be too eager to regulate them. He distinguished between those railroads that were honorably managed for the benefit of both stockholders and the public and others that were managed to the injury of both. He thought the most important objective of legislation should be to eradicate the practice of giving discriminatory rebates for the purpose of crushing competition, concluding with characteristic Jacksonian fervor: "It is a great public calamity when people in a free country are brought to believe that the tendency of public institutions is to make the strong stronger and the weak weaker."[24]

When Cooley was defeated for re-election to the Michigan State Supreme Court in 1885, one of the opportunities presented to him was the presidency of a railroad at a salary many times the amount of his combined former salaries as a judge and professor.[25] A few years earlier, John Forrest Dillon had taken the eye-opening step of leaving the federal judiciary in Iowa to become a very highly paid general counsel to the Union Pacific Railroad. Cooley manifested no interest in such a move, although he would presumably have commanded an even higher price than Dillon.

In December 1886, Cooley was appointed receiver for the Wabash Railway. In making this appointment, the United States Circuit Court discharged the receivers appointed earlier, who had conducted the receivership for the benefit of the owner, the scion Jay Gould, to the disadvantage of bondholders. The court selected Cooley as a "symbol of integrity"[26] to manage the railroad to meet its indebtedness. It was his standing as such a symbol that would lead, in 1887, to his final venture as a public servant.

13

The Advent of Federal
Administrative Law

By 1887, Cooley was burdened by substantial impediments of age. The preceding year, the year of his appearance at Harvard and of the Haymarket riot, he had begun to suffer from chronic, and sometimes acute, depression.[1] The cause of his depression was never determined. His illness might have been associated with organic deterioration; long decades of overwork; the sudden deprivation of his longstanding work commitments as teacher, judge, and scholar; his discomfort with the public events of the time; the failing health of his wife of over forty years; or more likely, a combination of some or all these.

One did not have to be afflicted with these burdens of aging to be depressed by the state of affairs in 1887. America was a glum place. The frontier was closing and, with it, the mythic opportunities it afforded to all having the desire and energy to exploit them. As noted, the advent of industrialization had brought new opportunities for the amassing of great wealth extracted from the labors of a new proletariat having no visible means of escaping grinding urban poverty,[2] while socioeconomic theorists were professing the inevitability of oppression in a Darwinist war of all-against-all.[3]

Industrial pollution was becoming a menace to both rural and urban landscapes.[4] The manufacture and sale of worthless medicines[5] was only one of many scams perpetrated on the public. Many industrial workers and their families were exposed to horrifying work hazards, were suffering cuts in wages needed to sustain high profit margins, or both.[6] Harsh means were employed to break unions.

Politics was increasingly a game played by the wealthy and the cynical; for twenty years and more, the nation's politics and law had been given over to the greed and mendacity of some of its most aggressive and resourceful citizens. Corruption in government had reached epic levels, awaiting the revelations of Lincoln Steffens and other muckrakers.[7] Public officials had begun to discover the rewards of mortgaging the future with public debt to pay for present enjoyments.[8]

Random criminal violence was beginning to make its appearance in newly urbanized communities;[9] a president of the United States[10] and a mayor of Chicago[11] had recently been murdered by persons seemingly motivated by revenge for their failure to secure public employment.

Meanwhile, the efforts to reconstruct the former slave states had come to an end[12] and the oppression of the former slaves and their descendants was becoming increasingly open and shameless.[13] The country's prospects seemed bleak in all directions.

At such a troubled time, the aged and failing Cooley was called to shape and direct the effort of the federal government to respond to the social and economic crisis centered on the railroads. The Interstate Commerce Act was signed by President Cleveland on February 4, 1887;[14] it was a major event in the political life of the country, because it was the federal government's first substantial step into the arena of business regulation. A major objective of agrarian politics had been achieved.[15] In part, the Act was a reaction to a Supreme Court decision reaffirming the impotence of state governments[16] and the regulatory agencies they had created.[17]

The Act established the Interstate Commerce Commission and authorized that body to regulate interstate rail transport, but with limited powers.[18] The Commission was the first of the important federal regulatory agencies to be created and it established a pattern for others.[19] It was

> not the product of a concerted reform movement. It did not reflect a coherent ideological approach to railroad regulation. And it was not one element in a more broadly perceived political agenda. Instead, [it] addressed a discrete set of immediate pressing problems in an equivocal fashion that reflected the difficult process of hammering out legislative compromise.[20]

Reflecting the ambivalence of Congress,

> the powers . . . conferred upon the Commission by the original legislation were found to be restricted in scope and feeble in effect. . . . Almost from the beginning the Commission encountered serious obstacles in the performance of its functions. Unwilling witnesses successfully took refuge in constitutional guaranties as a means of withholding essential testimony from the Commission. Moreover, at almost every step, the Commission was hindered by the open hostility of the railroads and the unsympathetic attitude by the courts. . . . The fact that the Commission was compelled to take the initiative for the enforcement of its orders, and that its rulings became binding only upon being judicially sustained by the courts of last resort, not only left the carriers free to ignore the Commission's orders, but afforded ample opportunity to the courts to become the real arbiters of contested issues.[21]

When it came to White House selection of the Commission's five members, there was a free-swinging imbroglio between diverse railroads (and their investors) and diverse users. What the president needed was someone, or five someones, who would apply the vague general policies established by Congress in "the coldest neutrality."[22] On advice from all sides, President Cleveland importuned Cooley to serve as founding chair. Reluctant for reasons not only of his own health, but also that of his wife, Cooley nevertheless answered the call. The appointment was widely hailed as one establishing the integrity of the Commission,[23] with one observer exulting that "the most daring experiment in constitutional law has been entrusted to the first constitutional lawyer of the country."[24] At the first meeting of the Commission, Cooley was promptly elected to the chair. During the first three years, when Cooley's health remained adequate, the other commissioners deferred to him on many important matters.[25]

Of course, Cooley was aware that the unsettled aims of the Commission, however the conflicts among them might be resolved, were impossible to attain, given the modest powers conferred on the agency. He had long conceded a need for public regulation of at least some kinds of businesses for the purposes of restraining predation. In his 1870 opinion in *People v. Salem*,[26] the least cautious constitutional decision of his court, he had proscribed public subsidies for railroad construction, but acknowledged the public's need to confer the power of eminent domain on some private businesses, such as railroads, and he recognized that such rights when conferred must be accompanied by enforceable duties to the public. In this respect, as in others, he adhered to the dictum of Lieber that all rights carry duties.[27]

While separating his public from his private self,[28] Cooley was mindful that there are private stakes in public policies, and that the line between public and private interests is elusive. The need to draw such a line was widely noted in 1872 when the Supreme Court of the United States decided *Munn v. Illinois*.[29] Illinois had enacted a scheme of rate regulation for grain elevators. The owner of an elevator protested, citing Cooley's *Constitutional Limitations*,[30] and arguing that such rate regulation denied him "equal rights," there being no satisfactory distinction between grain elevators and any other business. The Supreme Court upheld the state regulation, holding that businesses "affected with a public interest," such as grain elevators, might constitutionally be singled out for such controls. In 1878, Cooley published an article commenting on the decision.[31] While he did not question the result in *Munn*, he questioned the vacuous breadth of the term, "affected with a public interest," agreeing with the owner of the elevator that the public has some stake in the conduct of most, if not all, business.[32] But some enterprises did need to be regulated; thus, in the same article, he expressed agreement with a then-recent Wisconsin decision holding that railroad rates might be regulated by the state without regard for provisions in the railroads' corporate charters,[33] a position dissonant with *Dart-mouth College*, the one decision of the Supreme Court of the United States Cooley had allowed himself to question in his role as text writer. A few years later, he published another article for a general readership in which he explained that exceptionally high profits resulting from monopoly pricing could properly be taken into account in setting rates on public services facilitated by the power of eminent domain or by patent protection for new inventions.[34] Thus, in earlier years, Cooley had accommodated his Jacksonian politics to the concept of public utility regulation, but his approval of the idea was characteristically cautious.

Congressional diffidence about the wisdom of its dramatic step was manifested by its failure to confer a subpoena power on the Commission. On this account, the Commission lacked the ability to conduct an effective investigation of matters for which it had regulatory responsibility; it was substantially compelled to act on the basis of presentations of data made voluntarily by the railroads.[35]

The Act was also pitifully ambivalent in prescribing the regulatory aims it directed the Commission to pursue. As we might expect, Congress was trying to respond to diverse and conflicting political pressures. Some railroads sought regulation as protection against competition, while others saw benefits to themselves in remaining unregulated on the long hauls. Among those who wanted to be regulated, there was little agreement about the form or substance of the regulation that ought be applied. Many shippers also sought regulation as protection against the sometime monopoly power of the railroads, but there were equally sharp conflicts of interest among shippers who were as concerned with the rates charged their competitors as with rates they were themselves required to pay. Trunk-line passengers had interests that conflicted with those who rode on local trains. It was also recognized that consumers and workers had a stake in the regulatory issues, but even they were not united in their interests.

Cooley laid out a pattern of regulation based on the Act that resonated with Jacksonian notions of Equal Rights. The Commission did not, at the outset, undertake the task of setting long-haul rates, a task made Herculean by the complex economics of railroading, the constitutional division of authority between state and federal governments, and the random presence of unregulated non-rail competition on rivers and canals. However, the Commission established a requirement that rates be filed and made the same for all shippers and passengers equally situated, a principle that might today be welcome to many if imposed on airlines to preclude "frequent flyer" or other favoritism for upper-class travelers. And it entertained complaints by shippers that particular rates were excessive. In 1890, to the dismay of the railroads, the Commission ordered a reduction of rates on the carriage of grain in the Midwest.[36]

Although Cooley had in his 1883 article explained the economic benefits sometimes associated with long haul price "discrimination," his Commission, obedient to the expressed aims of Congress,[37] proscribed the practice,[38] even where the discrimination was a response to predatory pricing by a competitor.[39] The Commission cracked down on rebates for large shippers[40] and the issuance of free passes to preferred passengers,[41] a group that often included judges and others engaged in law enforcement. It also all but proscribed discrimination against African-American passengers on interstate runs,[42] allowing racial segregation only where the accommodations were identical,[43] a condition that could rarely be met. As a result, African-American citizens sometimes traveled in desegregated Pullman cars although every other facet of their social lives was segregated by local Jim Crow laws and practices. The Commission did, however, weaken in its resolve to enforce this standard after Cooley's retirement in 1891.[44] It also, in accordance with the Act, proscribed traffic pooling, again despite Cooley's personal opinion that the practice was sometimes necessitated by the diseconomies of competition. The Commission even opposed the proposed repeal of the statutory restraint on pooling,[45] despite the earnest entreaties of the railroads that such pooling was necessary, as Cooley had himself suggested in 1883.[46]

Although its policies disfavoring pooling and short-haul discrimination were injurious to the railroads, the Commission acknowledged a responsibility to assure a reasonable return on investments made in building the railroads, because disinvestment in them would disserve everyone. But the Commission was powerless to overcome the economic pressures driving the value of many local railroads so low that they were cheaply acquired by railroad monopolists such as Harriman, Hill, Morgan, and Vanderbilt, who emerged as business moguls in the early years of the twentieth century.[47]

Cooley's Commission sought,[48] but did not receive until 1920,[49] authority to regulate intrastate traffic.[50] Some of its policies were restrained by the courts,[51] some were modified by Congress, and others were indifferently enforced by later commissions. And the Commission was later criticized both for failing to assure an adequate return to railroads[52] and for failing adequately to protect shippers and consumers.[53] Sometimes these criticisms were made almost in one breath.[54]

The charge was also later made that the Commission had been captured by the railroads, an accusation that rested on the assumption that the only function of the Commission was to protect shippers and consumers from predation by the railroads, an assumption further supposing that shippers and consumers had no stake in the economic health of their carriers. Doubtless there were many advocates of national regulation of the railroads who hoped thereby to secure markedly lower rates on interstate consignments. Perhaps, as Charles and Mary Beard assumed, some of them thought that the 1887 Act marked the capture of a stronghold of public enemies; if so, the Beards were right that such persons deluded themselves.[55] Herbert Hovenkamp has recently observed that such critics often lacked understanding of the economics of railroads and the difficulties presented by state/federal relations, matters "far better" understood by Cooley "than many of the historians who have written about it since."[56] The circumstances precluded the possibility that "discrimination" in rates could be eliminated; inevitably remaining as victims would be those who were disfavored by whatever rates might be established. Virtually irresistible were the pressures on some roads to respond to some demands of some large shippers even though such demands were contrary to Commission policy.

Another objective of immediate concern to the Commission was safety in travel. Carnage on the roads was a national problem.[57] In 1879, Cooley in his *Torts* treatise had explained and justified such common law principles as the fellow servant rule that operated to deny compensation to industrial workers injured in the course of their employment.[58] But a decade later, and no longer writing in the restrained role of text writer, he was unwilling to rely on the benign motives of industrialists and the self-interest of workers to promote public safety. In 1889, the Commission conducted a national conference on the problem,[59] initiating an impulse that led to enactment of the Federal Safety Appliance Act of 1893,[60] requiring all railroads to maintain equipment reasonably assuring the safety of workers and passengers.

Meanwhile, in 1888, Cooley was afflicted with a severe and disabling case of pneumonia.[61] In 1889, he began to have frequent bouts with epilepsy.[62] In 1890, his wife died.[63] He was never thereafter capable of sustaining a work agenda and there were times when he was not lucid.

In 1891, at the end of his career as chairman, Cooley recommended federal legislation to provide for the compensation of injured railway workers.[64] Cooley's 1891 recommendation was adopted in the Federal Employers' Liability Act of 1906.[65]

Cooley's major contribution as chairman of the Commission had less to do with the substance of railroad regulation or the rights of passengers, shippers, and workers than with the creation of an administrative style and process that would guide future national institutions. Three features of his Commission have been emulated, or at least held out as models for emulation.

First, his Commission sought to resolve problems by mediation, avoiding wherever possible the use of the lash of its adjudicative power. It eschewed the power to make compensatory awards of damages as likely to lead to constitutional problems related to the right to trial by jury, turn the Commission into a police or small claims court, and diminish its moral influence.[66] These positions reflected Cooley's view (most vigorously advanced by Gladden) that the chief problem was one of business morality. During these years, Cooley traveled much, speaking to railroad men wherever they gathered and always adjuring them to higher standards of conduct in their performance of duties to all shippers, passengers, and shareholders. He spoke, he said, "as a clergyman might."[67] In this respect, he honored the advice of Henry Carter Adams, now on his staff at the Commission, who urged that it was a duty of the government to set the standards for industrial morality.[68] The Commission's conduct also reflected Cooley's long-standing belief that the law could modify behavior only if it in fact nurtured and drew upon the moral sources of human conduct, an idea of German ancestry and voiced by Lieber, Andrew Dickson White, and Charles Kendall Adams.

Cooley's preaching was not without effect. Even later critics have acknowledged that the Commission was at first relatively effective in securing voluntary compliance with its policies by many railroads.[69] Reliance on moral suasion has since been a keystone of much of our national law, notably in the administration of labor law by the National Labor Relations Board[70] and the Equal Employment Opportunity Commission.[71] In recent years, federal agencies, perhaps most notably the Environmental Protection Agency, have made a regular practice of overtly mediating between regulated industries and public interest groups to secure regulatory standards acceptable to both groups. That practice is descended from methods first employed by Cooley's Commission.

Second, Cooley developed the concept of a rulemaking process. His Commission was stunned by the opinion of the Supreme Court in *Chicago, Milwaukee and St. Paul Railway Co. v. Minnesota*[72] holding that state ratemaking decisions are subject to *de novo* judicial review as rulings on questions of law. This indicated that no weight would be given to the regulatory agency's decision when challenged by a railroad; each matter would be separately reconsidered anew by a court. The opinion of the Court, written by Justice Brewer, suggested that such review was required by the Due Process Clause. Cooley, contending against this reading of the Constitution, argued that Commission ratemaking decisions, like jury determinations of negligence, were too oriented to specific circumstances to admit of treatment as questions of law to be decided *de novo* by a traditional court.[73] Moreover, such intensive review conducted in diverse federal courts sitting in each federal district would severely impede the effort to maintain national consistency in the regulatory program. And it undermined the dignity of the Commission, making its proceeding a mere warm-up for the determinative proceeding to be conducted later in court.[74]

In response to the threat of intensive judicial review, Cooley proposed a procedure to protect disputants that he described as "administrative due process of law."[75] He urged that Commission decisions resulting from such a process ought, with respect to its findings of fact, to be as final as jury determinations, a recommendation that was finally adopted by Congress in the Hepburn Act of 1906.[76] This concept of administrative due process was imparted to the Federal Trade Commission when it was established in 1914[77] and was to become a keystone of the administrative process emerging in the New Deal. In this, Cooley was the forebear of James Landis,[78] an architect of New Deal government. The essential features of administrative due process are to afford affected parties notice of prospective agency action and an opportunity to be heard, basing even rulemaking action on the record of the evidence submitted, on which interested parties might comment. This concept was embodied in the Administrative Procedure Act of 1946.[79]

Third, Chairman Cooley's Commission set a standard for professional interpretation of a new law that was exceptional. Cooley's regulations and opinions were respected as models of clarity in providing guidance for regulated carriers. Judge Henry Friendly spoke of the Commission opinion in the short-haul matter:

> If Cooley had deliberately set out to write an opinion that would forever be a model for administrators, he could scarcely have done better. . . . [I]t is such an admirable illustration of what all commissions should do early in their careers, and then do again later on. . . . To get the full flavor of Judge Cooley's opinion, it ought to be read in full, as against the vacuous and weasel-worded utterances characteristic of our day. The railroad lawyer who studied it in June of 1887 must have come away feeling he had learned quite a lot; he had eaten meat, not gelatin.[80] The opinion did not settle every [Section 4] case for him, something that would have been manifestly impossible, but it told him pretty well how the land lay. Moreover, the Commission had provided the most effective possible answer to the fears, expressed in Congress, that the [Act] had endowed [the Commission with arbitrary power greater than that of] the Czar of Russia.[81]

Judge Friendly's remarks record a widely shared reaction against the disposition of federal regulators to preserve their discretion by favoring deliberate indeterminacy in making rules to which they might later be held by reviewing courts.[82] While "wide will wear, tight will tear" is a profound wisdom in drafting constitutions, it is not a doctrine to be honored in writing administrative regulations that are intended to guide business practices and that can be readily revised as their flaws are revealed by experience. Cooley therefore wrote rules that spoke directly to the most prominent issues. Alas, later commissioners in diverse agencies have not always been willing and able to follow his lead.

What Cooley had done was more than lay the groundwork for the New Deal.[83] His method was to conduct his agency according to moral conventions inhering in law, such as accessibility, comprehensibility, consistency, stability, and prospectivity. In aiming to meet these aspirational standards of law, Cooley's agency strove to obey the same "morality of law" later elegantly described by Lon Fuller.[84] Indeed, Fuller's morality was substantially derived from observing the conduct of virtuous public lawyers such as Cooley.[85]

The Commission under Cooley was conducted with substantially full knowledge of the economics of the railroad industry. But it maintained a wholesome perspective on the utility of that knowledge. Given the limits of its powers, and even the limits of government to deal with the economic complexities of the industry, it recognized that the immediate and overriding objective was not economic, but moral. Absent moral integrity in the law and especially in its processes, any objective of economic regulation, however modest, would be unattainable because effective regulation requires the voluntary cooperation of most of those to whom it is applied. No law, Cooley perceived, could go far to correct behavior if it lacked the reinforcement of moral suasion.

Scholars of the interaction of law and economics may sometimes fail to recognize that economic analysis is incomplete if it fails to take account of the moral context, that is, of the social and political culture from which any law, and thus any market, derives its being. Many involved in the "first law and economics movement," such as Newcomb and Sumner and other early social Darwinists, failed in their fatalism to undertake that disorderly and disconcerting synthesis. Some of their twentieth-century successors may have been no more sensitive than their predecessors to the interdependency of law, economics, and morals.[86]

14

Three Progressives

In 1893, Cooley was elected president of the American Bar Association. His health did not enable him to speak publicly, but he sent an address to be read to the membership at its 1894 meeting.[1] That address expressed his continuing concern for the incendiary relationship of capital to labor, still and again discomposing the Republic. In that address, he expressed his hopes for law as an alternative to economic predation, chaos, and violence, and placed responsibility on the bar for the fulfillment of those hopes. He observed that arbitration of labor disputes, then the best hope for industrial peace, could not work without the cooperation of employers, nor could any other means of resolving conflicts between capital and labor. He addressed the bar as he had spoken to railroad men, "as a clergyman might." He called on lawyers, in the performance of their professional duties, to educate their industrial clients to meet moral obligations to the public and to their workers and to secure enactment of laws reinforcing those moral duties. The profession ought, he concluded, to "endeavor to have all laws which specifically affect the interests of laborers just and right, and see that they are administered so as to secure to all whose daily labor must give them and their families the means of support, the just rewards of their labor."

Given the grim condition of the nation, it must have taken considerable will for the severely depressed Cooley to utter so hopeful a valedictory. Yet, as he spoke, a Progressive age was materializing. Class war would be averted. Government and the legal profession would play a role in securing that benign result. While they would never solve the substantive economic problem of railroad regulation, lawyers would bring a nourishing if impermanent peace to the transportation industry and to the American workplace as well. And they would achieve their results within the confining institutional framework of a constitutional republic.

In significant part, the Progressive Era was associated with the careers of three lawyers who may be regarded as Cooley's immediate moral, political, and intellectual successors: Louis Brandeis (1856–1941),[2] Ernst Freund (1864–1932),[3] and Learned Hand (1872–1961).[4] They are the subjects of the next three chapters. There is no evidence that any of the three read Cooley's valedictory address to the bar, but each pursued a career that was responsive to its challenge.

It would be incorrect to think of four such strong-minded persons as closely linked to any ideological persuasion. Each of them thought very much for himself. But their common aims make it possible to speak of them as sharing a common professional commitment to the idea of popular self-government. In this sense, if no other, all four were, as Cooley said, "conservatives."

Brandeis brought to his career moral and political values bearing the imprint of both a German-Jewish culture and the midwestern agrarian communities from which Cooley emerged. Hand, like Cooley, was a native of upstate New York and a descendant of Barnburners. Freund shared the German-Jewish heritage of Brandeis. Brandeis and Hand were acolytes of James Bradley Thayer, Cooley's contemporary, who shared many of Cooley's values and assigned his students Cooley's short text to read. Cooley and Freund consciously associated with many of the ideas voiced in antebellum times by Francis Lieber.

All four men aspired to practice the political morality expressed by Lieber in his 1837 works. In addition, all shared Jacksonian preferences for "free speech, free labor, and free schools."[5] None was much concerned about the fourth tenet advocated by Barnburners, "free trade." All were partisans of representative self-government, but not of direct democracy.[6] Their partisanship was not animated by confidence in the wisdom of the people, but by mistrust of judges or others putting themselves forward as possessors of superior moral judgment and by the sense that misgovernment by the people themselves was more readily borne and more easily corrected than misgovernment by an elite profession.

All shared the ambition to include as many citizens as possible within the emerging governing class. Each appears to have thought of himself as on the margins of that class, sharing bonds of common humanity with the outsiders. They shared a desire, not to be insiders, but rather "to dissolve the distinction."[7]

Also, as noted in chapter 1, the four shared characteristics that Anthony Kronman denoted as Aristotelian. The same moral traits were those identified by Lieber as important attributes for democratic leadership. All were admired for their capacity to separate their private self-interest or idiosyncratic morality from their acknowledged public responsibility. Excellence in the professional parlance to which they subscribed entailed the subordination of one's own personal interests, preferences, and tastes to those shared by the public. Legal texts provide an occasion for such subordinations.

While no person, however professional, can expect to achieve perfect mastery of self, "safe" judges can come close. Those who do, as Piero Calamandrei proclaimed, practice a form of restrained heroism.[8] As judges, Cooley, Brandeis, and Hand often did.

The ability of public lawyers such as Cooley, Brandeis, Freund, and Hand to separate their private selves from their public responsibilities was in part a product of their moral autonomy. They did not allow themselves to need much of what others must supply: money, sexual favors, or even public esteem. Hence, they were invulnerable to bribery or intimidation. This independence and disinterest enabled them better to reckon with reality in public affairs; their realism enabled or forced them to change their minds about public issues.

Another moral trait shared by Cooley, Brandeis, Freund, and Hand was substantial patience in attending to factual details of uncertain significance. God, it is often said, is in the details. Cooley's energetic assimilation of the intricate realities of the railroad industry made him a moral force in railroad law and politics, a status he could not have achieved had he lacked that discipline. His co-professionals shared it.

Finally, each of the four exemplars exhibited an eye for compromise and accommodation. Each accepted with maturity the reality of democratic government that no momentary majority, much less a judge, can compel others fully to accept as truth their view of reality and their moral values. In this respect, each might be denoted as a "deliberative" democrat.[9] Each moderated his Lockean regard for individual rights with an equal regard for Burkean communitarian duties of accommodation required to enable the center to hold.

15

Louis Brandeis

Louis Dembitz Brandeis was a descendant of a clan coming from Prague in 1849 who bore little resemblance to the Cooley boys who had cleared subsistence farms in Genesee County four decades earlier. They came to Madison, Indiana, as a group of twenty-six, with two grand pianos, trunks full of books, and the financial resources to build a cornstarch factory and a wholesale grocery business.[1]

The clan left Prague for a variety of reasons. The prospects for their businesses in Prague were not good, and as adherents of an unorthodox sect of Judaism in a German community in a Slavic region of the Hapsburg Empire, they were fourth-degree members of minorities within minorities.[2] Their enterprises in Madison had been planned by their scout, Adolph Brandeis. Their factory failed, but the grocery business succeeded. Adolph and Frederika Brandeis settled in the German community in Louisville. Adolph bought grain and other produce from farmers in the Ohio valley and shipped it on the rails newly laid to the East. Other members of the clan spread along the Ohio River.

The clan had been supportive of revolutionary politics in Europe, assisting democratic movements in Italy and Poland as well as Austria and participating at the margins of the attempted revolution against the Hapsburgs that was part of a general European uprising against monarchy in 1848, an event moving young Cooley in Adrian, Michigan, to poetic expression and Lieber in South Carolina to tears of exultation. In America, the Brandeis clan were antislavery Unionists, supporting first Henry Clay and then Lincoln.

Frederika Dembitz Brandeis was an exceptionally gifted member of this unusual group. She scarcely needed the resources of a college to confer on her children an extraordinary education. She was trilingual and also could read the classics in their original languages. She was competent as a musician, dancer, and dramatist. She wrote poetry. Her children were at an early age reading Schiller and Goethe and listening to her perform Mozart and

Beethoven. She forbade talk about business at dinner, but led the discussion to politics in America and Europe. Although not forgetting that she was Jewish, she did not educate her children in Judaism. She did not believe, she said, "that sins can be expiated by going to divine service." Consistent with the teachings of Finney and the midwestern revivalists, she believed "that only goodness and truth and conduct that is humane and self-sacrificing towards those who need us can bring God nearer to us."[3] So she instructed her children.

Her second son, Louis, born in 1856, was named for her brother, Lewis, a lawyer in Louisville who wrote a text on *Kentucky Jurisprudence*, read in twelve languages, translated *Uncle Tom's Cabin* into German, and was sufficiently competent as an astronomer to predict an eclipse of the sun to the minute.[4] Unlike his sister, Lewis became an orthodox Jew who described the Sabbath as "a foretaste of heaven."[5] His namesake adored him.

Louis and his older brother often rode in the wagon with their father to buy grain from farmers throughout the Ohio Valley and frequently fraternized with those from whom he bought. Louis formed an enduring affection and respect for those self-reliant folk and the institutions they erected in their "island communities," communities resembling Attica, New York and Adrian, Michigan, the towns from which Cooley had emerged a generation earlier.

In 1872, Adolph Brandeis prudently foresaw the Depression of 1873. He liquidated his business and took the family to Europe for fifteen months. Louis enrolled in the *realschule* in Dresden, where despite the school's reservations about the admission of a rustic from America, he was soon recognized as an exceptional student.[6] When the family returned to Louisville in 1875, Louis enrolled at Harvard Law School while his father and brother established first a cotton business and then a retail business in Louisville in the frustrated hope of regaining their former prosperity.[7]

Brandeis prepared himself for law school by making a close study of Kent's *Commentaries on American Law*,[8] in the edition prepared by Holmes. As a law student, he thrived on Langdell's case method, finding that it nurtured "intellectual self-reliance and the spirit of investigation."[9] But he regarded Thayer as his "best friend among the instructors."[10] It may have been Thayer who introduced him to the elite community on Beacon Hill, where he was soon warmly received. Brandeis found the Boston Unitarian culture on the Hill quite congenial to the secular Jewish values he brought from Louisville: Both placed high values on intellectual achievement and community service. He formed a fast friendship with Samuel Warren, a classmate of Brahmin standing who became his partner in a Boston law practice.

Despite his European and Jewish background, Brandeis was at the time of his graduation from law school as much a Jacksonian as Cooley had ever been. He was deeply committed to the idea of self-government, best conducted at the level of local communities. Indeed, it was long said of Brandeis, as it might have been said of Cooley, that "democracy was his religion."[11] As much as Cooley, he mistrusted remote governments, whom he believed to be predestined to subjection by monied interests.

Lacking the rusticity of Cooley, Brandeis soon attracted clients and also an offer of an appointment to the Harvard Law faculty, which he declined. He did occasional teaching at Harvard and at the Massachusetts Institute of Technology. With his partner, he wrote law review articles. One of these on tort liability for invasions of privacy by the press[12] was redolent of Cooley's earlier attention to the same subject and became an instant classic. But his law practice soon engaged all his energies.

The professional services of Brandeis were in great demand for several reasons. He was exceptionally attentive to what his clients said and he quickly assimilated the details of events and relations. He was known also for his prudent attention to practical consequences, including those to be foreseen in the not-so-immediate future. But what was most remarkable in Brandeis as a lawyer was his independence. He practiced consummate frugality in his private life, was never dependent on any client's fees, and was both willing and able to speak with an extraordinary candor that many clients valued very highly. He was no gun for hire, but gave his representation and advice only to those whose conduct he deemed acceptable. In this last respect, he resembled George Wythe, the first American law teacher, who was known to his contemporaries as Aristides, the Athenian statesman of legendary integrity, for his steadfast refusal to advocate a claim or defense he questioned on the facts.[13]

Brandeis made himself a public lawyer in 1886, the year of Harvard's recognition of Cooley, an event he likely witnessed. He was then thirty years old and in his ninth year at the bar. A transformative experience that year was his representation of a paper manufacturer disadvantaged by a Boston ordinance purporting to be a health measure. Brandeis perceived the ordinance to be corrupt favoritism for a local monopoly.[14] In that event and others, he formed a low opinion of lawyers who lobbied for legislation drafted to serve the selfish interests of clients, especially where, as was often the case, there was no adversary present to argue for the competing interests of unorganized citizens having individual stakes in the issues too small to warrant their attention. He, like Cooley, regarded the aggregation of such interests as "the public interest" that it is the responsibility of the public profession to protect. He came to regard as especially venal the work of lobbyist-lawyers who worked with the knowledge that their clients were manipulating the media and bribing legislators.[15] After 1886, he frequently shouldered his way into political affairs in which he perceived "the public interest" to be gravely underrepresented.

Just as Cooley's Jacksonian resistance to government had been eroded by the sight of the predatory practices of industrial employers, Brandeis was shaken in his anti-government convictions by the 1892 attack by Pinkerton strikebreakers on Andrew Carnegie's steelworkers, who were striking against a wage cut.[16] Again like Cooley, Brandeis formed the view that the issue was, in the main, a moral one. He spent much of the remainder of his career as a lawyer providing precisely the service to which Cooley in 1894 had summoned the bar. And in 1905, he made a speech at Harvard that, without mentioning Cooley, was an echo of Cooley's presidential address.[17] He came, like Cooley, to talk to lawyers, judges, and even business clients, "as a preacher might."

Brandeis regularly advised clients to practice, and indeed he insisted that they practice, what he denoted as "industrial democracy," encouraging rather than fighting unionization. He affirmed that "the sense of unrestricted power is just as demoralizing for the employer, as it is for the employee. Neither our intelligence or our characters can long stand the strain of unrestricted power."[18] He became an advocate of the cooperative movement appearing in England and Scandinavia in the early years of the century; that movement favored control of enterprises by workers and consumers.[19] On his advice, some of his clients experimented with variations on these ideas; notable among them was Filene Brothers, the largest mercantile establishment in Boston.[20]

Like Cooley, Brandeis, although generally realistic, was occasionally susceptible to irrational optimism about the possibilities of self-government. It seems to have been his admiration for midwestern farmers and his passion for their communitarian values that led him to be an ardent admirer of the Jewish *kibbutzim* being established in Palestine. Despite his disconnection from Judaism, he was among the first American Zionists.[21]

Brandeis also greatly admired Periclean Athens as an example of the possibilities of self-government.[22] He perceived that the revolutionary generation of Americans shared that admiration, linking as it did freedom with duty to community; thus, he was to hold that political discussion is not merely a right, but a duty,[23] a notion earlier expressed by Lieber. In the Brandeis view, a major object of public policy should be the attainment of leisure for self-development and self-expression by every citizen. Thus, as Dan Farber observed:

> Brandeisian citizens have the "right to be let alone," not so they can pursue lives of private fulfillment, but so they can develop their abilities and imaginations to be applied creatively to the needs of those around them, free from the deadening weight of government or group pressure.[24]

In the hope that it would supply greater opportunities for private fulfillment, Brandeis favored "scientific management" as advocated by efficiency engineers in the early years of the century.[25] Brandeis was attracted to the aim of providing stable employment with regular hours for workers. He also supposed, perhaps correctly, that greater efficiency in the use of labor would raise wages. In these respects, scientific management promised workers greater control over their own lives and hence more opportunity to serve family and community. He was not, however, successful in his efforts to persuade labor unions that they should support scientific management.

In 1898, Brandeis undertook an examination of the Massachusetts liquor lobby. When he confirmed that liquor interests were bribing legislators, he concluded that the bribery was largely defensive, being the result of unreasonable legislative restrictions imposed with the expectation that bribes would be paid to secure non-enforcement. He then undertook for a modest fee to represent the liquor interests to secure the repeal of that legislation, on condition that they cease spending money to influence public officials. He succeeded in the immediate purpose.[26] Whether this put a permanent end to the industry's efforts to bring illicit pressures to bear on legislators is unknown.

Brandeis went on from this triumph to others. His business clients had a stake in his struggle to secure lower fares for public transportation. He succeeded in persuading the city to authorize competing enterprises, arguing against regulated monopoly.[27] "The objections to despotism and monopoly are fundamental in human nature," he affirmed; "they rest upon the innate and ineradicable selfishness of man." This sort of activity attracted favorable notice among many of his co-citizens, but not among his former friends on Beacon Hill.

Other clients sought Brandeis's counsel in an insurance scandal;[28] he undertook an investigation without fee, drafted legislation to correct the problem, and secured its enactment. An enduring feature of his insurance law was the authorization of savings banks to sell life insurance as a means of diminishing the oligopolistic power of the large insurers.

In 1907, Brandeis encountered J. P. Morgan's New Haven Railroad.[29] He was retained by the Boston and Maine Railroad to resist the acquisition of its stock by the New Haven, an acquisition forbidden by Massachusetts law. He took the case, but concluded that it was a matter of "great public interest" and that he should therefore refuse a fee. He actually paid his firm for his own services, to assure that his partners were not deprived of income because of his refusal to take a fee. While this won the support of his partners, his efforts were not appreciated by all the Boston Brahmin, many of whom held New Haven stock or shared the social Darwinist views expressed by Herbert Spencer. This struggle against the New Haven continued for a period of seven years and in both state and federal courts, the Massachusetts legislature, the Interstate Commerce Commission, and the United States Department of Justice. In August 1914, the New Haven yielded and at last made the divestiture, thus vindicating Brandeis's prolonged efforts.

Among the objectives of Brandeis as a public interest lobbyist were humane labor laws, a cause in which his primary ally was Ernst Freund.[30] They worked together for minimum wage and maximum hour laws, although Brandeis was skeptical about the effectiveness of such regulations: He thought them a poor substitute for unionization, industrial democracy, and scientific management. Freund and Brandeis also lobbied for the enactment of industrial accident compensation laws such as Cooley had begun to advocate in 1891 while serving on the Interstate Commerce Commission.

In 1908, Brandeis accepted Florence Kelley's invitation to defend Oregon's law mandating a ten-hour work day for women.[31] His brief in that case, typical of his professional work, seemed to overwhelm the Court with social data gathered by Kelley to justify the Oregon policy as a reasonable one. The legal points in the brief were simple and succinctly stated. It assumed that the members of the Court ought be concerned with the practical consequences of their decisions; to those who viewed law in antiseptic Langdellian terms, this was a disturbing assumption, but it proved to be correct.

In these matters of labor law reform, Brandeis worked with state legislatures, not Congress. He regarded Congress as too remote from citizens to be suitably responsive. He was all his life an advocate of social experiments at the state and local levels; one of his most cited judicial opinions was an outcry for the power and responsibility of states to experiment with different resolutions of common problems to see what works best.[32] This was straight Cooley, much as Cooley (on this issue) had been straight Lieber. Yet Brandeis opposed much of the Progressive program for political reform, such as primaries and referenda, because he favored representative democracy over direct democracy, which he presciently feared as an empowerment of propogandists.[33]

Brandeis was convinced that the social ills accompanying industrialization were primarily the result of the excessive economic power amassed by such, to him, evil enterprises as United States Steel. He held the view that political freedom depended on the economic independence of farmers, merchants, and artisans.[34] Great accumulations of economic power would, over time, assure great accumulations of political power as well. He therefore fully shared the sentiment expressed in the Democratic platform of 1912, denouncing "the privilege-hunting and favor-seeking class."[35]

When Governor Woodrow Wilson won the Democratic nomination for president, Brandeis wrote to congratulate him. Wilson invited him to consult over lunch. The lunch was extended to three hours, and Brandeis emerged from it as the architect of Wilson's program, to be known as "The New Freedom." He persuaded Wilson that the aim of the Roosevelt Progressives to regulate those with great economic power was insufficient and even dangerous.[36] The regulators, he foretold, would become themselves oversized and would then be captured by those whom they were called to regulate—again straight Cooley as Cooley had been straight Jackson. What was needed was a program to so fragment economic power that all were brought down to what Brandeis, as the social and economic architect, deemed a suitable human scale, that is, that small amount of power that humans might be organically capable of exercising with prudence and humanity.

With this aim in mind, Brandeis advocated two reforms that were in due course effected by the Wilson administration. The first of these was the strengthening of the antitrust laws, the exemption of labor unions from their application, and the creation of the Federal Trade Commission to participate in its enforcement to break up oversized enterprises. The second was the establishment of the Federal Reserve Bank, whose aim was to break up what Brandeis saw as a money trust. Brandeis did not measure the importance of these enactments by their economic consequences; while he was not indifferent to consumer prices, his purposes were primarily moral rather than economic, and the moral issue was the measure of economic power some citizens would be permitted to amass and deploy to disempower others.

In 1913, while the New Haven controversy was still brewing, Brandeis was called to a role similar to that performed by Cooley in his role as chair of the Interstate Commerce Commission. He was retained by the Commission to advise it regarding a joint petition of fifty-two railroads for rate increases.[37] The railroads, knowing of the New Haven matter, feared Brandeis and reviled him in the press as a persecutor of honest business. Extended hearings were conducted. Brandeis reported that the railroads were, indeed, receiving too modest a return on their investments, but he recommended against a horizontal increase in rates such as those proposed and urged that the discount in the rates charged to big shippers be reduced or eliminated.

All this independence of thought and behavior was not, as Cooley's experience confirmed, a favored path to a Supreme Court appointment. Nevertheless, in January 1916, President Wilson nominated Brandeis to fill a vacancy on the Supreme Court of the United States. Wall Street was said to groan "like the echo of a national disaster."[38] The confirmation proceedings in the Senate were as bitterly contested as any in the history of the Republic. Six former presidents of the American Bar Association voiced objections to the nomination. One of the ABA presidents, Joseph Choate—a true Langdellian—centered his argument on the impropriety of the "Brandeis brief," which he condemned as an invitation to the Court to rest its constitutional decisions on concerns of policy rather than pure law.[39]

Walter Lippman explained the Beacon Hill opposition by describing Brandeis as "a rebellious and troublesome member of the most homogeneous, self-centered, and self-complacent community in the United States."[40] The ABA presidents were widely perceived to be mere grudge bearers. The complaint about the Brandeis brief brought forth a warm endorsement of Brandeis by Roscoe Pound, soon to be appointed dean of the Harvard Law School.[41] Brandeis was also supported by ten other members of the Harvard Law faculty, leaving only one in opposition.

As a justice, Brandeis did not disappoint those who expected him to sustain the authority of state legislatures to resist economic power. As a justice, he would also be identified with other causes. But he did not forsake the habits of mind and character that he exhibited as a lawyer. He remained a bear for facts. It was this quality that made him a powerful force on the Court, because lawyers or colleagues who skimped on their knowledge of matters in dispute were certain to be challenged. Charles Evans Hughes described him as "master of both microscope and telescope."[42] George Sutherland, while acknowledging that he detested Brandeis's ideas, proclaimed him "one of the greatest technical lawyers I have ever known."[43] Brandeis strove unsuccessfully to interest Holmes in facts and in data, and it may have been Holmes who said, "Brandeis weighs a ton."[44]

Like Cooley, but unlike Holmes, Brandeis retained little interest in abstract theory. He deemed broad principles to be the enemy of sound practical judgment. He once expressed to his protégé, Felix Frankfurter, concern that college students were studying philosophy, and thought perhaps that the people needed to be cautioned that this was a dangerous practice. "Philosophy, he warned, "is rather the cyclone cellar for finer souls. As it was in the declining days of Greece, and as the monastery was in the so-called Dark Ages."[45]

Brandeis was faithfully attentive to both sides of any conflict into which he was drawn, as a lawyer or judge. In this respect, he manifested what Holmes denoted an "exquisite moral susceptibility."[46] Given the moral precepts embodied in his law practice and in his politics, Brandeis was of course a champion of judicial self-restraint. It was the duty of judicial self-restraint that caused him to lead the Court in 1938 in overruling Justice Story's 1842 decision authorizing federal courts to apply their own interpretations of the common law in deciding issues arising in diversity litigation.[47] He reasoned that Story's position was an arrogation by federal courts of power properly residing in state courts, rendering unconstitutional the legislation it purported to interpret. For similar reasons, he dissented from the promulgation of the Federal Rules of Civil Procedure.[48]

Among his most cited opinions was that in *Ashwander v. Tennessee Valley Authority*,[49] in which he enumerated the many situations in which the federal courts were obliged to refrain from the exercise of their power to decide interesting and important constitutional questions. That opinion was in significant respects an echo of an 1893 essay by his mentor, James Bradley Thayer,[50] and of Cooley's *Constitutional Limitations*. Brandeis had in fact reiterated Cooley's advocacy of judicial restraint in 1892, the year before Thayer's famed lecture in Chicago.[51] But *Ashwander* was also characteristic of Brandeis's insistence on imposing upon himself restraints he deemed appropriate for others. It has been depicted as "the crowning statement of one of the major themes" of his judicial career: The Court "must take the utmost pains to avoid precipitate decision of constitutional issues."[52]

In recognition of the universality of human vanity, Brandeis opposed the construction of the Supreme Court building. He thought it too grand a structure and likely to cause the members of the Court to gain an oversized estimate of their own importance. He referred to it as the Temple of Karnak and refused to occupy the grand chambers provided for him, but continued to work out of his apartment.[53]

While a justice, Brandeis retained a lively interest in the issues that had attracted his notice as a lawyer and developed some new ones.[54] He valued many and diverse friendships. He and his wife regularly held "at-homes," events notable for the richness of the conversation and the poverty of the cuisine. The diversity of his friendships is suggested by the fact that one person frequently present on those occasions was a rustic, self-educated young senator from Missouri to whom Brandeis was attracted: Harry Truman. When the bright young men from Harvard and Yale arrived in 1933 as part of the New Deal promising to put an end to the Depression and transform American society, Brandeis told them to go home and help their communities in their hour of need instead of posturing about the "foreign aid" they were going to send them from remote Washington. Lieber and Cooley would likely have joined in that advice.

However they likely would not have approved of one aspect of Brandeis's career: As his years on the Court passed, he became increasingly unable to stifle his interest in politics.[55] He confided more than he should have in his protégé, Frankfurter, and financed some of Frankfurter's forays into public affairs. While this subsidy was not large, it was at best a strange connection. And through other friends in addition to Frankfurter, he gave sometimes insistent advice to other public figures in Washington. No one has suggested that in these matters Brandeis was animated by anything other than passionate concern for what he perceived to be the public interest. But it was a role that he himself had disowned in his early years on the Court as one not appropriate for a justice.

16

Ernst Freund

In 1890, a new University of Chicago was established to replace a failed predecessor; it commenced operation with a large gift from John D. Rockefeller.[1] William Rainey Harper, a theologian,[2] was its president and the person who had won the support of Rockefeller.[3] Harper was soon desirous of establishing a law school, and was therefore required to face the issues raised in the Hemenway Gymnasium that memorable evening in 1886.

One of Harper's advisors urged that the object should be to train students "to become leaders of the bar and ornaments of the bench, inspiring teachers, scientific writers and wise reformers, rather than to produce the greatest possible output of eager youths, quick to pick up the professional technicalities and careless of aught beyond professional emolument."[4] The curriculum envisioned by this advisor gave emphasis to public law and comparative law. Reckoning that a program in comparative law would encounter difficulty in attracting students, Harper for a time contemplated an institution chiefly devoted to legal research. With that in mind, he consulted a junior colleague, Ernst Freund.

Freund had been born in New York City, but was raised in Berlin. He held a doctorate from Heidelberg when he returned to New York in 1885. There, he studied law and politics with Frank Goodnow, a former student and successor to Lieber at Columbia. He completed his Columbia doctorate while serving as a founding member of Chicago's Political Science Department.[5] Freund had brought to Chicago many of Lieber's ideas. One of these, which Lieber had employed as a founder of the Columbia Law School in 1858, was that the academic and scholarly enterprise in law should be firmly rooted in the work of the practicing profession.[6] Freund shared that view with Harper. He later recalled that

> [t]here was quite a demand at the time that the school should not be "merely professional" but should set itself up as a school of jurisprudence; but those who made the issue were not entirely clear as to its implications. President

Harper wisely concluded that the vital thing was the establishment of the highest professional standards, leaving the question of jurisprudence in abeyance.[7]

Thus, on Freund's advice, Harper asked Dean Ames of the Harvard Law School, quoting words addressed to the apostle Paul, to "[c]ome over into Macedonia and help us."[8] Joseph Beale, a reliable Langdellian, was dispatched to Chicago as acting dean, on condition that Chicago promise to pursue Harvard's ideals and exclude politically sensitive persons such as Freund from the new school. Despite Ames's deep mistrust of Freund, Freund seems to have won Beale over. Contrary to the condition imposed by Ames, he was a founding member of the faculty and was soon its intellectual centerpiece. Among the others recruited was Floyd Mechem, a former student of Cooley's at Michigan and then perhaps the most widely published[9] member of the Michigan Law faculty. The Mechem appointment troubled Ames because Mechem had pioneered in empirical work and had admitted that he was not ideologically committed to the case method. He had, however, edited a casebook and written several treatises. One of Mechem's works was an innovative work, *The Law of Public Offices and Officers*.[10] It was devoted in part to searching the limits of the doctrine of sovereign immunity, a doctrine that Freund had questioned in an article published in 1893 in the then-new *Political Science Quarterly*[11] and that Cooley had questioned in 1875.[12]

That there were from the outset members of the Chicago faculty inclined to favor judicial jurisdiction to treat the misdeeds of governments and officers as occasions for the imposition of tort liability invites contrast to their counterpart at Harvard, Bruce Wyman.[13] Wyman began teaching at Harvard in 1900 and initiated a course in administrative law in 1902. His teaching was conducted without reference to Frank Goodnow's epic work, *Comparative Administrative Law;* he presented the doctrine of sovereign immunity as the overriding principle of Anglo-American administrative law and in his writing opposed virtually all forms of judicial oversight of administrative discretion.[14] This position fit neatly into the Langdell vision of law as separate from politics. Wyman was succeeded at Harvard by Felix Frankfurter and James Landis, both of whom joined him in advocacy of greater discretion and freedom from judicial oversight for administrative agencies.[15]

In 1903, Freund began teaching administrative law to second-year law students. He was agreeable to the use of the case method, but was something less than a master of that form of instruction. Some of his students dismissed him as a mere "continental or civil lawyer"[16] because his discussions were prone to focus on broader theories and principles than the conventional law school case discussion of the time. Yet, one knowledgeable student also attributed to Freund the professional lawyer's "natural revul-

sion against the nebulous speculation that often passes as legal philosophy."[17] And Freund was himself to question "Is jurisprudence something
better than law? Is scientific different from professional law?"[18] There was
no mistaking that Freund was a lawyer and, like Cooley, deeply concerned
with the condition of the institutions of democratic government.

In 1904, as we have seen, Freund published *The Police Power, Public
Policy and Constitutional Rights*, a work in many ways redolent of Cooley's *Constitutional Limitations*. But he did not limit his professional commitment to scholarship and teaching. As one of his students was later to
say:

> To him the mastery of legal principles was an incomplete accomplishment un-
> til dedicated to the progress of society. . . . While many good men sit at home
> not knowing that there is anything to be done, not caring to know, cultivating
> the feeling that politics are dirty and that government is ruled by vulgar politi-
> cians, Ernst Freund remembered that if the government is not to be mastered
> by ignorance, it must be served by intelligence.[19]

In 1905, Freund served as draftsman for the Illinois legislation obligating
employers to compensate workers for job-related injuries.[20] The next year,
he joined Louis Brandeis of Boston in founding the American Association
for Labor Legislation, a group committed to preparing and securing the enactment of laws protective of workers. In 1908, he was elected president of
that organization, a position he retained for many years.[21] In 1906, he
served as draftsman to rewrite the Chicago City Charter, working with the
reform government of Walter Fisher.[22] In the course of this work, he became an advocate of a constitutional right to municipal Home Rule, a favorite idea of Lieber and Cooley. In 1920, Freund represented the city of
Chicago in the state constitutional convention and drafted the provisions
bearing on municipal government.[23] His interest in municipal government
was later reflected in yet another prescient work questioning the use of
newly invented zoning boards to advance the interests of more prosperous
citizens at the expense of those less fortunate, [24] a position redolent of the
warnings of William Leggett and of President Jackson. In 1908, Freund was
a co-founder of the Immigrant Protection League, another organization
that he was to lead. In that work, he lobbied against laws requiring the reg-
istration of aliens and their deportation without judicial process. He later,
in 1921, took a particular interest in the rights of immigrant women.[25]

Also in 1908, Freund was appointed by the governor to represent Illinois
on the National Conference of Commissioners on Uniform State Laws. He
was a commissioner for twenty-four years, served as president of the conference in 1920, and drafted numerous statutes proposed for enactment by
state legislatures.[26] In that role, he took a special interest in laws protecting
the interests of illegitimate children and in the enforcement of obligations

for child support. His work in this field and in the field of immigration was animated by his association with Jane Addams and he served as champion within the university for the establishment of the school to train professional social workers who would emulate her pioneering work. Addams was later to say of him, that "He never once failed to be sensitive to injustice and preventable suffering."[27]

In 1919, Freund supported his fellow Chicagoan, Eugene Debs, when he was convicted for utterances in opposition to the war effort. When Debs's conviction was affirmed by a narrow vote in the Supreme Court, Freund was so critical of the Court's opinion[28] that its author, Holmes, acknowledged that the criticism had "cast gloom over his life."[29] In the same year, Freund rose to the support of victims of Attorney General Palmer's "Red Raids" against persons identified as "dangerous aliens" and was appointed to a "Committee of 12" who investigated the attorney general and found his actions unjustified.[30] In 1921, Freund supported efforts to provide a defense of the two immigrants, Sacco and Vanzetti, who were convicted and executed in Massachusetts for politically motivated murders.

All of these public involvements informed Freund's research and teaching. In 1917, he published *Standards of American Legislation: An Estimate of Restrictive and Constructive Factors*. In 1928, he published *Administrative Powers over Persons and Property: A Comparative Survey*, and in 1932, *Legislative Regulation: A Study of the Ways and Means of Written Law*. These three volumes, together with a number of short articles generally subsumed in the longer works, constitute a major contribution to the intellectual development of American public law. In its cultural relativism and practical sense, Freund's work strongly resembled that of Lieber and Cooley.

With respect to legislation, Freund's work reflected his Progressive political views, but was much more than a lawyer's brief in support of Progressive legislation. Although acknowledging that the constitutional scheme of separation of powers muddled responsibility for clarity in the writing of legal texts, Freund sought to devise means to assure a higher level of professional competence in drafting statutes. He elaborated principles for the guidance of professional draftsmen.[31] He argued for the use of social science as a predicate to enactment, insisting that regulatory legislation should come at the end of an analytical process.[32] Frequently he reiterated the law of unintended consequences, decreeing that any legal text, however carefully expressed, can and probably will affect the behavior of citizens in its secondary and tertiary consequences in ways that were never intended by the draftsman. Freund argued for legislative reference services, such as that being developed at the University of Wisconsin, and for legislative procedures that assured competing interests an opportunity to be heard on pending matters.

To the dismay of Langdellians, Freund argued that legislation was preferable to case law in its potential for thoughtful treatment of social and political issues. He affirmed that:

> Most of the common law has developed in that atmosphere of indifferent neutrality [to social consequences] which has enabled courts to be impartial, but also keeps them out of touch with vital needs. When interests are litigated in particular cases, they not only appear as isolated and scattered interests, but their social incidence is obscured by the adventitious personal factors which color every controversy. If policy means the conscious favoring of social above particular interests, the common law must be charged with having too little policy.[33]

Sounding not unlike Thucydides or Cicero, Freund decried "the common law attitude toward legislation, looking upon it as an inferior product of the non-legal mind to be tolerated and minimized in its effects."[34] Yet Freund urged the need for judicial responsibility and deliberation in interpretation "to balance legislative inadvertence."[35] He was rightly skeptical of judicial efforts to detect legislative intent from records of legislative deliberations, observing that such intent is, in reality, a fiction.

Following Lieber,[36] Freund urged the perpetual need to seek prudent compromise in legislative responses to social problems: "The choice between the second best and nothing at all is the normal situation."[37] He broadly opposed legislation bearing on moral conduct occurring in private, because he viewed such laws as impractical, ineffective, and a waste of legislative influence. He argued for what he described as the sound principles of legislation, principles seeming to be more than faintly Aristotelian:

> the non-partisan policy of justice in legislation, the observance of the limits of the attainable, the due proportion of means to ends, and moderation in the exercise of powers which by long experience has been shown to be wise and prudent, though it may be temporarily inconvenient or disappointing in the production of immediate results.[38]

In his work on administrative law, Freund was preoccupied with the problem of administrative discretion to which Cooley had given so much attention as chairman of the Interstate Commerce Commission. Freund's deep concern for individual rights, which for him included the right to own and enjoy property, led him to a Barnburner's mistrust of officials and to concern for "the shady and corrupt aspects of government."[39] He favored legislative prescriptions that limited the prerogatives of administrators as narrowly as possible within the limits of the legislature's wisdom to foresee the application of its texts to individual matters. He argued that administrators exercising power over individual rights are obliged to be consistent and to develop standards guiding future dispositions, much as courts evolve standards through the evolution of common law and much as Cooley had done at his Commission.

Freund contended that courts should review administrative decisions not merely to assure that the officer was exercising a power authorized by legislation, but also to assure that the decisions reflected not only the policy embodied in enabling legislation, but also its elaboration through administrative rules and decisions. He argued for closer review of administrative determinations on which the exercise of agencies' jurisdiction is based, providing the theory of review of jurisdictional facts that was expressed by the Supreme Court of the United States in 1932 in *Crowell v. Benson.*[40]

In his concern for administrative discretion and standards, Freund's thinking was dissonant with the practices of many American courts, which were then generally reluctant to review administrative decisions except on the narrowest of grounds.[41] Particularly in an age that celebrated technical competence above almost all else, courts were generally deferential to the supposed expertise of executive officers and reluctant to engage in the openly political process of evaluating the substance of administrative decisions, even where individual rights were at stake. This tendency of the courts was approved by Wyman, Frankfurter, and Landis. Their view would flourish during the era of the New Deal, only to have its weaknesses fully revealed. Freund's views would prevail by mid-century,[42] embodied in part in the Administrative Procedure Act of 1946.[43] In 1954, Frankfurter acknowledged that Freund had been the "voice crying in the wilderness" and proclaimed him to be one of the greatest of American law teachers.[44]

17

Learned Hand

The career of Learned Hand is more difficult to assess in the terms of this account than are those of Cooley, Brandeis, or Freund. Like Cooley, Hand was from upstate New York and a descendant of Barnburners. His father was, however, an Albany lawyer who could send him to Harvard.[1] After graduating from Harvard College and Harvard Law School, Hand practiced law for some years in Albany and in New York City.

In his law practice, Hand exhibited several personal characteristics shared with Cooley. Both as young men were lacking in social grace and slow to attract private clients and both were bookworms; both, however, overcame their natural reticence to win national audiences for their speeches.[2] For neither was law practice so demanding that he lacked time for politics or publishing his views. In 1908, Hand published an attack on *Lochner* rooted in the cautious position on judicial review earlier expressed by his mentor, Thayer, and by Cooley in *Constitutional Limitations*,[3] but also reflecting the Progressive politics of his time.[4] A few months later, he was appointed by President Taft to the United States District Court.[5] He was for a half-century thereafter a member of the federal judiciary; his political activities were accordingly subdued.

True to his Barnburner origin, Hand shared Cooley's distaste for arrogance in all its forms. In one of his final public utterances, he memorably decried rule by "Platonic Guardians," "even if I knew how to choose them."[6] On the other hand, he was not himself innocent of class bias; even when defending Jeffersonian ideals, he conceded that "[i]t is intolerable to feel that we are each in the power of the conglomerate conscience of a mass of Babbitts, whose intelligence we do not respect, and whose standards we may detest."[7] Moreover, perhaps as a consequence of many years tenured for life in high office, he was less courteous to fellow lawyers and judges than was Cooley and may at times have manifested a little arrogance of his own. Even colleagues as accomplished as Henry Wade Rogers[8] and Charles Clark[9] were the sometime objects of his ridicule.

But despite this shortcoming, sometimes counterbalanced by a capacity for self-ridicule, Hand was quick to detect pretense in others, and he aligned himself with those who were the object of unwarranted scorn. As were Cooley, Brandeis, and Freund, Hand was impulsively protective of the station of outsiders of all kinds. He reviled racism in the form best known to him, which was anti-Semitism,[10] and was like the others a staunch advocate of the rights of immigrants.[11] On the other hand, he, like Cooley, was slow to believe that a criminal prosecution was unfounded; comparable to Cooley's assumption that the persons accused in the Haymarket bombing were guilty was Hand's inclination to accept the guilt of Sacco and Vanzetti, despite their vigorous defense by Freund and Felix Frankfurter.[12]

Hand and Cooley were also alike in their tendency to political migration. Where Cooley changed from Jacksonian Democrat to Free Soil to Lincoln Republican to Mugwump Democrat, Hand changed from Jacksonian Democrat to Roosevelt Republican to Bull Moose Progressive to New Deal Democrat.[13] What this reflected in each instance was an exceptional measure of independence. Each did his own thinking and neither flinched at the consequences to his career of disowning political alliances in favor of what he perceived to be the public interest, that is, the health of democratic institutions and the protection of the aggregated interests of those who were doing the Republic's work and raising the Republic's children. Hand identified himself as a "conservative among liberals and a liberal among conservatives,"[14] an identification that Brandeis, Cooley, and Freund would willingly have shared. Hand paid the same price as Cooley for his independence: Both were denied appointment to the Supreme Court of the United States despite general recognition in the profession of their eminent qualifications for that office.[15] Indeed Hand, like Cooley, long presided over a United States Court of Appeals regarded by many in the profession as superior to the Supreme Court of the United States in its professional craftsmanship and moral judgment.[16] Like Cooley and Freund, he was occasionally prescient, anticipating legal developments occurring a generation or more later.[17]

Hand, apparently more than Brandeis or Freund, idolized Holmes. He attributed to Holmes a dedication to his work that Holmes did not lack, but which Hand possessed in even greater measure. He denoted Holmes as "the president of a Society of Jobbists" idealizing the job well done.[18] On the occasion of that remark, he spoke of his own guild:

> It is an honest craft, which gives good measure for its wages, and undertakes only those jobs which the members can do in proper workmanlike fashion, which of course means no more than that they must like them. [It] demands right quality, better than the market will pass.[19]

As that remark suggests, Hand in his later years disowned, with the elder Holmes, the ambition manifest in his early professional career, consciously to serve the public,[20] an instinct that his Barnburner culture may have taught him as one likely to lead some people to meddle in other people's affairs. However, if one were to judge Hand by deeds, not words, his standard of "workmanlike fashion" entailed earnest evaluation of the public's stake in matters he was called upon to decide. His words on this theme therefore seem best taken as a caution against the excesses of do-goodism. They assuredly were not a disavowal of the political content of the law he was called upon to interpret and enforce. In one of his most elegant and widely quoted utterances, he declared:

[E]verything turns upon the spirit in which [the judge] approaches the questions before him. The words he must construe are empty vessels into which he can pour nearly anything he will. Men do not gather figs of thistles, nor supply institutions from judges whose outlook is limited by parish or class. They must be aware that there are before them more than verbal problems; more than final solutions cast in generalizations of universal applicability. They must be aware of the changing social tensions in every society which makes it an organism; which demands new schemata of adaptation; which will disrupt it, if rigidly confined. . . . All I want to emphasize is the political aspect of the matter, of the opportunity to preserve that spirit of liberty without which life is insupportable.[21]

This is Lieber.

Hand's opinions and speeches rate highly as legal literature. Thus, he made Cooley's point at Harvard more elegantly than had Cooley; "The profession," he said, "must satisfy its community by becoming itself satisfied with the community. It must assimilate society before society will assimilate it; it must become organic to remain a living organism."[22] These were not words to counsel reaction; they were advice to the bar on the true source of its opportunity to influence humane reform.

Hand often exhibited a sufficient measure of rhetorical elegance to be so quotable and citable that Judge Posner ranked him a "great judge."[23] But, like Cooley and Brandeis, he seems not to have allowed himself to think in such terms. He perceived that respect for the institutions of self-government required judicial modesty. Ever alert to just the right metaphor, he put it best:

We are workers in the hive; we shall not be missed, nor shall we be able to point at the end to any perceptible contribution. But the hive goes on, an entity, a living thing, a form, a reality. So far as we cannot severally sink our fate in its fate, we shall not have our reward.[24]

Hand did not fully share the preference expressed by Lieber, Cooley, Brandeis, and Freund for local politics allowing more room for participatory democracy and experimentation. In his nationalism he followed the thinking of his teacher James Bradley Thayer,[25] the politics of Theodore Roosevelt,[26] and the social theory of Herbert Croly. This element of the Progressive ideology was driven by the recognition that state and local governments were impotent to regulate the employment and trade practices of firms operating in a national economy because effective local regulation led to a flight of capital and employment. Cooley, Brandeis, and Freund understood the centralizing pressures, but found them an additional reason to preserve localism whenever practicable.

Late twentieth-century observers are likely to be shocked by the knowledge that Hand, while sitting on the federal bench, in 1913 stood for election to the New York Court of Appeals.[27] This action may be evidence that he was not wholly out of sympathy with the Jacksonian principle that judges should be accountable to the people. On the other hand, he strove vigorously but unsuccessfully in 1912 to dissuade Theodore Roosevelt from his campaign for a constitutional provision favoring the recall of judicial decisions, a kind of appeal from the Supreme Court to popular referendum.[28] Hand's concern was the conventional one for the independence of the judiciary; he urged that on that account, it would be better to repeal constitutional provisions than to subject them to so degrading a process of enforcement. Nevertheless, he acknowledged that the judicial decisions evoking Roosevelt's response were grievous abuses of the judicial office. And, despite his difference with Roosevelt on this issue, his 1913 campaign for judicial office was conducted in an effort to support and sustain the Progressive Party led by Roosevelt.

In the mid-1920s, Hand's deference to democratic politics was dividing him from friends and former political allies.[29] A pivotal event was the holding of the Supreme Court that a Nebraska law forbidding elementary school instruction in German was invalid.[30] Hand was disappointed that Progressives who had joined him in denouncing the misuse of the Fourteenth Amendment now rejoiced at its use in a cause they favored. His alienation increased when his friends became active in attacking Tennessee legislation forbidding the teaching of biological Darwinism in public schools.[31] Walter Lippman, a close ally, denounced Tennessee as "these millions of semiliterate priestridden and parsonridden people" and favored application of the Fourteenth Amendment to compel them to embrace Lippman's preference for the teaching of respected science.[32] Hand rejected that view and the result was a permanent rupture in their relationship.[33] Hand, we can be sure, did not disfavor the reading of the German language or favor the rejection of Darwinist science, but thought these follies to be within the right of the people of Nebraska or Tennessee to commit.

In 1937, Hand opposed Franklin Roosevelt on his plan for court-packing.[34] Again, he was severely critical of the Court's decisions that had evoked the court-packing response, but he valued the political independence of the Court more highly than the New Deal program threatened by the Court's actions.

These experiences may have led Hand to take an extreme position on the need for restraint by judges holding office for life who are tempted to do good by imposing their personal wills on the laws they are commissioned to enforce. He came increasingly to share the anxiety expressed by Holmes that the federal judiciary was out of control in administering the Fourteenth Amendment, to a degree inviting such schemes as those favored by the two Presidents Roosevelt to bring the judiciary to heel. Going beyond Cooley, his mentor Thayer, or Brandeis, Hand, in his eighty-seventh year, virtually proposed the repeal of that amendment on the ground that it was an invitation to judicial mischief threatening the institutions of the Republic.[35] Alexander Bickel characterized his position as "radical," as indeed it was.[36]

Hand's caution was reflected in the increasingly moderate positions he took with respect to the First Amendment. When he ascended the bench, the First Amendment was given modest application, even to federal legislation,[37] but Hand courageously applied it to protect the access of a radical magazine to the United States mail.[38] Yet, decades later, when the First Amendment had evolved into a much more robust doctrine, he wrote an opinion that was regarded as reducing its scope.[39] Even in that sphere, he advocated caution; the primary protection of speech, in his view, ought be the judgment and tolerance of the people expressed through democratic legislation.[40] His advocacy of judicial caution seems to have become increasingly intense as he aged.[41] In some measure, his preference for democratic political solutions was intensified by the repugnant totalitarian regimes appearing in Russia, Italy, and Germany.

In 1958, in his eighty-sixth year, his position on judicial review led him to be critical of an icon, the Court's opinion in *Brown v. Board of Education*.[42] It was unfortunate that Hand at such an age expressed so radical a view about such a matter. His criticism of *Brown* was destined to create a firestorm.[43] The only support he received was from those generally favoring school segregation, an institution for which he had no regard whatever. His views were widely dismissed as reactionary. Even in hindsight, they seem on the surface to be so, especially recalling that Cooley had desegregated the Detroit schools ninety years earlier. At the very least, Hand's utterance was ill-timed.

There was, however, more to Hand's position than may be apparent. Although no less eminent a scholar than Cass Sunstein has declared "unacceptable" any constitutional interpretation questioning *Brown*,[44] it may now be possible to deliberate dispassionately about what the Court could have done other than what it did had Hand been making the decision. To fully evaluate the issue raised by Hand, it would be necessary to reconstruct the situation antecedent to *Brown*, a task far beyond the reach of this study, if indeed it could be done.

But it is possible to imagine a different sequence of events that would sustain Hand's criticism of *Brown* as a mistimed use of judicial power. The framework for such speculation is provided by conventional Jacksonian politics favoring equal rights and equal duties to participate in state and local government. Such rights and duties could have been prescribed and enforced by the most cautious of life-tenured judges without offense to the institutions of self-government, because they were, as Cooley had emphasized, clearly expressed in the Fifteenth Amendment.

The decision to challenge Jim Crow laws first in the field of public education was not made by the Court, but by the leadership of the National Association for the Advancement of Colored People Legal Defense Fund, then led by Charles Hamilton Houston.[45] From their perspective, this was an eminently reasonable choice. It forced the Court to address the issue within that framework, not the one that Hand or others of like mind might have preferred.

It was, however, arguably an unfortunate choice. There is at least the possibility that the legal assault on Jim Crow would have proceeded more smoothly had the first target been not schools, but voting rights. A Court devising remedies to end racial discrimination in the voting precincts would have been acting not only within the framework of a clear constitutional text, but also to enforce rights directly involved in the democratic process, which is unquestionably a direct concern of the federal courts.[46] President Truman had in 1948 advocated legislation to facilitate enforcement of voting rights and in this he had the support of the Republican Party.[47] Only the Southern filibuster stood in the way of its enactment. Had the Court been asked in 1946 to devise broad remedies to protect voting rights, it very likely would have done so[48] and would have been skating on thick political ice. The remedies could, moreover, have been applied at once, with no concession to "all deliberate speed." While enforcement of judicial decrees would have been a problem requiring support by the executive, as it was with school desegregation,[49] resistance might well have been overcome much more easily, at least in most Southern states.

Enforcement of equal voting rights would have been more effective to end racial segregation if the Court had also earlier reapportioned Congress and the state legislatures. In 1946, the Court refused to set aside the Illinois law creating congressional districts with glaringly unequal populations.[50] Justice Frankfurter led three justices in holding the case non-justiciable, an extreme exercise of judicial self-restraint that would be overruled in

1960.[51] While the text of the Constitution did not speak directly to the issue, the equal protection doctrine later applied is a reasonable inference from the provisions bearing on congressional and legislative elections. A Court enforcing the right to participate in the political process on reasonably even terms is strengthening the democratic process and giving added legitimacy to the other branches and levels of government.

If the Court by 1954 had achieved the democratization of lower houses of state legislatures and school boards in much of the South, resistance to school desegregation would have been far less solid. Indeed, the Court could then have effected desegregation in most communities throughout the South by strict enforcement of the admittedly objectionable but irresistible standard of "separate but equal." Of all the Southern states, it may be that only South Carolina could make a serious argument that its separate schools were equal in the financial support they received. Most states and school districts simply could not afford the diseconomies of "separate but equal" and would not have been able to marshal the votes even to try if a substantial portion of the electorate were opposed. One might reasonably have hoped to lay Jim Crow to rest in most states by democratic means.

The charm of this alternative approach for lawyers and judges such as Hand, or Cooley or Brandeis or Freund, is that it would have enabled the people themselves to do by democratic means most of what had to be done. The problem with *Brown,* as Hand perceived, lay in the fact that a very good and necessary reform was achieved by the wrong institution. While Professor Sunstein is right that the merits of school desegregation are beyond debate, perhaps Hand was not wrong to question whether the destination was reached by the best possible route. An unfortunate, secondary, and unintended consequence of the route taken was that it weakened rather than strengthened the democratic process and inflated the pretensions of the anti-democratic judiciary. Those unwelcome consequences are still felt.

18

A New Age of
Judicial Heroism

As described in chapter 7, the Supreme Court of the United States was throughout the nineteenth century in thrall to harsh social Darwinist politics. After ratification of the Fourteenth Amendment in 1868, the Court treated the Due Process Clause as its commission to enforce unenacted principles of natural law impeding the efforts of state legislatures to restrain predation by monied interests.

The Court also placed the power of the federal judiciary on the side of economic might in opposing the labor movement.[1] In over half a century, until Congress intervened in 1932,[2] the federal courts broke over 4,000 strikes (one every four and one-half days)[3] by arresting and imprisoning strike leaders for acts found by judges to have been in contempt of their decrees.[4] The justices played hero to the predatory class.

Thus, rivaling *Lochner* in its indifference to the elementary requirements of self-government and federalism was the decision of the Court in *United States v. Debs.*[5] In that case, a federal court broke a Chicago rail strike at the request of the attorney general of the United States, despite the lack of any legislative authority for the attorney general to be involved in the matter and despite the fact that federal intervention was contrary to the wishes of Illinois Governor Altgeld, who affirmed that there was no danger of serious violence. Despite the absence of any legislation authorizing the Department of Justice to proceed in such a matter, the Court found judicial authority to enjoin the strike and arrest Eugene Debs for contempt of court. It found this authority in the constitutional provision authorizing the United States to conduct a postal service: A federal court could, on its own, make it a crime for Debs to be an indirect cause of delay in the delivery of the mail.

Also, Court thus found in the Fourteenth Amendment its commission to invalidate numerous state enactments to protect workers.[6] Among the laws states were forbidden to enact were minimum wage laws. Thomas Reed Powell aptly characterized these cases as resting on "mythical" constitutional standards.[7]

In addition, for almost a half-century, the diversity jurisdiction of the federal courts remained a primary tool of barons of industry seeking to avoid or minimize responsibility to their workers.[8] Adhering to the constitutionally dubious doctrine voiced by Justice Story in *Swift v. Tyson*, the federal judiciary, with the Court's approval, imposed on personal injury claims a body of federal tort law that was notably less generous than the laws of most states. Claims removable to federal court were therefore worth materially less in settlement than identical claims headed for adjudication in state courts, so the removal jurisdiction[9] was a major weapon in the defense against workers' claims. By such means, the Court protected the titans of industry against the claims of those on whose backs industry was created.

The social Darwinist Court shouted its last hurrah in the 1930s by invalidating New Deal legislation.[10] Many who voted for the National Industrial Recovery Act of 1933 thought it invalid[11] and were not surprised when the Court unanimously held it to be so. But a majority of the Court, led by four superannuated members, soon appeared to be on the verge of invalidating other enactments more cautiously designed to restore hope and trust in the face of a devastating economic collapse and massive unemployment.[12] Franklin Roosevelt and others in 1937 feared that the Court's decisions invalidating the efforts of the president and Congress to reinvigorate the economy might cause the Republic itself to unravel. The advent of Mussolini in 1925,[13] the collapse of the German republic in 1933,[14] the murder of the prime minister of Japan in 1936,[15] and the Fascist crushing of the Spanish Republic underway in 1937[16] were visible examples of democratic disintegration. Although the "kingfish," Huey Long, had been assassinated in 1935 for his pretensions, other potential tyrants lurked offstage, rehearsing their lines promising more heroic solutions to the nation's distress.[17] Roosevelt, as desperate as Lincoln had been with the Taney Court in 1863, proposed to enlarge the Supreme Court to dilute the influence of the "Nine Old Men" whose willful resistance threatened the ability of the Republic to make a serious response to economic calamity. If the fears of Roosevelt and those who supported his plan, such as Senator Hugo Black,[18] were factually justified, then court-packing was warranted, despite the ardent protests of Learned Hand, the American Bar Association, and others that the action sacrificed the traditional independence of the federal judiciary.[19]

Although the court-packing plan was defeated, the proposal may have momentarily intimidated the Court.[20] Justice Roberts, perhaps at the urging of Chief Justice Hughes, reversed the position he had taken only months earlier and voted to uphold a state minimum wage law.[21] Also, older members of the Court soon retired. The New Deal program was thus saved and the long era of judicial Darwinism came to an unceremonious end.

The Court, however, merely redirected its attentions and reformulated its political role. It acknowledged a presumption of constitutionality for legislation regulating business and the economy, but in a celebrated footnote to an opinion of the Court, Justice Stone suggested that it would give closer scrutiny when legislation (1) appears on its face to be within a specific prohibition of the Constitution, such as those of the first ten amendments, which are deemed equally specific when held to be embraced within the Fourteenth; (2) restricts those political processes that ordinarily can be expected to bring about repeal of undesirable legislation such as restraints on the right to vote or in the dissemination of information; or (3) is directed at ethnic, racial, or religious minorities unable to secure protection from the majority of an electorate.[22]

These impulses were consonant with Jacksonian politics. Yet, Cooley, Brandeis, and Freund would have been troubled, as Hand was, by the role the Court thus undertook to play, not because they would have disagreed with the substance of the Court's initiatives, but because they respected the limits of the role that a national judiciary having no accountability to an electorate can play in a federal republic. Vigorous protection of the interests enumerated in the classic footnote can prevent a more legitimately democratic address of those interests.[23] On that account, Justice Brandeis recorded his dissent.[24] Thus, the Court, having recast itself as hero to beleaguered individuals and classes, was no more respectful of the imperatives of self-government than was its predecessor. There would be justices (Felix Frankfurter, John Marshall Harlan, Byron White, and sometimes Hugo Black, most obvious among them) who would voice objections, but the Court would soon become another "bevy of Platonic Guardians." The difference lay in the interests they chose to guard.

Indeed, the triumph over court-packing initiated an era of judicial presumption suggesting comparisons to *Dred Scott*, the forgotten emblem of nineteenth-century judicial arrogance. In the course of his deliberation in *Brown*, Justice Stanley Reed asked his law clerk whether he favored "krytocracy." The clerk unsurprisingly required the use of the *Oxford English Dictionary* to learn that the word means "government by judges."[25] As a form of government, it has not been in common use. The concept of a "liberal" krytocracy—one fired by a desire to transform the social order it governs—may have been unique at the time of its advent in post–World War II, post-*Brown* America.

Perhaps the leading twentieth-century practitioner of constitutional lawmaking in disregard of the rights of citizens to govern themselves was William Brennan. He has been admiringly described as a "great judicial

statesman."[26] Because he was a Catholic justice,[27] some may have wondered at the time of his appointment if he might be subject to papal authority in his interpretations of the Constitution of the United States. In a way,
such a concern was validated by his career, because the inflated sense of the
Court's role he seems to have brought to its work[28] helped to make the
Court resemble a College of Cardinals telling members of the faith what to
believe and how to live. The Brennan "encyclicals" *required* the community
to respect a broad range of individual and minority rights, and left little discretion to local congregations or constituencies to believe, or to act upon
the belief, that somewhat more communitarianism and less individualism
or pluralism might be preferable. The encyclicals were not presented as serious interpretations of a written legal text,[29] but were rooted in natural
law sanctioned by reference to the indeterminate text of the Fourteenth
Amendment and to what Justice Brennan presumed to be the better instincts and ideals of the people. He was fairly said to be a non-interpre-
tavist[30] engaged in "a search for political-moral knowledge, for answers to
the various questions as to how we, the polity, should live our public, collective life, or life in common"[31] and sometimes our not so public life, too.
Unlike Cooley or Brandeis, Brennan seldom if ever gave weight to the political judgment of elected officers, perhaps especially those elected at state or
local levels. Frankfurter only somewhat unjustly described the Brennan
Court as animated by "self-willed, self-righteous power lust."[32] Whether
lustful or not, the Court embraced the belief that anything a legislature
could do, it could do better.[33]

There is irony in the denotation of this anti-democratic restoration of judicial supremacy as "liberal," a sort of code word for the moral preferences
of the recently emerged "national class."[34] As Christopher Lasch explained
the irony,[35] many ruling meritocrats revolted against the moral values of
those less-esteemed persons who merely vote, pay taxes, bear and raise the
Republic's children, and put themselves at risk in its defense. A visible
means of avoiding the noisome duty of persuading these lesser persons of
the correct world view was to constitutionalize political issues that would
otherwise be subjects of popular governance.[36] The meritocracy in revolt
may, if Lasch is correct, have supplied the receptive audience needed to induce high court judges to discard the caution advocated by earlier "liberals" favoring the right of self-government. Indeed, Frankfurter despaired
that his colleagues were determined to be immortalized in "the Valhalla of
liberty" and "in the meantime to have the *avant-garde* of the Yale Law
School . . . praise them."[37]

A different interpretation is that of Michael Sandel, who blames the
Supreme Court for displacing the earlier American tradition of shared
power with a new vision of "freedom" elevating individual autonomy and
governmental neutrality at the expense of the bonds uniting us in a com-

mon venture.[38] Evidence to support his hypothesis can be found not only in the conduct of the Court, but also in legal scholarship disregarding the possibility that life-tenured judges ought to or could be influenced in the formulation of doctrine by "the common thoughts of men" or other communitarian concerns,[39] expressing wonder that anyone should be concerned about the Court's "anti-majoritarianism"[40] and dismissing the concern as platitudinous.[41]

Whatever the social-psychological origins of this anti-democratic "liberalism," it called into question the validity and integrity of the traditional political rhetoric of the Republic.[42] Life-tenured judges are not in any useful sense "we, the people," however much one might wish to believe otherwise.[43] To speak of krytocracy as a government of or by the people is a transparent fraud on citizens' political rights.[44] While none can deny, as Justice Robert Jackson affirmed, that the "very purpose" of constitutions is "to withdraw certain subjects from the vicissitudes of political controversy,"[45] when "certain subjects" include many or most of those of greatest interest to citizens, the effect, as he noted,[46] is to withdraw the life-giving oxygen from the air sustaining self-government.

As we have seen, our exemplars were mindful of at least three grave problems inherent in political rule by judges. First, as Cooley's message at Harvard reflected, they believed that a judiciary disregarding the "common thoughts of men" will be resisted by those whose thoughts it disdains. In this view, people do not change their minds, and often not even their behavior, because of the utterances of senior citizens in black robes, especially if they are imbued with the individualist spirit of Protestantism. Judgments of high courts purporting to effect social change are therefore often useless and sometimes counterproductive. On the other hand, Cooley and his successors supposed that people will more readily adapt to policies debated and decided by democratic methods in which they participated, especially if their dissenting views have been prudently accommodated.

Second, my exemplars recognized that judges as a class are not selected for their political and moral wisdom, nor is there reason or experience to suggest that they acquire it in office. "Wayward" as Hand observed the "vagaries of popular assemblies" to be, judges of all political persuasions are capable of equally colossal political blunders. There are at least three reasons for this. One is that the judicial process is not well suited to the presentation and assimilation of political wisdom.[47] The Brandeis brief to the contrary notwithstanding, legislatures and administrative rulemakers are, as Freund observed, structurally more adept at "mastering statistics and economics," as Holmes prescribed, because they have direct access to technical expertise as well as to popular estimates of such expertise and have no obligation to address an imminent dispute when they have well-founded doubt about the right solution. A second reason, as Freund emphasized, is that the judiciary can seldom broker prudent compromise between competing values, and compromise is more often than not the wisest policy. That "the best is the enemy of the good" is an adverse comment on much judicial policymaking. A third reason is that the doctrine of precedent to which American courts are necessarily committed dictates that they cannot readily correct their policymaking mistakes. Having written, the judicial hand moves on. For all these reasons, political blunders by the judiciary may be more likely and more costly, even though they are more likely to bear the marks of principled decisionmaking.

Finally, my exemplars genuinely believed in the wisdom of separating powers. They recognized that courts assuming the role of third chamber to bicameral legislatures invite political attacks threatening their independence, and hence their qualifications, for their more humdrum, but more essential, work of resolving disputes by enforcing legal rights and duties. As high courts enter the fray to displace legislatures as policymakers, they leave behind no organ independent of politics that is free of improper influence and qualified to decide pertinent "cases and controversies" according to law.

These insights were for a time lost to the Court. Forgotten by the Court as it became a College of Cardinals was its experience with court-packing and the reaction against *Dred Scott* or *Debs*. It became intoxicated with the idea that the Fourteenth Amendment is its commission to enforce natural law and bring into being an America conforming to the presumably elevated moral values owned by the justices. While the Fourteenth Amendment was loosely drafted and had an ambiguous history,[48] the Court's treatment of that text was "extravagant interpretation"[49] of the sort Lieber had denounced as a usurpation of the right to self-government.

The moral arrogance of judicial heroism is perhaps most dramatically illustrated by the response of heroic justices to the adjudication of claims of constitutional right with respect to family relationships and sexual mores. Political views on these subjects are, of course, very much in ferment, owing in large measure to scientific and technological developments. Those views are diverse and often strongly held.[50] The texts of federal and state constitutions do not speak to the subject.

For an extreme example of judicial hubris, I advert to Justice Brennan's dissenting opinion in *Michael H. v. Gerald D.*[51] The case involved the claim of a biological father to visitation rights to a child born to a woman married, at the time of both conception and birth, to another man. Although the mother had taken her baby for some months to live with the biological father, his claim was resisted by her as well as by her husband, who had legitimated the child. Over Justice Brennan's dissent, the Supreme Court upheld California law denying to biological fathers the right to establish their relationship by scientific proof. So may the law of every other jurisdiction in the world, for Bronislaw Malinowski recorded it as one of the very few moral principles universal among human societies that "no child should be brought into the world without a man—and one man at that—assuming the role of sociological father, that is, guardian and protector, the male link between the child and the rest of the community."[52] While we are familiar with successful instances of children being raised cooperatively by fathers and step-fathers, no one can doubt that this is seldom optimal for the children, who are thus endowed with an opportunity to pit one against the other in a game of competitive indulgence; such competitive fatherhood can and often does result in alienation, neglect, and even hostility on both sides. The universal practice to which Malinowski points is thus rooted in common sense. It is, of course, possible that the universal principle has diminished applicability to contemporary American culture. Common sense will not be the same when children can be created without the inconvenience of intercourse and can be raised by caring institutions. Nevertheless, it is truly extraordinary for Justice Brennan to proclaim such an ancient and universal principle to be so unreasonable as to be unconstitutional and to so hold without a supporting word in the text of the Constitution. So much for self-government!

19

Ineffective Judicial Heroics

The ascendancy of Justice Brennan and other justices disdainful of self-government has been so often praised and condemned that an elaborate account seems unnecessary,[1] but a brief review is offered here for the limited purpose of illuminating its effect on the role of lawyers and judges as stewards of democracy.

Justice Brennan himself was a man of great personal charm and humanity. Nothing said here should be taken as personal criticism of him or of other justices. The purpose of the next three chapters is to make the limited point that efforts of judges to transform the social order without the general moral support of citizens are not very effective and are often counterproductive.[2] To spare the reader, I will not balance criticism of the Supreme Court's disdain for democracy with a full account of the benign but misguided motives that have frequently caused the Court to take a good thing too far.

After *Brown*, it seemed that every beleaguered individual or group in America, including perhaps some beleaguered only in their own perceptions, fancied that the Court in its anti-democratic role might relieve their distress. Their hopes often lay in a generous application of natural law enforced by the English chancellors' traditional contempt power. No longer the heroic defender of the monied class, the Court would, with fanfare, play hero to any who were overborne, not merely to the racial minority that was the immediate subject of the Fourteenth Amendment, but to all who were said to lack access to political power, even convicts and prisoners. "Equality" was for a time given a share of the place previously reserved for "liberty" in the Court's pantheon.[3] Thus, the idea of popular sovereignty came to be viewed by many American lawyers (seeing with the eyes of Governeur Morris) as a mere impediment to social reform.[4] And the role of the federal judiciary became once again redolent of the overbearing and pretentious role of the chancellor wielding power in the name of the king's (now nominally the people's, but really the judges') conscience.[5]

While *Brown* stands as the shining example of the good deeds that politically animated, life-tenured judges may on occasion perform when their decisions are congruent with widely shared moral precepts, even the Court's performance with respect to racial segregation is mixed and can be said at times to manifest misuse of its political power. When the Court at last ordered lower federal courts to reorganize and manage the public schools, and not merely in the South where segregation was *de jure*,[6] it pitted its authority broadly against self-government in communities spread across the continent.

To what effect? Some have mistakenly credited the Supreme Court with most of the advances in race relations occurring in the United States after the decision in *Brown*.[7] *Brown* itself was widely anticipated and approved; by 1950, only a well-placed minority of Americans thought it right that Linda Brown be excluded from her neighborhood school because of her skin pigmentation. The politics of world war and the economic changes resulting in mobility of people of all colors had undermined the social conditions from which Jim Crow had emerged.[8]

Moreover, desegregation gained its major legal impetus, not from *Brown*, but from the Civil Rights Act of 1964.[9] That legislation was less the product of *Brown* than of the assassination of John Kennedy; the political skill of Lyndon Johnson; Johnson's willingness to sacrifice the loyalty of the Old South to the Democratic Party; the moral support of citizens aroused by such leaders as Martin Luther King, Jr.[10] Rosa Parks,[11] and Jackie Robinson;[12] and the enduring influence of the moral rhetoric of Jefferson and Lincoln. The historical depth of the public morality was cogently observed by Leon Higginbotham, who said of the Declaration of Independence:

> The unsophisticated might argue that [it] had no ultimate impact of significance in eradicating slavery or diminishing racial discrimination. Yet in the corridors of history, there is a direct nexus between the egalitarian words uttered, even if not yet meant, and many of the changes that later took place. . . .
>
> The irony of the unfulfilled American dream of equality is that of all those in the long line of dreamers who have sought the ultimately just society, none had to seek out alien sources for moral authority. They had only to say to the American people: fulfill the largest promise in your first statement as a nation.[13]

While the federal courts were a useful instrument, "destroying apartheid in America"[14] was not primarily their achievement, but that of the American people (including, especially, African Americans who protested persuasively) and the Congress they elected.

Notwithstanding the contribution of *Brown* to the cause, there were costs. *Brown II*,[15] the decree that desegregation should proceed "with all deliberate speed," has been fairly appraised as a disaster.[16] It was an exhibition, among other things, of poor political judgment resting on Justice Frankfurter's unfounded belief, formed on the basis of his many private discussions in Cambridge with Harvard law students, that Southern lawyers would rise up in support of the Court.[17] Alas, that did not happen.

Although Linda Brown herself was never admitted to her neighborhood school in Kansas, many local schools and the school districts governing them, including many outside the South, were in time forced into something like judicial receivership, with a federal judge displacing elected officials in making a wide range of decisions affecting the conduct of schools.

The spirit of Southern rednecks who wanted to impeach Earl Warren was nationalized in the politics of George Wallace, the angry governor of Alabama, who by denouncing the "pointy-headed intellectuals" marshaled a huge vote in the 1968 Democratic primaries in northern states.[18] Many individual federal judges were subject to strenuous efforts to intimidate them;[19] numerous Michigan bumper stickers called not for the impeachment, but the assassination, of Judge Stephen Roth for ordering bussed integration of all the schools in metropolitan Detroit,[20] one of many cities in which school populations reflected segregated housing patterns caused in minor part by historic misuses of local political power reflecting racist impulses. That extremely hostile reaction was most visible in the westside suburbs, which were populated by the offspring of twentieth-century immigrants from eastern Europe who bore no responsibility for historic racisms and who perceived no reason why their children should bear the burden and inconvenience of desegregating African-American children for sins they did not commit. Judge Roth, himself an immigrant, was likely responding in his order to the evidence that the burden of desegregation, if limited to the city of Detroit, would fall entirely on those least responsible for it and leave free of any inconvenience the monied, "national" class residing in Grosse Pointe and Bloomfield Hills. While an appeal from his order was pending, he died of a heart attack, quite possibly caused by the stress associated with the odium attached to his decision.

The effect outside the South was to uproot neighborhood schools in black neighborhoods as well as white.[21] Sacrificed in the effort to promote racial integration was the traditional relationship between public education and the family.[22] Derrick Bell made the point that it was not merely white parents, but also black, whose responsibility and authority over the education of their children was diminished.[23] There is even reason to suspect that the psychological justifications for desegregation were harmfully self-fulfilling,[24] perhaps even foreseeably so.[25] While it would be unjust to suggest that there was a clearly superior approach to the achievement of public school desegregation or to blame the Court for the poor estate of public education in America at the century's end, *Brown II* and its progeny surely made a contribution to the demise of public schools. And, over the longer term, public education as a means by which citizens share the tutelage of their children may be more vital to the Republic than the Constitution itself. On that account, the federal courts have substantially but belatedly abandoned the goal of racial integration of school children as one that is both unattainable and counterproductive.[26] In the extensions of its application, *Brown II* has indeed been silently overruled.

School desegregation was the defining moment for the "liberal" Court and profession, but it was only a point of departure. With equally high purpose, the Court soon undertook by judicial decree to transform other aspects of American society.

Near the top of the agenda was the transformation of state and local police. The Court still has not gone so far as to incorporate every detail of the first eight amendments into the Fourteenth, but it has incorporated selectively those provisions "implied in the concept of ordered liberty,"[27] a position initially conforming to Cooley's 1873 interpretation of the Civil War amendments. That standard was, however, given an increasingly expansive interpretation.[28] Thus, all the provisions bearing on criminal procedure are now applied to the states, except perhaps the prohibition of excessive bail[29] and the requirement of indictment by grand jury.[30] Often in the forefront of this initiative was Justice Frankfurter, who disfavored broad incorporation of the first eight amendments into the Fourteenth, but who took a strong position on the application of the Fourth Amendment to the states.[31] In this field, if no other, Justice Frankfurter was an adherent to natural law.

As in *Brown II*, the Court was in its work on criminal procedure initially on high moral ground commanding widespread support in the "common thoughts of men." As early as 1936, the Court had held that it was a denial of due process of law for a state court to admit an unreliable, coerced confession as evidence of guilt.[32] Few Americans would have questioned the result in that case, the sheriff having admitted to beating the accused, "but not too much for a Negro." By 1944, however, the Court exhibited less concern with the unreliability of coerced confessions than with the purpose of disapproving and deterring dangerous police methods.[33]

Cooley, in his *Constitutional Limitations,* had argued for the right of indigent persons charged with serious crime to representation by appointed counsel;[34] in 1932, his politically reactionary former student, George Sutherland, led the Court in holding that Alabama could not deny the right of persons charged with a capital offense to be represented by counsel.[35] In 1938, the Court held that the federal government was required by the Sixth Amendment to supply counsel to an indigent accused of a felony,[36] but in 1942, it held that the Constitution did not require an appointment of counsel by a state court for a confessed robber sentenced to eight years of confinement.[37] That decision was overruled in 1963,[38] with the support of twenty-two states that already provided for the appointment of counsel in such a case.[39] Due process was explained as a dynamic principle having its roots in popular notions of justice, an explanation challenged by Hugo Black, who unsuccessfully resisted the importation of natural law into the Constitution of the United States.[40]

The Court in 1964 went beyond its moral and political support in regulating police conduct. In a pivotal case, it held that the Fourteenth Amendment prohibited a state from using a confession secured by questioning conducted before the accused consulted his counsel.[41] And, a year later, it held that the state must advise the accused of his right to counsel before questioning, else a conviction based in part on his confession must be reversed.[42] These decisions were not well-received by those whose obedience was required, for at least three reasons. First, they appeared to require radical change in the customary practices of local police departments everywhere. Second, they coincided with a precipitous increase in violent crime in most American cities. Third, they resulted in the release of persons, many or most of whom were almost certainly guilty of serious crime.

President Nixon fully exploited the political opportunity presented,[43] and Congress soon enacted legislation providing that confessions voluntarily secured shall be admissible in federal court "if voluntarily given."[44] The Senate Judiciary Committee recommending the legislation predicted that it would be upheld as a result of changes in the Court.[45] While the issue has never squarely arisen because of the circumspect behavior of the Department of Justice, there have been intimations that the Court no longer thinks of the right to counsel in the station house as one having constitutional rank.[46] Moreover, the principle proved to have meager practical effect, because police were quick to learn ways of formal compliance with the requirement. The authors of the interrogation manual disapproved by the Court were soon able to boast that "all but a few of the interrogation tactics and techniques presented in our earlier publication are still valid."[47] Thus, the effort to conform the conduct of state and local police with respect to persons in custody to a standard higher than that most citizens would endorse was at best partially successful.

Meanwhile, the Court had extended the Fourteenth Amendment to prohibit not only police misconduct in handling persons in their custody, but also the use of evidence otherwise unlawfully obtained, without regard to its reliability as proof of serious crimes or the gravity of the police misconduct by which the evidence was obtained. This stringent method of enforcement had been applied *in federal court* as early as 1914 to exclude the product of searches conducted in violation of the Fourth Amendment.[48] It was resisted in many states that found it objectionable that a criminal was "to go free because the constable blundered."[49] In 1961, for the first time, the Court concluded that the Due Process Clause of the Fourteenth Amendment prohibits states from using such evidence,[50] no matter how persuasive or even irrefutable. The stated purpose was to deprive enforcement officers of any incentive to engage in misconduct, such as warrantless searches. The Court assumed that no other effective method of policing the police could be devised.[51]

It is likely that some state and local police are more cautious than they were in 1961 in breaking into and entering the homes of citizens and are more likely to secure the permission of a judicial officer prior to the conduct of a search. The exclusionary rule was, however, modified in 1984 to allow states to use evidence where the police conduct was only technically illegal[52] or was in good faith.[53] The degree to which any improvement in police behavior in the conduct of searches for evidence is owing to the Court's decrees remains uncertain.

There were and are other methods of enforcing the Fourth Amendment. The tort liability of both municipal governments and their individual officers for abusive police conduct was expanded by aggressive civil enforcement of the Civil Rights Act of 1868.[54] These tort remedies have led to the creation of administrative mechanisms for controlling police misconduct.[55] In combination, these developments seem likely to have had more influence on police conduct than the Court's constitutionalization of the exclusionary rule. These other remedies have the reassuring feature that they are no benefit to convicted felons. Moreover, they are within the power of elected representatives to revise; hence the citizens affected by police conduct and misconduct share responsibility for them.

It remains certain that in every instance of the exclusionary rule's application by the Court, a conviction is set aside on the basis of an error having no bearing on the innocence or guilt of the convict. That feature of the rule is, of course, distasteful to those citizens most sensitive to the dangers of violent crime. Politicians reacting against the alleged "softness" of the Court's treatment of felons have advanced their careers by enacting laws providing for increasingly brutal sentences. Also in part a reaction against the exclusionary rule is the Victims' Rights movement,[56] which may succeed in amending the Constitution for the purpose of elevating conviction rates.

The Court's extravagant interpretations of the Fourteenth Amendment applicable to criminal law enforcement were not limited to the regulation of police conduct. The Court also undertook the reformation of state prisons.[57] There can be no doubt of the squalid conditions of many of them, but whether judges run materially more humane prisons than wardens remains open to debate.

Also, for a time the Court indicated that it would prohibit capital punishment.[58] In 1972, it vacated 600 death sentences, finding that the executions would constitute cruel and unusual punishment proscribed by the Eighth Amendment as incorporated into the Fourteenth. Each of the thirty-seven states using that form of punishment re-enacted their statutes with procedural modifications and there was an epic increase in the number of capital sentences and executions.[59] There is some reason to believe that there is a causal connection between these events.[60] It is certain that the Court backed away from the implications of its 1972 decision in the face of a strong political reaction.[61] It then covered its retreat by imposing elaborate procedural requirements in capital cases that may have given an advantage to prosecutors seeking the death penalty and created an agenda of specific questions for jurors to consider, perhaps concealing from some the reality that there is, underneath the verbiage, a human life at stake.[62]

Nevertheless, Justice Brennan in his retirement cheerfully forecast that "[o]ne day the Court will outlaw the death penalty. Permanently."[63] It seems never to have occurred to him that the abolition of capital punishment is properly a task for those who write and amend the constitutions and laws of the states and not for his College of Cardinals to decide without regard for citizens' rights to self-government.

As earlier noted, the Court did at last in the post-war era render a constitutional decision protective of the majority's right to vote: It ordered the states to realign legislative and congressional districts to equalize their populations in conformity with constitutional provisions.[64] The benefits to democratic traditions even of this obvious step are in some doubt, for it has not prevented political parties from locking up safe seats.[65] But the Court in any case was unable to refrain from overdoing a good deed. It soon followed its first, readily defensible decision with another much harder to justify. The people of Colorado had voted by referendum overwhelmingly and explicitly to retain in one house of their legislature a scheme for giving substantial representation to rural counties likely to be disregarded on important issues by the representatives of much more numerous urban voters. The effect of such an organization of a house of the legislature is modestly to empower local government by giving it a role in state government comparable to that given to state government in the federal scheme by the composition of the Senate of the United States as envisioned at the Founding. Despite this needful purpose, the Court held that Colorado was obliged by the Fourteenth Amendment to organize both houses of its legislature alike, in accordance with its seemingly Jacksonian slogan, "one man, one vote."[66]

The direct effect was to reduce the political status and influence of counties. Why the people of Denver should be denied the right to confer such status on the rural counties of Colorado can be explained only by uncritical reference to the slogan. Thus was "one man, one vote" made into anti-democratic dogma. Among those who were appalled by this decision was winning counsel, Archibald Cox, then the solicitor general of the United States.[67] One knowledgeable and sympathetic observer referred to it as "the second American Constitutional Convention."[68]

Not perceived at the time were the indirect effects of the "one man, one vote" principle. A secondary effect is an extraordinary opportunity for gerrymandering legislative districts; the possibilities for manipulation to produce a particular result in an assembly are not unlimited, but may at times seem so because of the denial of legitimacy to ancient county and precinct boundaries. A tertiary effect has been to place the highest state courts in a political cockpit, because they generally have the final say when an apportionment scheme is challenged. Accordingly, unwelcome partisan interest in the membership of those courts has been elevated.

A similar intrusion on state sovereignty was the 1995 decision invalidating state-imposed term limits on members of the United States Senate and House of Representatives. Such legislation may have been ill-advised; certainly it tended to weaken the ability of a state enacting such a law to secure a full share of pork barrel benefits. For the latter reason, there was no cause to suspect an illicit motive of the state legislators enacting term limits. Quite unnecessarily, the Court interpreted the state law as a "qualification for office" in conflict with those provided in Article I of the Constitution.[69] Term limits are not "qualifications," but disqualifications established to serve aims unrelated to those served by the constitutional requirements. The Court was seemingly unable to contain its impulse to decide an interesting political question. The result was to block a lively movement of political reform.

Arguably the most lawless of Justice Brennan's opinions was his decision to savage by subtle means the popular institution of the right to jury trial in civil cases.[70] Flying not only in the face of ancient tradition expressed in the Seventh Amendment, but also into the teeth of two federal statutes and a rule promulgated by the Court itself, the Court held that a federal district court could, by local rule, cut the size of the jury in half. Geoffrey Hazard aptly described Justice Brennan's opinion as "monumentally unconvincing."[71] An effect of the decision was to make jury verdicts more idiosyncratic and less predictable, evoking cries of anguish over outlying verdicts that must be corrected by judicial intervention and impede settlement negotiations.[72] Justice Thurgood Marshall, in his dissent, was incredulous that the Court could have so little regard for an institution so integral to the role of the federal judiciary in the constitutional scheme.[73]

The restructuring of the upper houses of state legislatures and the civil jury in federal courts were radical transformations serving no important public purpose, yet they evoked no popular response. That was, of course, not true of *Roe v. Wade*.[74] Whatever its merits as policy, the principle espoused by the Court in that case had even less foundation in the text or tradition of the Fourteenth Amendment than had *Lochner*.[75]

Unlike *Dred Scott* or *Debs*, those two pieces of nineteenth-century extravagance in constitutional interpretation, *Roe* lacked the justification of a crisis to be confronted; there was no civil war or revolution in sight that the Court could have thought it was averting. On the contrary, as the Court noted, many state legislatures were actively entertaining arguments for abortion rights; four states, including New York, had recently revised their law to accommodate abortion rights and the number of legal abortions in the United States was in a perpendicular climb.[76] A substantial reform commissioned by the Texas legislature giving the plaintiffs in *Roe* most of what they wanted was in the advanced stages of development, presentation, and probable enactment.[77] There was scattered resistance to legislative reform, chiefly among Catholic organizations, but it lacked force in most states. After all, women were then as now a majority in the electorate; those favoring abortion rights were not disadvantaged in their access to a political forum in any sense within the contemplation of the Court's 1938 footnote.

The Court in *Roe* eschewed a narrow holding. The Texas statute challenged was nineteenth-century legislation allowing no exceptions to its proscription of abortions; its manifest purpose was not to protect the life of the fetus, but the health of pregnant women. Had the Court adhered to the cautious practices of Cooley or the counsel of Brandeis in *Ashwander*, it could have limited its holding to such enactments, or the statute might have been invalidated on grounds of desuetude.[78] Either holding would have accelerated the democratic political debate on abortion rights instead of pretermitting it. But a majority of the Court was beguiled by its seemingly simple and seemingly popular[79] answer to a complex social and moral problem and supposed themselves justified in imposing it on the political institutions of the states in the broadest possible terms.

Not least among the deficiencies in the Court's opinion was its arrogance in dismissing the complexities of a profound moral issue. As Robert Burt observed, the decision, like that in *Dred Scott*, sought to resolve political conflict "by awarding definitive and conclusive victory" to one side, an authoritarian method reflecting the Court's distorted conception of itself as a College of Cardinals.[80] Such arrogance was well-calculated to evoke opposition and defiance.

Indeed, if members of the Court thought they would persuade the public to their view, they were soon disabused of that notion. Their opinion in *Roe* had no more persuasive effect than did that of their predecessors in *Dred Scott*. The Right to Life movement has been in large measure a reaction against the Court's imprudence. Doubtless there were persons in 1972 who thought that abortion is murder, but they were fewer in number and far less outspoken than they are today. Once the Court had foreclosed the political forum to them, their numbers were increased and the voices became shrill. Few members of Wiebe's "national class" or Lasch's "elite" share the view that abortion is murder, but that view is commonly held by citizens who do not see themselves as members of a ruling class.

Some of the Court's resisters practiced defiance,[81] while others took to the streets and became violent.[82] Those violent reactions have no counterpart in the politics of other nations, even predominantly Catholic ones in which abortion rights have been established by parliamentary means.[83] Because of the violent reaction against the Court's ukase, it may still be more difficult in many communities for a woman to secure an abortion today than it was when *Roe* was decided.[84] To confront the violence of the response, pro-choice forces invested great energy in organizing protection and in seeking injunctive protection,[85] a process well-calculated to raise tempers on all sides and further diminish the prospects for satisfactory resolution of the controversy. The Republic is reduced to using the criminal law to suppress opposition to the Court that is too boisterous.

Considerations similar to those involved in *Roe* inform the debate about the constitutionality of "the right to die." So far, the Supreme Court has prudently withheld support for the precept that such a right can be discerned in the Due Process Clause.[86] There is of course much to be said in favor of permitting physician-assisted suicide by the desperately sick. But drawing subtle distinctions between suicide and homicide in all the diverse circumstances in which the issue arises is beyond the competence of even the wisest judges.[87] Legislated solutions have the enormous advantages of expressing "the common thoughts of men" better than courts ever can and of leaving ample room for changing the law as better insights become available.[88]

It is perhaps too harsh to declare that extended school desegregation, the reform of the criminal justice systems of the states, the reorganization of state legislatures and federal civil juries, and the enlargement of "reproduction rights" were all failed heroics. There were benign consequences. But a significant price was paid in thrusting the Court and the Constitution into political cockpits where they do not belong, jeopardizing the independence of the Court and the integrity of the Constitution. And in different ways and to different degrees, all of these heroic initiatives at social reform backfired in precisely the ways that Cooley, Brandeis, Freund, and Hand foretold.

20

First Amendment Heroics

Enforcement of the First Amendment is among the most solemn duties of the Supreme Court and some of its most admirable moments have come in the performance of that duty.[1] Cooley, Brandeis, Freund, and Hand were all passionately committed to its principle as an indispensable element of the democratic political process. In 1925, Brandeis joined in extending First Amendment restraints to state and local government by incorporating that provision into the Due Process Clause of the Fourteenth Amendment,[2] although the textual and historical basis for that extension was inconclusive.[3]

The compass of the First Amendment at the time it was incorporated into the Fourteenth was, however, narrow.[4] The idea was largely confined to a thought expressed by John Milton in 1644:

> Give me the liberty to know, to utter, and to argue freely according to conscience above all liberties . . . . And though all the winds of doctrine were let loose to play upon the earth, so Truth be in the field, we do injuriously by licensing and prohibiting to misdoubt her strength. Let her and falsehood grapple; who ever knew Truth put to the worse in a free and open encounter. Her confuting is the best and surest suppressing.[5]

The amendment's protection extended to speech related to religious observance and political expression motivated by conscience and a regard for truth; even that protection was not expressed in absolute terms.

As we have seen, state constitutions contained provisions very similar to the First Amendment and were the subject of a significant part of Cooley's *Constitutional Limitations*. As Cooley had explained it in 1873, the Fourteenth Amendment provided a redundant but perhaps occasionally important means of enforcing political rights that might in some states be jeopardized by timid or corrupt judicial administration.[6] But no one, in 1873 or 1925, reckoned that the Fourteenth Amendment had to do with symbolic speech, obscenity, commercial speech, campaign finance, or even defamation. The "liberal" Supreme Court constitutionalized all of those subjects and thereby imposed its libertarian views on state and local governments, foreclosing political debate on the wisdom of the principles it applied. Our freedom of expression is not derived from the tolerance of the communities in which we express ourselves, but from what Brandeis might have denoted as "foreign aid" imposed by a distant and imperial oligarchy.

To some extent, the enlargement of First Amendment protection was prompted by the narrowest and most legitimate of Fourteenth Amendment concerns about the right of African-American citizens to express their indignation at segregation.[7] But the Court went far beyond considerations of a vibrant political process and did not attempt to reconcile its reasons for doing so with the contrary politics expressed by the vote of the people.[8]

One of the Court's anti-democratic excursions was the use of the Fourteenth Amendment to invalidate pornography laws. In 1957,[9] the Court reversed a conviction under a federal statute forbidding the use of the mails to convey obscene material. Justice Brennan, writing for the Court, upheld the statute by interpreting it to be applicable only to matter altogether lacking redemptive social importance; the mail in question did not meet that standard and so was not subject to the postmaster's control. In 1973, the Court modified the standard to apply to "works taken as a whole."[10]

Insofar as that decision affects only the federal government, no exception is taken to it here. The issue appears in a different light, however, when the standard is applied to state or local government. No doubt the application of a local standard by a jury or local censor evaluating artistic "works taken as a whole" can threaten the values articulated by Milton and embodied in the First Amendment. The arts, prized as instruments of social change, not infrequently offend and ought not in a free society be suppressed. There is also, however, a wide range of material offensive to the moralities prevailing in many communities for which the claim can be only colorably made that a work as a whole has *some* nominal intellectual content or literary value, but which falls far short of making a contribution to the enduring struggle between truth and falsehood.

Finding the distinction between art and smut elusive, Justice Harlan repeatedly advocated, without success, that some accommodation ought to be made to allow for the discretion of state and local officials in drawing that line.[11] As a consequence of the Court's failure to observe his caution, the power of the state to restrain the circulation of "adult" materials was closely confined. States and communities were substantially disempowered to regulate a wide range of commercially motivated activity exploiting diverse sexual urges, including violent ones, that do not comport with the hopes of many communities to channel sexuality into a strict framework of Victorian family life or some postmodern alternative social structure.

A more current and even more questionable application of the First Amendment is its use to bar site-blocking software to prevent Internet access to child pornography on public access computers in public libraries.[12] While the Supreme Court has not ruled on that precise issue, the lower court decision may well be upheld on the basis of the Court's prior ruling. One result will be that fewer children will be seen in public libraries.

As Justice Harlan observed, the federal interest in imposing such constraint on state officers is at best attenuated. Very little is known about the social consequences of pornography. It may be, as many believe, harmless or even benign. But the contrary position has not been disproved; it is at least possible that much is, as some contend, degrading to women[13] as well as hostile to widely favored norms of sexual conduct and therefore a provocation to antisocial conduct. The "common understanding of men" asserted by Cooley to be the basis for sound law may still be that literary freedom ought to be compromised to protect "family values." That sort of compromise is what state and local officials are elected to achieve.[14] There is no expertise in the federal judiciary qualifying them to make the necessary artistic assessment, and the testimonies of academic experts on artistic value are notably unpersuasive to any but other experts. Doubtless, even the Victorian Thomas Cooley would subscribe in substance to some of the Court's holdings protective of literary freedom,[15] but it seems certain that he, with Justice Harlan, would allow more room for political resolution of the issues. By their lights, if a particular work of art is censored in a community, the primary forum in which to grieve should be a legislature, a city council, or a jury; a judge holding tenure for life ought to become involved only in matters of extremity. If the city fathers of Atlanta are so unwise as to prevent the exhibition of so excellent a film as *Carnal Knowledge*, the most appropriate response is for the voters to throw the rascals out. Likewise, if a library board concludes that there will be a net gain in community access to information if certain unwelcome material is excluded, that is a decision that any court should be slow to overrule on the basis of such ephemeral law as the Due Process Clause.

The Court has virtually forbidden state or local government to encourage even a generalized religious faith. Many of the Founders, Washington and Jefferson not least among them, shared a loose deism bordering on unbelief, but perceived religion to be a necessary element in democratic life.[16] Cooley and Brandeis, although not themselves committed to any religious faith, also shared the belief that the morality of citizenship was for many citizens dependent on such faith and that the democratic state therefore had a self-interest in encouraging healthy religious institutions.

There is no principle of natural law by which the line between church and state can be judged.[17] While justices may suppose that "the dissemination of science" is a "sufficient agent" of civic moral education to sustain a community capable of self-government,[18] theirs is a "culture of disbelief."[19] The contrary belief of the Founders that religious life is needed to sustain the ties of community essential to democratic government is another that has not been falsified.

Most controversial of the Court's decisions in this area is that forbidding prayer in schools,[20] a stricture that has often been defied. There is no question that a requirement that school children participate in faith-specific religious services is an offense against the core values of the First Amendment. But the Fourteenth Amendment is not a commission to the Court to stamp out every religious impulse manifested by public institutions. Providing textbooks to students in parochial schools is probably bad policy, but the constitutional values at issue are minimal and do not call for the application of the Court's heavy hand.[21] Likewise, the lighting of a Christmas tree on the courthouse lawn alongside a crèche and Chanukah menorah may be in poor taste,[22] but it hardly threatens the values of religious freedom and free public discourse. There is some evidence that the Court has begun to perceive that it has overstepped its role in preventing almost all relations between state or local government and religious institutions.[23]

The Court has also used the First Amendment to control actions of state and local governments bearing on practices denoted as symbolic speech. Especially extraordinary was its holding that nude dancing in a bar is a constitutionally protected activity.[24] It found that dancing, being an expressive activity, must be protected, despite the lack of connection between that protection and any purpose that might reasonably be attributed to the First or Fourteenth amendments.

Constitutional protection for the burning of crosses is another example.[25] A state or city could reasonably perceive that such a gesture is an intimidation and a provocation to violence, with no visible redeeming value. And then there is flag burning.[26] Not only are citizens entitled to withhold their respect for national symbols, but the Court has proclaimed the individual's right to destroy them.[27] Many believe that ceremonial honor to the symbols of the Republic is an important means of reinforcing civic virtue.[28] That belief, too, has not been falsified.

While this author would not criminalize nude dancing, cross burning, or flag burning, the political choices to punish such acts are reasonable ones that the Constitution of the United States has not clearly withdrawn from state and local governments. It is not the place of life-tenured federal judges to foreclose them on the basis of the ephemeral text of the Fourteenth Amendment.

Another misguided excursion is the Court's extension of the First Amendment to commercial advertising.[29] Until the post-*Brown* era, it was assumed that commercial advertising was unprotected by any constitutional entitlements.[30] Commercial advertising, after all, has nothing to do with conscience and very little to do with truth. Nevertheless, the Court's present doctrine is that advertising that is not false or deceptive and does not concern unlawful activities may be restricted only in the service of a substantial public interest.[31] This standard disempowers states and communities from dealing with a considerable range of highly debatable matters.

A useful illustration of the difficulties with the Court's new standard is the problem of lawyer advertising.[32] Even simple price advertising by lawyers often threatens to mislead because of the absence of any means to provide information about the relative quality or utility of the service that a lawyer seeks to sell for the stated price. There is also a public interest of ancient dignity expressed in laws against champerty and barratry that accords with widely shared moral judgment in forestalling activities seeking to cause or perpetuate civil disputes. While it is fairly contended that much litigation is in the public interest and ought to be promoted, there are many claims that potential plaintiffs are ill-advised to assert, not only because they lack merit, but also because the transaction cost, in heartache as well as treasure, makes their assertion improvident even if successful. Any experienced lawyer is acquainted with instances in which considerable public and private expense was incurred in litigation, foreseeably to the benefit of no person except the lawyers; indeed, an Italian proverb has it that a lawsuit is a fruit tree growing in the yard of a lawyer. Moreover, the public has a special claim to regulate lawyers to prevent the degradation of the profession by commercialism. This is so because trust in lawyers is a public resource affecting the trust in other institutions of the Republic.[33] In addition, lawyer advertising appears to have strengthened a tendency for remunerative law practice, like other commercial enterprises, to be concentrated in fewer hands.

Whether, despite all these concerns, lawyer advertising is on balance useful, and whether or to what extent its regulation is warranted, are questions eminently suited to resolution by officers entrusted by the people to decide them. There is no reason to suppose that national uniformity is useful. Life-tenure judges, however educated and experienced, have no special qualifications to appraise the issues. Nevertheless, the Court has constitutionalized the field, disabling state courts, bar associations, and legislatures from exercising responsibility except that limited to constraining the most blatant abuses.

If lawyers have a constitutionally protected right to advertise, a reasonably compelling argument can be made for a constitutionally protected right to beg.[34] Recognition of such a right would entail a Court-crafted law of vagrancy equally suitable for application to every community, neighborhood, and street in the United States. Humane consideration of the needs and interests of the most impoverished citizens is as important as any of the values enshrined in the Constitution, but it would be improvident of the Court to take upon itself the responsibility for controlling the means by which those needs and interests ought be considered and recognized.

A grave example of the Court's hubris in extending the First Amendment is the Court-created right to spend money to influence the result of elections. While many of us are willing to supply small sums of money to support a political cause, the "common understanding of men" is that large political contributions are generally made in expectation of a *quid pro quo* from the recipient. There have been rare occasions when wealthy persons acting in what they perceived to be a public spirit have financed an expensive campaign because they believed in a cause. Sometimes, no doubt, what is sought by a large contributor from a favored candidate is congruent with the public interest. But there is no reason to expect this to be so; many campaign contributions, we cannot know how many, are repaid out of public stock in the form of special consideration in lawmaking or enforcement.

We can be grateful that such a relative few of our officials are known to accept bribes, but large campaign contributions resemble that evil. For example, it is the frequent practice of many firms and persons of means to contribute substantial sums to rival candidates so that whichever candidate wins, the donor wins. On the face of it, such contributors are expressing no idea and favoring no policy other than preferential treatment for themselves. Perhaps the clearest example of the evil is the federal subsidy to sugar growers, which serves no imaginable public purpose, but lines the pockets of a few families who subsidize the political campaigns of many, many legislators on both sides of any aisle.[35] Other generous patrons of political campaigns include gambling casinos, tobacco companies, highway contractors, and real estate developers, none of whom can be suspected of spending to promote any policy other than self-interest.

The problem of campaign finance was a problem in earlier times, but it did not become acute until the advent of television. The electronic media are capable of providing a *blitzkrieg* of political advertising, but only for a high price paid to the media and to consultants who are expert in the relevant arts. Political advertising on commercial television is much more effective, and much more pernicious, than any other form of campaigning because the disinformation supplied through sonorous and artistic spot advertisements broadcast between innings or between soap opera conversations "melts down" in the minds of viewers, who are prone to forget its unreliable source and attribute it to a reliable one.[36]

The result of such an insidious electronic *blitzkrieg*, or even the possible threat of a *blitzkrieg*, because of its effectiveness, is to impose a similar cost on rival candidates. Indeed, candidates face a prisoner's dilemma compelling them to resort to high-tech, high-cost, negative campaigning. To compete for many public offices, the serious office seeker is therefore compelled to do whatever is necessary to secure a large campaign fund. Money, big money, has truly become the mother's milk of politics.[37]

The problem of campaign finance lies at the center of First Amendment concerns. The Court was not wrong to perceive that any regulation of political campaigning is a constitutionally sensitive matter. On the other hand, the need for constraints on corruption and fraud is equally obvious. One line seems clear to many, perhaps most, citizens: There is a difference between a voluntary expression of an idea owned by the person expressing it and expressions made for hire. The former is entitled to absolute protection, because citizens have duties as well as rights to share their wisdom, or their ignorance, with fellow citizens. Another line that many people might draw is between communication to a volunteer audience and to a captive audience that merely wants to watch a ball game or a soap opera. The former may have an absolute right to hear, whereas the latter may be entitled to some protection from pernicious disinformation that will "melt down" so that its source will be forgotten, with a resulting distortion of citizens' political judgment.

The Republic, as Brandeis so frequently emphasized, requires debate for its very life. But when large sums of money are used to hire others to express, publish, or broadcast ideas that they may or may not share to audiences who do not choose to receive them, more than debate is involved. In such circumstances, the right to free expression ought to be balanced against competing values bearing on the integrity and fairness of democratic elections.

In *Buckley v. Valeo*,[38] the Court distinguished between contributions to candidates' campaign funds and so-called issue advocacy conducted by groups ostensibly to advance political ideas. Experience suggests that this distinction is not administrable. Groups purportedly advancing their ideas by hiring others to express them, particularly if during a contested campaign they identify candidates as favoring or opposing their ideas, create an arms race, placing irresistible pressure on their opponents to raise equivalent sums in self-defense. The corrupting effect of this so-called soft money is not less than that of hard money contributed directly to a candidate.

An additional consideration in the regulation of campaign finance is the diversion of energy of incumbent public officials to fundraising activities. It may be that the average congressperson or legislator now spends half of his or her time on that mission; to that extent, there is a misappropriation of the salary and expenses paid by the Republic in exchange for his or her full-time service.[39]

Moreover, there is a dissonance with the Equal Protection Clause, the even more venerable Jacksonian doctrine of Equal Rights, and the premise of the "one man, one vote" doctrine, in allowing wealthy citizens to outspend and thus overbear their less resourceful co-citizens. The Constitution, as Cooley warned, may come reasonably to be regarded "by considerable classes as an instrument whose office is to protect the rich in the advantages they have secured over the poor, and one that should be hated for that reason."[40]

These, too, are complex considerations eminently suited to resolution by compromise through a democratic process. There is no need for national uniformity. There is no professional expertise making one person's judgment better than another about where the lines ought be drawn. Nevertheless, the Court imposed its view of "Truth" to invalidate a city ordinance limiting contributions to groups advocating approval or disapproval of referenda.[41] Issue advocacy by electronic *blitzkrieg* therefore appears to be invulnerable to regulation, even at the state or local levels.

The problem of campaign finance is most acute with respect to judicial elections. In such elections, voter interest is low, political content is limited, and the appearance, if not the risk, of quasi-bribery to secure preferred treatment is especially great. Nevertheless, since the 1980s, multi-million dollar campaign funds are required to secure election to some states' highest courts.[42] Citizens are not wrong to doubt the independence of the judiciary in such circumstances. The practice is a fulfillment of the cynical view expressed in public choice theory that elected judges are virtually indistinguishable from legislators in their vote-maximizing behavior.[43]

Indeed, a reasonable citizen might well wonder: If people have the right to use money to buy influence with a legislature, why should they not be equally entitled to buy a court, or even the Supreme Court? Frederick Grimke noted that all the arguments for life tenure for judges are nearly equally applicable to legislators and executives;[44] if free spending to bribe and intimidate the latter officers is protected, it is reasonable to contend for the free exercise of those rights to influence the work of the judicial branch. Perhaps even Supreme Court justices should be elected in high-cost, high-tech campaigns in which big spenders can secure consideration of their interests.

The problem of campaign finance is further compounded by what the Court has done with the law of defamation.[45] In *New York Times v. Sullivan*,[46] it embraced a position earlier taken by Cooley,[47] holding that a public official must prove malice to recover for alleged defamation uttered in public debate. That holding, as applied to political campaigns, took no account of our vast postmodern abilities to publish derogatory material requiring a victimized candidate promptly to refute it or the large sums required for effective refutation, funds that can often be acquired only by inappropriate sacrifice of the candidate's integrity as a public officer. Meanwhile, *Sullivan* establishes another parameter within which states are confined in their efforts to secure the public's right to make informed selections of its representatives.

In 1997, some states enacted new legislative schemes, some of them involving public finance of some campaigns.[48] In 1998, voters in two more states adopted that principle by referendum.[49] Perhaps public funding can be used as leverage to secure compliance with acceptable campaign laws. Yet it remains unclear what, if anything, a state can do to protect its elected officers, even elected judges, from the corrupting burden of disinformative, high-tech, high-cost campaigns.[50]

With government disabled from sheltering informative and constructive political discourse, the Court has contributed to a degradation of our politics that is now itself sometimes invoked as the justification for resort to constitutional adjudication as a preferred method of resolving contentious public issues. The Court having corrupted legislation, the argument goes, there is no choice but to leave our political decisions to it.

Alas, the heroics of the Court with respect to the First Amendment have in no sense failed. Although enthusiastically approved by the media who profit by them and heralded by many academics and libertarians,[51] the Court's decisions have not only seriously overstepped its legitimate role, they have made the revered First Amendment an instrument of oppression. Many of the issues evoking the strongest political passions have been seemingly forever resolved by the Court, leaving citizens with nothing to say about them.

All of the substantive policies the Court has imposed on the people are reasonable, perhaps even desirable policies. But such policies are the stuff of democratic politics. Quite possibly, individuals ought to be free not only to dance naked, burn flags and crosses, or supply pornography to the public library, but also to spend millions to influence elections by "issues advocacy" that incidentally defames public officials. A state or community choosing to confer such rights on individuals is indeed a free society.

That cannot be said when the choice to confer the rights is made by life-tenured judges, because the issues resolved are precisely the issues that free societies should contest and debate. They should retain the right to modify the decisions they make in accordance with the changing preferences of the electorate. With respect to all these matters, there is no basis for presuming the wisdom of the Court, or of pundits of the media, or other members of the "national class." As Cooley, Brandeis, Freund, and Hand would have urged, the Court should have exercised more self-restraint.

21

The Contagion of
Judicial Heroism

The Supreme Court of the United States was not, in its new heroic age, the only judicial usurper of the political prerogatives of state and local governments. The highest state courts sometimes attempted political feats no less grand. Some courts appeared to be competing for recognition as a junior Warren Court, as they had been encouraged to do by Justice Brennan.[1] It came to be the ambition of some state court judges, as well as federal judges, to be the author of "impact decisions," that is, those that would attract favorable notice of the media. Their initiatives were diverse,[2] but one apt account was that many states' courts opened "a forum-shopping opportunity for liberals."[3]

The heavy involvement of state supreme courts in the making of state policy was scarcely new.[4] As early as the eighteenth century, several courts were deeply embroiled in matters calling attention to the political nature of their work. To secure the independence of courts from governors and legislatures, Jacksonians had required many judges, like Cooley, to stand for election. In the early years of the twentieth century, a wave of Progressive reform had sought to re-establish the "independence" of the state judiciaries from excessive popular control by diverse reforms. Among the reforms adopted was "merit selection," a scheme authorizing a credentialed panel to screen judicial nominees. Such a scheme was adopted for the California Supreme Court in 1934.

These successive waves of reform transformed the diverse constitutions of the states, so that the doctrine of separation of powers often took on a form different from that established in the federal Constitution. High-court judges are selected in diverse ways; they enforce constitutions that are in some cases much more elaborate in their details than the federal Constitution and that sometimes explicitly confer powers on them that the Supreme Court of the United States does not possess. For example, the highest courts in several states have a constitutional power to enact procedural rules for use in inferior courts,[5] a power conferred on the Supreme Court of the United States only in limited form and only by delegation from Congress.[6] Some state courts have gone so far as to hold that procedural matters are beyond the ken of legislatures and are their own exclusive responsibility.[7] And courts in many states have successfully invoked their power to compel legislatures to provide funds needed for their operation, a power never claimed by the federal courts.[8]

It is also the case that state constitutions are more easily amended to correct high-court errors.[9] Easy amendment diminishes the risk of grave consequences resulting from failures of judicial self-restraint. The issue of independence or political accountability is therefore a somewhat different issue in each state and different for any state court than for the federal judiciary.[10] Interpretative practices may reasonably differ in these various environments.[11] That being so, generalizations about the prudence of particular political decisions of state courts are especially hazardous. Certainly, state courts have duties to enforce their states' constitutions as they are written[12] and not as an echo of the Supreme Court of the United States and the Constitution it enforces.

Nevertheless, the heavy political involvement of the Supreme Court of California was extraordinary and reflected the professional leadership of the Warren Court.[13] Under the leadership of Chief Justice Donald Wright, that court frequently invoked ephemeral constitutional language to decide troublesome political issues. One member of the court boasted that he and his colleagues were using the Equal Protection Clause of the Fourteenth Amendment to remake California as an egalitarian society.[14] It was seemingly of no matter whether the people favored the new social order being created by him. The number and dimensions of the court's reforms of California law left little room for doubt that it had, for a time, overtaken the state legislature as the place where state policy was most likely to be made. It had thus also displaced the right of the people through elected representatives to decide for themselves what sort of place California ought to be.

Some of the reforms achieved by that court were humane, but many were of doubtful prudence. And by casting itself as a primary player in the political process, the court called into question its fitness impartially to decide legal controversies having significant political aspects of general interest to citizens.

Among the California court's endeavors in its heroic era was a reorganization of the state's public school finance system, which the court found to be inequitable and therefore unconstitutional.[15] The state was ordered to bring the system into compliance with the court's decree. The legislature did so reluctantly. The resulting increase in school taxes evoked a taxpayer revolt. A referendum expressing the taxpayers' dissatisfaction cut deeply into the sinew of the state's previously abundant public fisc,[16] a blow from which public education and other institutions in California have not recovered. The court meanwhile ordered the state to pay fees of $800,000 to the prevailing counsel in the school finance case,[17] an order that the legislature defiantly refused to obey for many years, thus challenging the legitimacy of the decision and the efficacy of judicial power.

Numerous state supreme courts followed the California court's lead in undertaking to reorganize the school finance systems of their states.[18] The New Jersey court was the first to do so,[19] going beyond the California court in the means deployed to enforce its policy when the legislature was unable to agree on a suitable financial scheme.[20] Other state supreme courts followed.[21]

Few persons knowledgeable about public education would deny that local finance of public schools is problematic:[22] Differentials in tax bases of local districts are reflected in the financial resources available to schools, thus resulting in sometimes severe inequalities in the educational services provided. However, state courts undertaking to solve this problem by stringent equalization decrees ignored strong evidence that (1) there is a meager correlation between the social and economic status of the families of schoolchildren and the abundance of the tax base of their local schools and (2) there is little connection between the size of public school budgets and the educational outcomes they produce.[23] Moreover, local taxation is linked closely to local control of the public schools, a tradition reflecting the reality that schools are an extension of, as well as a surrogate for, the family. The best schools tend to be those in which parents take the most interest. In state after state, when the issue has been put to voters, they have voted for local control and against statewide equalization; that preference has been shared by voters in school districts having scant financial resources, who (perhaps wisely) seem generally to prefer local control to additional revenue that must come with the attached string of greater involvement of state bureaucracy.[24] It appears that the chief advocates for state finance and control are the teachers' unions, not parent-teacher organizations or community groups.

At a time when public faith in the institutions of public education seems to be declining despite relatively high expenditures and millions of the most concerned parents are keeping their children home or electing to pay private school tuition, centralization of public schools may be precisely the policy that is not needed.[25] Whatever may be the most prudent method of financing locally controlled schools, the issue is one best resolved by state legislatures that are in touch with the desires of the local electorates who care most about their schools and are equipped to compromise the conflicting values and correct their mistakes.[26]

This is not to say that no state court was justified in taking notice of the inequities of school finance. But a court led by Cooley or Brandeis would have avoided proclaiming large constitutional doctrines and would have limited the impact of any remedy it might have provided to those school districts in genuine need as a result of their lack of tax base, leaving it insofar as possible for the state legislature to accommodate those real needs.[27] What such a minimal remedy might be would depend on the configurations of state law within which it would be fashioned.

Public school finance is but one example of the misguided heroics of the California Supreme Court. In 1972, it made another large splash in the state's politics by holding that capital punishment violated the "cruel and unusual punishment" provision of the state constitution.[28] In part, this holding was animated by concern for a situation that had accumulated over a period of many years. There were over 150 persons on California's death row awaiting execution; the court's decision thus prevented an unseemly slaughter of prisoners. It was, however, promptly reversed by a popular initiative amending the state constitution.[29] Despite this rebuke, the court continued to prevent executions for reasons unpersuasive to those who had supported the amendment. Chief Justice Rose Bird, the successor to Wright, was later forthright in expressing her unwillingness to affirm any sentence of death.[30]

In 1975, the California court fearlessly and imprudently took on yet another political issue arousing strong passions. It did so by reinstating an order of a California trial judge ordering the Los Angeles schools to initiate a desegregation plan.[31] The judge who had issued the order had already been resoundingly defeated at the polls, one of the few California superior court judges ever to fail of re-election.[32] There had been no evidence presented in the case of *de jure* segregation by the Los Angeles school board. It was unlikely, on the facts presented at trial, that any federal court enforcing the federal Constitution would have made the decision that had been made by the defeated state judge. An organization known as Bustop had mounted stout political resistance and secured a reversal in the intermediate court of the trial judge's decree, only to have it reinstated by the Wright court.[33]

The court in the 1970s also stretched the California law of torts to facilitate the compensation of previously non-compensable harms.[34] All forms of liability insurance became notably more expensive and a wag waspishly described the court as having adopted the "doctrine of proximate solvency," that is, that the nearest supply of money should be tapped to compensate whatever harms any citizen might experience.

In addition, the California court held unconstitutional a standard clause in most of the mortgages on residential real estate; the offending clause required that loans be repaid on sale of the residence and thus required home buyers to negotiate new mortgages at interest rates current at the time of resale. As a result of the court's decision, most purchasers of California homes could assume existing mortgages with lower interest rates, rather than acquire new mortgages that would in the prevailing market bear much higher rates.[35] This decision conferred a windfall on some home buyers, but their windfall came at the expense of mortgage lenders throughout the state and resulted in a general elevation of long-term interest rates because lenders could no longer expect an opportunity to recalculate interest in light of current economic prospects.

In all these endeavors, the California court attempted to bring reality into accord with the moral and political values of a majority of its members.[36] Principles not widely shared by the people of the state were forcibly read into the state's constitution. The court was enormously overconfident both of its wisdom and of its ability to modify the beliefs and conduct of the people. The court failed, as other courts often have, to recognize the reality that few people change their morals or their politics, or often even their behavior, on the instruction of senior citizens in judicial robes.

A secondary result of these activities was to alter the political environment in which the court worked. One assessment was that:

> In the fifties and beyond, controversial judicial decisions had been defended by a broad spectrum of politicians on the ground that what the courts ordered was the law and deserved support even if the substance of a decision were distasteful. As time went on, however, political leaders tended to defend particular decisions only if they agreed with the result. As a consequence, the California court became identified with the liberal side of the political spectrum, and attacking the court became easier for the extreme right as moderates tended to withdraw from the debate.[37]

Accordingly, the California court was undone in 1986 when three of its members were voted out of office in retention elections.[38] The campaign against the sitting judges was financed by thousands of small contributions by individuals opposed to their retention. The efforts of the bar and the media to protect the independence of the court were vigorous, but doomed to fail.

Other state courts have undergone similar turmoil resulting from bold judicial decisions. As the California experience indicates, courts making politically unwelcome "impact" decisions invite political reactions threatening to their independence. When those decisions can be explained as forthright enforcement of legal texts, a strong and effective defense against political intimidation can be maintained by the profession. When, however, such decisions rest on attenuated interpretations of highly indeterminate texts, the charge of political usurpation is perceived to be valid, and the courts are vulnerable to partisan politicization.

Despite this hazard, other state supreme courts have made bold decisions foreclosing consideration by legislatures and local governments of salient political issues. Among these are some constitutionalizing of the law of torts, thereby foreclosing democratic resolution of the issues presented by personal injury litigation. Thus, in 1997, the Supreme Court of Illinois set aside elaborate tort reform legislation that was the product of prolonged political debate and deliberation, holding that caps on general damages are unconstitutionally discriminatory against those suffering the most.[39]

Other courts have discovered previously unrecognized welfare rights in state constitutions.[40] The Supreme Court of Alaska daringly affirmed the right under the Alaska Constitution to possess and use marijuana in one's home,[41] while the Supreme Court of Hawaii suggested that it might recognize and enforce same-sex marriages.[42] Such bold decisions tend to beget bold reactions. In 1998, Alaska and Hawaii amended their constitutions to provide that a union of persons of the same sex is not a marriage.[43] Meanwhile, the Hawaiian legislature created a status of "reciprocal beneficiaries" for partners in same-sex unions,[44] a solution that would have strongly appealed to Ernst Freund as an admirable second-best for both sides of the controversy, but one beyond the competence of a court to craft.

Also worthy of note is the example of the New Jersey Supreme Court's correction of the abuse of exclusionary zoning. While the Supreme Court of the United States has on occasion invalidated zoning laws as applied to a particular land use,[45] it has prudently stayed its hand from broad rulings requiring a federal court to assume responsibility for controlling land uses. The New Jersey legislature, however, had ignored the caution expressed by Ernst Freund and had unwisely conferred zoning power on boards created by small communities. Some of these were populated only by prosperous homeowners who were apparently supportive of zoning laws having the effect of excluding the poor from their communities. Invoking the "general welfare" clause of the state constitution, the New Jersey court invalidated some of these zoning actions and created an elaborate mechanism of private enforcement to compel boards to accommodate diverse housing.[46]

Although it seems likely that most citizens of New Jersey would have at least some sympathy for the court's political aim, even if motivated only by a selfish interest in not having the poor forced into their own neighborhoods, the court's scheme evoked vigorous opposition. While there was abundant litigation seeking to enforce the court's contrived system, little change in housing patterns resulted. In due course, the court's mandate was displaced by a New Jersey Fair Housing Act that seems to receive somewhat greater acceptance.

Whether the court's coercive role was beneficial or not is a matter remaining in dispute. Two members of the court responsible for the decision encountered serious resistance in a retention election, and even very sympathetic observers have been critical. Charles Haar, a vigorous critic of exclusionary zoning, limited his criticism to the court's effort at public relations.[47] But it is by no means clear what the court could have done, consistent with its role, to promote better public understanding of its decision. Perhaps a better opinion of the court might have been written, but would judicial press conferences help? John Payne found the court's holding to be too complex, too arbitrary, and too counterintuitive to be comprehensible to the public.[48] Payne suggests that the court might better have dealt with the problem by remanding the issue to the legislature, much as Cooley, as we have seen, did on several occasions. This could have been achieved by disapproving legislative delegation of the zoning power to small, homogeneous communities, thereby requiring those desiring exclusionary zones to return to the legislature for new authority. The legislature would then be called upon to reconsider the appropriate dimensions of local governments so empowered.

Such recent experiences of high state courts tend again to confirm Cooley's 1886 dictum at Harvard that law not expressing the common thoughts of men is feeble. Such law can also be mischievous, especially in its more remote consequences, as Freund emphasized. When courts, state as well as federal, sound common thoughts, they play a useful role in reinforcing the moral stature of democratic law. When they ignore the ancient wisdom of Thucydides and try to exhibit their political genius to solve problems seemingly neglected or mistreated by the legislators elected to solve them, they are likely to lack sufficient support to achieve their aims.

Moreover, extravagant judicial decisions undermine the process of democratic legislation. It is a serious matter when judicial institutions have become the place to go with political concerns, leaving legislatures and city councils as gatherings of inconsequential folk. Not only is the independence and disinterest of the courts called into question, but political energy and interest is directed to seek partisan control of the judiciary.

The nature of the harms resulting from misplaced judicial involvement was illustrated in 1998 by the settlement of claims brought by state and local governments against cigarette companies to recover the public costs of health care incurred as a result of smoking. The merit of the states' claims was, to say the least, dubious. All states had long taxed the sale of cigarettes and many a highway had been paved with the proceeds. A justification for such taxation had been that cigarettes are harmful to health, a fact well known for centuries. At any time, any state could have raised its tax and spent the proceeds on public health initiatives, including renewed efforts to discourage teen-aged smoking.

In lieu of such forthright policymaking, bogus cases were filed in state courts by states' attorneys general and then settled for billions of dollars to be paid over a period of twenty-five years, in substance as an additional tax on the product. The settlement was celebrated with much fanfare and public beating of breasts by the attorneys general.

It seems apparent, however, that the transaction was chiefly an effort of tobacco companies to resolve a mounting political and legal crisis by co-opting the attorneys general and some members of the private bar known for their representation of personal injury plaintiffs, who have been re-

warded for their participation with mind-boggling fees paid by tobacco
companies. The settlement is a smoke-and-mirror device to circumnavigate
state legislatures, the institutions designed to consider such matters, and for
which the electorate has full responsibility, and to impose political responsibility on the courts.

Although many involved with public health have mounted an ambitious
effort to eliminate the use of tobacco (much as we have previously eliminated the use of alcohol, marijuana, and cocaine?), it is not clear that they
have the support of the electorate or of state legislatures. Two gubernatorial candidates supporting their initiative were defeated in 1998 elections in
Massachusetts and Minnesota. A troublesome feature of this initiative is
that it conflicts with the spirit of individual responsibility suffusing many of
the judicial heroics recounted in the previous two chapters. Cigarette smok-
ers are the group having the most direct interest in the issue, and although
abashed, they possess political influence sufficient to prevent the election of
a gubernatorial candidate hostile to their interests.

Because the result of the initiative was apparent settlement of a noisome
issue, one is inclined to cheer. Yet concern for the effect on the integrity of
the courts is warranted. It has been made to appear that the state courts
have, in effect, imposed a substantial tax on the sale of a pack of cigarettes.
That appearance is not only misleading, it also reinforces the impression
that litigation is the primary instrument of politics. The responsibility is vis-
ited upon the courts for an issue lying clearly within the purview of state
legislatures. At the very least, it tends to disqualify courts required to decide
other matters involving claims arising from the sale of tobacco products.

Just as tobacco settled, the cities of New Orleans and Chicago have sued
the makers and sellers of guns for the cost of treating gunshots. To many,
this seems a stronger case even than that against the tobacco companies.
But there can be little doubt that the political ramifications are enormous
and almost certainly beyond the capacity of any state's judicial system to
manage. Using the courts to circumnavigate the influence of gun lobbies is a
recipe for political disaster. As the editors of *The Economist* have remarked, "[I]f America is ever to get its priorities right on tobacco, guns, or
any other issue, it will do so only in the debating chamber of democratically elected legislatures, not through threats of mass litigation."[49]

22

Academic Law and
Judicial Heroics

The new age of judicial heroics tracked the advent of the legal academy. It is tempting to believe the connection to be causal. Felix Frankfurter once declared that "[i]n the last analysis, the law is what the lawyers are. And the law and lawyers are what the law schools make them."[1] His was a cheerful conceit; the law schools did not make themselves, but were made by lawyers and university administrators in response to diverse social forces bearing on the profession.[2]

The underlying causes producing the twentieth-century American legal academy are numerous and not readily sorted, but it seems likely that the development was caused most forcefully as a tertiary effect of industrialization creating Americans' appetite for technical competence certified by academic credentials. That appetite brought on the nationwide boom in higher education, forcing change in the legal profession.

Holmes in his *Path of the Law* correctly foresaw the advent of academic law.[3] It emerged as a distinct subprofession apart from the judiciary and the practicing bar no later than the time of the founding of the Association of American Law Schools in 1900.[4] The earliest sign was the appointment of James Barr Ames in 1872 to a full-time position at Harvard almost immediately upon graduation. He rose to the deanship without devoting a day of his professional life to a non-academic pursuit.[5] By 1900, the number of full-time law teachers was substantial, and some, like Ames, lacked sustained contact with what President Eliot dubbed derisively as "the real world."[6]

Since that time, the legal academy has been drifting into the academic profession and away from the legal profession, amidst growing anxiety about its mission.[7] Academicians have tended to substitute Holmes's indifference to the "real world," typical of life in the cloister, for the commitment to the Republic that antebellum law teachers aimed to nurture. A reason for this substitution is that the academic profession in America has at least since 1950 outranked the legal profession in social status; to those preoccupied with affect, the doctorate in philosophy in any discipline is a more luminous achievement than a mere law degree and license.[8]

Academization has brought significant benefits to the law.[9] Holmes elegantly stated the aim of academic law in almost Cartesian terms to be

> to follow the existing body of dogma into its highest generalizations by the help of jurisprudence; next, to discovery from history the ends which the several rules seek to accomplish, the reasons why those ends are desired, what is given up to gain them, and whether they are worth the price.[10]

Such pursuits were not new, but were exemplified by earlier American legal writers, especially by Francis Lieber, who was himself not a licensed lawyer, but held a German doctorate, and by the juriconsults in the baths of Rome. Yet the institutionalization of those academized aims in the emerging legal academy helped to break down the empty formalism that Langdell and some of his adherents sought to establish in the late nineteenth century as a scientific legal method.[11] Academization facilitated and encouraged the use of genuinely scientific methods to examine the factual premises of laws and proposed laws. At least in theory, it provided a bridge between other academic disciplines and the realities of public life that are the stuff of the lawyer's discipline. And it gave job security to a substantial number of ministers without portfolio having the time and responsibility to serve as critics to those employed to attend to the Republic's affairs.

On the other hand, academization threatens the very benefits it confers by reducing the prospect that studious authors will be taken seriously by those bearing public responsibility. If Holmes's lightning of genius should strike a law professor today, it is unlikely that "the real world" would notice. The reasons for this are enumerated below.

First, academic lawyers achieve status within their profession less by performing useful service to the Republic than by meeting conventional academic standards requiring the utterance of novel ideas pitched to a high level of abstraction. "The remoter and more general aspects of the law are those which give it universal interest," Holmes said. In pursuing what seem to be issues of universal dimension, academicians tend to forego study of those lesser ones that they might be able to solve and on which public officers are likely to accept their counsel.[12]

The tendency to engage in cosmology, or what Linda Mullenix has denoted as "metarealism,"[13] is likely reinforced by the increase in the number of law teachers holding doctorates in other more esteemed disciplines. Ironically, metarealism, even in the extreme form of nihilism denying the integrity of legal texts, is in post-modern diction often denoted as "pragmatism."[14] Yet, as Charles Collier noted,[15] there is very little legal scholarship today resembling three prosaic articles appearing together in an early issue of the *Harvard Law Review*: Brandeis and Warren, "The Law of Ponds"; Beale, "Tickets"; or Williston, "Successive Promises of the Same Performance." Instead, legal scholars are prone to exhibit their mastery of almost any other discipline than law.[16]

Second, most large legal ideas were entertained in the time of Justinian, if not even in the time of Hammurabi. There are no new continents of law to explore. Academic lawyers are in this respect in an unfortunate position not unlike that of gross anatomists, who have no hope of discovering a new organ in the human body and are therefore scorned by their medical research colleagues who have large mysteries to pierce and whose literature may achieve seeming miracles. This appears to be the realization expressed by Holmes when he quit academic life for the bench.

Third, as Cooley remarked at Harvard, and as Cicero and Thucydides had previously observed, sound, useful legal ideas are generally conventional ones. So even Holmes conceded that law must respect "the habits of a particular people at a particular time."[17] "The life of the law is not logic, but experience," he said in his most famous utterance. Good law expresses the culture of which it is a part and is therefore confined by the moral premises of that culture. Ernst Freund made the point that:

> It is not possible to work a [legal] system successfully if its fundamental justification is constantly questioned; or putting it the other way, a great system that has established itself will convert its disciples from skeptics into votaries, or will quickly get rid of them. Law, like other human institutions, is a working compromise, and the very fact that it is an appeal to reason demands assumptions that must not be too closely questioned. [18]

This reality is odious to academicians of pure heart who regard it as their duty and their privilege to question all the premises of the social order. In this respect, there is a fundamental, but seldom noted, conflict of interest in academic law.

Fourth, cloistered scholars are physically isolated from the universe in which real decisions are made. Sound moral judgment on public issues is an attribute not easily acquired within the academic cloister. To be useful advisers and critics to those exercising public responsibility, legal scholars would need to involve themselves in active politics to a degree that few do. Thus, in 1896 Woodrow Wilson, then president of Princeton University, deplored the tendency of professional academics to treat texts as "material" and "not life"; they do not, he said, reflect, so much as "they set forth schemes, [and] expound with dispassionate method." "Their minds," he perceived, "are not stages, but museums; nothing is done there, but very curious and valuable collections are kept there."[19] This may be especially so for those who follow Langdell in the belief he expressed that evening in 1886 that all that is worth knowing about law is in books.

Fifth, for reasons implicit in the foregoing observations, the academic enterprise encourages utopian dogmatization. It does not reward the practice of moral compromise, which, as Freund so insistently observed, is the objective of democratic politics and law. The complex constitutional structure of the Republic was designed precisely to prevent the political implementation of dogma, to compel compromise.[20] Utopian legal critics who disapprove of compromise are out of tune with the realities of democratic government. Utopianism in the academy has been reinforced by the tendency of the heroic judiciary to perform the role of Cardinals willing to issue decrees to effect all manner of benign results. Dogmatism can take forms so extreme as to undercut the intellectual and political foundation of academic freedom, an institution that assumes that Truth has not yet been discovered.[21]

Sixth, public decisions, especially those made by judges, are reactive to immediacies. De Tocqueville observed in this context, "[t]he world is not led by long or learned demonstrations: a rapid glance at particular incidents, the daily study of the fleeting passions of the multitude, the accidents of time, and the art of turning them to account, decide all its affairs."[22] On that account, even judges and lawyers sympathetic to positions taken by academics infrequently have time or energy to consult academic literature with the care required by turgid academic prose.

Seventh, academic authors are often disinclined to accept the modest role embraced by Cooley and Freund as mere secondary authorities. With due respect to such excellent works as those of Charles Alan Wright[23] and Lawrence Tribe,[24] there is no work done in this century on a subject so laden with political implications that is the equal of *Constitutional Limitations* in commanding the trust of its users as an accurate account of the law. To write such work, authors must eschew novel thoughts and to that extent disavow not only academic status seeking[25] but the more immediate satisfactions of self-expression. As close as contemporary academic work can come to that standard are the Restatements of the Law prepared under the auspices of the American Law Institute; those works have no individual authors and are for the most part devoted to less intensely political fields.

Eighth, work on intellectual frontiers of the sort implicitly suggested by Holmes often employs the professional jargon of another academic discipline,[26] a jargon likely to impede, if it does not prevent, comprehension by judges and practicing lawyers who might otherwise presume to read it. While it is true that legal academics tend to seek normative applications of interdisciplinary insights, this can distort those insights and often results in a frustrating disconnection.[27] As Francis Allen observed some years ago, the university law school is increasingly a colonial outpost of the graduate school.[28] A self-respecting law school serving the "national class" would be ashamed not to have on its faculty a broad sampling of scholars whose interests in law is incidental to a primary intellectual interest in another more academically respectable field, an interest certified by a doctorate in that field. Their work is often difficult to communicate effectively to persons outside the pertinent intellectual community.

Ninth, academic status is seldom acquired by work on the law and politics of local institutions. For the most respected academic lawyers, only the federal government or the international order is worthy of study. Work of the sort done by Freund with state and local governments is out of fashion because it does not command the attention and admiration of the "national class."[29]

These enumerated circumstances have an aspect of self-fulfilling prophecy. Teachers and writers who do not expect a hearing from those in power tend not to invest themselves in the effort to address the nonexistent audience in ways that would be helpful to it. As a consequence, as Harry Edwards[30] and Mary Ann Glendon[31] have observed, much that now passes for scholarship by law professors is not written with an expectation that it might be read and used by those having public responsibility, with whom academic authors find little or no common ground. It is often discourse addressed to small audiences of specialized academic readers having little involvement in the immediate cares of the world.[32] Academic lawyers therefore frequently achieve the fate of being ignored by those whom they ignore.[33]

Indeed, it may be questioned whether many legal academics are still lawyers or instead have become political philosophers. As such, they may be subject to the complaint made against some of the most eminent members of that esteemed discipline by Benjamin Barber:

> [T]hey have served the ideal of the enlightenment better than they have informed our political judgment. In substituting reason for common sense, they have declared the sense of commoners to be nonsense. Rights are philosophically vindicated, but only as abstractions that undermine democratic communities that breathe life into rights; justice is given an unimpeachable credential in epistemology, but no firm hold on action or on the deliberative process from which political action stems; talk is revivified as the heart of the political process and then recommended to citizens, but in a form that answers to constraints not of citizenship but of philosophy; civility is celebrated, but construed as incompatible with the sorts of collective human choice and communal purposes that give civility its political meaning; the past is resurrected, but only in order to disdain the present and mock the future.[34]

While many legal philosophers do, as Barber asserts, disdain the present and mock the future, most, like justices, are prone to suppose that their views are more consequential than in reality they are.[35] They are disinclined to accept the reality that most audiences are no more influenced by moral reasoning than by what passes as legal reasoning. Richard Posner has observed the self-preoccupied aspect of work in moral philosophy:

> Moral philosophers pick from an ala carte menu the moral principles that coincide with the preferences of their social set, and they have both the intellectual agility to weave an inconsistent heap of policies into a superficially coherent unity and the psychological agility to honor their chosen principles only to the extent compatible with their personal happiness and professional advancement.[36]

Of course there are popular prophets who articulate a moral precept whose time has come, but whether the time for that precept has come is heavily dependent on the experience of those to whom it is addressed. As Lieber put it, "millions have died for similes . . . [but] politics are matters of realities not suppositions."[37] And many are the prophets of great eloquence and intellect who have been unable to find a receptive audience.

A lively effort to confirm a larger consequence for moral theory is the recent work of Amy Gutmann and Dennis Thompson, who strove to summon conflicting and passionately held political views to the mediative authority of academic theory.[38] As Judge Posner suggests,[39] the result of the effort seems to be largely rhetorical flourish: "No one is going to surrender his moral intuitions to moral theory, nor should he."[40] The discipline of Gutmann and Thompson may suffice to resolve such matters as the legitimacy of laws against infanticide or domestic violence, but it is seldom if ever helpful in deciding hard cases. As Cooley so forcefully stated that evening in Cambridge, morality, although an unmistakably different form of social control, undergirds sound law and causes it to be obeyed. Therefore, it is the morality of the people who do the obeying that matters, not the morality of their theorists.

Holmes usefully cautioned us against relying too heavily on the moral language of the law, because it is chiefly an appeal to obedience[41] and not an invitation to remake legal texts on the basis of more elevated moral reasoning. Changes in the moral language of the law will seldom if ever induce substantial changes in behavior or belief.

Despite these enumerated disabilities, it remains a widely shared impulse of legal academics to discover, like astronomers, a new source of natural law, a new constellation of individual rights, to be invoked by life-tenured judges to decree the transformation of a gravely defective social order formed by an ignorant *lumpenproletariat*. An eminent example is Robin West, who finds in the inexhaustible text of the Fourteenth Amendment "antisubordinationist" rights to be imposed as restrictions on democratic government.[42] An overstated but pertinent criticism of her efforts is that

Many of the new progressive strategies—especially the suppression of free speech and the insistence that a radical vision is superior to that which the populace has developed over the years—are based on a profoundly antidemocratic mistrust of the people's choices. . . . [West] is ultimately an authoritarian in the deepest sense of the word, adopting traditional conservative tools to impose her outdated personal views on a public that has already soundly rejected them.[43]

There is, as one might expect, and as West exemplifies, a correlation between the moral theorizing of legal academics and the dogma of "liberal" political correctness,[44] because academic theory consistently favors, as Duncan Kennedy has listed:

Brown without delay and racial quotas, but civil disobedience, nonprosecution of draft card burners, the explicit consideration of distributive consequences rather than reliance on efficiency, judicial review of apportionment decisions, extensive constitutional protection of criminals' rights, the constitutional protection of the right of homosexuals to engage in legislatively prohibited practices, the right to produce and consume pornography, and abortion rights.[45]

As Judge Posner has observed, there is often unresolved tension in this conventionality:

[They] favor abortion . . . [but t]hey are against capital punishment. . . . They are for the theory of evolution when the question is whether creationism should be taught but against the theory of evolution when the question is whether there is a biological basis for differences in behavior between men and women. They want to regulate cigarette smoking out of existence, but they want to permit the smoking of marijuana. They are for the strongest possible public measures for safety and health, but they are against quarantining persons who are infected by the AIDS virus.[46] . . . They denounce their predecessors for indifference to the fate of the Jews in Nazi Germany or the blacks in South Africa during apartheid [but] have been for the most part indifferent to the genocides in Cambodia, Bosnia and Africa.[47]

West and others of like mind are thinking and writing about law. That is not visibly the case for some contemporary legal academics who, apparently despairing of their lack of influence on those who exercise political power, have withdrawn into a self-obsessive genre of literature celebrated as legal storytelling.[48] Arthur Austin denotes them as Outsiders, against whom the "Empire Strikes Back."[49] While such art forms as legal storytelling may indeed be as irrelevant to law[50] as Andy Warhol's Campbell Soup cans are to artistic mastery, the Outsiders, like Andy Warhol, may be on to something. As a comment on the social utility of some of what passes for advanced legal scholarship, the Outsiders may have it about right.

On the other hand, one might wish to divert some of the energy of Outsiders to the vast and neglected opportunities to bring their humanity and intellect to the conduct of the more obscure public officers who run our cities, counties, school districts, and states, where modest gains in the pursuit of justice might be achieved, albeit without reward in the coin of academic status. Ernst Freund provided the model. The career of Catherine MacKinnon, an Outsider in many ways but the premier exponent of sexual harassment law,[51] provides another. MacKinnon has deigned to seek to influence more city councils. For another example, Erwin Chemerinsky has helped draft a city charter for Los Angeles.[52]

These disjunctions between academic thought about law and the work of courts or legislatures suggest that the legal academy bears little responsibility for the overbearing tendencies of the judiciary remarked in the previous chapters. What we may see are parallel, not sequential, developments within the legal profession. On the other hand, Frankfurter may have been accurate in describing the Supreme Court in its moments of hubris as seekers of the approval of the intellectual avant-garde.

While there were many academic critics of the Warren Court's tendency to overreach its commission, their number diminished as those who remembered the 1930s were replaced by those who were attracted to law by their youthful hope to participate in broad social reform through constitutional litigation in federal courts.[53] Those academicians who speculate as wishful Platonic Guardians are disposed to prefer that the Republic's judges sit on a woolsack of discretion such as that of the feudal Court of Chancery and to applaud those who presume to do justice according to a king's conscience or natural law that is at best the presumed wisdom of a ruling class.

For this reason, a vast amount of academic energy has been invested in the task of reconciling the constitutional role of the judiciary with democracy.[54] Most of what can be usefully said on that subject was said at the time of ratification. For judges such as Cooley and Brandeis, the task of reconciliation was not especially difficult: Their view was that democratic legislation is valid unless explicitly proscribed by the text of a constitution ratified by the people and subject to modification by them; judicial review in their view is avowedly anti-democratic and should therefore be practiced with restraint assuring the moral and political primacy of legislation. However, the task of reconciliation becomes difficult and worthy of heroic intellectual efforts when thinking proceeds from the contrary premise that restraint should not be practiced and judges should be encouraged to enforce not only the text of constitutions, but also principles of natural law developed by academic discourse in political and moral philosophy.

Thus, an extensive academic literature argues that judicial review should be ever more intensive because of the deficiencies inherent in democratic legislation.[55] Legislatures, it is said, are chiefly known as places in which we express our selfish impulses,[56] an observation it would be difficult to contest. Because venal interest groups influence legislation, it is reasoned, government by decree emanating from the life-tenured elite is theoretically superior to democratic self-government. Others have striven to justify the overbearing conduct of the Supreme Court as a fulfillment of eighteenth-century republican expectations; these arguments tend to rest on the alleged congruence of the substance of the Court's agenda with the politics of some Founders.[57] In essence, it has been suggested, the Court is somehow the real voice of the people, much as the king's chancellor was the real voice of the Crown. Justice Brennan himself apparently deemed his principles to have the sanction of democratic self-government so long as the self-governing citizens accepted them, that is, did not rebel against his decisions.[58] While he acknowledged the law he created and administered to be the product of his generation's "experience and understanding, its passion and reason,"[59] he was apparently untroubled that his passions were the product of his own experience and were not widely shared except among a limited professional class. Theories in this vein have been multiplied by academic authors, but a common theme has been that the Court should be more attentive to the advice of the moral philosophers of the academy and less attentive to "the common thoughts of men."

Despite the enumerated limitations and overconfidence of legal academic theorists, their work has a synergistic effect. Academic theorists do, as Frankfurter observed, provide a receptive, sometimes even a fawning, audience for heroic judges and give less frequent applause to text-bound legal drones.[60] Justice Brennan, for example, could seemingly do no wrong. Even his extraordinary dissent in *Michael H. v. Gerald D.* received uncritical acceptance among theoreticians. Ronald Dworkin,[61] Frank Michelman,[62] and Kathleen Sullivan[63] celebrated it as an exemplary "moral reading" of the Constitution, without expression of serious concern that such a moral reading is a finger in the eye of self-government.

While most theoreticians will on occasion acknowledge that not all morally correct opinions are also law,[64] Judge Posner is not wrong to observe a tendency to conflation.[65] That conflation is the risk feared by Brandeis when he questioned the teaching of philosophy. It tends to be a reason for the occasional attractions of academic moral philosophy to judges and the lawyers who appear before them. They, for the reasons stated by Mill, tend to be attracted to ideas empowering themselves. If the Holmesian lightning bolt of genius is that courts ought to be less constrained and more aggressive in the exercise of their powers, many judges and lawyers will experience a self-inflationary gratification from the message.

A dramatic example of academic theory that may be taken too seriously by judges and lawyers is the discovery by academicians of international human rights law as a category of our national law. Philip Jessup was perhaps the Copernicus of this discovery;[66] Louis Sohn,[67] Louis Henkin,[68] Harold Koh,[69] and Anne-Marie Slaughter[70] its leading observers. These scholars reveal customary international law as yet another form of unenacted natural law to be enforced by life-tenured judges. That law is based on what judges can discern about current international conventions not ratified by the United States, or conceptions of justice in other countries around the world, about which the primary sources of information are the academic authors who urge its enforcement. For example, the South African Constitutional Court in 1995 was induced to decide the constitutionality of capital punishment substantially on the basis of international precedents;[71] this is presented as a model for a global system to be enforced in the United States by the federal judiciary.[72]

In early times, the federal courts were charged to enforce the law of admiralty having its origins in international practice and understanding and the customary law governing the relations between nations, such as the law of diplomatic immunity. In recent years, lower federal courts have in addition asserted jurisdiction to enforce customary international law of other sorts.[73] The American Law Institute has now lent its support[74] to the idea that customary international law, as discerned by the federal judiciary, is federal law, perhaps superseding even prior federal legislation.[75]

While not long ago it was possible to suppose that customary international human rights law was narrowly limited to such matters as genocide and torture, we are now told that the list is not closed and has, due to improved communications around the globe, grown to include gender discrimination, religious rights, rights relating to sexual orientation, and the right to be free from "hate speech."[76]

We are also told by contemporary Langdells that life-tenured judges "find," and do not "make," such customary international law, and we are assured that, also among the rights to be protected, is the right to live in a democratic society.[77] The irony of this last assurance seems to be invisible to those who give it, nor does it dissuade life-tenured federal judges from repairing to Colorado in the summertime to attend seminars on customary international human rights law conducted by experts in that field.[78] Or constrain other efforts to persuade the judiciary that they are members of "a global community"[79] and that an international outlook on moral issues is more appropriate than obedience to the conventionalities of insensitive American Babbitts.[80]

When it was observed that the expansion of customary international law to include unenacted laws regarding "human rights" threatens to effect a vast displacement of state law made by judges and legislators who are accountable to the people they serve,[81] Harold Koh responded by expressing disdain for state and local law, and for the right to self-government. For him, any matter having even secondary international effects is an appropriate subject for federalization pursuant to the foreign affairs powers of the federal government. If the federal courts have long decided the scope of diplomatic immunity, then it is in this view but a modest step for them to decide whether capital punishment violates an international norm. Nor should it matter that the United States has refused to ratify a particular convention, or has ratified it only subject to conditions precluding its application to displace state law.[82] Koh seems to fear that if the life-tenured federal judiciary were not to impose as customary international law of their own devising (reflecting the presumably elevated morality of human rights scholars), American states might practice genocide on their citizens.

There was for a time a substantial evangelical campaign to transfer American legal traditions to developing countries.[83] That campaign was aborted when its champions recognized that the economic and social infrastructure of the receiving nations is so different with respect to such matters as class and tribal rivalries that the American experience was simply inapplicable.[84] It is for the same reason nonsense to suppose that the issue of capital punishment, much less that of "hate speech," can be universalized. It is amply difficult for American judges to resolve such issues in the context of an American culture of which they have at least some knowledge; to involve them in the administration of natural law principles derived from the whole of human experience is a form of cultural imperialism. It is also an invitation to judicial arrogance desensitizing the American legal profession to its responsibility for our own democratic institutions.

What is frequently lacking in much academic legal discourse is attention to those aspects of legal institutions that generate the loyalty of the citizens expected to sustain them by their obedience. As Burke said, "[i]n the groves of their academy, at the end of every vista, you see nothing but gallows. Nothing is left which engages the affections on the part of the commonwealth."[85] Rarely is recognition given in academic literature to the role of law as a confirmation of conventional morality and as a message of reassurance to the good citizens who do the Republic's work that it is indeed *their* Republic.[86]

While there is thus a synergy between these phenomena, the inter-relationships between heroic judging and theoretical scholarship are likely minor effects. As Lieber (who learned it from Savigny) and his adherents would have been quick to affirm, both developments are surely driven by larger forces operating within the legal profession and derived from the larger culture of which they are a part. Judges and professors, as well as many lawyers, are members of Wiebe's "national class." Their thoughts are the product of an industrial era, an age that believed all things possible, even the remaking of a self-governing society into a utopia "void of crime and poverty" by technical experts on the bench. And they are also the product of a time when the Republic came to fill the role of a global empire threatened by an evil adversary that in important respects personified the horrors of mob rule. Just as earlier times produced Cooley and Brandeis, so it is the imperial America that has made the legal profession what it is at the end of the twentieth century, not the legal profession that made America what it is.

23

Byron White,
Outcast Justice

Justice Byron White served as contrarian to the Supreme Court in the heroic age of Justice Brennan. As Mary Ann Glendon noted, his was the ordinary heroism of a sort that won few plaudits from the "national class" of academics and media observers.[1]

White was raised in the beet-farming community of Wellington, Colorado, a village of less than 600 persons close enough to the foothills metropolis of Fort Collins that the mountain ranges were a constant presence on the western horizon.[2] His parents were natives of Iowa; his mother the daughter of German immigrants. His father managed the small lumberyard next to the depot; the family, which included two sons, lived in a modest frame house nearby.

By extraordinary initiative, tiny Wellington High School managed to field competitive teams in football, basketball, and track. The White brothers both proved to be excellent athletes as well as earnest students. Both went on to the University of Colorado, were star athletes there, compiled almost perfect academic records as undergraduates, were student leaders, and were Rhodes Scholars. Byron may have been the best college football player in America in 1937; having acquired the unwelcome sobriquet, "Whizzer," he was a national celebrity at twenty. In 1939 and 1940, he was the highest-paid player and the leading rusher in the National Football League. He led his class at Yale Law School in the intermittent semesters in which he was in residence there.

At Yale, White was naturally attracted to the teaching of Arthur Linton Corbin, an elderly Kansan who had practiced law in the mining town of Cripple Creek, Colorado, for four years at the turn of the century. Corbin was the senior member of the Yale Law faculty, in influence as well as age.[3] He was a renowned critic of the formalist, apolitical approach to law associated with Langdell and he taught the law of contracts as an experience in the application of non-ideological practical judgment. Karl Llewellyn, the ringleader of the ill-defined group self-acclaimed as Legal Realists,[4] had earlier been powerfully smitten by Corbin's teaching,[5] as were many others. Indeed, it may be said that Corbin was the individual most responsible for the advent of Yale Law School in the late 1920s as a premier academic institution.

Corbin explained to an anxious alumnus the Yale Law School as it stood in the late 1930s; the faculty, he said, taught law as the

> continually changing product of our evolutionary process. If we avoided discussion of those social and economic forces which cause our law to change and to be what it is, we would be incompetent for our job; and yet our classroom discussions deal primarily with the facts of cases and the reasons given by the courts for their decisions.[6]

Despite his parental identity with Legal Realism, Corbin was, as was Brandeis, mistrustful of the New Deal and impatient with younger colleagues, such as Bill Douglas, Abe Fortas, and Thurman Arnold, who were prone to employ the rhetoric of pragmatism to clothe a political ideology sometimes no less overconfident and inflexible than that of Langdell and his followers. That political ideology of Yale's Young Turks was broadly rooted in the shallow soil of evanescent New Deal policies and was generally labeled by undiscerning observers as "liberal."[7] Corbin, so far as appears, always did his own thinking and there is no evidence that any of his antecedents had a direct influence on him. It is possible, however, to see a similarity between his thought and that of Francis Lieber, whose writings were still being assigned to students when Corbin was a Yale Law student in the 1890s.[8]

By the time of his encounter with Corbin, White was himself a highly autonomous person, so secure in his notoriety as a football player that he had little need to prove himself to any person. At least in hindsight it was predictable that he would be attracted to the independent, non-ideological approach to law exhibited by Corbin.

White studied constitutional law with Edwin Borchard in the wake of the court-packing controversy. Borchard, like many others at the time, was relieved to see the Court taken down a notch and the Fourteenth Amendment put back on the shelf where in his view it belonged.[9] White was personally attracted to Myres McDougal, an outspoken advocate of greater use of social science in the formulation of law. That relationship was somewhat adversarial; classmates recalled numerous spirited classroom arguments between the two.[10] White later celebrated the teaching of Wesley Sturges,[11] an exceptionally tough-minded teacher who shared Corbin's lack of ideological commitment and who took few prisoners in his frequent assaults on soft-minded cant when he detected it in his students' utterances. Indeed, Sturges showed no mercy on cant, whatever its place on any political spectrum.

Celebrity status never wore well on White. It was later said that he would as soon have played football with twenty-one other guys in an empty stadium.[12] He was repelled by hype and, at least by the time he was nineteen, he did not respect or pursue fame. As a professional athlete, he recognized that publicity was a part of his job and he patiently endured the efforts of sports journalists to earn their livings, but without acquiring a taste for their attentions.

Likewise, his high earnings[13] as an athlete did not cause him to acquire much of an appetite for the things that money buys. His children were raised in a modest home (in which he is still living) and attended public schools. It would doubtless be incorrect to say that he did not respect fortune any more than he respected fame, but never did he seek it.

White's law school career was interrupted by three years in the Navy. While serving in the Solomon Islands campaign as a junior officer, he was assigned the task of assessing the responsibility of another junior officer for the loss of a torpedo boat in circumstances not easily explained or justified.[14] His report absolved the commander of the boat, who was Lieutenant John F. Kennedy, a person whom White had previously met while in England as a Rhodes Scholar.

After the war, White married, completed his law study, served as law clerk to Chief Justice Vinson, and practiced law in a Denver firm. Much too reserved in manner to be an effective public speaker, he seldom appeared in court, but acquired a worthy list of clients who regularly sought his legal advice. While he recognized that he would be likely to win any initial election in Colorado, he thought it unlikely that he would win a second one; this self-judgment was probably accurate, given his incapacity for the artifices of public relations.

When Kennedy sought the Democratic nomination for president in 1960, White managed his campaign in Colorado. It was a successful campaign and the Kennedys were impressed with his political judgment.[15] After the election, the president named his youthful brother, Robert, as attorney general and White as his deputy. White quickly became a force in the Department of Justice and won favorable notice for presiding over federal efforts to protect Freedom Riders in Alabama from violent mobs.[16] When a vacancy on the Supreme Court arose, he was appointed to fill it.

The *New York Times* was, however, from the outset unimpressed. Pontificating that a justice should be "a man of intellect and compassion and—because the Court must be a teacher—[able] to articulate," it expressed the editorial opinion that White's lack of "scholarly distinction prevented his appointment from being a great one."[17] *The New Republic* also feared that he was insufficiently liberal.[18] These expressions accurately foretold White's relationship to the media and to the legal academy.

As a justice, White was quick to separate himself from the "liberals" revered by *The New Republic*, such as Chief Justice Warren and Justices Black, Brennan, and Douglas, with respect to the appropriate role of the Court sitting in judgment on the constitutionality of laws enacted by Congress or the state legislatures. He did not accept the sharp distinction suggested in Chief Justice Stone's immortal footnote 4,[19] but gave deference to *social* policies of the states as well as the *economic* regulations at issue in the days of the social Darwinist Court that had come to an end in the court-packing crisis. This was evidenced in his first dissent, in 1962, to an opinion of the Court holding that it was "cruel and unusual punishment" for California to criminalize narcotics addiction.[20] He disputed the Court's characterization of the offense as one of status rather than conduct and deplored its novel interpretation of the constitutional language.

It was also soon evident that Justice White was not a literary stylist. His prose was unpretentious, like that of Cooley and Brandeis. Like the English House of Lords,[21] he did not cite academic literature, nor did he appear to write for an academic audience. His plain words seemed to be addressed more to legislators or county-seat lawyers than to an intellectual elite. In opinions of the Court, he seemingly preferred the passive voice and sentences made intricate by his apparent effort to avoid making doctrine broader than necessary to decide the case presently before the Court. His dissents, on the other hand, sometimes resembled the work of a road grader leveling everything in front of him.

His first dissent prefigured others in the field of criminal procedure, including a ringing dissent in *Miranda*[22] in which he questioned the whole line of Warren Court decisions imposing a set of constitutional requirements on criminal law enforcement by state police and state courts, requirements that have since been relaxed. He aligned himself with Justice John Harlan on these and many other matters. They shared the conviction, reflecting the teaching of Cooley, Thayer, Brandeis, and Hand, that dramatic reforms of society by judicial decree are mischievous; that representative government however frustratingly slow and inept is in the end the only reliable and effective method of achieving genuine social reform; and that federalism and home rule are not outdated, but are, as Lieber had proclaimed them to be, the soul of democratic life.[23] Yet White was marginally less cautious than Harlan, for example, in extending the Sixth Amendment right to jury trial in criminal cases to state courts.[24] Those who thought him inconsistent in rendering the latter decision failed to note that his opinion empowered the most democratic of institutions, the jury.

Justice White did not lack compassion when confronted with the problem of implementing *Brown*, but he had the practical wisdom, as many did not, to sense the limits of judicial influence. A pivotal case was *Green v. New Kent County Board of Education*,[25] in which the Court held that freedom of choice was an inadequate means of desegregation. He joined in the decision, but not without concern that the Court, by requiring numerical results, was embarking on a course that would prove counterproductive in its effects on race relations. He also repeatedly upheld legislative efforts to promote affirmative action,[26] at least so long as such action did not impose significant costs on individuals having no responsibility for past discrimination.[27]

White dissented with passion in *Roe v. Wade*.[28] Although acknowledging privately that he would as a legislator favor the right of a woman to discontinue a pregnancy, he denounced the Court for inventing such a right out of whole cloth. His opinion was brief and rested on considerations of federalism, asserting that such moral issues were left by the Constitution for resolution by state governments. Some found his position in *Roe* inconsistent with his earlier vote joining in the holding that married couples have a constitutionally protected right to practice contraception.[29] The opinion of the Court in the earlier case had supplied sufficient authority for the decision in *Roe* that Justice Stewart, who had dissented in the earlier case, felt obliged to follow it in *Roe*. But as William Van Alstyne emphasized, the earlier case had involved marital privacy and the contraception prohibited had little effect except on the consenting partners whose privacy right was asserted.[30] Destroying a human fetus by a medical procedure bore little resemblance to contraception in its consequences to others and was scarcely a private act. Moreover, the difference in the practical consequences of the constitutionalization of the right claimed was immense. The political reality was that there had been no significant political constituency vigorously opposed to contraception; although it violated Catholic doctrine, few, if any, even of the holy fathers, regarded contraception as a grave evil. Many citizens of diverse religious persuasions regarded abortion as murder.

Although otherwise faithful to the doctrine of precedent, White never ceased voting to overrule *Roe*. It was almost predictable that he would write the opinion of the Court in *Bowers v. Hardwick*[31] holding that there is no constitutionally protected right to engage in homosexual conduct. When he used the word "facetious" to characterize the contrary argument, he invited the severe judgment that he was "vituperatively homophobic."[32] That may be. However, the wisdom of his decision has perhaps been demonstrated by the peaceable transformation of American mores that has occurred since he wrote *Bowers*. Perhaps indirectly because of *Roe*, few Americans have changed their minds about abortion since 1972, while despite *Bowers*, popular attitudes toward homosexuality have changed markedly since 1986. It is possible that a reason is that the Court left citizens free to think for themselves and take full responsibility for their own moral judgments about homosexuality.[33]

Justice White joined in Justice Brennan's sweeping opinion in *New York Times v. Sullivan*,[34] a vote that he later concluded was his worst vote in thirty years on the Court. For many years, he sought opportunities to restore (without punitive damages) the law of defamation in its application to political discourse. He sensed, as many (including Thomas Cooley)[35] did not, that even the First Amendment, the holiest-of-holy principles to civil libertarians, could be overborne and that it was a mistake to strip our political discourse of effective restraint on false or misleading information about candidates for public office. He affirmed a public need for a forum in which candidates victimized by political disinformation could call their unjust assailants to account.

Also revealing a restrained view of the constitutional entitlements of the media was the opinion White wrote for the Court in *Branzburg v. Hayes*,[36] denying the right of journalists to refuse to identify their sources. He also wrote the opinion of the Court in *Zurcher v. Stanford Daily*,[37] holding that newsrooms are not sheltered from reasonable searches for evidence conducted pursuant to warrants. And again in *Herbert v. Lando*,[38] he wrote for the Court, upholding the right of civil litigants to compel the disclosure of unpublished material in the possession of journalists. These decisions earned him the unrestrained hostility of the media[39] and of others emotionally invested in the First Amendment. Their hostility did not abate when he expressed the opinion that a knowingly false attribution of a quotation is actionable defamation[40] and when he led the Court in holding that a promise of confidentiality by the press is an enforceable contract.[41]

Strangely, almost irrationally, bitter was the press response to the opinion of the Court, written by White, holding that the Fourth Amendment does not prohibit warrantless searches of garbage left outside the house for collection.[42] The decision seems debatable, but unimportant. Garbage is available to rats, cats, dogs, homeless itinerants, and journalists; why not to an energetic detective investigating a heinous crime? Yet the *New York Times* and the *Washington Post* railed against the decision and it led the generally temperate Tom Wicker of the *Times* to denounce White personally as "the bitterest legacy of the Kennedy Administration."[43]

White resisted efforts of journalists and academic observers to psychologize or strategize the work of the Supreme Court or attach ideological labels to its decisions. Indeed, on that account, he appears to have regarded aggressive journalists associated with highly regarded publications as a malign influence on the integrity of the Court. Stuart Taylor, an arch practitioner of that form of journalism, portrayed White as an arrogant misanthrope whose "unspoken message" to the press was, "You want to know what the case was about, maggots? Then go downstairs and stand in line for a copy of the opinion."[44] As is so often the case with harsh words, Taylor's comment reveals more about the commentator than about the object of his observation.

Judges, unlike legislators or executive officers, are bound to publish in their opinions what they can in support of their decisions and to resist the influence of other considerations. It is not unreasonable to believe, as White apparently did, that the proper role of legal journalism is to report and criticize legal events, not to speculate on unstated motives. To a person of that conviction, no good purpose is served by justices sitting for interviews by the media, and Taylor, if persistent, may well have seemed to be a maggot.

Two White opinions reflected his sense of the appropriate role of the media in shaping political discourse. One was an opinion of the Court in *Red Lion Broadcasting*, upholding the authority of the Federal Communications Commission to impose its fairness doctrine on licensed broadcasters.[45] The other was his dissent in *Buckley v. Valeo*, expressing his full approval of federal laws limiting campaign contributions and expenses.[46] Those opinions affirmed the right of citizens to participate in the political process on even terms, undistorted by the insistent intrusions of those controlling the media or those having money and willingness to spend it to dominate weaker voices. Both threaten the annual revenues of the media. They were written even before the development of the industry of highly compensated campaign consultants who have mastered the technology of the electronic media and the spot commercial to degrade our political discourse.[47]

On White's retirement, the *New York Times* editorially dismissed him as an inconsequential enigma, forgetting that it had in the past deplored his influence, especially with respect to the immunity from the law's burdens that it was prone to claim for the media.[48] Indeed, nothing the *Times* had to say on the subject of White's career reflected any comprehension of a judge's duty to democratic decisionmaking.[49] Even after having five years to reflect on White's stellar self-discipline, Linda Greenhouse of the *Times* described his career as "ambiguous and indistinct" and pitied him as one who had "nearly disappear[ed] into the anonymity of the Supreme Court,"[50] never noticing that her observations were the highest possible praise for a judge genuinely committed to the institutions of self-government.

White's experience calls attention to the growing role of the media in shaping our law. While Cooley, Brandeis, and Hand were public men and familiar with the journalists of their day, none of them was ever required to suffer daily contact with those whose livelihood depended on their reportage of influences lying behind the actions of the court and the reasons stated in their judicial opinions.[51] That type of reportage is a recent development; while desirable in some respects, and even sometimes arguably necessary, as a pervasive technique it has almost surely had a malign effect on the professional conduct of judges making newsworthy decisions because it provides a powerful motive for "impact decisions" by judges seeking public notice. To be lionized by the media is an irresistible attraction to many public persons, and few indeed are so nearly immune to it as was White.

Not only do the media stimulate the urge of judges to be celebrated, but they also direct public attention to the subterranean aspects of judicial work. The media have a self-interest in fostering the perception that the opinion of the Court is mere window-dressing to a story remaining to be told by investigative journalists. If the published opinion were to be seen as the real story, there would be no role for the journalist to play. Indeed, conventional journalists do not rely on, and seldom even report, what legislators or executive officers say, unless the fact of their statement is itself a subject for remark. Having their own unstated agenda (to uncover a story that sells), they are motivated to uncover the secret agendas of others, such as the unexpressed ideological impulses of judges. Judges who merely express "the common thoughts of men" make poor copy; indeed, to members of the media, a judge without an ideological center, who is merely an honest public servant, is a menace to their livelihood.

In some measure, the hope of the media that subterranean influences on courts are the real story is self-fulfilling. Not only do judges seeking media approval have reason to conform to the media's expectations, but they are also caused, as readers and viewers, to be more conscious and more tolerant of their own ideological impulses and those of other judges.

As White appeared to sense, this is an unwelcome influence. Good judges and prudent lawyers are steeped in self-knowledge and in control of their idiosyncratic impulses, but they are also unselfconscious, a trait difficult to sustain in the presence of a journalist. By the standards of professionals such as White, if there is such a person as a "great judge," he or she would be one who seeks and expects *never* to provide good copy. He or she will pass and be forgotten with the rest and be no more interesting to the media than Learned Hand's drones who manage their hive for a time and then quietly subside. To pursue a career in this way requires at least a measure of the trait White possessed in such abundance. As Mark Tushnet remarked about White,[52] such a person regards judging as what he does, not as who he is. It would be a good thing if more judges were "inner-directed" as White was. And, for that reason, it would not, on balance, be a bad thing if Stuart Taylor and Linda Greenhouse were required to stand in line to read the Court's opinions as the basis of their reportage.

In contrast to White, most justices in recent times have indulged in some public relations work, seeking a favorable press by making themselves available to the media. Not surprisingly, some of the young law clerks in their employ have done the same, supplying the media with tips about the justices and their relationships. Carrying this practice to the extreme, one former law clerk in 1998 published 500 pages of gossip, leading the Court to seek a method of preventing such disclosures in the future.[53] The former clerk's work was in a sense a reprise to the 1979 book, *The Brethren*,[54] which Byron White reviled.[55] Whether the public knowledge created by such illuminations is sufficiently valuable to warrant the cost to the institution is a question.

A related question is the appropriate relationship between members of the Court and future historians. A tendency of justices has emerged in recent years to preserve internal correspondence for use by future scholars. When White left the Court, he shredded his files.[56] While he gave no reason, it was obvious that he deemed his official utterances and those of his colleagues as all that ever needed to be said by them about the Court's rulings. Again, there is a question whether the value to the Republic of widely shared knowledge of the internal workings of the minds of justices and the relationships among them is worth the cost of revealing it. Among the perceived costs likely to weigh in White's mind is an unwelcome effect on the motivations of justices. Justices who write for future historians, like those who provide interviews to reporters, are likely to become more self-conscious in the process and thus more given to heroic posturing.

These apparent quiddities of Justice White aside, what "liberals" were most prone to revile in his judicial work was his unwillingness to certify the superiority of the moral judgment of the credentialed class to that of their less-august fellow citizens. Although a member of that class and sympathetic with most of its prevailing values, he was reluctant to impose them on citizens of lesser status who did not share them. In this respect, it is fair to say that Justice White had the courage of Justice Harlan's convictions. While Harlan often practiced the same caution and was always careful to express it, he did on more than one occasion succumb to the heroic temptation. Robert Nagel has tellingly depicted Harlan's form of deference to lower-class political and moral judgment in his account of *Cohen v. California*,[57] upholding the right of an individual to wear a "scurrilous epithet" on his jacket:

> Harlan dismisses the notion that the display of the words *fuck the draft* was inherently likely to cause a violent reaction as "plainly untenable . . . reflecting an undifferentiated fear or apprehension . . ." He is confident that the sensibilities of passersby could be adequately protected if they would just (why didn't the local officials think of it?) avert their eyes. By contrast, what is at stake in protecting this "trifling and annoying instance of . . . disgraceful abuse of a privilege" is, if only enough thought is applied, momentous. Protecting individual freedom here will serve to "produce a more capable citizenry and more

perfect polity. . . ." In fact, "no other approach would comport with the premises of individual dignity and choice upon which our political system rests." Plainly, the officials of California had made an enormous error; the moral underpinnings of our political system were at risk; only the measured reflections of a few justices lay between us and eventual calamity. This was a small decision, reluctantly and carefully arrived at, but it would serve the highest, not to say the most grandiose, purposes.[58]

Another, unrelated, and seldom-noted sphere in which White's cautious approach to the judicial role was prominent, is the validity of federal legislation creating novel political structures not authorized by the Constitution. Challenged as inconsistent with conventional separation of powers doctrine were bankruptcy judges with limited terms,[59] one-house legislative vetoes of administrative action,[60] the comptroller general as budget-deficit policeman,[61] the independent counsel appointed by a special court,[62] and the sentencing commission.[63] White regarded all these devices as practical (if perhaps mistaken) legislative responses to difficult problems of public administration, for which Congress should be given full political responsibility.

On the other hand, White was apparently concerned about the changing relationship of the Court to lower federal courts. For years, he was the primary advocate of the Court's duty to resolve significant conflicts in the interpretations of federal law by the intermediate courts of appeals.[64] Perhaps in part because White retired, there has been a steady decline in the number of cases the Court agrees to hear. It now decides about ninety cases a year, many fewer than it decided in the 1980s,[65] and it refuses to decide scores of cases in which the lower courts have differed in their interpretations of the national law.[66] While this course may be explained by the need of justices to have time to consider the decisions they do make, it reflects a substantial but unacknowledged delegation of its constitutional responsibility. It encourages the United States Courts of Appeals to think of themselves as junior varsity supreme courts whose primary function is making national law for their respective territories, a function very different from that which they were created to perform and one they are not organized to perform well.

White did not articulate the reasons for his concern about this development. Most members of the federal judiciary approve it; a reason is not hard to discern, because it discreetly enhances the power and discretion of the life-tenured judges sitting on lower federal courts. Judges exercising discretion and making law have more fun than those who read transcripts of evidence to assure that previously established law has been faithfully applied. And the adverse consequences of this change in the job description of circuit judges are too subtle to evoke outcry. Its direct effect is a balkanization of the national law. This adds complexities to the law, and complexity fosters game playing by lawyers and causes billable hours to increase. The delegation also creates an odd and questionable form of government for the regional circuits: Each is given a life-tenure judiciary of its own without corresponding executive and legislative branches, a situation resembling the one Louis Brandeis declared to be unconstitutional in *Erie*.[67] This absence of balancing powers elevates the lack of political accountability of law-making, life-tenured federal judges.

The courts of appeals sit in small, isolated groups and lack effective means of controlling idiosyncratic members. They can optimistically express what they believe and hope is the law, but they are structurally unable to assure compliance with their expressions by dissenting members sitting in other panels who are free to decide later cases without opinion[68] or by opinions obfuscating differences. In the unquestionably honest belief that pressures of time require it, and to conserve energy for the more pretentious role of making law, those courts may give short shrift to less interesting matters being brought to their attention. They can do so by pretermitting argument, dispensing with explanatory opinions, or delegating opinion writing and even decisions to their staffs. One circuit judge has acknowledged that in reality a federal appeal is now a matter of grace and might as well be recognized for what it is by giving the courts of appeals the same power to control their dockets as the Supreme Court enjoys.[69] Thus, if litigants defeated in federal courts ever had the right to know the reasons for their defeat, that entitlement is presently being given scant recognition.

This also means that district judges are increasingly free to indulge their personal preferences in managing cases in the trial court. The result, as White seems to have recognized, is to defeat the purpose Congress had in mind when it created the courts of appeals in 1891, which was to inhibit "the kingly power" of the life-tenured judges sitting as chancellors of federal justice.[70] A consequence of unsteady federal law conferring more discretion on lower court judges is to diminish the fields in which citizens and local governments can function without regard to a federal presence. Explicit, clear, predictable law is a source of freedom, White understood, not only for individuals but for their self-governing communities.

24

The Political Economy of
Legal Education

Chapter 4 contrasted Cooley's Jacksonian vision of open legal education as an instrument of democratic government with the class-ridden, technocratic vision displacing it in the late nineteenth century. Cooley, Brandeis, Freund, and Hand were in their own times reconciled to Langdell's reformation of professional education, in part, surely, because in practice, at least for a time, it could be made to serve the ends of moral education preparing lawyers for stewardship of democracy. We now consider whether university education in law at the end of the twentieth century can still be said to serve that traditional aim. Anthony Kronman has decried the loss in recent decades of the commitment of lawyers to the commonwealth[1] and Macklin Fleming has documented the profession's growing preoccupation with income as a measure of self-worth.[2] To what extent may such trends be linked to changes in professional education?[3]

Langdell's program of 1870 entailed three reforms of the Harvard Law School: the introduction of the case method, the elevation of admissions requirements extending pre-professional higher education to four years, and the extension of the law curriculum to three years. The purpose of these reforms, singly and together, was to elevate the status of the Harvard Law School within the legal profession and, less urgently, to elevate the relative status of the legal profession. His purposes were largely achieved.

Yet, it is clear that Langdell, like many other reformers, only dimly understood what he had wrought. As Grant Gilmore has observed, if Langdell had not existed, it would have been necessary for America to invent him,[4] because his motives resonated strongly with those of the members of an industrial society aspiring to be human capitalists. Yet his achievement did not defeat the moral impulses of Cooley, Brandeis, Freund, Hand, and their many antecedents who undertook the professional responsibility for providing stewardship of self-government.

Thus, the case method, despite its faint resemblance to hazing, proved to be far more than an initiation ceremony. It was embraced enthusiastically by many professionals who did not share Langdell's feudal values. Among them were his colleague Thayer, Thayer's students Brandeis and Hand, and even Freund. What they and others discovered is that Langdell's method was a superior instrument for moral education nurturing the traits required for effective service to democratic institutions.[5]

Laura Kalman is one of many who have spoken for those overwhelmed by anxiety at the requirement of student participation in public class discussions.[6] Joel Seligman noted with restraint that "[o]n occasion, some law school professors have been insensitive to the emotional vulnerability of their students."[7] For decades, psychiatrists and psychologists have questioned the consequences of aggressive case method law teaching for the mental health of students.[8] No one has denied that the "cold call" on students to participate in class discussion is a stressful challenge. But the stress of engaging in intellectual combat with an 800-pound gorilla was, for those who survived (and most did), preparation for dealing with judges and adversaries not available to students receiving instruction in a nurturing environment. Students such as Kalman much prefer the personal warmth of teachers such as Cooley, but it was for most less useful as preparation for a life in public law.

The case method and the cold call were keys to making university legal education more than a filling of empty vessels with information about transient legal doctrine that could as well be acquired without a teacher. In almost any of its many forms, the case method provided a focus to discussion between teacher and student and among students in which a useful intellectual and moral toughness was fostered. Even the most militant opponent of the case method, Simeon Eben Baldwin, emphasized the need for the sort of exchange fostered by it; law students, he conceded, "are not to be treated like school-boys"[9] if they are expected to become persons on whom others rely for judgment in contentious circumstances. The importance to novitiates in law of the kind of experience the case method affords was understood by gentle George Wythe, whose students learned quickly both to fear and to value their exposure to an audience of fellow students.[10]

Moreover, studying cases, unlike reading texts expressing doctrine, lends a practical bent to the thinking required of the student. Cases are problems and students reading cases are, like lawyers, trying to solve problems. The method thus hones the student's sense of relevance as he or she acquires the habit of distinguishing between ideas that are useful to the solution of particular problems and those that are not. It enhances the skill of predicting what those who apply the lash of power will do with it in a given foreseeable circumstance. To read carefully and understand an opinion of a court is to enter the mind not only of its author, but also of others who signed it, and still others who will read it and invoke it as precedent. So to predict the use of power by others, a lawyer must lay aside his or her own idiosyncratic impulses, suppress wishful thinking, and think professionally as those likely to exercise the power are likely to think. For dogmatic persons, this is an especially difficult discipline to master, but, as Anthony Kronman notes,[11] all the more valuable on that account.

The case method also has the virtue of supplying an accurate account of American law, for it reveals graphically that courts have a social and political responsibility; their responsibility is performed by publishing institutional opinions giving assurance to readers of their fidelity to legal texts; the utterances of those institutional opinions are themselves legal texts; law so made is an aggregation of atomized rules, each containing the seed of its own revision; the political responsibility so exercised is generally inferior to that of other officials elected by vote of the people; and the political responsibility of the courts is necessarily shared by the profession of whom the judiciary is a part.

In addition to this accurate revelation of the nature of American law, there is a subtle, moral subtext to learning acquired from casebooks and case discussion that is of special value in the training of public lawyers. An unstated premise of useful classroom discussions of law cases is that there is, for most cases, a resolution that is more nearly correct for that time and place than are the other answers proposed. That correct answer is faithful to the pertinent legal texts read in light of the dominant and emergent values of those governed and serves their longer-term interests. This is the premise of the judicial role to which law students are socialized by the case method.

More specifically, students often acquire from the method at least some of what Lon Fuller described as a morality of aspiration.[12] The reader of a thousand opinions of the court is likely to gain the impression that judges and other legal decisionmakers are more often than not, within the limits of their capacities, striving to make decisions that conform to professional expectations and to the general public welfare as rationally assessed. This impression may be fortified when the class discussion of judicial efforts is critical and proceeds from the premise (generally unstated) that judges can and should be criticized when they indulge themselves or disserve the common interest.

Among the moral precepts to be observed in judicial conduct and shared by students are those Fuller identifies as the morals of law. Opinions are subject to just criticism if they lack generality, if their utterances are unclear or self-contradictory, command the impossible, are inconstant, or are incongruent with the actual application of the lash of power. A total failure to meet one of these moral requirements, Fuller affirmed, "does not simply result in a bad system of law; it results in something that is not properly called a legal system at all, except perhaps in the Pickwickian sense in which a void contract can still be said to be one kind of contract."[13]

In fact, few who have experienced it would deny that nine months or so of close reading and public discussion of legal cases is a morally transformative experience.[14] It is perhaps for this reason that American law teaching has been perceived by some as destructive of student idealism.[15] But, as Kronman again observed, the youthful idealism impaired is often associated with adherence to abstractions and absolutes.[16] By separating the young idealists from such beliefs and stripping them of dogmatism, the case method sometimes leaves them for a time in a state of mistrust of their own convictions, but what was thus lost is the overconfident idealism of youth doomed in any event to shatter against the rocks of reality. Meanwhile, many students learned that the frustrations and even the occasional humiliations of vigorous public discourse are momentary and that moral courage has its rewards. As Byron White's response to his teachers, Corbin and Sturges, demonstrates, he was a grateful beneficiary of the method at its most rigorous.

The method is hardly sure fire. There are finite limits to what any mere educators can hope to achieve by any method. The legal profession, not the academy, is the most influential moral teacher of law students, and it is in turn subject to powerful moral influences from the culture it serves.[17] Whether a novitiate will comprehend or accept the moral teaching of the case method is determined by all the cultural (and even genetic) forces bearing on the formation of character. We can say with confidence only that law schools are more likely to produce graduates sharing the democratic values of Cooley, Brandeis, Freund, Hand, and White with the case method than without it.[18]

While the case method was a benefit to the public profession, the effects of Langdell's other reforms were far more ambiguous. They have tended to separate the profession from the constituency it serves. The most direct effect was to substantially elevate the initiation fee for admission to the profession. This has had malign secondary and tertiary effects.

Some elevation of academic standards in law was necessary in the early decades of the twentieth century. Thayer was a leader in the effort to elevate the almost non-existent standards prevailing in the nineteenth century in states that had experienced Jacksonian law reform.[19] Freund's law school in Chicago was the first to award the juris doctor degree as a novel form of academic pretension; a Brandeis daughter was among the early candidates for that degree.[20] Brandeis, Freund, and Hand, like Cooley before them, were superbly competent legal technicians who respected the technological element in the work of a legal profession devoted to effective public service. All three were also fully aware of the boom in higher education marked in its inception by the initiative of Charles Eliot in appointing

Langdell to his position and all were aware of its relationship to social status in an industrial society and its implications for law and the legal profession. It seems clear that they approved of Thayer's efforts and those of his associates in the American Bar Association and related organizations.[21]

There was class bias, and perhaps a touch of racism,[22] in the elevation of academic standards as it occurred in the early decades of the twentieth century, but everywhere in America, in all professions, standards were being elevated.[23] A profession's standing in the community was perceived to depend on the number of years its members invested in academic pursuits. It is not imaginable in such a social context that American law could have been left to those with meager formal education of the sort experienced by Lincoln and Cooley.

Nevertheless, those regarding American law and the legal profession as a service to the Republic might well take a skeptical view of the moral premises of professional education in law as it continued to evolve after 1950. It has become an increasingly elaborate but ever less demanding enterprise of escalating cost, increasingly preoccupied with the indicia of academic status and the short-term gratification of student desires and convenience.[24]

Cooley expressed his skepticism about the isolating effect of professional pretensions in his remarks at Harvard. Brandeis acquired, in later years, an enlarged interest in legal education and by his deeds expressed a similar skepticism.[25] As a university trustee, he offered advice and support, not to Harvard, but to Charles Hamilton Houston's Howard Law School.[26] He opposed the tendency toward centralization of professional education in national institutions. Despite his continuing loyalty to his friends and admirers at Harvard, he rejected Dean Pound's call for support and advocated the creation of twenty such institutions in lieu of a pre-eminent few. He became a major benefactor and advisor to the University of Louisville and took a keen interest in its law school. When he died in 1941, he was buried in the Law Building at that university[27] and that school now bears his name.

Brandeis's reasons for opposing the ambitions of the Harvard Law School were similar to those prompting him to oppose much of the New Deal, Chief Justice Stone's celebrated footnote 4, and the promulgation in 1938 of the Federal Rules of Civil Procedure. While these positions now seem anachronistic, they reflected the Jacksonian impulses he shared with Cooley. If the nine justices moving into the elegant, new Supreme Court building struck Brandeis as beetles in the Temple of Karnak, one wonders what metaphor might have come to his mind as he contemplated the ornate, even rococo, institutional architecture of American legal education in the late twentieth century.

Throughout the century of professional status seeking, there have been occasional sounds of caution. An earnest argument against artificial minimum standards for entry to the bar was advanced in 1921 in the name of a Carnegie Commission.[28] In sum, the argument (redolent of Cooley's 1863 reflections on the virtues of the open law school he was conducting)[29] was that law is part of the political system and must in a democracy be accessible to the people governing themselves. If law must be the "common thoughts of men," then men and women who are well acquainted with those diverse thoughts must be included among those admitted to law's inner sanctum.

Perhaps as a result of that 1921 report, law did not follow medicine to require four years of postgraduate study plus at least two more of apprenticeship, but it has settled for a more modest commitment of time serving. The Jacksonian wisdom was that time-serving requirements, for them expressed in apprenticeship requirements and other aspects of "the pursuit of excellence," have costs to be borne chiefly by those outside the profession. Those costs, in their estimation, exceeded any perceived public benefit.

In confirmation of their premise, we can see at least four social, political, and moral problems that might not have arisen, at least in the form they did, but for the extension and elaboration of university legal education: (1) the rising real cost of entry for novitiates entering the legal profession; (2) the decline in social mobility reflected in the demography of the legal profession; (3) the rising real cost of legal services; and (4) the rising levels of dissatisfaction of young law graduates with their employment. The three items last mentioned are largely derived from the first.

Most bar leaders, accreditors, and legal educators have been oblivious to these moral, social, and political costs. The "pursuit of professional excellence" is almost always presented by them as an absolute good. Thus, an influential and otherwise admirable report on legal education produced in 1992 by the American Bar Association group led by Robert MacCrate[30] is replete with costly suggestions and void of any consideration of how those costs might be borne or their indirect consequences.

The fact is that university legal education in the late twentieth century is difficult to justify as an instrument of democratic government. Its real cost has been steadily rising throughout this century without a corresponding increase in its beneficial results. The increase in cost is a direct result of the elevation of academic standards reflecting the legal profession's acquisition of academic status. The increase is partly a consequence of the time-serving requirements associated with the nomenclature of the J.D. degree and partly a consequence of a steady increase in instructional costs.

In the days of Lincoln, the price of becoming a lawyer was the price of a book and the value of the time it took to read it.[31] At the time of Cooley's presidency of the American Bar Association, the median number of years of academic study by American lawyers was zero. That is to say, more than half had never seen the inside of a college. That median rose from zero to seven over a period of about seventy years. Thus, the amount of income foregone to pursue studies required of credentialed lawyers grew rapidly and steadily to approximate five years of earnings. This number can be somewhat discounted in light of the simultaneous substantial increase in life expectancy extending the likely period of earning. But the income foregone has to be foregone in a lump at the outset of a career in the hope of enlarged earnings later and thus constitutes a large entry cost.

This massive increase in the cost of foregone income has been almost matched by the increasing cost of instruction. Until 1960, tuition charges, even in the most elite private law schools, were modest. The increases since then have been breathtakingly large, frequently as much as five-fold in real dollars.[32] That change in part reflects the decline in the willingness of private and even some public universities to subvent the professional education of those with high earnings prospects and a resulting increased ability of students to pay. But it also reflects a dramatic increase in the real cost of instruction.

A novitiate can avoid some of the out-of-pocket cost by attending a part-time program imposing less cost in foregone income or a less luminous school that incurs lower instructional cost,[33] but the likely consequence of doing so has been to consign oneself to a subordinate social status within the legal profession and thus to restrict access to high-earnings employment. In most states, it is still possible for some who seek careers in law to secure a public subvention by attending a state university law school. To the extent that this is so, the social costs are not less, but are borne in different ways.

The benefits acquired in exchange for this huge increase in the cost of entry are depressingly difficult to demonstrate. Some of the cost might be justified as consumption rather than investment because the expenditures have made the environment of professional education more pleasurable for teachers and students than it otherwise would be. There would be nothing wrong in this were it not for the fact that the higher level of consumption is required as a condition of entry into the public's profession. The cost is not generally borne by those who enjoy the consumption, but by those who later consume their services as professionals.

If one looks for benefits in university legal education other than those associated with a rigorous case method, benefits that can fairly be denoted as sound investments resulting in law that is more efficient, more democratic, or more just, the search is frustrating. Langdell himself had difficulty justifying a three-year curriculum. His means of doing so was to require those seeking a Harvard degree tediously to examine the whole corpus of judge-made common law by the case method. This was so transparently unwarranted that relatively few students in the nineteenth century remained to complete their degrees.[34] Gradually, other courses of instruction were found to fill out a plausible curriculum so that the time was not an utter waste. But given the unavoidable necessity that lawyers of all kinds must, from the start of their careers, assume responsibility for their own instruction as to the law controlling a particular dispute or transaction at a particular moment, there is an early point of diminishing return in filling the heads of students with legal doctrine that will be forgotten by the time, if ever there is a time, when knowledge of that doctrine is needed. Given that the impact of the case method is substantially fixed for most novitiates in one academic year, it requires a leap of faith to suppose that the third year is in any sense needed by novitiates to become competent lawyers. The purpose of the requirement was not and is not substance, but affect.

The same assessment might be made of the fourth year of required undergraduate instruction. That requirement is not imposed by the bar associations, but is imposed by many universities, including all those of status. Given that the fourth year can be spent in almost any undergraduate curriculum at almost any college, it would be impossible to explain a connection between the requirement and the usefulness of the services to be performed by the profession. Again, the explanation lies on the side of affect: Its function is to warrant the denotation of a law degree as a kind of doctorate. In sum, if the utility of the services rendered by the profession were the sole measure, universities could readily do as well in five years what they now take seven to do.

Turning to the high cost of instruction, the justification in terms of practical benefits to the public is only marginally stronger. The strongest point to be made is that some of the increased cost relates to clinical education aiming to improve the technical competence and professional ethics of the profession. That was the aim of the MacCrate Report. There is, of course, nothing new in that purpose. Jacksonian law teachers such as Cooley invested much of their own energy as teachers in moot courts. At Michigan, moot courts early came to include moot trial work.[35] Indeed, at William and Mary and Transylvania, students were required to participate in moot legislative work.[36] But good contemporary clinical legal education resembles good apprenticeship training and often bears the same demerit of cost ineffectiveness. Good clinical legal education consistently involves intimate teaching relationships that are more expensive, often very much more expensive. The MacRate Report advocated more skills training. To the extent that salable skills can be transmitted by clinical methods, they may often be more efficiently acquired by on-the-job training of the sort experienced by members of most trades. The Report gave no consideration to such possibilities.[37]

The need for expensive clinical training is in part the result of the academization of the full-time law faculty. Teachers lacking professional experience are seldom effective mentors nurturing sound professional habits and ethics.[38] Many are in fact repelled by what lawyers do and are refugees from active lawyering.[39] In turn, the availability of clinical training reduces the academized faculty's responsibility for professional training, liberating them for the more abstruse intellectual pursuits favored by searchers for Truth.[40]

The increase in clinical education is a minor source of the increased cost of instruction. Other causes include the widespread use of full-time teacher-scholars to staff most university law school curricula. In this century, it has been presumed, but never demonstrated, that the instruction of full-time teachers is in all respects superior to that of part-timers such as Cooley or Brandeis. Full-time teachers are generally much more expensive than part-time ones; this is so because universities have felt the need to accommodate the ambitions of the full-time faculty to engage in non-teaching activities. As teaching ratios have gone down, so have teaching loads. A university that desires a faculty to produce scholarship-winning peer esteem and to retain those who produce it, must assure its faculty of more modest teaching responsibilities.

One form of compensation for full-time faculty is to allow them to teach what they please, with minimal regard for curricular needs or the desires of students. Such teaching as may be required of those most favored is frequently conducted in specialized seminars that are often even more intimate and costly than elegant clinical education.

It is not only the ambition of the academized legal scholar that leads to costly proliferation. An additional factor elevating the real cost of a university legal education has been the desire of students for what may be described as "boutique instruction." For most students, curricular choice seems an absolute good and discussions in small classes are less stressful than in large ones. Students are attracted to the very questionable premise that knowledge of a particular field acquired in law school will help them acquire and perform well-compensated employment. Proliferating the curriculum is therefore a response to consumerism. Even a law school of negligible status would in 1998 be ashamed to exist if its curriculum did not contain an array of highly specialized offerings unknown to law schools as recently as 1970 and attracting no more than a relative handful of students.

Even more than with respect to clinical education, the positive consequences of this development are speculative. It is doubtful that the conduct of the boutique seminar often contributes significantly to the quality of the professional services later delivered by participants.

Lightening the usual teaching load of full-time teachers has contributed to a material increase in gross production of scholarly writings. For reasons stated in the previous chapter, one could question whether the additional volume of material has added greatly to the social utility of such work. Like the present utterance, much is doomed to almost certain inconsequentiality. And there is a question whether novitiates to the profession should as a cost of entry, through higher tuition, bear the expense even of the most useful and admirable scholarship. [41]

In fact, students, and their clients, would almost surely be better served by simpler, more comprehensive, and less expensive curricula providing broad and systematic acquaintance with law and the environment in which it functions and by more abundant experience in handling the stress of performing before a large, critical audience of fellow students. That is especially true for students planning careers in narrowly specialized fields, who are not likely later to educate themselves with a breadth of perspective, and for students such as Cooley and Langdell, who were as young persons afflicted with shyness. But law schools dependent on their social or academic status have little choice but to incur the cost of curricular "enrichment," if that is what it is, if they are to compete for the ablest students and faculty and maintain their place in the status pecking order.

As noted, this steep ascent of the real cost of entry into the American legal profession has contributed in turn to secondary adverse social consequences. Let us briefly examine them.

The first of these has been an adverse effect on the demography of the profession. Perhaps the connection is obvious, but it may be illuminated by a description in economic terms. The elevation of academic standards in the twentieth century made all American lawyers human capitalists. To become a lawyer, one is required to make an investment in one's self by forbearing income and paying tuition. To make a sizable economic investment in one's self requires personality traits that are not evenly distributed among citizens. Those raised in families that are accustomed to investing are more prone to be human capitalists than those who are raised in families with subsistence incomes.

To diminish the exclusionary effects of high entry cost into professions, the United States established the guaranteed student loan program.[42] It is, however, far from clear that the program works as it was intended. At least with respect to professional law schools, it seems to have added fuel to the fire of rising real costs. By enabling more students to pay more tuition, the loan programs have enabled schools to compete by further improvements in teaching ratios, reductions in teaching loads to attract and retain more elite faculty, and increased proliferation of more costly seminars and clinical programs. Close study would likely confirm that the chief effects of guaranteed loan programs in law schools have been to enhance the tuition revenues of the schools and to add to the debt burden of novitiates, with ineffable if any improvement in the quality of the services delivered by novitiates to their clients. If this is correct, the GSL program is the fulfillment of the Jacksonians' worst fears about government programs, that their benefits will be gathered to the bosoms of the wealthy and will seldom reach the offspring of the working class who are, or ought to be, the intended beneficiaries. GSLs, like the Bank of the United States so despised by President Jackson, mostly make the rich richer.

Among the consequences of a high initiation fee was a brake on the entry of women into the legal profession. In 1875, there was a mere handful of women lawyers. By 1910, the number had reached 558.[43] By 1940, it was 4,187.[44] But female participation in higher education generally was growing much more rapidly. Particularly in state universities west of the Alleghenies, there were about as many women as men in college. Women were not generally admitted to a few "national" law schools that were part of older, all-male universities, but few sought admission to the many law schools such as Cooley's Michigan or to New York University,[45] another institution of Jacksonian origins, where they were perhaps especially welcome. A reason that the numbers of women in law schools did not rise at the same pace as in undergraduate colleges is that the investment required was greater for law than for the newer and rapidly feminized professions of education, social work, nursing, and librarianship. Women who expected to bear children did not see themselves as likely to have a full quotient of income-earning years to provide a suitable return on their investment.

Women at last began entering the profession in large numbers in the 1970s, not merely because they were given greater legal protection against discrimination, but also because by that time fewer planned to devote substantial time to child bearing and child care. This development diminished the effect of elevated standards as an impediment to female entry into the profession.

In 1865, there was only a handful of African-American lawyers. In 1900, there were 728.[46] This reflected significant social change. This growth continued, but as professional standards were elevated, the rate of growth was sharply reduced. In 1940, the number was only 1,052.[47] As a percentage of the licensed bar, there was no increase in the intervening four decades. The reason was the lack of access of African-American students to higher education; law schools outside the South were open to them, but at a price that few could bear. Also largely absent from the legal profession were persons of Asian, Hispanic, or southern European origins. In short, the elevation of standards was a substantial impediment to social mobility in the legal profession.

To confirm the demographic effect of rising entry cost, one need only look at old class pictures at schools like Michigan or Kansas. Throughout the nineteenth century, when Jacksonian or Populist notions prevailed, there were steady trickles of minority and women graduates of such institutions. The flows diminished as academic standards began to rise and ever larger investments were required to gain entry into such schools.

To secure minority participation in the legal profession, law schools began in 1965 to engage in affirmative action with respect to admissions and financial aid. That effort has succeeded in producing a respectable and growing number of African-American lawyers.[48] But such programs have not been without social and political costs and they have encountered increasing resistance.[49] Among the costs, affirmative action tends to isolate its beneficiaries and reinforce their sense of caste. That sense of isolation may be the driving force behind a resegregative impulse sometimes euphemistically described as multiculturalism.[50] True racial integration in the legal profession would likely have come faster and with far less grief had admission standards not been elevated as much as they were.

Next, there is the related problem of the steadily rising real cost of legal services. The rising cost of entry has likely contributed to that increase. It has certainly fed a steady elevation of the income expectations of lawyers. In the nineteenth century, those expectations were low. Joseph Baldwin reported of the "flush times" in Alabama that the lawyers were all incompetent, but their failures were redeemed by the reluctance of clients to pay for their services.[51] Neither lawyer nor client had much to complain of. Even as recently as 1960, students entering law school seldom expected high earnings, especially not in their first decade of practice.[52] As the realities of human capitalism have been recognized, the buyers of legal services have come to expect to pay fees sufficient to provide a return on the investment made in training.

I do not suggest that low earnings for lawyers is a social good. But high income expectations impede the distribution of services, which is a social ill. The Legal Aid movement is a creature of this century.[53] So likewise are The Legal Services Corporation and Neighborhood Legal Services programs.[54] These are beneficial, indeed essential, remedies for a problem of which the high price of university legal education is a cause. Lawyers working in those programs are underpaid relative to their classmates and are so few in number that they are unable to meet any but the most urgent needs of their clienteles; they are also often underappreciated by their clients, who manifest a preference for "real lawyers" whose services they buy with their own money.[55] These programs would be less needful and their deficiencies less significant if the profession of which they are a part were less exclusive.

It is not only the working poor who are affected by the price of legal services. A motive of some of the leaders of the movement to use alternative methods of dispute resolution is the reduction of legal costs. While other purposes may also be served by ADR,[56] an aim is to reduce the amount of expensive lawyer-time invested in the resolution of disputes, perhaps especially those routine matters that affect the interests of individual citizens. The price of legal services has thus so impaired the ability of our courts to deal with the legal problems of citizens that they are driven into a private market.

Indeed, the ADR movement is animated by concern not only for the routine legal costs of ordinary citizens. Even multinational corporations are interested in ADR or any other means of reducing their legal costs. They report, and it seems not unlikely, that their legal costs are several multiples of those borne by their international competitors.[57] One reason, in addition to others more deeply embedded in different cultures, is that lawyers are everywhere trained less elegantly than in the United States. Rising pressures must be withstood by graduates who are increasingly sheltered from stress in the prolonged period of their formal education and are thus less well prepared to withstand them.

Finally, there is the growing dissatisfaction of young lawyers with their jobs, and perhaps, too, of employers with their work. Its existence is confirmed by the unprecedented mobility of young lawyers. The problem may be related to the others noted. Persons making large investments to secure entry have higher expectations not only of income, but also of enjoyment, than do those who qualified merely by reading a couple of books. Moreover, those who pay salaries or legal fees needed to provide a suitable return on the investments of the human capitalists may have rising expectations about the utility or effectiveness of the services they are buying at higher cost. A partial and tertiary consequence of these developments is that the legal profession increasingly reflects the values of a "winner-take-all" society[58] in which the rewards received by a few private lawyers are comparable to those received by prize athletes and rock stars while equally competent and energetic lawyers are being expelled from their firms for their inability to "make rain," that is, to earn fees, sufficient to support a corps of costly associates. Meanwhile, the relative compensation of the judiciary and other public officers declines.

The fact that the capital investment is made by law students with borrowed money intensifies the disappointment when the expectations are not fulfilled. To continue paying interest to retire a loan taken to secure a job that one does not like or was unable to hold must be even more dispiriting than paying one's credit card charges for last year's vacation. Worse, the need to repay loans compels behavior motivated by concern for economic outcomes.[59] To repay loans, graduates seek and secure jobs that pay more and foreseeably give less gratification. Worst, indebtedness diminishes professional independence and pressures lawyers to perform professional misdeeds.[60]

A number of law schools have sought to respond partially to this problem of debt burden with loan forgiveness programs.[61] These are designed to encourage students hoping to use their professional talents to serve public needs.[62] Necessary as these programs are, they are meager palliatives.

High tuition may have another unwelcome secondary effect on the usefulness of university legal education as training for professional work. As previously noted, there appears to be a trend that has grown over several decades for law students to think of themselves as consumers entitled to immediate gratification from the law school experience. The demands of rigorous case-method teaching are resisted and that method is increasingly displaced by less rigorous, illustrated lectures that are more gratifying and less stressful for students. Law students today encounter fewer teachers such as the Wesley Sturges who taught Byron White at Yale, who do not suffer their students to engage in naïve, uncritical, sanctimonious, or self-congratulatory thinking. Students paying more may thus get less enduring benefits.

The democratic values motivating the careers of Cooley, Brandeis, Freund, Hand, and White are at odds with the increasing credentialization of the profession. Had their Jacksonian moral judgment been brought more heavily to bear on the transformation of the legal profession in the twentieth century, the problems reviewed here would have been of lesser dimensions and the Republic would have been equipped in the future with a profession better suited to its service.

Is there a solution to any of the problems raised in this chapter? I dare suggest one comprehensive solution that is, alas, unlikely to gain serious consideration. A well-endowed university or law school could reduce or even renounce tuition income, thereby rejecting the moral premises of human capitalism. To do that without invading corpus, it would be necessary to cut their costs severely. For a law school now covering half its cost with public funds or endowment income, the objective of restoring tuition to its 1960 level (in real dollars) could be reached by reducing the faculty by a third and eliminating administrative frills.

There are a few law schools in America that could go further, and like Thomas Cooley's Michigan, charge no tuition at all. Such an institution would be communicating to its students precisely the professional morality that the traditions and institutions of self-government require and that democratic educators since the time of Jefferson and Wythe have sought to nurture. It would be making a large gift to the Republic.

Would the graduates of such a school be less well-equipped to compete in the profession? Not likely. Would they make better career choices and have more gratifying careers? Surely. Would such an institution and its alumni lose status or gain it? I believe the latter.

25

Prospect

There are few portents of a regeneration among American lawyers of the faith in the stability of democratic government or of commitment to the role of stewardship to its institutions. As Benjamin Barber has observed, philosophers are today more numerous than citizens.[1] The voices of Cooley, Brandeis, Freund, and Hand have occasional echoes, but they are often inaudible in a clamor of self-aggrandizement and self-advertisement. State and local governments are not yet the "lifeless skeletons" Cooley feared they would become, but they may be nearly so. Richard Sennett states that we have lost interest in civic affairs while yet longing for community.[2]

Meanwhile, the profession becomes more a preserve of a ruling class, while judges, scholars, and teachers are increasingly isolated in their pretensions of class. With the ruling class, they tend to live and work in a gated community in which the unwashed are unwelcome. It may also be that class lines within the profession are intensifying, because the twentieth-century preoccupation with academic credentials seems to continue on its upward course. As one would expect, those trends reflect what is happening in America as new technologies and the imperatives of free trade impose an ever-deepening cleavage of class lines dividing the aristocracy of human capitalists who can sell services valued in the world market from their countrymen who cannot. For the foreseeable future, those lawyers undertaking with my exemplars the responsibility to shelter and nurture the institutions of self-government must perform that duty against the march of events.

On the other hand, "it is a long road that has no turning." The Progressive movements of a century ago saved industrial society, capitalism, the market economy, and the institutions of the Republic from the inferno of class war. A century ago, a more technocratic and elite legal profession embedded in serviceable universities was a constructive response to the social and political problems of the day. It was recognized as serving a common good; its emergence helped enable the center to hold.

That seems to be no longer true. A legal profession overdeveloped in its technocratic expertise, with an overconfident judiciary and a professoriate withdrawn from its affairs into an equally overdeveloped academic profession, may have little to contribute to the stability of an increasingly divided post-industrial society. The existing profession may instead be viewed as a growing liability serving to invigorate feelings of hostility and alienation on the part of citizens who, not without reason, increasingly see themselves as the non-participating object of a government and a profession indifferent to their hopes, values, and interests.

Marx may be dead, but class struggle was endemic in human society for thousands of years before he wrote and has surely survived him. "Don't tread on me" is a slogan now reappearing on the heraldry of those who perceive that the vestiges of American self-government are a hoax and a new opiate of the people.

At such a time, the American legal profession has its traditional duty to perform. That duty was simply stated by Timothy Walker in Cincinnati when Thomas Cooley was a boy:

> We are trying the greatest political experiment the world ever witnessed; and the experience of all history warns us not to feel too secure. A voice from the tombs of all departed republics tells us that if our liberty is to be ultimately preserved, it is at the price of sleepless vigilance. I refer not to foreign aggression, for this we have nothing to fear; our only foes are those of our own household. Domestic aggression may come from two quarters. On the one hand, power [and wealth are] always tending to augmentation. Those who have some, employ it to gain more; and if not seasonably withstood, become too strong to be resisted. And on the other hand, liberty is always tending to licentiousness. The more men have, the more they are likely to want. Being free from many restraints, they would do away with all. Now when dangers threaten, from either of these quarters; when [the powerful] would trample the law under their feet, or mobs would rise to overthrow it; who are the sentinels to give the alarm? Do I assume too much in saying [those] whose profession it is to watch over the law?[3]

How might the profession hope to perform this mission in the century to come? Self re-examination might be the first step. It would require the profession to give greater collective and individual attention to the social and political consequences of demarcations of class lines that it presently fosters and diminish its preoccupation with the paste jewelry of academic credentials.

Regeneration would also seem to require a genuine devolution of power to local and state governments, because it is only at such levels that citizens can effectively participate in making political decisions they can rightly perceive to be their own. Federalism must be revalued.[4] In state and local governments, to borrow a phrase from architecture, political power can be exercised on a human scale, that is, within the limits of our understanding and prudence. Such a devolution would require, among other things, a compromise with the ambitions of the imperious "national class" to impose its will without regard to the consent of the governed.

Finally, regeneration would also require devolution of power away from the judiciary to the political branches of governments at all levels, because it is these political institutions that best know and best implement "the common thoughts of men." Some of the attention of academic lawyers, our "ministers without portfolio," might usefully be redirected to the work of legislative bodies and government agencies, even those of state and local governments. Even more needed is a reduction in the grandiosity of the judiciary, who have been too often encouraged to make decisions other than "on a human scale" that are beyond the limits of their wisdom and of their real power to influence events.

Such devolutionary changes would require lawyers and even law professors to spend more time with people owning conventional moral and political values and less with intellectuals and word processors. In short, it would require a general injection into the profession of modesty and sociability, if not humility.[5] Even some "cause lawyers" who are invested in the representation of ideas or causes[6] rather than people might usefully devote less effort to litigating claims rooted in the mists of natural law and more to lobbying in Capitols and city halls.

In turn, rehabilitation of legislative bodies would seem to require a transformation of the electoral process transmogrified by the advent of electronic media. Especially in need of re-examination is constitutional protection for pricey, spot political advertising on commercial television, where large audiences can be reached while inattentive to the sources of the disinformation with which they are supplied. Even viewers who are not successfully manipulated are alienated from the democratic process and thrust into a "spiral of cynicism"[7] disparaging not only to the law but to the sense of common citizenship; they cannot fail to notice that democratic politics has been made a preserve of the wealthy. Democracy requires the judiciary to recede from its excessive deference to the individual rights of those willing and able thus to spend money to influence outcomes.[8]

There is at least one legal system appearing to exemplify many of the characteristics that ours needs to regain. Ironically, it is the German. Law plays a large role in German culture, as it does in ours. The Basic Law of the Federal Republic promulgated in 1949 has been "a resounding success."[9] That law was drafted with a view to our experience. The judges of their Constitutional Court are appointed, half by each house of the Parliament, and serve non-renewable terms of twelve years;[10] their decisions can be reversed by amendments approved by two-thirds of both houses of the Parliament.[11]

An important mission of the Constitutional Court is to protect the institutions of federalism[12] and Home Rule[13] that our Prussian émigré, Francis Lieber, assured us long ago to have been a vital organ of our Republic. While German *landers* are sometimes prone to return power to the central government, they remain a useful check on the universal tendency to centralize. The German court is also responsible for enforcing an impressive list of individual rights expressed in the text of the Basic Law, including rights to "life" and to "physical integrity."[14] For a half-century, it has performed its role with vigor, but with little pretension that it is possessed of moral judgment superior to the elected representatives of the citizens it serves.

While judges and law professors are given extended training, education in law is available in Germany without an extraordinary investment of time or money and the social and professional pecking order among German universities has little bearing on the status or employability of lawyers. Individual judges are endowed with relatively modest discretion, because there is an extended appellate hierarchy responsible for close oversight of the exercise of judicial power.[15]

Germany remains a class-ridden society, perhaps still more class-ridden than America, but the feelings of all Germans toward their law and government were strikingly exhibited in 1998 when 86 percent of the eligible voters went to the polls to elect a new Parliament, an achievement unimaginable in America.

Reversals of direction by whole societies or classes do not occur merely as an act of will. There must be an external cause or a shared experience inducing a reaction before the increasingly divisive condition of our law and legal profession can begin to heal. What might be such a cause or experience? One possibility is that some citizens who are experiencing a substantial loss of status and sense their exclusion from the "national class" will in a time of crisis pose a sufficiently dramatic threat to the self-anointed that the latter will experience a Burkean epiphany not unlike that resulting in the Progressive era. If that should occur, it is not unlikely that any next round of Progressivism will disfavor the elevated pretensions of the legal profession and its judges, will devolve political power on local governments and legislatures, and might even find the will and the means to restore substantive civil dialogue to our national life.

Perhaps such a next round has been set in motion by the collapse of the Soviet Union, an event that has transformed relationships and expectations in fundamental ways that we have not yet fully felt. One tertiary effect of that event is to stimulate localism around the world. Communities can better be afforded a measure of independence. It could happen here.[16]

Another hopeful possibility is that the same technologies that nurtured and reinforced the vision of Langdell and the intellectual aspiration of Holmes may themselves set parameters to those developments. Rococo professional education in law, diminished in its effect by demands for emotional comfort and reassurance to the fragile self-esteem of its consumers, may be genuinely threatened by "distance learning." New institutions are arising to employ the internet to transmit the rudimentary education once supplied by Thomas Cooley and his colleagues. No less a competitor than the Kaplan Education Center of the Washington Post Company has entered the field,[17] and other well-capitalized organizations can be expected to join Kaplan. Their elegantly illustrated, high-tech, visual presentation can be recorded and transmitted almost anywhere on the planet. A mere handful of law professors can provide that form of instruction to an entire cohort of novitiates without either lecturers or students leaving their homes or offices. This would make thousands of other law teachers dispensable except to those who value the case method dialogue, and even that can be supplied by anonymous gnomes paid by the hour whom students can encounter in chat rooms. For that form of education, resident study requirements will be hard to defend and maintain, and the American Bar Association has conceded the applicability of the antitrust laws to such accreditation requirements.[18]

The primary remaining function of the university law school may then be the one performed in admissions offices. But those who employ lawyers may deduce that that, too, can be performed as well outside the university by employment agencies that compete in price. University law schools competing in such an environment would be under pressure to strip their curricula to the essentials, if indeed essentials can be identified. Thus, as distance learning displaces the boutique seminar, the real price of entry into the profession could diminish. We might be on the verge of discovering that professional education as we presently know it is a dinosaur. Imaginably, this might lead to the rediscovery of a moral purpose to professional education in law, as preparation for the role of stewardship illustrated by the careers celebrated here. While the academic pursuit of Truth in law cannot justify requiring many years of resident study as a precondition to the performance of professional services, the hope of nurturing public Virtue might.

Also, as Judge Posner has observed, our judges have substantially delegated some or perhaps even much of their work to law clerks with little noticeable depreciation in its quality. "It is," he said, "a little as if brain surgeons delegated the entire performance of delicate operations to nurses, orderlies, and first-year medical students—and patients were none the worse for it."[19] A comparable development has been the advent of paralegals in law firms. If the time comes when it is perceived that paralegals and parajudges are competent to do much of what highly trained lawyers and judges do, the reaction may resemble the Jacksonian reforms of the 1840s. In an age of deregulation of airlines, power companies, and other utilities, it is not unimaginable that excessively pretentious professions may also be deregulated.

Such a reaction would strip the profession as a whole, especially the judiciary, of the pretense that long years of study have enabled it to know best the answers to such imponderable questions as whether there is a right to live or a right to die, how differences in religious faith should be reflected in common schools, whether purported art is or is not smut, what should be advertised, what the highway patrol should say when it makes an arrest, or what professional school admissions offices should do about race, and a thousand other issues on which William Leggett's sturdy farmer or our neighborhood auto mechanic is essentially as well informed as the "sallow accountants" and lawyers who presume to impose their collective wills on such matters.

No doubt such an erosion of status and power would be resisted by much of the organized profession and the academy. Yet, it would not be without benefits to many lawyers or many who aspire to be lawyers. Most, at least, who presently presume (like this author) to be philosopher-kings are doomed to experience professional frustration and perhaps personal unhappiness. That doom will generally be avoided by those who define their professional tasks on a more nearly human scale. Success and professional gratification are far more likely to attend the careers of those who see themselves as Thucydides and Cicero would have wished them to.

Despite such benefits, other pressures will surely be needed to turn some of the judiciary away from their antidemocratic habits: perhaps the likes of the Presidents Roosevelt to advocate the recall of judicial decisions or a plan to pack the Court or some other crackpot idea for bringing more of the judiciary and the profession to recognize that they are commissioned not to rule the Republic, but to mediate among the forces seeking to do so. Such a political leader is not likely to appear until times are hard and the public is willing to entertain radical thoughts, but such a time could be in the not-so-distant future.

All that seems certain is that the present trend lines cannot be projected to infinity. Judges and lawyers can serve a Republic, but can never rule one. It would have been difficult in Cooley's time to foresee the evolution, one can almost say revolution, that was beginning to be visible that night in 1886 when he encountered Langdell and Holmes. However, there was forming at that time an irresistible tide of political, social, and economic reform that swept across much of America in the first decade-and-a-half of this century.

We are therefore entitled to hope for better times ahead, less in terms of enhanced gross domestic product and more in the communitarian impulses of democratic self-government. And an optimist might perhaps see a twinkling star of hope in the return of some contemporary art, literature, religion, and science to the stabilities and self-imposed constraints of the not-so-distant past. If such fields can experience that kind of renaissance, why not law?

Notes

Author names and short titles are used in these notes; full source information is in the References.

Chapter One: An Embattled Faith

1. De Tocqueville, Democracy in America, 296–306.
2. See generally Carrington, *Revolutionary Idea.*
3. For an account, see generally Carrington, *Theme of Early American Law Teaching.*
4. Lieber, Political Ethics, 19; Perry, Life and Letters, 416.
5. United States v. United Mine Workers, 330 U.S. 250, 308 (1947).
6. Kronman, Lost Lawyer, 175–180.
7. The phrases come from the Preamble to the Constitution of the United States.
8. Quoted in Peterson, Thomas Jefferson, 697.
9. This concern is to be distinguished from that of D. Kennedy, who finds class bias primarily in teaching methods that I defend. See his Legal Education as Training for Hierarchy.
10. This is the theme of Wiebe, Self-Rule.
11. *When Lawsuits Make Policy,* 17.
12. *George Washington Rides Again,* 18.
13. Glendon, Nation under Lawyers.
14. B. Friedman, Turn to History, 958–960; compare Cloud, *Searching Through History.*
15. Such lawyers are the subject of Sarat and Scheingold, Cause Lawyering.
16. Carrington, *A Tale of Two Lawyers,* 625–626.

Chapter Two: A Celebration

1. See Record of Commemoration.
2. A full biography of Cooley is A. Jones, Constitutional Conservatism; see also the briefer works of Hutchins, *Cooley;* McLaughlin, *Written Constitution;* and Rogers, *Cooley.*
3. In 1869–1870, Michigan had 308 law students, Harvard 120. Reed, Training for the Public Profession, 452. Their admission standards were then the same: literacy was the requirement.
4. *Book Review, Michigan Reports,* 883; A. Jones, Constitutional Conservatism, 180.
5. Wise, *Ablest State Court,* 1532–1534.

6. The American Law Review, edited in Boston by John Chipman Gray and then by Oliver Wendell Holmes, gave much attention to the decisions of the Supreme Court of Michigan. See, for example, Book Notice, 3 Am. L. Rev. 141 (1868); Book Notice, 3 Am. L. Rev. 757 (1869); Book Notice, 6 Am. L. Rev. 558 (1872). And see Mr. Justice Cooley, 32 Am. L. Rev. 916 (1898).

7. Rogers, *Cooley*, 217–219. See also Note, 22 Am. L. Rev. 477 (1888).

8. A. Jones, Constitutional Conservatism, 303–305.

9. Quoted by A. Jones, Constitutional Conservatism, 122.

10. Book Note, 27 Alb. L. Rev. 300 (1883).

11. This was the fourth edition of Story's Commentaries.

12. Cooley, Treatise on the Law of Taxation, iv. For contemporary comment on the taxation treatise, see Horwitz, Transformation of American Law, 20–22.

13. A. Jones, Constitutional Conservatism, 247.

14. His then most recent publication was a social and political history of his state. Cooley, Michigan.

15. Cooley, Elements of Torts.

16. *Record of Commemoration*, 95.

17. Public law became a subject of professional discourse in the era of the Marshall Court beginning in 1803; its emergence was marked in 1833 by the publication of Story's Commentaries on the Constitution, which emphasized case law as a source of constitutional doctrine. See Powell, *Loyalty to the Law*, 116–119 and Bloomfield, *Law and Politics*.

18. See the remarks in Record of Commemoration: Mr. Carter, 79; Justice Holmes, 65, and Dean Langdell, 84.

19. Address in Holmes, Collected Legal Papers, 272.

20. G. E. White, *Canonization*, 588–596.

Chapter Three: The Brahmin Hosts

1. Morison, Three Centuries of Harvard.

2. See generally D. Williams, Wilderness Lost.

3. Carrington, *Revolutionary Idea*, 541–568.

4. Sutherland, Law at Harvard, 92–139.

5. Id., 236–299.

6. 1 Warren, History of Harvard Law School, 292–296.

7. The proposal was advanced by John Lowell. Morison, *Dissent*, 18–26. Timothy Pickering had promoted New England secession as early as 1803. Greenslet, Lowells, 135–136.

8. In *Natural History of Intellect*, quoted in Brooks, Flowering of New England, 93.

9. 2 Martineau, Society in America, 188.

10. Full accounts of the events are in Fuhrner, Advocacy and Objectivity and Haskell, Emergence.

11. A Jones, Constitutional Conservatism, 31 n. 80.

Chapter Four: The Barnburner Persuasion

1. A. Jones, Constitutional Conservatism, 1–2.

2. Cooley, Michigan, 240–241. The description is of Michigan in the 1830s, but he was describing immigrants from New York and Ohio whose ancestors were from New England, and the account is indirectly autobiographical.

3. Horton, James Kent, 130.

4. Id., 126.

5. 4 Dwight, Travels, 3–4. The letter quoted was written in 1804. President Dwight was given to such jeremiads. L. Friedman, 183.

6. Carrington, *Law and Chivalry*, 712–714. For a critical assessment of the novel, see Ferguson, Law and Letters, 119–128.

7. See Notions and Letter to Lafayette.

8. Letter to Countrymen; Homeward Bound is a fictional statement of the aristocratic views expressed in these political tracts.

9. Ferguson, Law and Letters, 300.

10. Home as Found, 66–67.

11. Id., 210.

12. O'Dea, The Mormons, 2–4.

13. Cross, Burnt Over District, 112.

14. H. Starr, *Finney.*

15. 1 Fletcher, History of Oberlin College, 11.

16. An account of revivalsim is Cross's Burnt Over District.

17. Greenstone, Lincoln Persuasion, 260–262.

18. See Metaphysical Elements of Justice.

19. 1 de Tocqueville, Democracy in America, 101–160.

20. Martineau, Retrospect.

21. 1 de Tocqueville, Democracy in America, 292.

22. Chapman, Garrison, 34–157; Thomas, Liberator, 114–366; Walters, Antislavery Appeal, 3–18.

23. *Second Reply to Hayne, January 26, 1830* in 3 Webster, Works, 342.

24. Leggett was born in New York City in 1801. He died in 1839. His friend and admirer, Theodore Sedgwick Jr. promptly collected and published his work. Leggett's influence was assessed in Hofstadter, *William Leggett*. See also Meyers, Jacksonian Persuasion, 141–157. For a sampling of his own work, see Leggett, Democratick Editorials.

25. See Leggett, Democratick Editorials, 271–272.

26. Id., 255.

27. *First Inaugural Address, March 4, 1801* in 3 Jefferson, Writings, 317 (Bergh).

28. Schlesinger, Age of Jackson, 257.

29. 2 Compilation of Messages and Papers, 590.

30. Enumerated in Novak, *Public Economy*. For a compilation, see Dane, General Abridgement, 728–755.

31. Generally set forth in Sedgwick, Public and Private Economy.

32. Wealth of Nations. Smith's social views were not dissimilar to those of Barn-burners; he was not, as many may assume, a social Darwinist or a eulogist for unre-strained predation by wealth. Viner, *Adam Smith*.

33. Devised by Henry Clay, "The American System" was a scheme to collect a tariff protecting local industry and providing revenue to fund internal improve-ments such as roads and canals. For a brief description, see Peterson, Great Tri-umvirate, 68–84.

34. 2 Leggett, Democratick Editorials, 289–292, 296, and 315.

35. The Panic and its aftermath are described by Rezneck in *Social History*.

36. 2 Leggett, Democratick Editorials, 162–163.

37. P. Starr, Social Transformation, 30–59.

38. For brief accounts, see Haber, Quest for Authority, 91–116 and Bloomfield, American Lawyers, 32–58.

39. Coke, *Prohibitions, 65*.

40. Indiana Constitution of 1851, Art. VII, § 21.

41. For an example, see Kent, Memoirs, 235.

42. 2 Chroust, Rise of Legal Profession, 245ff.

43. Even in Massachusetts, local bar organizations were dissolved. Gawalt, Massachusetts Lawyers, 145.

44. Goebel, History, 52–53, 104–108.

45. Haynes, Selection and Tenure of Judges, 96–97.

46. The best statement of the case for the election of judges may be Grimke, Na-ture of Free Institutions, ch. 7.

47. In *Constitutional Machinery* and *Route to Hell*, Hall describes reform poli-tics in numerous states.

48. Haynes, Selection and Tenure of Judges, 101–135.

49. This is the point made by Hartz, Liberal Tradition in America.

50. Carlyle, Past and Present, 168.

51. A. Jones, Constitutional Conservatism, 25.

52. Cooley, *Consider M. Stacy*, 268.

53. 2 Chambers's Information for the People, 697.

54. Id., 696–697.

55. A. Jones, Constitutional Conservatism, 37 n. 13.

56. 16 Western Literary Messenger 65 (1851).

57. A. Jones, Constitutional Conservatism, 72.

Chapter Five: Legal Education for the People

1. Brackenridge, Modern Chivalry, 419.

2. Quoted in 4 Clay, Papers, 818.

3. Woodburn, History of Indiana University, 280–281.

4. Carrington and King, *Wisconsin Idea*.

5. Carrington, *Legal Education for the People*.

6. The first two presidents of Cornell, Andrew Dickson White and Charles Kendall Adams, were Michigan colleagues of Cooley. Adams's plan for a law school reflected the Michigan tradition. See Report of Special Committee . . . Cornell Uni-

versity. The founding dean at Cornell was Harry Burns Hutchins, who came from Michigan and later returned to Ann Arbor. Hutchins, *Cornell Law School.*

7. The group was for a time known as "The Club." For Albert Gallatin's description, see J. A. Stevens, Albert Gallatin, 379ff.

8. T. Jones, New York University, 6.

9. Bellot, University College, 10–37.

10. Especially important was the report of George Tichnor of Harvard. Morison, Three Centuries, 232–238.

11. Albert Gallatin, quoted in H. Adams, Life of Gallatin, 648.

12. Report quoted by T. Jones, New York University, 12.

13. 9 Wendell (N.Y.) 224.

14. His biography is Driscoll's Benjamin Butler.

15. J. Curtis, Fox at Bay, 61.

16. Proctor, Bench and Bar of New York, 751–755.

17. The program may have attracted as few as fifteen students. Reed, Training for the Public Profession, 152.

18. Tompkins, New York Law School, 11–14.

19. Allison, Historical Sketch, 15–20.

20. Id., 40.

21. Documentary History, 196.

22. For an expression of his views, see Lathrop, Address.

23. He was born at Catskill in 1822; he was the grandson of Timothy Dwight, the president of Yale. *Goebel* 33–43.

24. 1 Fletcher, History of Oberlin College, 117.

25. Other American colleges had earlier received African-American students without fanfare. Thus, the first student enrolled at Lafayette College in Easton, Pennsylvania, happened to be an African American. 1 Skillman, Biography of a College, 66.

26. A brief account is Fairchild, *Professorship of Law.*

27. 2 Fletcher, History of Oberlin College, 705.

28. George Vattel '44 was the first African-American lawyer in Pittsburgh, and practiced for several decades in Syracuse. 2 Fletcher, History of Oberlin College, 533. John Mercer Langston '50 was the first African-American lawyer in Ohio and the founder of the law school at Howard University. His autobiography is From Virginia Plantation. His experiences at Howard are recounted by Logan in Howard University.

29. E. G. Brown, Legal Education at Michigan, 3–6.

30. Michigan Constitution of 1837, Art. X, § 5.

31. Cooley, *Founding*, 93.

32. Schlesinger, Age of Jackson, 159–176.

33. Schoenberger, *Tappan.*

34. E. G. Brown, Legal Education at Michigan, 269–270.

35. Reed, Training for the Public Profession, 195.

36. Hutchins, *Cooley*, 435.

37. One account is in Fessenden's *Rebirth.*

38. 2 Warren, History of Harvard Law School, 409–413.

39. The metaphor is not original. B. Currie, *Materials of Law Study,* 20. Another comparison is to geometry, suggested by Hoeflich in *Law and Geometry*.

40. He was, however, cognizant of mercantile custom as a source of contract law. Kimball, *Warn Students,* 58.

41. J. Clay Smith, Emancipation. The two African-American students graduating from the University of Michigan Law School in 1872 were both from Adrian, suggesting that Cooley had a hand in their arrival. E. G. Brown, *Initial Admission*.

42. Robinson, *Women Lawyers*.

43. Drachman, Sisters in Law, 64–71.

44. R. Stevens, Law School, 35–72.

45. A. Jones, Constitutional Conservatism, 222–226.

46. Boyd, Cooley Bibliography, 4.

47. Published in five volumes in 1803. Tucker elided the most offensive of Blackstone's royalisms and added notes descriptive of American law.

48. J. Kent, Commentaries.

49. Harris, *Fronter Lawyer's Library,* 241.

50. Another edition was prepared by William Gardiner Hammond, the founder of two law schools, at the University of Iowa and at Washington University.

51. Ames, *Langdell,* 466–467.

52. Seligman, High Citadel, 30.

53. Williston, Life and Law, 200.

54. LaPiana, Logic and Experience, 77.

55. Elkins and McKittrick, Age of Federalism, 92–132.

56. Quoted in 2 Warren, History of Harvard Law School, 397.

57. La Piana, Logic and Experience, 24; Sheppard, *Casebooks,* 599–604.

58. This last is an idea often associated with John Austin, but it is not known that Langdell ever read Austin.

59. Record of Commemoration, 86.

60. Id.

61. Carrington, *Langdell,* 716–739.

62. Letter of January 8, 1883, quoted in Howe, Justice Holmes, 158. See also LaPiana, Logic and Experience, 18–20.

63. Quoted in Baker, Justice from Beacon Hill, 208–209. His published review of Langdell was less harsh. Book Notice, 6 Am. L. Rev. 354 (1872) and Book Notices, 14 Am. L. Rev. 14 (1880). The latter, a review of the second edition, was unsigned. For attribution of authorship, see Touster, "Holmes," 695 n. 91.

64. Book Note, 14 Am. L. Rev. 233 (1880).

65. E. G. Brown, Legal Education at Michigan, 102–103.

Chapter Six: Law and the Lightning of Genius

1. Holmes, Collected Legal Papers, 276–277.

2. Cooley, *Lawyer's Duty,* 87.

3. Cooley, *Sources,* 520–521.

4. Thucydides, History of the Peloponnesian War, Bk. III, § 37 (quoting Cleon, the son of Claenetus). Cooley elaborated on this theme in *Lecture I*. Compare Lincoln, *Perpetuation of Political Institutions,* 112.

5. This is the theme of Wiebe in *Self-Rule.*

6. Croly, Promise of American Life, 134.

7. Scalia, *Common Law Courts,* 13.

8. Id., 9.

9. Holmes, *Path of the Law.*

10. Alschuler, *Descending Trail,* passim.

11. Id., 409.

12. For example, Posner, *An Economic Theory of Criminal Law,* 1205–1208.

13. For example, Singer, *Player and the Cards,* passim. For a response, see Stick, *Can Nihilism Be Pragmatic?*

14. See generally Grey, *Holmes.*

15. Howe, Justice Holmes, 261.

16. Holmes, *Law in Science,* 59–60.

17. Quoted in Baker, Justice from Beacon Hill, 270.

18. Holmes, *Path of the Law,* 474.

19. Mill, *On Liberty,* 163.

20. For an expression of this view, see Croley, *Majoritarian Difficulty.*

21. E. S. Brown, *Contribution,* 363.

22. For current provisions in American jurisdictions, see Book of The States, 127–128; for a collection of foreign constitutions, see The Constitutions of the Countries.

23. Mill, *On Liberty,* 140.

24. Holmes, *Twenty Years in Retrospect,* 157.

25. Southern Pacific v. Jensen, 244 U.S. 205, 221 (1917) (Holmes, J., dissenting); see Grey, *Molecular Motions.*

26. Holmes, Common Law, 106.

27. Gordon, *Comment,* 570.

28. The question asked, for example, in McIntyre, Whose Justice?

29. Millon, in *Objectivity,* makes a similar observation.

30. Hamilton et al., Federalist, No. 71.

31. 198 U.S. 45 (1905).

32. Lochner v. New York, 198 U.S. 45, 75 (1905). See Sunstein, *Lochner's Legacy.*

33. White, Justice Holmes, 140. See also Ross, Origins, 66.

34. Letter to Alice Stepford Green, August 20, 1909, quoted in Holmes, The Essential Holmes, 116.

35. Cooley, *The Influence of Habits.*

36. Cooley, Law as *Educating Force.*

37. Holmes, *The Gas Stokers' Strike,* 582, 583.

38. 1 Ackerman, We the People, 4.

39. See generally Farber and Frickey, Law and Public Choice.

40. For example, Michelman, *Law's Republic.*

41. Galanter, *Portable Soc 21, 259.*

42. See Jacobs, Law Writers, 23–63; Corwin, Liberty Against Government, 67–8; Fine, Laissez-Faire, 128–129; Haines, Revival of Natural Law, 117; Hall, Magic Mirror, 222–223; Hyman, More Perfect Union, 354–355, 516–519; Leedes, *Justice Sutherland;* Lerner, *Supreme Court;* Paludan, *Law and Failure of Reconstruction;* Paul, Conservative Crisis, 142–146; Siegel, *Historicism,* 1516 n. 503; Syed, Political Theory, 64; Tribe, American Constitutional Law, 571 n. 4; Twiss, Lawyers, 34. Of these, Twiss is perhaps most extreme in describing Cooley's treatise as a "direct counter" to Das Capital (Twiss, 18). Jacobs, apparently basing his observation wholly on frequency of citation, nominated Cooley as "the principal contributor to the cause of constitutional laissez-faire in the era following the Civil War." (Jacobs, 27). Those who later saw ratification of the Fourteenth Amendment as a conspiracy to secure property rights against socialism regarded Cooley as one of the conspirators, his treatise being the evidence. (See, e.g., Graham, Self-Inflicted Wound.) See also Hurst, Growth of American Law, 338; Paschal, Justice Sutherland, 9. More balanced in their presentation of Cooley are A. Jones, Constitutional Conservatism and *Thomas M. Cooley;* Barnes, *Introduction* to Cooley, Treatise on Constitutional Limitations; Baskerville, Law and Limitations; Benedict, *Laissez Faire;* Friedman, 545–546; Gillman, Constitution Besieged, 55–59; Gold, Shaping Law, 137–139; Nelson, Roots of Bureaucracy, 5 and passim; and Nelson, Fourteenth Amendment, 14, 110, 192; White, American Legal Tradition, 115–122; J. Williams, Constitutional Vulnerability, 1485–1514.

43. White, American Legal Tradition, 151.

44. For example, Hartz, Liberal Tradition; Bickel, Morality of Consent, 3–30.

45. Freidel, Francis Lieber; B. Brown, American Conservatives.

46. Rawls, Political Liberalism. For yet a different use of the term "liberal," see Kalman, Strange Career. Kalman, like Rawls, makes no effort to define the term. She seems to equate "liberal" with a set of views held by late-century academics sometimes scorned as "political correctness."

47. An effort to supply a definition is S. Holmes, Passions and Constraint.

48. Shklar, Ordinary Vices, 5.

49. Cooper, Letter to Countrymen, 99.

50. Cooley, *Address,* 10.

51. Cooley, *Lecture I.*

52. Cooley, Michigan, 371.

53. His remarks are quoted by A. Jones, *Cooley and the Court,* 121.

54. Lieber, Legal and Political Hermeneutics, 195. For an earlier expression of the same point, see Brackenridge, Modern Chivalry, 45.

55. Lasch, Revolt of the Elites.

Chapter Seven: The Supreme Court in Jacksonian Perspective

1. Act of Settlement of 1701, 12 & 13 Will. 2, c.2, § 3(1700) (Eng.).

2. Dawson, Oracles, 12.

3. R. Stevens, Independence, 3–4.

4. Goldfarb, Contempt is an account of this development.

5. Haynes, Selection and Tenure of Judges, 80, 99–100.

6. Quoted by William Plumer, in turn quoted by Bloomfield, American Lawyers, 57.

7. Winters, *Selection of Judges,* 1081; Haynes, Selection and Tenure of Judges, 98–99.

8. Henderson's *Background* and Wolfram's *Constitutional History* provide full accounts.

9. Wolfram, *Constitutional History,* 657, 662–673. And see 1 de Tocqueville, Democracy in America, 307–314.

10. See F. Strong, Judicial Function, chapter 1.

11. Act of June 18, 1798, 1 Stat. 566; Act of June 25, 1798, 1 Stat. 570; Act of July 6, 1798, 1 Stat. 566; and Act of June 25, 1798, 1 Stat. 586. For an account of this episode, see J. M. Smith, Freedom's Fetters; for its background, see Levy, Legacy of Suppression.

12. Francis Wharton, *State Trials in the United States During the Administrations of Washington and Adams,* quoted in D'Alemberte, *Searching for the Limits,* 626.

13. Warren, History of Supreme Court, 191; see generally 187–230. For a recent defense of Chase, see Jay, Rehabilitation.

14. Ellis, Jeffersonian Crisis, 33; J. E. Smith, John Marshall, 301, 372.

15. 1 Cranch 137 (1803).

16. An account is 2 Beveridge, Life of John Marshall, 168–220.

17. 1 Warren, History of Supreme Court, 295.

18. Carrington, *Butterfly Effects,* 753–754.

19. Letter to Governor John Tyler, May 26, 1810, in 12 Writings, 391, 392 (Bergh).

20. D. Dewey, Marshall, 170–174.

21. 4 Wheat. 316 (1819).

22. Id. at 324–325, 326–327, 377–376.

23. Second Reply to Hayne, 5 Webster, Writings, 248.

24. *Andrew Jackson Nullification Proclamation,* 2A Compilation of the Messages of the Presidents, 640.

25. 2 Story, Commentaries, 543–555 (1833); and see Powell, *Story's Commentaries,* 1293.

26. See generally Freehling, *Prelude to War.*

27. Created Equal?, 119–121.

28. The Douglas position is examined in Johansen, Frontier.

29. Marshall wrote nine essays in the exchange. Marshall's Defense (Gunther ed.) collects them.

30. Published in Richmond in 1820.

31. Details are provided in The Responsible Judge, 247–255.

32. 4 Wheat. 518 (1819).

33. Section 10.

34. Federalist, No. 44.

35. Charles River Bridge Co. v. Warren Bridge Co., 11 Pet. 420 (1837).

36. Id. at 629.

37. For example, Hunter v. Pittsburgh, 207 U.S. 161 (1907).

38. 91 U.S. 216 (1842).

39. See especially Holmes's *Address* in John Chipman Gray, 49–50.

40. Gray, Natures and Sources of Law, 253.

41. Erie v. Tompkins, 304 U.S. 64 (1938). The story is more fully told in Freyer, Harmony & Dissonance.

42. Scott v. Sandford, 19 How. 393 (1857).

43. M. Siegel, Taney Court, 66–68.

44. A recent comment on the opinion is Deane, *Reassessing Dred Scott*. See generally Fehrenbacher, Dred Scott.

45. Frank, Lincoln, 115–123, 135–140.

46. *First Inaugural Address, March 4, 1861* in 8 Compilation of Messages of the Presidents, 3210.

47. *Ex parte* Merryman, 17 Fed. Cas. No. 9487 (Cir. Ct. Md. 1861). See Jackson, 324–327.

48. Kens, Justice Field, 95–96.

49. For example, Hurtado v. California, 119 U.S. 516 (1884); Mugler v. Kansas, 123 U.S. 623 (1887).

50. Kens, Justice Field, 245.

51. Pollock v. Farmers' Loan & Trust Co., 157 U.S. 479, 607 (1895).

52. For discussion, see Corwin, Court Over Constitution, 177–209.

Chapter Eight: Deference to Democracy

1. Grimke, Nature of Free Institutions, 457.

2. Hutchins, *Cooley*, 458.

3. The story is told by G. Edwards in *Why Cooley Left*.

4. Wiebe, The Search for Order. Wiebe begins his account with the recovery from the depression of 1873 and the aftermath of the Grant administration.

5. White, American Legal Tradition, 114.

6. Cooley, *Uncertainty*. To this reader, the reassurance was not especially convincing. This was one of Cooley's more pedestrian works. The theme, however, is also that of Llewellyn in Common Law Tradition.

7. This was not so extraordinary as some twentieth century observers may have supposed. See Scheiber, Instrumentalism.

8. People v. Blodgett, 13 Mich. 163 (1865).

9. 13 Mich. at 173.

10. Compare Lincoln, *Perpetuation of Political Institutions*.

11. G. E. White, Marshall Court, 927–964.

12. A. Jones, Constitutional Conservatism, 172.

13. Cf. Scalia, *Originalism*, 851–852.

14. Stuart v. School Dist. #1 of Kalamazoo, 30 Mich. 69, 80 (1874).

15. 30 Mich. at 85.

16. Barron, *Promise of Cooley's City*.

17. Cooley's position on home rule is examined in J. Williams's *Constitutional Vulnerability* and Gere's *Dillon's Rule.*

18. 24 Mich. 44 (1871). For background, see A. Jones, *Cooley and the Court,* 115–117.

19. Art. XV, § 14.

20. Cf. Bickel & Wellington, *Legislative Purpose,* 34, 38.

21. See Krotoszynski, *Constitutional Flares.*

22. 24 Mich. at 44, 109.

23. Civil Liberty and Self-Government, passim.

24. 24 Mich. at 108.

25. Id. at 107.

26. Cooley, Treatise on Constitutional Limitations, 192.

27. Mich. Pub. Acts No. 392, 1873 Laws of Michigan 175.

28. Park Comm'rs v. The Mayor, 29 Mich. 343 (1874).

29. Robertson v. Dexter, 57 Mich. 127 (1885). See also Allor v. Wayne County Comm'rs, 43 Mich. 76 (1880).

30. Board of Park Comm'rs v. Common Council of Detroit, 28 Mich. 227, 241 (1873).

31. For the present status of Home Rule provisions, see Callies, *Home Rule.* For an analysis of the judicial role in enforcing such provisions, see Sandalow, *Limits of Municipal Powers.*

32. Hunter v. City of Pittsburgh, 207 U.S. 161 (1907).

33. For example, see San Antonio Indep. Sch. Dist. v. Rodriguez, 411 U.S. 1 (1973); cf. Milliken v. Bradley, 418 U.S. 717 (1974).

34. People v. Board of Educ. of Detroit, 18 Mich. 400 (1869).

35. Id. at 414.

36. Treatise on Constitutional Limitations, 393. He did, however, acknowledge the force of a state constitutional provision limiting the elective franchise to whites. Id., 394. The Fifteenth Amendment to the Constitution of the United States trumped this Michigan constitutional provision, but not until 1870.

37. 163 U.S. 537, 557 (1896) (Harlan, J. dissenting). Cf. Strauder v. West Virginia, 100 U.S. 303 (1880) (holding that the Equal Protection Clause precludes state from restricting jury service to white persons).

38. Treatise on Constitutional Limitations, 393.

39. 46 Mich. 341 (1881).

40. 376 U.S. 254 (1964).

41. The next year, the court upheld a privilege of the press against a claim by a judge whom the newspaper had accused of confining a man without a charge and setting excessive bail. Miner v. The Detroit Post and Tribune, 49 Mich. 358 (1882).

42. 46 Mich. at 383. Compare Kalven, A Worthy Tradition, 205. In MacLean v. Scripps, 52 Mich. 214 (1883), Cooley joined in affirming a judgment in favor of a professor of medicine accused by the press of adultery.

43. See, for example, Near v. Minnesota, 283 U.S. 439 (1911).

44. A. Jones, *Cooley and the Court,* 101–106.

45. See Schaefer, *State Investment.*

46. A Republican governor had vetoed such legislation in 1866 and 1867. Constitutional revision was proposed in 1868 to authorize such aid and the revision was defeated by vote of the people. A. Jones, Constitutional Conservatism, 174.

47. People v. Salem, 20 Mich. 452 (1870).

48. Id. at 477–479.

49. Id. at 483–484.

50. Id. at 485.

51. Id. at 486–487.

52. A. Jones, Constitutional Conservatism, 181, n. 41.

53. There was a somewhat similar holding in Hansen v. Iowa, 27 Iowa 28 (1869).

54. See, for example, C. Kent, *Municipal Subscription;* Note, 7 Am. L. Rev. 126 (1870). The Supreme Judicial Court of Maine reached a similar result relying upon the explicit language of the Maine Constitution forbidding takings without compensation. Allen v. Jay, 60 Me. 124 (1872).

55. A. Jones, Constitutional Conservatism, 183.

56. Quoted in id., 180.

57. See, for example, Township of Pine Grove v. Talcott, 86 U.S. 666 (1874) (holding that state subsidization of railroad construction is not a violation of the Fourteenth Amendment).

58. 54 Mich. 350 (1884) (also cited as State Tax-Law Cases).

59. Id. at 360–361.

60. For example, Cooley, *The Administration of President Grant,* 170.

61. For example, Cooley, *The Method of Electing.*

62. "Blaine, Blaine, James G. Blaine, continental liar from the state of Maine!" was a popular cry. Hirsch, *Election of 1884,* 1561. For a contemporaneous account of the Blaine-Cleveland campaign, see Goodrich, Life and Public Service, 386–387.

63. The case was McLean v. Scripps, 52 Mich. 250 (1883). The attack of the paper on Cooley is described in Edwards, *Why Cooley Left.*

64. Id., 1568 (quoting *Evening News,* March 16, 1885 at 2, col. 1). When he lost the election, the *Evening News* crowed that he had been "unmercifully slaughtered" by 20,000 votes, "[j]ust the number of dollars that were given in a celebrated judgment." Id., 1572 (quoting *Evening News,* April 6, 1885 at 2, col. 1).

65. Vander Velde, *Cooley,* in Michigan and the Cleveland Era, 92.

Chapter Nine: A Nineteenth-Century Classic

1. Cooley, Treatise on the Law of Taxation, iv. See also his Editor's Preface to Story, Commentaries on the Constitution (4th ed), v–vi.

2. The civil law tradition has long treated scholarly synthesis as an important source of law. See Dawson, Oracles of the Law, 100–147.

3. Carrington, *Butterfly Effects,* 795–805; see generally Simpson, *Rise and Fall;* Rubin, *Practice and Discourse.*

4. Lawyers also sometimes forget. For example, Erickson, *Muller v. Oregon,* 232–233.

5. Contrast the training and experience of the English judiciary. Atiyah and Summers, Form and Substance, 336–358.

6. Rogers, Unpublished Biography (quoting Judge Graves).

7. Note, *Cooley's Constitutional Law,* 328.

8. Friedman, History of American Law, 545.

9. McLaughlin, *Cooley.* See also Hutchins, *Cooley,* 472–473.

10. Hurst, Growth of American Law, 203.

11. 1 Cranch. 137 (1803).

12. Perry, Life and Letters, 55–60.

13. Id., 77.

14. Id., 140.

15. Harley, Francis Lieber, 78.

16. Lieber, Political Ethics.

17. Lieber, Legal and Political Hermeneutics.

18. Lieber, Civil Liberty and Self-Government.

19. Id., 242.

20. Lieber, Manual of Political Ethics (2d ed); Legal and Political Hermeneutics (3d ed); Civil Liberty and Self-Government (2d ed.)

21. Carrington, *William Gardiner Hammond.*

22. His biography is Altschuler's Andrew D. White. He remained a close, lifelong friend of Cooley. A. Jones, Constitutional Conservatism, 383.

23. This Adams founded the political science department at Michigan before following White to the presidency of Cornell. Haddow, Political Science, 189–192, 205–208. He concluded his career as the president of the University of Wisconsin.

24. See generally Fuhrner, Advocacy and Objectivity; Haskell, Emergence.

25. Constitutional Limitations, iv. [All references are to the 1868 edition unless otherwise noted.]

26. Jacobs, Law Writers, 23–63; Lerner, *Supreme Court,* 692.

27. Constitutional Limitations, 38–84.

28. Sedgwick III, Treatise on the Rules. This Sedgwick was a fellow adherent of the Equal Rights doctrine. His father was the author of a work acclaimed by Jacksonians as perhaps the best expression of their dogma. Bridenbaugh, *Theodore Sedgwick.* Stephen Field was the father's research assistant while Field was a student at Williams. Swisher, Stephen J. Field, 16–17. The son attended Columbia and practiced law in New York City, where he was active in politics with David Dudley Field, notably in the Constitutional Convention of 1846, which abolished the apprenticeship requirements for admission to the bar. Heck, *Theodore Sedgwick.* Sedgwick's treatise was revived in a posthumous edition prepared by John Norton Pomeroy in 1874.

29. Constitutional Limitations, 38 n. 1.

30. For example, "Give effect to the whole instrument." Id., 57–59.

31. Id., 71, n. 2.

32. People v. Hurlbut, 24 Mich 44, 107 (1871).

33. But see S. Siegel, *Historicism,* 1488–1514.

34. Constitutional Limitations, 73.

35. Id., 73–74.

36. A. Walker, History of Sherman Law, 12.

37. Constitutional Limitations, 159–188.

38. Scott v. Sandford, 19 How. 393 (1857).
39. Constitutional Limitations, 169–172.
40. Citing more than a score of cases from as many different states and quoting Justice Lemuel Shaw of the Supreme Judicial Court of Massachusetts. Id., 182.
41. Thayer, *Origin and Scope,* 140.
42. For comment on this aspect of Thayer's doctrine, see Nagel, *Name Calling.*
43. Cf. 1 Story, Commentaries, x: "A constitution of government is addressed to the common sense of the people and never was designed for trials of logical skills or visionary speculation."
44. A. Jones, Constitutional Conservatism, 247. On the possible influence of Thayer's essay on a trio of justices, see Mendelson, *Influence.*
45. Tushnet, *Thayer's Target.* But compare Allen, *Constitutional Adjudication.*
46. Grey, *Thayer's Doctrine;* G. E. White, *Revisiting Thayer.*
47. For a brief account of his activities, see Carrington, *Hail! Langdell!,* 719. One may find in his concerns for Native Americans and Filipinos a measure of patronization, see Hook, *Brief Life,* 7, but if paternalism is a badge of reaction, then the New Dealers must also qualify for that label. Thayer also actively opposed the war with Spain as an unwelcome venture into imperialism. Thayer, *Our New Possessions.*
48. Bork, 54.
49. See Kyvig, Explicit and Authentic Acts; Chemerinsky, *Amending the Constitution.*
50. 410 U.S. 113 (1973). I cite this case as perhaps the most aggressive use of the Court's power in the twentieth century.
51. See Thayer, *Origin and Scope.* See Tushnet, *Thayer's Target,* 27.
52. For example, People v. Hurlbut, 24 Mich. 44 (1871).
53. Constitutional Limitations, 192.
54. Id., 189.
55. Id., 195.
56. Id. at 196–197.
57. This is the theme of Lieber, Civil Liberty and Self-Government.
58. J. Williams, *Constitutional Vulnerability,* 137–149.
59. For example, Eaton, *Right to Local Self-Government,* passim; Syed, Political Theory, 53–75.
60. For a brief account of his career, see Goebel, History, 84–85. Dillon shares with Cooley and Tiedeman the distinction of being the object of attack by Jacobs, Law Writers.
61. J. Williams, *Constitutional Vulnerability.* And see Gere, *Dillon's Rule.*
62. She described Dillon as "an academic ally of the robber barons of the Gilded Age." J. Williams, *Constitutional Vulnerability,* 90.
63. Id., 149.
64. Cooley, *Lecture I.*
65. 20 Mich. 452 (1870).
66. Constitutional Limitations, 211–235.
67. Constitutional Limitations (4th ed), 260–261 and 289.
68. Barron, *Promise.*

69. Constitutional Limitations, 334. But see his reference to Webb v. Baird, 6 Ind. 13, at 394. Contrast Mallard v. United States District Court, 490 U.S. 296 (1989).

70. Johnson v. Zerbst, 304 U.S. 458 (1937); Gideon v. Wainwright, 372 U.S. 335 (1962).

71. Constitutional Limitations, 351.

72. Id., 355, quoting Bank of Columbia v. Okely, 4 Wheat. 235 (1819).

73. See, for example, Underkuffler-Freund, *Perfidy of Property*, reviewing Nedelsky, Private Property; F. Strong, Judicial Function.

74. Twiss, Lawyers, 18.

75. Constitutional Limitations, 392, quoting Locke, Of Civil Government, § 142.

76. Id., 393.

77. 520 U.S. 681.

78. Constitutional Limitations, 390, 393.

79. Erickson, *Muller v. Oregon,* 233.

80. Muller v. Oregon, 208 U.S. 412 (1908).

81. Constitutional Limitations, 414–466.

82. Id., 573.

83. Id., 574–580.

84. Dartmouth College v. Woodward, 4 Wheat. 518 (1819).

85. Constitutional Limitations, (2d ed., 1871) 335. See also Cooley, *State Regulation.*

86. See generally Degler, Age of Economic Revolution.

87. Montgomery, Beyond Equality and The Fall of The House.

88. For example, Slaughterhouse Cases, 16 Wall. 36 (1873); Butchers Union v. Crescent City, 111 U.S. 746 (1883); Barbier v. Connolly 110 U.S. 127 (1884); Yick Wo v. Hopkins, 118 U.S. 356 (1886); Powell v. Pennsylvania, 127 U.S. 678 (1888).

89. For example, Chicago B. & Q. R. Co. v. Chicago, 166 U.S. 226, 236, 239 (1897); Davidson v. New Orleans, 96 U.S. 97, 99 (1878); Richmond F. &. P. R. Co. v. Richmond, 96 U.S. 521, 525 (1877); Boston Beer Co. v. Massachusetts, 97 U.S. 25, 26 (1877); Munn v. Illinois, 94 U.S. 113 (1877).

90. For biographies, see Kens, Justice Field; McCurdy, *Justice Field*; and Swisher, Stephen J. Field.

91. Swisher, Stephen J. Field, 428.

Chapter Ten: The Civil War Amendments

1. Donald, Charles Sumner, 262–264.

2. All editions were published by Little, Brown in Boston.

3. 1 Story, Commentaries, v.

4. [Cooley's footnote:] 20 State Trials 1; Lofft 18, Broom, Const. Law, 105.

5. 2 Story, Commentaries, 645.

6. Id., 689–690.

7. United States v. Reese, 92 U.S. 214 (1876); United States v. Cruikshank, 92 U.S. 542 (1876).

8. For example, *Ex parte* Yarbrough, 110 U.S. 651 (1884).

9. Upheld as late as Grovey v. Townsend, 295 U.S. 45 (1935), *overruled in* Smith v. Allwright, 321 U.S. 649 (1944).

10. See generally E. Foner, Reconstruction.

11. 2 Story, Commentaries, 648–649.

12. Id., 649. See Section 4 of the Fourteenth Amendment.

13. 2 Story, Commentaries, 653–656.

14. Id., 657.

15. Id., 658.

16. In Corfield v. Coryell, 6 Fed. Cas. 546 (1823), Justice Washington held that this clause did not preclude a state from limiting fishing rights in its streams to its own citizens, there being no federal right to fish.

17. The Slaughterhouse Cases, 16 Wall. 36, 74 (1873). In his opinion, Justice Miller enumerated some federal privileges, such as the right to travel to the seat of the government.

18. Field's position was developed in his dissenting opinion in The Slaughterhouse Cases, 83 U.S. 36 (1873). See also Bertemeyer v. Iowa, 85 U.S. 129 (1874).

19. Butchers' Union v. Crescent City Livestock Lending and Slaughterhouse Co., 111 U.S. 746, 756 (1884).

20. Paludan, *Law and Failure of Reconstruction,* 608.

21. 2 Story, Commentaries, 657–658, quoting 2 Speeches of Sumner 341.

22. 2 Story, Commentaries, 661–662.

23. Id., 662–663.

24. Id., 667.

25. Paludan, Covenant with Death.

26. This was the premise of both majority and dissenting opinions in the Slaughterhouse Cases, 83 U.S. 36 (1873).

27. Story, Commentaries, 671.

28. Id., 672.

29. Gitlow v. New York, 268 U.S. 652 (1925).

30. Farber and Sherry, History of Constitution, 263–271.

31. 2 Story, Commentaries, 676.

32. 5 Cush. 206 (1850). In the context of the Magna Carta, the term had a narrow meaning; it assured only equal access to the royal courts to enforce contracts and protect property rights. This narrow meaning was the one employed by Chief Justice Shaw, who quoted Edward Coke. Shaw's opinion was the source of the separate-but-equal doctrine. See Levy, The Law of the Commonwealth, 109–117.

33. 2 Story, Commentaries, 677.

34. H. Carter, Angry Scar, 346–347; see generally Franklin, Reconstruction.

35. See chapter 7.

36. 2 Story, Commentaries, 677. See Act of April 20, 1871, 17 Stat. 13.

37. 2 Story, Commentaries, 683–685.

38. Baldwin v. Missouri, 281 U.S. 686, 695 (1930).

39. 198 U.S. 45 (1905).

40. And six years after the death of Field.

41. Brief for plaintiff in error at 16, 24–27.

42. 198 U.S. at 56.

43. People v. Beattie, 89 N. Y. Supp. 193 (App. Div. 1904).

44. Bessette v. People, 193 Ill. 334 (1903).

45. 198 U.S. at 57.

46. McLean, William Rufus Day, 18.

47. 198 U.S. at 70.

48. Id. at 60.

49. For example, Dunscomb, Police Power.

50. Pound developed his thesis in *Do We Need a Philosophy?*, *Need of Sociological Jurisprudence*, and *Liberty of Contract*.

51. See, for example, McLaughlin, *Cooley*. McLaughlin graduated in law at Michigan and then became an historian, first at the University of Michigan, but concluding his career at the University of Chicago. When Cooley resigned from the law faculty in 1884, McLaughlin assumed responsibility for instruction in constitutional law. Note, 2 Michigan Alumnus.

52. McLaughlin, Court, Constitution, and Parties, 3–4.

53. McLaughlin, *Written Constitution*, 620.

54. Freund, *Limitation of Hours*, 416.

55. Muller v. Oregon, 208 U.S. 412 (1908). For a contemporary feminist review of that decision, see Erickson, *Muller v. Oregon*, 233.

56. For example, Adair v. United States, 208 U.S. 161 (1908); Coppage v. Kansas, 236 U.S. 1 (1914); Adkins v. Children's Hosp., 261 U.S. 525 (1923).

57. D. Currie, Constitution in Supreme Court, 47. See also Urofsky, *Myth and Reality*. For an account of the demise of the doctrine of legislative equality, see Gillman, Constitution Beseiged, 147–194.

58. 198 U.S. at 45, 75.

59. Spencer, Social Statics. On the influence of Spencer, see Fuhrner, Advocacy and Objectivity, 31, 43, 199, 231, 290, 308; Ross, Origins, 55–56, 64, 105–106.

60. White, Justice Holmes, 360.

61. Pound, *Liberty of Contract*, 464.

62. Cooley, Constitutional Limitations, 595.

63. Cooley, *What Can the Law Do?*

64. "Best known," Cass Sunstein concludes, "for its apparent humility." *Lochner's Legacy*, 879.

65. For example, Paludan, *Law and Failure of Reconstruction*.

66. 347 U.S. 483 (1954).

67. Graham, Everyman's Constitution, 295–336; ten Broek, Equal under Law, 94–108.

68. Tiedeman, Treatise on Limitations. Also significant was Wharton, Commentaries. Herbert Hovenkamp assigns substantial importance to Wharton's work. *Political Economy*, 396.

69. Hofstadter, Social Darwinism. This work tends to support the view of Hovenkamp that Social Darwinism was "the most overrated of Gilded Age ideologies." Hovenkamp, *Political Economy*, 418.

70. Tiedeman, Treatise on Limitations, vii–viii. The author also expresses the Spencerian view that "[l]aw can never create social forces." Id., 571. He also explains the subordination of married women as a right made by might. Id., 545. Cf. Spencer, Social Statics, 188.

71. Tiedeman, Treatise on Limitations, 6.

72. Id., 7.

73. Id., 537.

74. Thayer, *Origin and Scope.*

75. Freund, Police Power.

76. The first social worker. For her biography, see A. Kennedy, *Jane Addams.*

77. The first president of the American Federation of Labor and the Socialist candidate for president of the United States in 1912, who polled almost a million votes. Ghent, *Eugene Debs.*

78. The Chicago lawyer who won fame defending labor organizers and others accused of crime. For a biography, see I. Stone, Clarence Darrow.

79. Police Power, v.

80. Id., 755.

81. Id., 626–755.

82. Id., 721.

83. Id., 298–299.

84. Seagle, Quest for Law, 416.

Chapter Eleven: Industrialization

1. 1 P. Foner, History of the Labor Movement, 18–22.

2. A full account of Pinkerton tactics is Morn, Eye That Never Sleeps.

3. Aurand, *Anthracite Coal Strike.*

4. Eggert, *Railroad Strikes.* And see Bruce, 1877.

5. Quoted by Nelles, *Strike and Its Consequences,* 21–22.

6. The Anti-Chinese movement is described in Saxton's Indispensable Enemy.

7. 1 P. Foner, History of the Labor Movement, 490.

8. See generally Hofstadter, Social Darwinism.

9. For a biography, see H. Starr, Sumner.

10. Ross, Origins, 110–111.

11. Rostow, Theorists of Economic Growth, 153–208.

12. Cooley, *Lecture IV,* 40–41.

13. Cooley, *Labor and Capital.*

14. Cooley, *Lecture II,* quoted by A. Jones, Constitutional Conservatism, 219, n. 33.

15. Cooley, *Labor and Capital,* 512.

16. Id., 514.

17. A Jones, Constitutionalism Conservatism, 263. And see Gladden, Applied Christianity. On the social gospel movement, see Hopkins, Rise of Social Gospel.

18. A Jones, Constitutional Conservatism, 288.

19. The story of the Knights is told in Fink, Workingmen's Democracy.

20. 2 P. Foner, History of the Labor Movement, 49.

21. Id., 52–54.

22. For a full account of the tragedy, see Avrich, Haymarket.

23. For example, Anarchy at an End; for an account of political sentiments aroused by events in Chicago of that era, see Carl Smith, Urban Disorder; B. Nelson, Beyond the Martyrs.

24. Weir, Beyond Labor's Veil.

25. McLaurin, Knights of Labor, 131–148.

26. Saxton, Indispensable Enemy, 18; 2 P. Foner, History of the Labor Movement, 58–59.

27. His ideas were expressed in his *Past and Present*. For an account of this movement, its origins in Protestant theology, and its relationship to socialism, see Ross, Origins, 98–122.

28. A. Jones, Constitutional Conservatism, 287, n. 132.

29. Fuhrner, Advocacy and Objectivity, 91.

30. Id., 48–53.

31. A. Jones, Constitutional Conservatism, 290.

32. It was a half-time appointment; he was then teaching one semester each year at Cornell and one at Michigan.

33. For an account of this Adams's career, see Fuhrner, Advocacy and Objectivity, 49–54, 70–79, 100–104, 128–142, 247–264. On Cooley's support of Adams, see A. Jones, Constitutional Conservatism, 286–287.

34. A Jones, Constitutional Conservatism, 289.

35. Cooley, *Arbitration*.

Chapter Twelve: Rails

1. Cooley, Letter to Collum.

2. Wiebe, Search for Order, 43–45.

3. Haskell, Emergence, 37.

4. G. Taylor, Transportation Revolution and Fishlow, American Railroads are full accounts.

5. A graphic presentation of this data is provided by Haskell, Emergence, 33. The Erie Canal stopped charging tolls in 1882. Kirkland, Business, 375.

6. Their pervasive importance is the subject of Chandler's Railroads.

7. By 1895, one-fourth of the nation's rail assets were in the hands of receivers. Hovenkamp, *Regulatory Conflict*, 1043; see also Crowell, *Railway Receiverships*.

8. For example, C. Adams, *Railroad System*, 360–366.

9. Hovenkamp, *Regulatory Conflict*, 1044.

10. For early advocacy of rate regulation, see Redfield, *Regulation of Interstate Traffic*.

11. For a brief account of the Party, see Kirkland, Business, 432–436.

12. Benson, Merchants, Farmers, 29–54.

13. Purcell, *Ideas and Interests,* 561.

14. Rabin, *Federal Regulation*, 1207.

15. Hovenkamp, *Regulatory Conflict*, 1057–1062.

16. Cf. Gibbons v. Ogden, 22 U.S. (9 Wheat.) 1 (1824). In 1886, the Supreme Court held that a state could regulate rates only if both terminal points were within

the state. Wabash St. L. & Pac. Ry. Co. v. Illinois, 118 U.S. 357 (1886), qualifying an earlier more permissive holding in Peik v. Chicago & N.W. Ry., 94 U.S. 164 (1877).

17. For example, Smyth v. Ames, 169 U.S. 466 (1898).
18. Thurman et al., Constituting Advisory Commission.
19. Railroad Commission, Bullion (January 1883), quoted by A. Jones, Constitutional Conservatism, 297.
20. Ford, *Charles Francis Adams.*
21. See Kirkland, Business, 3–20.
22. Cooley, *State Regulation,* 215.
23. Cooley, *Popular and Legal Views.*
24. Quoted by A. Jones, Constitutional Conservatism, 298–300.
25. Id., 252.
26. Id., 303.

Chapter Thirteen: The Advent of Federal Administrative Law

1. A. Jones, Constitutional Conservatism, 291.
2. Wiebe, Search for Order, 13, 47.
3. For example, see Sumner, Folkways and What Social Classes Owe.
4. Pinchot, Fight for Conservation, 3–4.
5. P. Starr, Social Transformation, 81–112.
6. 1 P. Foner, History of Labor Movement, 18–22.
7. Steffens, Shame of the Cities.
8. For example, see Keating, History of Memphis, 32–33.
9. McKelvey, Urbanization, 92–94.
10. James A. Garfield (1831–1881); a biography is Peskin, Garfield; an account of his murder is Rosenberg, Trial of Guiteau.
11. For an account of the mayor's murder, see 2 Pierce, History of Chicago, 378–379.
12. E. Foner, Reconstruction, 580–582, 586.
13. Id., 588–601.
14. 24 Stat. 379.
15. R. Stone, Interstate Commerce Commission, 6.
16. Wabash Ry. Co. v. Illinois, 118 U.S. 557 (1886).
17. On the omnipotence of state agencies, see Benson's Merchants, Farmers.
18. For a brief account of the early history of the Commission, see Judson, Law of Interstate Commerce, 49–54, 58–60.
19. Landis, Administrative Process, 10.
20. Rabin, *Federal Regulation,* 1207–1208.
21. 1 Sharfman, Interstate Commerce Commission, 23–24.
22. Interstate Commerce Comm'n v. Chicago, R. I., & Pac. Ry., 218 U.S. 88, 102 (1910).
23. 2 Sharfman, Interstate Commerce Commission, 459.
24. Chaney, *Supreme Court of Michigan,* 391.

25. A. Jones, Constitutional Conservatism, 309–310, 316.

26. 20 Mich. 452 (1878).

27. Lieber, 1 Manual of Political Ethics, 386; *Ancient and Modern Teacher*.

28. For consideration of the difficulty in this distinction, see Cohen, Law; Gordon, *Independence;* Jaffe, *Law Making by Private Groups;* Rhode, *Ethical Perspectives,* 643–647; Sennett, Fall of Public Man, passim.

29. 94 U.S. 113 (1877).

30. Id.U.S. at 120.

31. Cooley, *Limits to State Control.*

32. For a later endorsement of Cooley's view, see Frankfurter, The Commerce Clause, 87.

33. The Attorney General v. Railroad Companies, 35 Wis. 425 (1874).

34. Cooley, *State Regulation.*

35. This lack was soon supplied, but the congressional authorization was challenged as unconstitutional. The statute was upheld in Brown v. Walker, 161 U.S. 591 (1896).

36. *In re* Alleged Excessive Freight Rates and Charges on Food Products, 4 I.C.C. 48, 116.

37. Section 4 of the 1887 Act forbade railroads to "charge or receive any greater compensation in the aggregate for the transportation of passengers or of like kind of property, under substantially similar circumstances and conditions, for a shorter than for a longer haul over the same line." 24 Stat. 380.

38. *In re* Southern Ry. & S. S. Ass'n, 1 I.C.C. 278 (1887). The complaint was filed on April 5, the day the Act took effect and decided on June 15. See generally R. Dewey, Long and Short Haul, 65–73.

39. *In re* Louisville & Nashville R.R., 1 I.C.C. 31 (1887). This decision was overruled in Interstate Commerce Comm'n v. Alabama Midland Ry. Co., 168 U.S. 144 (1897), holding that competitive pricing created dissimilar "circumstances and conditions." The latter decision resulted in an amendment of the statute making explicit that the result earlier reached by the Cooley commission was the national law. 2 Sharfman, Interstate Commerce Commission, 443.

40. For example, Providence Coal Co. v. Providence and Worcester R.R., 1 I.C.C. 107 (1887).

41. Cooley spoke to this subject at Harvard in 1889; his remarks are reported in the Railroad Gazette, May 10, 1889.

42. Relying on Section 3 of the Act that prohibited "any undue or unreasonable prejudice or disadvantage" to any passengers. The Commission also relied in part on the Civil Rights Act of 1875.

43. Council v. Western & Atl. R.R., 1 I.C.C. 638 (1887); Heard v. Georgia R.R., 1 I.C.C. 428 (1888).

44. Welke, "All Women are White," 143–144.

45. Interstate Commerce Commission Report, 19–30 (1888).

46. Cooley, *State Regulation*; and see Hadley, *Railroad Business.*

47. The rise of the railroad titans is recounted in E. G. Campbell's Reorganization.

48. Interstate Commerce Commission Report, 73(1889).

49. Act of February 28, 1920, ch. 91, 41 Stat. 456.

50. For an argument for continuation of state regulation by one of Cooley's students, see Rogers, *The Constitution*.

51. The Commission experienced many defeats in the Supreme Court in the early years of the century. Ripley, Railroads, 463.

52. The financial plight of regulated railroads is the subject of Martin, Enterprise Denied.

53. For example, Kolko, Railroads; and see Beard and Beard, Rise of American Civilization, 566–568; Faulkner, Decline of Laissez-Faire, 187–191; Kirkland, History, 286–301.

54. For example, Kirkland, History. Kirkland chastises the ICC for failing to prevent discrimination and other abuses (187–191), for failure to prevent consolidation (191–198), and for neglecting the interests of the carriers and for insisting on competition (209).

55. Beard and Beard, Rise of American Civilization, 566.

56. Hovenkamp, *Regulatory Conflict,* 1025–1026.

57. Friedman, *Civil Wrongs,* 353.

58. Cooley, Treatise on Torts, 541–545.

59. 1 Sharfman, Interstate Commerce Commission, 246.

60. 27 Stat. 531, 45 U.S.C. § 7.

61. A. Jones, Constitutional Conservatism, 333.

62. Id.

63. Id., 337.

64. Interstate Commerce Commission Report, 325–333 (1891).

65. Act of June 11, 1906, 34 Stat. 232.

66. Interstate Commerce Commission Report, 27–28 (1887). Cooley wrote this report.

67. A. Jones, Constitutional Conservatism, 326.

68. H. C. Adams's *Relation of State* is an expression of this sentiment.

69. For example, Faulkner, Decline of Laissez-Faire, 187.

70. Labor Management Relations Act of 1936, §§ 201–204. Section 203(c) created the Federal Mediation and Conciliation Service. Also, Section 8(d) requires "bargaining in good faith," an elusive moral concept. For a brief account, see Wellington, Labor and the Legal Process, 30–39.

71. 29 U.S. C. § 629(a)(2). Cf. Increase Minority Participation by Affirmative Change Today, Inc. v. Firestone, 895 F. 2d 1189 (11th Cir. 1990).

72. 134 U.S. 418 (1890).

73. Interstate Commerce Commission Report, 15–20 (1890).

74. This consideration moved the court to limit review of ICC orders to the record made in the Commission. Cincinnati, New Orleans & Tex. Pac. Ry. Co. v. ICC, 162 U.S. 196 (1896).

75. He had earlier, as a judge, proclaimed that "[t]here is nothing that necessarily implies that due process of law must be judicial process." Weimar v. Bunbury, 30 Mich. 203 (1874).

76. Hepburn Act, Act of June 29, 1906, 34 Stat. 584.

77. 38 Stat. 717.

78. Landis, Administrative Process, 89–122.

79. 60 Stat. 237, 5 U. S. C. §§ 1101 et seq.

80. Judge Friendly was not the first to remark on the clarity of Commissioner Cooley's regulatory utterances. For a series of illustrations, see Meyer, *Judge Cooley,* 144–146.

81. Friendly, Federal Agencies, 29, 31.

82. See Horwitz, Transformation, 213–246.

83. Vander Velde, *Cooley,* 879.

84. Fuller, Morality of Law, passim.

85. See also Freund, *Substitution of Rule for Discretion,* and Frankfurter, *Task.*

86. Schmalbeck, *Justice of Economics;* Jolls et al., *Behavioral Approach;* Ellickson, *Law and Economics.*

Chapter Fourteen: Three Progressives

1. *Address of the President,* 17 A. B. A. Rep. 181, 242 (1895).

2. Mason, Brandeis; Strum, Brandeis: Justice for the People.

3. Kraines, World and Ideas.

4. Gunther, Hand.

5. See chapter 3.

6. Baude, *Comment;* for a contemporary statement of their position, see S. Clark, *Populist Critique.*

7. Burt, Two Jewish Justices, 87.

8. Calamandrei, Procedure and Democracy, 37–38.

9. The term is employed by Gutmann and Thompson in Democracy and Disagreement.

Chapter Fifteen: Louis Brandeis

1. Strum, Brandeis: Justice for the People, 4–6.

2. Baskerville, Law and Limitations, 34–36.

3. Strum, Brandeis: Justice for the People, 9.

4. Id., 10.

5. Id., 11.

6. Id., 12.

7. Id., 13.

8. Baskerville, Law and Limitations, 62.

9. Strum, Brandeis: Justice for the People. 19.

10. Id., 20.

11. Richberg, *Industrial Liberalism,* 233.

12. Brandeis and Warren, *Right of Privacy.*

13. An account of Wythe's legendary integrity is I. Brown, American Aristides.

14. Strum, Brandeis: Beyond Progressivism, 17.

15. Strum, Brandeis: Justice for the People, 41.

16. Strum, Brandeis: Beyond Progressivism, 24–25.

17. Brandeis, Business, 342.

18. Id., 27.

19. For a contemporaneous account studied by Brandeis, see Potter, Cooperative Movement.

20. Strum, Brandeis: Beyond Progressivism, 39.

21. Id., 100–115.

22. Strum, Brandeis: Justice for the People, 237.

23. Whitney v. California, 274 U.S. 357, 375 (1927).

24. Farber, *Reinventing Brandeis,* 185.

25. Strum, Brandeis: Beyond Progressivism, 43–47.

26. Id., 18.

27. Id., 19; Mason, Brandeis, 106–107.

28. Strum, Brandeis: Beyond Progressivism, 18–19.

29. Mason, Brandeis, 177–214.

30. Kraines, World and Ideas, 50–59.

31. Muller v. Oregon, 208 U.S. 412 (1908).

32. Dissenting in New State Ice Co. v. Liebmann, 285 U.S. 262 (1932).

33. Strum, Brandeis: Beyond Progressivism, 77.

34. Urofsky, Mind of One Piece, 55–57.

35. Strum, Brandeis: Beyond Progressivism, 83.

36. 1 Link, Wilson, 489.

37. Mason, Brandeis, 335–352, Urofsky, Brandeis and Progressive Tradition, 68–86.

38. A reporter quoted in the Kansas City Post, and by Mason, Brandeis, 465.

39. Todd, Justice on Trial, 228–229.

40. Quoted by Mason, Brandeis, 484.

41. Todd, Justice on Trial, 207–209.

42. Mr. Justice Brandeis, 3.

43. Konefsky, Legacy, 278n.

44. Urofsky, Mind of One Piece, 146.

45. Strum, Brandeis: Beyond Progressivism, 156.

46. Letter to Felix Frankfurter, August 14, 1916, quoted in Bickel, Unpublished Opinions, 222.

47. Erie R.R. v. Tompkins, 304 U.S. 1 (1938).

48. Order of the Supreme Court, December 20, 1937.

49. 297 U.S. 288 (1936).

50. Thayer, *Origin and Scope.*

51. Baskerville, Law and Limitations, 109.

52. Bickel, Unpublished Opinions, 2–3.

53. Mason, Brandeis, 628–629.

54. Strum, Brandeis: Justice for the People, 372–405.

55. See generally Murphy, Brandeis-Frankfurter Connection.

Chapter Sixteen: Ernst Freund

1. Storr, Harper's University, 1–17.

2. Goodspeed, William Harper.

3. Storr, Harper's University, 18–52.

4. Ellsworth, Law on the Midway, 33.

5. His biography is Kraines, World and Ideas; or see Carrington, *Ernst Freund.*

6. On Lieber's role at Columbia, see Goebel, History, 44–67.

7. Woodward, *Ernst Freund,* 149.

8. Williston, *Joseph Henry Beale,* 687.

9. Among his works were Elements of Partnership and Treatise on Law of Sales.

10. Law of Public Offices and Officers.

11. Freund, *Private Claims.*

12. Cooley, *Liability of Public Officers.*

13. Wyman, Principles of Administrative Law.

14. Chase, American Law School, 64–65.

15. For example, Frankfurter, *Task;* Landis, Administrative Process.

16. Sayre, *Common Law,* 254.

17. Cohen, Law, 316.

18. Freund, *Law School.*

19. Leo Wormser, quoted in Kraines, World and Ideas, 148–149.

20. Kraines, World and Ideas, 5.

21. Id., 5, 50–59.

22. Id., 4.

23. Id., 129–132.

24. Freund, *Some Inadequately Discussed Problems;* cf. Babcock, Zoning Game, 3.

25. Kraines, World and Ideas, 5.

26. Id., 60–63.

27. Quoted in id., 148.

28. Freund, *The Debs Case.*

29. 2 Holmes, Holmes-Pollock Letters, 14; G. E. White, Justice Holmes, 421–427.

30. Kraines, World and Ideas, 201–203, n. 466.

31. For example, Legislative Drafting. Freund concerned himself with such humdrum matters as the ambiguity inherent in the use of "shall." Freund, Legislative Regulation, 225.

32. He even went so far as to suggest the need for empirical treatment of the law of future interests. A. Kent, *Ernst Freund,* 149.

33. Freund, Standards, 48.

34. Id., 312.

35. Freund, *Interpretation.*

36. Lieber, Manual of Political Ethics, 352–353.

37. Freund, *Legislation.*

38. Freund, *Problem of Intelligent Legislation,* 78. See also D. Horowitz, Courts and Social Policy.

39. Freund, *Substitution of Rule for Discretion,* 670.

40. 285 U.S. 22 (1932).

41. Jaffe, Judicial Control, 320–353; Pound, Administrative Law, 27–56; Goodnow, Principles, 378–441.

42. Horwitz, Transformation, 213–246.
43. 60 Stat. 237, 5 U. S. C. §§ 551 et seq.
44. Frankfurter, Freund Lecture, 1.

Chapter Seventeen: Learned Hand

1. Gunther, Learned Hand, 3–71.
2. Id., 344–415.
3. Hand, *Due Process of Law*.
4. Purcell, *Learned Hand,* 839.
5. Gunther, Learned Hand, 123–133.
6. Hand, Bill of Rights, 73.
7. Hand, *To Yale Law Graduates,* 72.
8. Gunther, Learned Hand, 278–279.
9. Id., 522–523.
10. Id., 116–117.
11. Id., 365.
12. Id., 387–396.
13. Id., 190–269.
14. Id., 352.
15. Id., 416–434.
16. See generally Schick, Learned Hand's Court.
17. In Hand's case, see Gunther, Learned Hand, 153–170.
18. Id., 403.
19. Hand, *Mr. Justice Holmes,* 862–863.
20. Gunther, Learned Hand, 400–402.
21. Hand, *Sources of Tolerance,* 7.
22. Hand, *Speech of Justice,* 619.
23. Posner, *Hand Biography,* 22.
24. Hand, *To Yale Law Graduates,* 69.
25. Thayer, *Origin and Scope,* 154; see also Thayer, *Case of Gepcke.*
26. Gunther, Learned Hand, 213.
27. Id., 233–237.
28. Id., 224–235.
29. Id., 376–377.
30. Meyer v. Nebraska, 262 U.S. 390 (1923).
31. For an account of the controversy, see E. Larson, Summer for the Gods.
32. Gunther, Learned Hand, 482.
33. Id., 489–502.
34. Id., 457–460.
35. Hand, Bill of Rights.
36. Bickel, *Judicial Restraint.*
37. Rabban, First Amendment, 9–18.
38. Masses Publishing Co. v. Patten, 244 Fed. 535 (S. D. N. Y.), *rev'd,* 246 Fed. 24 (2d Cir. 1917).

39. United States v. Dennis, 183 F.2d 291 (2d Cir. 1950), *aff'd,* 341 U.S. 495 (1951).

40. Blasi, *Learned Hand,* 11–16.

41. Purcell, *Learned Hand,* 896–918.

42. 357 U.S. 483 (1954).

43. Id. at 660–664.

44. Sunstein, *In Defense,* 26.

45. Tushnet, Making Civil Rights Law, 116–150.

46. For a contemporary review of the corpus of law that might have been developed earlier, see Issacharoff, Kaplan, and Pildes, Law of Democracy.

47. McCullough, Truman, 586–587.

48. See United States v. Classic, 313 U.S. 299 (1941); Smith v. Allwright, 321 U.S. 649 (1944).

49. For an account of the watershed event in Little Rock, see Freyer, Little Rock Crisis.

50. 328 U.S. 549 (1946).

51. Baker v. Carr, 369 U.S. 86 (1962).

Chapter Eighteen: A New Age of Judicial Heroism

1. See generally Ross, Muted Fury.

2. Norris-LaGuardia Act, 47 Stat. 70.

3. Forbath, Law and Labor Movement, 192–198.

4. Frankfurter and Greene, Labor Injunction, 17–46.

5. 158 U.S. 564 (1894).

6. For example, Adkins v. Children's Hosp., 261 U.S. 255 (1923) (a Fifth Amendment case involving federal law).

7. For contemporaneous comment, see T. Powell, *Judiciality of Minimum Wage Legislation.*

8. Purcell, Litigation and Inequality, 104–126.

9. Now 28 U. S. C. § 1441.

10. Purcell, Litigation and Inequality, 132–162.

11. Shamir, Managing Legal Uncertainty, 16–18.

12. The alarming decisions were Carter v. Carter Coal Co., 296 U.S. 238 (1936) and Morehead v. New York *ex rel.* Tipaldi, 298 U.S. 587 (1936).

13. Gallo, Mussolini's Italy, 204–244.

14. A telling account is Halperin, Germany Tried Democracy.

15. The story is told by Toland, Rising Sun, 3–33.

16. Goldston, Civil War in Spain, 184–209.

17. See generally Brinkley, Voices of Protest; a biography of Long is Fineran, Career of a Tinpot Napoleon.

18. Newman, Hugo Black, 210–211.

19. Some saw the plan as the first step in establishing an American fascist state. Leuchtenberg, Supreme Court Reborn, 137.

20. For an argument that the change would have occurred without the court-packing proposal, see Cushman, Rethinking the New Deal Court.

21. West Coast Hotel Co. v. Parrish, 309 U.S. 379 (1937); Leuchtenburg, Supreme Court Reborn, 140–142.

22. United States v. Carolene Prods. Co., 304 U.S. 144, 148 n.4 (1938).

23. R. Jackson, Supreme Court, 76.

24. 304 U.S. at 311.

25. Kluger, Simple Justice, 656.

26. Post, *Democracy*, 442.

27. Marion, Jurisprudence of Brennan, 1.

28. See, for example, Brennan, *Equality Principle.*

29. See generally Grey, *Do We Have an Unwritten Constitution?*

30. Bittker, *Interpreting the Constitution*, 41–51.

31. M. Perry, *Authority of Text*, 573. See also Brest, *Misconceived Quest;* Chemerinsky, *Amending the Constitution.*

32. Frankfurter, Letter to Hand, June 30, 1957, quoted by E. White, Earl Warren, 181.

33. See Chayes, *Role of the Judge.*

34. Nichol, *The Left, the Right, and Certainty.*

35. See generally Lasch, Revolt of the Elites.

36. A shrill statement of the point is Graglia, *Constitutional Law.*

37. Frankfurter, Letter to Hand, June 30, 1957, quoted by E. White, Earl Warren, 181 n. 27.

38. See Sandel, Democracy's Discontent.

39. See, for example, Rubin and Feeley, *Creating Legal Doctrine;* Dworkin, Freedom's Law; Macey, *Promoting Public-Regarding Legislation.*

40. For example, B. Friedman, *History of Countermajoritarian Difficulty.* Croley, in *Majoritarian Difficulty,* expresses the concern that majoritarian-elected judges might be too indifferent to countermajoritarian values.

41. For example, Ackerman, *Storrs Lecture.*

42. Baker, *Exercising Amendment Power.*

43. As Frankfurter, for example, did. Levinson, *Democratic Faith of Frankfurter,* 444. And see Dahl, Democracy and Its Critics.

44. For an argument that Justice Brennan should have been impeached for usurping power, see F. Strong, Judicial Function, 159.

45. West Virginia Bd. of Educ. v. Barnette, 319 U.S. 624 (1943).

46. R. Jackson, Supreme Court, 76.

47. But see Chayes, *Role of the Judge.*

48. See Bickel, *Original Understanding.*

49. Lieber, Legal and Political Hermeneutics, 59.

50. For five views on law and sexual orientation, see Carrington, *A Senate of Five.*

51. 491 U.S. 110, 139 (1989).

52. Malinowski, Sex, Culture and Myth, 63.

Chapter Nineteen: Ineffective Judicial Heroics

1. For example, Berger, Government by Judiciary; Bork, Slouching Towards Gomorrah; Cox, Role of Supreme Court; Lusky, *Government by Judiciary*.

2. A theme also developed by Gardbaum in *Why the Liberal State.*

3. Fiss, Liberalism Divided, 4.

4. Post, *Equality and Autonomy*, 1541.

5. Chayes, *Role of the Judge*. Subrin, *How Equity Conquered*.

6. An account of the meager results from 1954 to 1964 is G. Rosenberg, Hollow Hope, 41–71.

7. G. Rosenberg, Hollow Hope, 39–41; Balkin and Levinson, *Canons of Constitutional Law*, 1022–1023.

8. Lemann's Promised Land is an account of the migration.

9. See generally Orfield, Reconstruction.

10. See generally Garrow, Bearing the Cross.

11. Id., 11–14.

12. Robinson's influence is described in Ranpersad's Jackie Robinson.

13. Higginbotham, In the Matter of Color, 383–384.

14. Robert Cover, quoted in Fiss and Resnik, Procedure, 730.

15. 349 U.S. 294 (1955).

16. For example, Wilkinson, From Brown to Bakke.

17. Urofsky, Frankfurter, 141.

18. On the Wallace phenomenon, see generally D. Carter, Politics of Rage.

19. For an account of some of them, see Bass, unlikely Heroes.

20. Bradley v. Milliken, 338 F. Supp. 582 (E. D. Mich. 1975), *rev'd in part,* Milliken v. Bradley, 418 U.S. 717 (1974); see generally Hain, *Sealing Off the City* and *Symposium: Milliken v. Bradley.*

21. See generally Limits of Justice. On African-American concern, see Bell, *Serving Two Masters.*

22. Tyack, One Best System, 15–21.

23. Bell, *Serving Two Masters;* see also And We Are Not Saved, 112–113.

24. Scott, Contempt and Pity explores the effects.

25. Brewer, *Scientific Testimony*, 1558.

26. Accounts of the modification of judicial decrees are Orfield and Eaton, Dismantling Desegregation and Douglas, *Limits of Law.*

27. Palko v. Connecticut, 302 U.S. 319 (1937); Adamson v. California, 332 U.S. 46 (1947).

28. For example, Duncan v. Louisiana, 391 U.S. 145 (1968).

29. But cf. Schilb v. Kuebel, 404 U.S. 357 (1971).

30. Hurtado v. California, 110 U.S. 516 (1884).

31. Urofsky, Frankfurter, 157.

32. Brown v. Mississippi, 197 U.S. 278 (1936).

33. Ashcraft v. Tennessee, 322 U.S. 143 (1944); and see Watts v. Indiana, 328 U.S. 49 (1949).

34. See chapter 8.

35. Powell v. Alabama, 287 U.S. 45 (1932).

36. Johnson v. Zerbst, 304 U.S. 458 (1938).

37. Betts v. Brady, 316 U.S. 455 (1942).

38. Gideon v. Wainwright, 372 U.S. 335 (1963).

39. Israel, Kamisar, and LaFave, Criminal Procedure, 252.

40. Yarbrough, Mr. Justice Black, 90. See especially his dissent in Adamson v. California, 332 U.S. 46 (1947).

41. Escobedo v. Illinois, 378 U.S. 478 (1964).

42. Miranda v. Arizona, 384 U.S. 436 (1965).

43. F. Graham, Self-Inflicted Wound, 10–26.

44. Crime Control Act of 1968, 18 U. S. C. § 3501.

45. F. Graham, Self-Inflicted Wound, 316.

46. For example, Michigan v. Tucker, 417 U.S. 433 (1974); Oregon v. Elstad, 470 U.S. 298 (1985).

47. Inbau and Reid, Criminal Interrogation, 1.

48. Weeks v. United States, 232 U.S. 383 (1914).

49. Cardozo, J. in People v. Defore, 184 N.Y. 13, 21 (1946).

50. Mapp v. Ohio, 367 U.S. 643 (1961), *overruling* Wolf v. Colorado, 338 U.S. 25 (1949).

51. See Oaks, *Studying Exclusionary Rule;* but see also Amsterdam, *Supreme Court.*

52. Massachusetts v. Shepherd, 468 U.S. 981 (1984).

53. United States v. Leon, 468 U.S. 497 (1984).

54. 42 U. S. C. § 1983.

55. Blalock, Civil Liability, 171–176.

56. Mosteller, *Essay* and Barajas and Nelson, *Proposed Amendment.*

57. For example, Cooper v. Pate, 378 U.S. 546 (1964); Johnson v. Avery, 393 U.S. 483 (1969); Wolff v. McDonnell, 418 U.S. 539 (1974).

58. Furman v. Georgia, 408 U.S. 238 (1972).

59. Death Row USA, 733–739.

60. Steiker and Steiker, *Sober Second Thoughts.*

61. Gregg v. Georgia, 428 U.S. 153 (1976).

62. See Dragich, *Justice Blackmun.*

63. New York Times, Sec. 4, p. 13, col. 1, April 28, 1996.

64. Baker v. Carr, 369 U.S. 186 (1962).

65. Issacharoff and Pildes, *Politics as Markets.*

66. Reynolds v. Sims, 377 U.S. 533 (1964).

67. Gormley, Archibald Cox, 174–177.

68. Id., 176.

69. U.S. Term Limits, Inc. v. Thornton, 514 U.S. 779 (1995).

70. Colgrove v. Battin, 413 U.S. 149 (1973).

71. James and Hazard, Civil Procedure, 53; see also Carrington, *The Seventh Amendment,* 51–53.

72. For an excellent account of the adverse effects, see Arnold's *Trial by Jury.*

73. 413 U.S. at 166.

74. 410 U.S. 113 (1973).

75. Noonan, *Raw Power*; Dixon, *"New" Substantive Due Process*; J. Ely, *Crying Wolf*; Epstein, *Substantive Due Process*; Monaghan, *Comment*; and Van Alstyne, *Closing the Circle*.

76. G. Rosenberg, Hollow Hope, 179.

77. Alschuler, *Descending Trail,* 402, n. 66. And see Sunstein, Legal Reasoning, 180.

78. On desuetude, see Calabresi, Common Law, 17–24.

79. Nelson, *History and Neutral Principles,* 1270–1275.

80. Burt, *Alex Bickel's Law School,* 1869.

81. G. Rosenberg, Hollow Hope, 189–195.

82. Forres and Henshaw's *Harassment* is an account.

83. Glendon, Abortion, 40.

84. For an account of the threat of violence in peacable Oregon, see News Hour, February 9, 1999. But see also Garrow, *All Over But the Legislating.*

85. Van Dyk's *Pro-Choice Mobilization* is an account of the response.

86. See, for example, State of Wash. v. Glucksberg, 521 U.S. 202 (1997); Vacco v. Quill, 521 U.S. 793 (1997).

87. Kamisar, *On the Meaning and Impact*; Sunstein, *Right to Die.*

88. Posner, *Problematics,* 1700–1702.

Chapter Twenty:
First Amendment Heroics

1. An encomium is Kalven, A Worthy Tradition.

2. Gitlow v. New York, 268 U.S. 652 (1925). See Farber and Sherry, History of the Constitution, 366–367.

3. See Fairman, *Fourteenth Amendment* and Berger, Government by Judiciary, 155–190; but see also Nelson, Fourteenth Amendment and M. Curtis, No State.

4. See generally Rabban, First Amendment.

5. Milton, *Aeropagitica,* 408–409.

6. See chapter 8.

7. See generally Kalven, Negro and The First Amendment. Examples are New York Times v. Sullivan, 376 U.S. 254 (1964) and NAACP v. Button, 371 U.S. 415 (1963).

8. Bollinger, *Elitism* notes the paradox.

9. Roth v. United States, 353 U.S. 476 (1957).

10. Miller v. California, 413 U.S. 15 (1973).

11. Alberts v. California, 353 U.S. 476, 503 (1957); Smith v. California, 361 U.S. 147, 169 (1959); A Book Named John Cleland's Memoirs of A Woman of Pleasure v. Attorney General of Mass., 383 U.S. 413, 455 (1966).

12. For example, Mainstream Loudoun v. Board of Trustees of the Loudoun County Library, E. D. Va., http://lw.bna.com/#1208 (November 23, 1998).

13. MacKinnon, Feminism Unmodified, 146–228.

14. Accord, Post, *Constitutional Concept.*

15. For example, Jenkins v. Georgia, 418 U.S. 153 (1974).

16. Washington, *Farewell Address of 1796,* 307–308.

17. See Fish, *Mission Impossible.*
18. Lindsay, in *Defending Liberalism,* seems to share such a supposition.
19. The term is Stephen Carter's; see his Culture of Disbelief.
20. Engel v. Vitale, 405 U.S. 421 (1962).
21. Lemon v. Kurtzman, 403 U.S. 602 (1971).
22. County of Allegheny v. American Civil Liberties Union, 492 U.S. 573 (1989).
23. Agostini v. Felton, 117 S. Ct. 1997, 2016–2017 (1997) *overruling* Aguilar v. Felton, 473 U.S. 402 (1985).
24. Barnes v. Glen Theatre, Inc., 501 U.S. 560 (1991).
25. R. A. V. v. City of St. Paul, 505 U.S. 377 (1992).
26. See generally Ward, *Free Speech.*
27. Texas v. Johnson, 164 U.S. 397 (1989).
28. Parker, *Statement re Flag-Burning.*
29. Virginia State Bd. of Pharmacy v. Virginia Citizens Consumer Council, 425 U.S. 748 (1976).
30. Valentine v. Christensen, 316 U.S. 52 (1941).
31. Central Hudson Gas & Elec. Corp. v. Public Serv. Comm'n of N.Y., 447 U.S. 597 (1980).
32. Bates v. State Bar of Ariz., 433 U.S. 350 (1977); *In re* R. M. J., 455 U.S. 191 (1982); Zauderer v. Office of Disciplinary Counsel, 471 U.S. 626 (1985).
33. Selinger so contends is *Public's Interest.*
34. It is made by Hershkoff and Cohen in *Begging to Differ.*
35. See generally Harper and Aldrich, *Political Economy.*
36. Jamieson, Dirty Politics, chapter 2.
37. See Lewis, Buying of Congress and L. Nelson, Democracy for Sale.
38. 421 U. S. 1 (1976).
39. Blasi, *Free Speech,* 1282.
40. Cooley, *Labor and Capital,* 514.
41. Citizens Against Rent Control v. Berkeley, 454 U. S. 290 (1981).
42. For data see Champaign, *Contributions in Texas Races;* Johnson and Uris, *Judicial Selection;* America's Third Party; and Report of Pennsylvania Special Commission, 20. It is reported that almost $11 million was spent on three campaigns for the Texas court in 1994 and that $4.3 million was spent on one race in Alabama in 1996.
43. See Hazen, *High Court Wrongly Elected,* 1313.
44. Grimke, Nature of Free Institutions, 444.
45. See generally Smolla, Suing the Press.
46. 376 U.S. 274 (1964). See generally A. Lewis, Make No Law.
47. See chapter 8.
48. Me. Rev. Stat. § 1121–1128; 1997 Vermont H. B. 28 enacted June 26, 1997. For an account, see Campion, *Maine Clean Election Act.*
49. New York Times, No. 5, 1998, B2.
50. See Fiss, *Money and Politics.*
51. See Post, *Community; Equality.*

Chapter Twenty-One: The
Contagion of Judicial Heroism

1. Brennan, *State Constitutions.*

2. Holland, *State Constitutions,* 464; R. Shepard, *Maturing Nature of State Jurisprudence;* Grodin, *Rediscovering.*

3. Kahn, *State Constitutionalization.*

4. C. E. Smith, Courts, Politics, and Judicial Process.

5. For example, Article V, § 2, Constitution of the State of Wyoming.

6. Rules Enabling Act of 1934, Act of June 19, 1934, 48 Stat. 1064.

7. For example, Winberry v. Salisbury, 5 N.J. 240, 74 A.2d 406 (1950).

8. J. Jackson, *Judicial Independence.*

9. Tarr and Williams, *Foreword: Western State Constitutions.*

10. See Peters, *Getting Away.*

11. See Gardner, *Southern Character;* Van Cleave, *State Constitutional Interpretation.*

12. Accord, Linde, *First Things First.*

13. A full account of the Bird court's early years is Stolz, Judging Judges, 1–192.

14. See Mosk, *Emerging Agenda.*

15. Serrano v. Priest, 18 Cal. 3d 728, 135 Cal. Rptr. 345, 557 P.2d. 929(1975); contrast San Antonio Indep. Sch. Dist. v. Rodriguez, 411 U.S. 1 (1973). For elaboration on the issue, see Carrington, *Financing the Dream.*

16. Fischel, *How* Serrano *Caused Proposition 13.*

17. Serrano v. Priest II, 20 Cal. 3d 24, 569 P.3d 1303, 141 Cal. Rptr. 315 (1977).

18. See Jensen, *Advancing Education.*

19. Robinson v. Cahill, 62 N.J. 473 (1973).

20. Robinson v. Cahill, 79 N.J. 464 (1976); see generally Tarr, *Robinson v. Cahill.*

21. Examples are Claremont Sch. Dist. v. Governor, 142 N.H. 462, 703 A.2d 1353 (1997); Opinion of the Justices, 624 So. 2d 107 (Ala. 1993); Roosevelt Elementary Sch. Dist. No. 66 v. Bishop, 877 P.2d 806 (Ariz. 1994); McDuffy v. Secretary of Educ., 615 N.E.2d 516 (Mass. 1993); Helena Elementary Sch. Dist. No. 1 v. State, 769 P.2d 684 (Mont. 1989); Edgewood Indep. Sch. Dist. v. Kirby, 804 S.W.2d 491 (Tex. 1991). See generally Enrich, *Leaving Equity Behind.*

22. For a statement of the obvious problems, see Note, *Unfulfilled Promises.*

23. A review of the evidence is Fischel, School Finance Litigation.

24. See Campbell and Fischel, *Preferences.*

25. See Fischel, School Finance Litigation.

26. See Hanushek, *When "Reform" May Not Be Good.*

27. An approach is suggested by Savanna R-III Sch. Dist. v. Public Sch. Retirement Sys. of Mo., 950 S.W.2d 854 (Mo. 1997).

28. People v. Anderson, 6 Cal. 3d 628 (1972).

29. Cal. Const., Art. I, § 27, approved by voters on November 7, 1972.

30. Uelman's *Review of Death Penalty* reviews the preformance of Chief Justice Bird and the Supreme Court.

31. Crawford v. Board of Educ., 17 Cal. 3d 280 (1976).

32. Stolz, Judging Judges, 33; Twardy, *Justice Roger Traynor.*

33. Stolz, Judging Judges, 35–36.

34. For example, Li v. Yellow Cab Co., 13 Cal. 3d 804 (1975) (adopting comparative negligence doctrine); for contemporaneous comment, see England, *Yellow Cab Co.*

35. Wellenkamp v. Bank of America, 21 Cal. 3d 943 (1978).

36. For an account by a member of the Court, see Grodin, In Pursuit of Justice.

37. Stolz, Judging Judges, 82.

38. The event is recounted in Culver and Wold's *Judicial Reform.*

39. Best v. Taylor Mach. Works, 179 Ill. 2d 367, 689 N.E.2d 1057 (1997).

40. Hershkoff, *Rights and Freedoms;* Kaufman, *Note, Cultural Meaning.*

41. Ravin v. State, 537 P.2d 494 (Alaska 1975); cf. State v. Kentner, 53 Haw. 327, 493 P.2d 306 (1972). But see State v. Erickson, 574 P.2d 1 (Alaska 1978) (cocaine distinguished).

42. Baehr v. Lewin, 852 P.2d 44 (Haw. 1993), *modified by* 852 P.2d 74 (Haw. 1993); *accord,* Braese v. Bureau of Motor Vehicles, No. 3AN–95–6562 CI, 1998 WL 88743 (Alaska Super. Ct. 1998). For discussion, see Wiggins, *Maine's Act;* Destro, *Law and Politics.*

43. New York Times, November 5, 1998, B7.

44. 31 Haw. Rev. Stat. Ann. § 572C (Michie Supp. 1997).

45. City of Cleburne v. Cleburne Living Ctr., 473 U.S. 432 (1985).

46. Southern Burlington County NAACP v. Township of Mount Laurel, 33 A.2d 713 (N.J. 1975) and 456 A.2d 390 (N.J. 1983); for discussion, see Kirp et al., Our Town; Haar, Suburbs under Siege.

47. Haar, Suburbs under Siege, 50.

48. Payne, *Lawyers, Judges.*

49. The Economist, November 21, 1998, 18.

Chapter Twenty-Two: Academic
Law and Judicial Heroics

1. Quoted in Jack and Jack, Moral Vision, 156.

2. See Carrington, *Butterfly Effects.*

3. Holmes, *Path of the Law;* Symposium, *Path of the Law After One Hundred Years.*

4. R. Stevens, Law School, 96–98.

5. Sutherland, Law at Harvard, 187.

6. Letter to W. C. Sawyer, May 14, 1874, quoted in Veysey, Emergence, 62.

7. H. Edwards, *Growing Disjunction;* Bergin, *Law Teacher.*

8. See Jencks and Riesman, Academic Revolution.

9. See Priest, *Increasing Division.*

10. Holmes, *Path of the Law,* 466.

11. See Grey, *Langdell's Orthodoxy* and Schlegel, Langdell's Legacy.

12. But see Ellickson, *New Institutions* and Chemerinsky, *On Being a Framer* for counterexamples.

13. Mullenix, *God, Metaprocedure, and Metarealism.*

14. Stick, *Can Nihilism Be Pragmatic?*

15. Collier, *Use and Abuse of Humanistics Theory,* 196.

16. Leff, *Law And.*

17. Holmes, *Path of the Law,* 460.

18. Freund, *Law School,* 150. See also Farber, *Case Against Brilliance* and Farber and Sherry, *200,000 Cards.*

19. Wilson, Mere Literature, 12.

20. 2 de Tocqueville, Democracy in America, 411ff.

21. Byrne, *Academic Freedom;* Rabban, *Can Academic Freedom Survive?*

22. Id., 43.

23. Wright, Federal Courts.

24. Tribe, American Constitutional Law.

25. Glendon, A Nation Under Lawyers, 204.

26. See Rubin, *Law and Methodology.*

27. See Schlag, *Normativity.*

28. Allen, *Dolphin and Peasant,* 184–185.

29. But see Ellickson, New *Institutions.*

30. H. Edwards, *Growing Disjunction.*

31. Glendon, Nation under Lawyers, 199–229.

32. Rubin, *Practice and Discourse;* Langbein, *Scholarly Objectives;* Post, *Lani Guinier.*

33. Evidence is supplied by Margulies in *Citing Law Reviews.*

34. Barber, Conquest of Politics, 193.

35. See, for example, Fried, *Philosophy Matters.*

36. Posner, *Problematics,* 1864.

37. Lieber, Manual of Political Ethics, 168–169.

38. Gutmann and Thompson, Democracy and Disagreement.

39. Posner, *Problematics,* 1677–1678.

40. Id., 1673. And see Gross, Ethics and Activism.

41. Holmes, *Path of the Law.*

42. For example, West, Progressive Constitutionalism.

43. Sherry, *Progressive Regression,* 1114–1115.

44. Eisele, *Taking Constitution Seriously,* 1819.

45. D. Kennedy, Critique, 127–128.

46. Posner, *Problematics,* 1686–1686.

47. Id., 1679.

48. For an account, see Abrams, *Hearing the Call.*

49. Austin, Empire Strikes Back, 33–62.

50. See R. Kennedy, *Racial Critiques;* S. Carter, *Academic Tenure;* but see, for example, Delgado, *Coughlin's Complaint.*

51. See MacKinnon, Sexual Harassment.

52. Chemerinsky, *On Being a Framer.*

53. Kalman, Strange Career, 12–131.

54. For example, Ackerman, We the People; Amar and Hirsch, For the People; Bickel, Morality of Consent; Dworkin, Freedom's Law; Post, *Democracy;* Michelman, *Law's Republic.*

55. This literature is reviewed and refuted by Elhauge, *Does Interest Group Theory Justify—More Intrusive Review?*

56. Karst, Belonging to America, 224.

57. Ackerman, We the People; Amar, *Philadelphia Revisited*; Amar, *Consent of the Governed*; Michelman, *Supreme Court 1985*; Michelman, *Law's Republic*. For criticism of this use of history, see Kalman, Strange Career, 132–229.

58. Michelman, *Brennan and Democracy*, 426.

59. Brennan, *Reason, Passion*, 962.

60. As Eisele observed in *Taking Constitution Seriously*.

61. Dworkin, Freedom's Law, 2–4 and passim.

62. Michelman, *Brennan and Democracy*, 414–415.

63. Sullivan, *Epistemic Democracy*, 450–451.

64. Dworkin, *Darwin's New Bulldog*, 1721, n. 12. And see Dworkin, Freedom's Law, 36.

65. Posner, *Problematics*, 1686, n. 28.

66. P. Jessup, *Doctrine*.

67. Pasqualucci, *Louis Sohn*.

68. Henkin, International Law.

69. Koh, *Transnational Law*.

70. See, for example, Helfer and Slaughter, *Toward a Theory*.

71. S. v. Makwanyane, 1995 (3) SA 391 (CC).

72. Helfer and Slaughter, *Toward a Theory*, 370–373.

73. The pivotal case is Filartiga v. Pena-Irala, 630 F.2d 876 (2d Cir. 1980).

74. Restatement (Third) of the Foreign Relations Law of the United States §§ 111, 115.

75. Maier, *Bases and Range*, 140; Henkin, International Law, 164–165.

76. Bradley and Goldsmith, *Customary Law*, 840–842.

77. Id., 854.

78. Id., 876, n. 365.

79. Helfer and Slaughter, *Toward a Theory*, 370.

80. Id., 372–373.

81. Bradley and Goldsmith, *Customary Law*.

82. Koh, *Is International Law State Law?*; a reply is Bradley and Goldsmith, *Federal Courts*.

83. Gardner, Legal Imperialism.

84. See Trubek and Galanter, *Scholars*.

85. Edmund Burke, quoted by Liebmann, Gallows, iii.

86. But see Balkin and Levinson, *Canons of Constitutional Law*.

Chapter Twenty-Three: Byron White, Outcast Justice

1. Nation Under Lawyers, 170–173.

2. Hutchinson, Man Who Was Whizzer White, 11–24.

3. Kalman, Legal Realism at Yale, 98–107 and *passim*.

4. His biography is Twining, Karl Llewellyn.

5. Id., 27–34.

6. Quoted in Kalman, Legal Realism at Yale, 135–136.

7. Id., 138–140.

8. Lieber's work on the Constitution, On Civil Liberty and Self-Government, was published in 1853. A posthumous third edition was edited by Theodore Dwight Woolsey, the Yale president, in 1877, and was the basis of his teaching in the law school. A fourth edition was edited by his son, Theodore Salisbury Woolsey, and published in 1901; he also taught constitutional law and was almost certainly the teacher of Corbin.

9. See, for example, Borchard, *Supreme Court.*

10. Hutchinson, Man Who Was Whizzer White, 154.

11. See B. White, *Mr. Justice White.*

12. Hutchinson, Man Who Was Whizzer White, 448.

13. His astonishingly high salary, off the charts at the time, was $15,800 dollars a year. Id., 97–102.

14. Id., 173–179.

15. Id., 241–259.

16. Navasky, Kennedy Justice, 20–22.

17. New York Times, April 2, 1962.

18. The New Republic, April 9, 1962, 7.

19. United States v. Carolene Prods. Co., 304 U.S. 144, 148 n.4 (1938).

20. Robinson v. California, 370 U.S. 660 (1962).

21. Atiyah and Summers, Form and Substance, 407.

22. Miranda v. Arizona, 384 U.S. 436 (1966).

23. Accord Harlan, *Thoughts at Dedication.*

24. Duncan v. Louisiana, 391 U.S. 145 (1968).

25. 391 U.S. 430 (1968).

26. Regents of the Univ. of Cal. v. Bakke, 438 U.S. 265 (1978); Fullilove v. Klutznick, 448 U.S. 448 (1980); Metro Broadcasting v. FCC, 497 U.S. 547 (1990).

27. Johnson v. Transportation Agency, Santa Clara County, 480 U.S. 616 (1987).

28. 410 U.S. 113 (1973).

29. Griswold v. Connecticut, 381 U.S. 479 (1965).

30. Van Alstyne, *Closing the Circle,* 1679–1683.

31. 478 U.S. 186 (1986).

32. Hutchinson, Man Who Was Whizzer White, 451.

33. For an account of the issue as one fit for local politics, see Carrington, *Senate of Five.*

34. 376 U.S. 254 (1964).

35. See Atkinson v. The Detroit Free Press, 24 Mich. 44 (1871), discussed in chapter 7 at note 18.

36. 408 U.S. 665 (1972).

37. 436 U.S. 547 (1978).

38. 441 U. S. 153 (1979).

39. Hutchinson, Man Who Was Whizzer White, 382–383, 412–413.

40. Mason v. New Yorker Magazine, 501 U.S. 546 (1991).

41. Cohen v. Cowles Media, 501 U.S. 663 (1991).

42. California v. Greenwood, 486 U.S. 535 (1988).

43. New York Times, June 7, 1988.

44. Legal Times of Washington, July 3, 1989.

45. Red Lion Broadcasting v. FCC, 395 U.S. 367 (1969).

46. 424 U.S. 1 (1976).

47. See generally Jamieson, Dirty Politics.

48. New York Times, May 20, 1993.

49. Hutchinson, Man Who Was Whizzer White, 440–441.

50. New York Times Book Review Section, October 11, 1998, 35.

51. This refelects a general pattern in journalism; see Cappella and Jamieson, Spiral of Cynicism.

52. Tushnet, *Byron White*, 423.

53. Lazarus, Closed Chambers.

54. Woodward and Armstrong, Brethren.

55. Hutchinson, Man Who Was Whizzer White, 2.

56. Id., 3.

57. 403 U.S. 15 (1971).

58. Nagel, Judicial Power, 136–137 Nagel's footnotes omitted.

59. Northern Pipeline Constr. Co. v. Marathon Pipe Line Co., 458 U.S. 50 (1982).

60. Immigration and Naturalization Serv. v. Chadha, 462 U.S. 919 (1983).

61. Bowsher v. Synar, 478 U.S. 714 (1986).

62. Morrison v. Olson, 487 U.S. 654 (1988).

63. Mistretta v. United States, 488 U.S. 361 (1989).

64. Hutchinson, Man Who Was Whizzer White, 400–401.

65. Dragich, *Once a Century.* And see Strauss, *One Hundred and Fifty Cases.*

66. In recent years, U. S. Law Week has regularly published a feature called "Circuit Split Roundup," listing numerous circuit conflicts. See 67 U.S. Law Week 2206–2208 (October 13, 1998), listing thirty-six arising in the month of August 1998 and 67 U.S. Law Week 2334–2336 (December 8, 1998), listing thirty-two more arising in October.

67. Erie R.R. v. Tompkins, 304 U.S. 64 (1938).

68. Gulati and McCauliff, On Not Making Law.

69. Parker and Chapman, *Accepting Reality.*

70. Carrington, *A New Confederacy?,* 934, quoting Culberson in 21 Cong. Rec. 3403, 3404 (1890).

Chapter Twenty-Four: The Political Economy of Legal Education

1. Kronman, Lost Lawyer.

2. Fleming, Lawyers, Money, and Success. See also Erlanger, *Law Student Idealism.*

3. For further reflection on the question, see H. Edwards, *Role of Legal Education.*

4. Gilmore, Ages of American Law, 44.

5. Carrington, *Hail! Langdell!* 754–749.

6. Kalman, *To Hell with Langdell.*

7. Seligman, High Citadel, 155.

8. For example, A. Stone, *Legal Education on the Couch;* Watson, *Quest.*

9. S. Baldwin, Young Man, 128.

10. See remarks of Senator John Brown quoted in E. Shepard, *George Wythe,* 753.

11. Kronman, Lost Lawyer, 155–158.

12. Fuller, Morality of Law.

13. Id., 39.

14. Kronman, Lost Lawyer, 113–116.

15. See J. Elkins, *Rites de Passage.*

16. Kronman, Lost Lawyer, 156.

17. See Carrington, *Butterfly Effects.*

18. But see D. Kennedy, *Legal Education.*

19. That was the year Thayer was elected as the founding president of the Association of American Law Schools.

20. Strum, Brandeis: Beyond Progressivism, 20.

21. R. Stevens, Law School, 92–111.

22. Id., 100–101; Auerbach, Unequal Justice, 74–124; Abel, American Lawyer, 83–108.

23. Larson, Rise of Professionalism, 166–176.

24. See Kissam, *Decline of Professionalism.*

25. Larson, Rise of Professionalism, 397–402.

26. Logan, Howard University, 314; McNeil, Groundwork, 70–72.

27. Strum, Brandeis: Beyond Progressivism, 332.

28. Reed made the argument in Training for Public Profession.

29. Cooley, *Address.*

30. Legal Education and Professional Development.

31. Frank, Lincoln as a Lawyer.

32. In 1997, the annual tuition at Michigan was $17,148 for residents and $23,148 for non-residents.

33. Reed, Training for Public Profession, 410–416.

34. 2 Warren, History of Harvard Law School, 523.

35. E. G. Brown, Legal Education at Michigan, 232–233.

36. I. Brown, American Aristides, 203–204.

37. A critique of the report is Costonis, *MaCrate Report.*

38. See Schiltz, *Legal Ethics.*

39. Glendon, Nation under Lawyers, 217.

40. For example, in *God, Metaprocedure, and Metarealism,* Mullenix attributes the abstracted treatment of civil procedure by Fiss and Resnik to the assumption that practical training is provided elsewhere.

41. Cramton, *Next Century,* 1279.

42. Duffy and Goldberg, Crafting a Class, 169–204.

43. J. C. Smith, Emancipation, 627.

44. Id., 636.

45. On NYU as a center of feminism, see Drachman, Sisters in Law, 119–148.

46. Id., 625.
47. Id., 635, 636.
48. Carrington, *One Law,* 586–591.
49. Carrington, *Diversity!;* cf. Hopwood v. Texas, 78 F.3d 932 (1996).
50. Id., 1109–1128.
51. J. E. Baldwin, Flush Times, 52.
52. Carlin, Lawyers, is an account of the modest circumstances of many Chicago lawyers in 1960.
53. R. H. Smith, Justice for the Poor and Growth of Legal Aid.
54. Free Legal Services.
55. Carrington, *Right to Zealous Counsel.*
56. Carrington, *ADR Primer.*
57. Quayle, *Agenda,* 980.
58. The term belongs to Frank and Cook; see their Winner Take-All Society.
59. Chambers, *Burden of Educational Loans;* J. White, *Impact of Law Student Debt.*
60. See generally Chambers, *Burden of Educational Loans.*
61. Kornhauser and Revesz, *Legal Education,* 823.
62. Vernon, *Educational Debt Burden.*

Chapter Twenty-Five: Prospect

1. Barber, Conquest of Politics, 263.
2. Sennett, Corrosion of Character.
3. T. Walker, Introduction, vii.
4. B. Friedman, *Valuing Federalism;* and see Bednar and Eskridge, *Steadying the Court.*
5. Compare Posner, *Problematics,* 1709.
6. Sarat and Scheingold, Cause Lawyering.
7. Cappella and Jamieson, Spiral of Cynicism.
8. For example, Buckley v. Valeo, 424 U.S. 1, 15, 21, 47 (1976).
9. D. Currie, Constitution of Germany, 339.
10. § 4(1), (2) Statute Respecting the Constitutional Court (1953).
11. Article 79.
12. Articles 27–38.
13. D. Currie, Constitution of Germany, 81–84.
14. Article 2(2).
15. D. Currie, Constitution of Germany, 74–77.
16. Cf. Printz v. United States, 117 S. Ct. 2365, 2383–2384 (1997); Barnett, *Necessary and Proper.*
17. Wall Street Journal, Feb. 25, 1999, B4.
18. See Kolovos, *Antitrust Law* and Reske, *ABA Settles;* but see also Cassens, *Law School Loses.*
19. Posner, Overcoming Law, 57.

References

Listed first are all authored works cited in the notes, in alphabetical order by the last name of the author. Unauthored works that have been cited, other than cases or statutes, are then listed in alphabetical order by title.

Authored Works

Abel, Richard L., The American Lawyer (1989)

Abrams, Kathryn, *Hearing the Call of Stories,* 79 Cal. L. Rev. 971 (1991)

Ackerman, Bruce A., *The Storrs Lecture: Discovering the Constitution,* 93 Yale L. J. 1013 (1984)

_____, We the People: Foundations (1991)

Adams, Charles Francis, *The Railroad System,* in Chapters of Erie and Other Essays (Boston, 1871)

Adams, Henry, Life of Albert Gallatin (Philadelphia, 1879)

Adams, Henry Carter, *Relation of the State to Industrial Action,* 1 Publications of the American Economic Association 465 (1887)

Allen, Francis A., *The Dolphin and The Peasant: Ill-tempered, but Brief, Comments on Legal Scholarship,* in Property Law and Legal Education: Essays in Honor of John E. Cribbet at 183 (Peter Hay and Michael H. Hoeflich, eds., 1988)

Allen, Ronald J., *Constitutional Adjudication, The Demands of Knowledge, and Epistemological Modesty,* 88 N. W. Univ. L. Rev. 436 (1993)

Allison, Charles Elmer, A Historical Sketch of Hamilton College (Yonkers, 1889)

Alschuler, Albert W., *The Descending Trail: Holmes' Path of the Law One Hundred Years Later,* 49 Fla. L. Rev. 353 (1997)

Altschuler, Glenn C., Andrew D. White—Educator, Historian, Diplomat (2 vols., 1979)

Amar, Akhil Reed, *The Consent of the Governed: Constitutional Amendment Outside Article V,* 94 Col. L. Rev. 457 (1994)

_____, *Philadelphia Revisited: Amending the Constitution Outside Article V,* 55 U. Chi. L. Rev. 1043 (1988)

Amar, Akhil Reed, and Alan Hirsch, For the People: What the Constitution Really Says About Your Rights (1998)

Ames, James Barr, *Christopher Columbus Langdell,* in 8 Great American Lawyers 465 (William D. Lewis, ed., 1908)

Amsterdam, Anthony, *The Supreme Court and The Rights of Suspects in Criminal Cases,* 45 N.Y.U. L. Rev. 785 (1970)

Arnold, Richard S., *Trial by Jury: The Constitutional Right to a Jury of Twelve in Civil Trials,* 22 Hofstra L. Rev. 1 (1993)

Atiyah, Patrick S., and Robert S. Summers, Form and Substance in Anglo-American Law: A Comparative Study in Legal Reasoning, Legal Theory, and Legal Institutions (1987)

Aurand, Harold, *Anthracite Coal Strike of 1875,* in Labor Conflict in the United States: An Encyclopedia 15 (Ronald L. Filipelli, ed., 1990)

Auerbach, Jerold, Unequal Justice: Lawyers and Social Change in Modern America (1976)

Austin, Arthur, The Empire Strikes Back: Outsiders and the Struggle Over Legal Education (1998)

Avrich, Paul, The Haymarket Tragedy (1984)

Babcock, Richard F., The Zoning Game: Municipal Practices and Policies (1966)

Baker, Liva, The Justice from Beacon Hill (1991)

Baker, Thomas E., *Exercising the Amendment Power to Disapprove of Supreme Court Decisions: A Proposal for a "Republican Veto,"* 22 Hastings Const. L.Q. 325 (1995)

Baldwin, Joseph E., The Flush Times in Alabama and Mississippi (New York, 1858)

Baldwin, Simeon Eben, The Young Man and the Law (1930)

Balkin, J. M., and Sanford Levinson, The Canons of Constitutional Law, 111 Harv. L. Rev. 963 (1998)

Barajas, Richard, and Scott Alexander Nelson, *The Proposed Crime Victims' Federal Constitutional Amendment: Working Towards a Proper Balance,* 49 Baylor L. Rev. 1 (1997)

Barber, Benjamin, The Conquest of Politics: Liberal Philosophy in Democratic Times (1988)

Barnes, Thomas G., *Introduction,* in Thomas M. Cooley, Constitutional Limitations (Thomas G. Barnes, ed., 1987)

Barnett, Randy E., *Necessary and Proper,* 44 UCLA L Rev. 745 (1997)

Barron, David J., *The Promise of Cooley's City: Traces of Local Constitutionalism,* 147 U. Pa. L. Rev. 487 (1999)

Baskerville, Stephen W., Of Laws and Limitations: An Intellectual Portrait of Louis Dembitz Brandeis (1994)

Bass, Jack, Unlikely Heroes: The Dramatic Story of the Southern Judges of the Fifth Circuit Who Translated the Supreme Court's *Brown* Decision into a Revolution of Equality (1981)

Baude, Patrick L., *A Comment on the Evolution of Direct Democracy in Western State Constitutions,* 28 N. Mex. L. Rev. 313 (1998)

Beard, Charles, and Mary Beard, The Rise of American Civilization (1928)

Bednar, Jenna, and William N. Eskridge Jr., *Steadying the Court's "Unsteady Path":* *A Theory of the Judicial Enforcement of Federalism,* 68 S. Cal. L. Rev. 1447 (1995)

Bell, Derrick A., Jr., *Serving Two Masters: Integration Ideals and Client Interests in School Desegregation Litigation,* 85 Yale L. J. 470 (1976)

_____, And We Are Not Saved: The Elusive Quest for Racial Justice (1987)

Bellot, Hugh Hale, The University College, London, 1826–1926 (1929)

Benedict, Michael Les, *Laissez Faire and Liberty: A Re-evaluation of the Meaning and Origins of Laissez Faire Constitutionalism,* 3 Law & History Rev. 293 (1985)

Benjamin, G. Andrew, Alfred Kozniak, Bruce Sales, and Stephen B. Shenfield, *The Role of Legal Education in Producing Psychological Distress Among Law Students and Lawyers,* 1986 Am. B. Found. Res. J. 225

Benson, Lee Merchants, Farmers, and Railroads: Railroad Regulation and New York Politics 1850–1887 (1955)

Berger, Raoul, Government by Judiciary: The Transformation of the Fourteenth Amendment (2d ed., 1997)

Bergin, Thomas, *The Law Teacher: A Man Divided Against Himself,* 54 Va. L. Rev. 637 (1968)

Beveridge, Albert, The Life of John Marshall (4 vols., 1917)

Bickel, Alexander M., *Judicial Restraint & The Bill of Rights,* New Republic 6 (May 12, 1958)

_____, The Morality of Consent (1975)

_____, *The Original Understanding and the Segregation Decision,* 69 Harv. L. Rev. 1 (1955)

_____, The Unpublished Opinions of Mr. Justice Brandeis (1957)

Bickel, Alexander M., and Harry Wellington, *Legislative Purpose and the Judicial Process: The Lincoln Mills Case,* 71 Harv. L. Rev. 1 (1957)

Bittker, Boris I., *Interpreting the Constitution: Is the Intent of the Framers "Controlling" If Not, What Is?,* 19 Harv. J. L. & Pub. Pol'y 9 (1995)

Black, Charles L., Jr., The People and the Court: Judicial Review in a Democracy (1960)

Blackstone, William, Commentaries on English Law (St. George Tucker, ed., 5 vols., Philadelphia, 1803)

Blakely, Edward J., and Mary Gail Snyder, Fortress America: Gated Communities in the United States (1997)

Blalock, Joyce, Civil Liability of Law Enforcement Officers (1974)

Blasi, Vincent, *Free Speech and the Widening Gyre of Fundraising: Why Campaign Spending Limits May Not Violate the First Amendment After All,* 94 Colum. L. Rev. 1281 (1994)

_____, *Learned Hand and the Self-Government Theory of the First Amendment: Masses Publishing Co. v. Patten,* 61 U. Colo. L. Rev. 1 (1990)

Bloom, Lackland H., Jr., *Hopwood, Bakke, and the Future of Diversity Justification,* 29 Tex. Tech L. Rev. 1 (1998)

Bloomfield, Maxwell, American Lawyers in a Changing Society 1776–1876 (1976)

_____, *Law and Politics: The Self-Image of the American Bar, 1830–1860,* 12 Am. J. Leg. Hist. 306 (1968)

Bollinger, Lee C., *Elitism, The Masses and The Idea of Self-Government: Ambivalence About the "Central Meaning" of the First Amendment,* in Constitutional Government in America at 99 (Ronald K. L. Collins, ed., 1980)

Borchard, Edwin, *The Supreme Court and Private Rights,* 47 Yale L. J. 1051 (1938)

Bork, Robert H., Slouching Towards Gomorrah: Modern Liberalism and American Decline (1996)

_____, *Styles in Constitutional Theory,* Y.B. of the Supreme Court Historical Soc'y 53 (1984)

Boyd, Leroy S., Cooley Bibliography (Mimeo, Interstate Commerce Commission, 1933).

Brackenridge, Hugh Henry, Modern Chivalry (Claude M. Newlin, ed., 1937)

Bradley, Curtis A., and Jack L. Goldsmith, *Customary International Law as Federal Common Law: A Critique of the Modern Position,* 110 Harv. L. Rev. 816 (1997)

Bradley, Curtis A., and Jack L. Goldsmith, *Federal Courts and the Incorporation of International Law,* 111 Harv. L. Rev. 2260 (1998)

Brandeis, Louis D., Business—A Profession (1914).

Brandeis, Louis D., and Charles Warren, *The Right of Privacy,* 4 Harv. L. Rev. 193 (1891)

Brennan, William J., *The Equality Principle: A Foundation of American Law,* 20 U. Cal. Davis L. Rev. 673 (1987)

_____, *Reason, Passion, and the Progress of the Law,* Rec. of the Ass'n of the Bar of the City of New York 948 (1987)

_____, *State Constitutions and the Protection of Individual Rights,* 90 Harv. L. Rev. 489 (1977)

Brest, Paul, *The Misconceived Quest for the Original Understanding,* 60 B.U. L. Rev. 981 (1980)

Brewer, Scott, *Scientific Testimony and Intellectual Due Process,* 107 Yale L. J. 1535 (1998)

Bridenbaugh, Jessica Hill, *Theodore Sedgwick,* 16 Dictionary of American Biography 551 (Dumas Malone, ed., 1935)

Bright, Stephen B., *Political Attacks on the Judiciary: Can Justice Be Done amid Efforts to Intimidate and Remove Judges from Office for Unpopular Decisions?* 72 N.Y.U. L. Rev. 308 (1997)

Brinkley, Alan, Voices of Protest: Huey Long, Father Coughlin and the Great Depression (1982)

Brooks, Van Wyck, The Flowering of New England, 1815–1865 (1936)

Brown, Bernard, American Conservatives: The Political Thought of Francis Lieber and John W. Burgess (1951)

Brown, Elizabeth Gaspar, *The Initial Admission of Negro Students to the University of Michigan,* 2 Mich. Q. Rev. 233 (1963)

_____, Legal Education at Michigan, 1859–1959 (1959)

Brown, Everett S., *The Contribution of Thomas M. Cooley to Bryce's American Commonwealth,* 31 Mich. L. Rev. 353 (1933)

Brown, Imogene, American Aristides (1981)

Bruce, Robert, 1877: Year of Violence (1959)

Burt, Robert A., *Alex Bickel's Law School and Ours,* 104 Yale L. J. 1853 (1995)

_____, Two Jewish Justices: Outcasts in A Promised Land (1988)

Byrne, J. Peter, *Academic Freedom and Political Neutrality in Law Schools,* 43 J. Legal Educ. 315 (1993)

Calabresi, Guido, The Common Law in the Age of Statutes (1980)

Calamandrei, Piero, Procedure and Democracy (John C. Adams and Helen Adams, trans., 1956)

Callies, David L., *Home Rule,* in 1 Local Government Law, ch. 4 (C. Dallas Sands, Michael E. Libardi, and John Martinez, eds., 1994)

Campbell, Colin D., and William A. Fischel, *Preferences for School Finance Systems: Voters Versus Judges,* 49 Nat'l Tax. J. 1 (1997)

Campbell, Edward G., The Reorganization of the American Railroad System 1893–1900 (1938)

Campbell, John, The Lives of the Chief Justices of England (London, Murray, 1849)

Campion, Michael E., T*he Maine Clean Election Act: The Future of Campaign Finance Reform,* 61 Fordham L. Rev. 2391 (1998)

Cappella, Joseph A., and Kathleen Hall Jamieson, Spiral of Cynicism: The Press and the Public Good (1997)

Carlin, Jerome, Lawyers on Their Own: A Study of Individual Practitioners in Chicago (1962)

Carlyle, Thomas, Past and Present (London, 1843)

Caro, Robert A., The Years of Lyndon Johnson (1982)

Carrington, Paul D., *ADR and Future Adjudication: A Primer on Dispute Resolution,* 15 Rev. Litig. 1 (1996)

_____, *Butterfly Effects: The Possibilities of Law Teaching in a Democracy,* 41 Duke L. J. 741 (1992)

_____, *Diversity!,* 1992 Utah L. Rev. 1105 (1992)

_____, *Ernst Freund,* in American National Biography, vol. 7 (1999)

_____, *Financing the American Dream: Equality and School Taxes,* 73 Colum. L. Rev. 1227 (1973)

_____, *Hail! Langdell!,* 20 L. & Soc. Inq. 691 (1995)

_____, *Law and Chivalry: An Exhortation from the Spirit of the Hon. Hugh Henry Brackenridge (1748–1816),* 53 U. Pitt. L. Rev. 705 (1992)

_____, *Legal Education for the People: Populism and Civic Virtue,* 43 Kan. L. Rev. 1 (1994)

_____, *Meaning and Professionalism in American Law,* 10 Const. Commentary 297 (1993)

_____, *The Missionary Diocese of Chicago,* 44 J. Leg. Educ. 467 (1994)

_____, *A New Confederacy? Disunionism in the Federal Courts,* 45 Duke L.J. 929 (1996)

_____, *One Law, The Role of Legal Education in the Opening of the Legal Profession Since 1776,* 44 Fla. L. Rev. 501 (1992)

_____, *The Revolutionary Idea of Legal Education,* 31 Wm. & Mary L. Rev. 527 (1990)

_____, *The Right to Zealous Counsel,* 1979 Duke L. J. 1291 (1980)

_____, *A Senate of Five,* 23 Ga. L. Rev. 859 (1989)

_____, *The Seventh Amendment: Some Bicentennial Reflections,* 1990 U. Chi. L. Forum 33.

_____, *A Tale of Two Lawyers,* 91 Nw. U. L. Rev. 615 (1997)

_____, *The Theme of Early American Law Teaching: The Political Ethics of Francis Lieber,* 52 J. Leg. Educ. 339 (1992)

_____, *William Gardiner Hammond and the Lieber Revival,* 16 Cardozo L. Rev. 2135 (1995)

Carrington, Paul D., and Paul H. Haagen, *Contract and Jurisdiction,* 1996 Sup. Ct. Rev. 351

Carrington, Paul D., and Erika King, *The Wisconsin Idea,* 57 J. Leg. Educ. 297 (1997)

Carter, Dan. T., The Politics of Rage: George Wallace, the Origins of the New Conservatism, and the Transformation of American Politics (1995)

Carter, Hodding, The Angry Scar: The Story of Reconstruction (1959)

Carter, Stephen L., *Academic Tenure and "White Male" Standards: Some Lessons from the Patent Law,* 100 Yale L. J. 2065 (1991)

_____, The Confirmation Mess: Cleaning Up the Federal Appointment Process (1994)

_____, The Culture of Disbelief: How American Law and Politics Trivializes Religious Devotion (1993)

Cash, W. J., The Mind of the South (1941)

Cassens, Debra, *Law School Loses Appeal Against ABA,* 84 A.B.A. J. 31 (1998)

Chambers, David L., *The Burdens of Educational Loans: The Impacts of Debt on Job Choice and Standards of Living for Students at Nine American Law Schools,* 42 J. Leg. Educ. 187 (1993)

_____, *Educational Debts and the Worsening Position of Small-Firm, Government and Legal Services Lawyers,* 39 J. Leg. Educ. 709 (1989)

Champaign, Anthony, *Contributions in Texas Judicial Races,* 17 Crime, L. & Soc'y J. 91 (1992)

Chandler, Alfred Dupon, The Railroads—The Nation's First Big Business (1965)

Chaney, Henry A., *The Supreme Court of Michigan,* 2 Green Bag 377 (1890)

Chapman, John Jay, William Lloyd Garrison (1921)

Chase, William C., The American Law School and the Rise of the Administrative State (1982).

Chayes, Abram, *The Role of the Judge in Public Law Litigation,* 89 Harv. L. Rev. 1281 (1976)

Chemerinsky, Erwin, *Amending the Constitution,* 96 Mich. L. Rev. 1561 (1998)

_____, *On Being a Framer,* 2 Green Bag 2d 131 (1999)

Chroust, Anton, The Rise of the Legal Profession (2 vols., 1965).

Clark, Sherman J., *A Populist Critique of Direct Democracy,* 112 Harv. L. Rev. 434 (1998)

Clay, Henry, The Papers of Henry Clay (9 vols., J. Hopkins, ed., 1965–   )

Cloud, Morgan, *Searching Through History, Searching for History,* 63 U. Chi. L. Rev. 1707 (1996)

Cohen, Morris R., Law: A Century of Progress 1835–1935 (1937)

_____, *Property and Sovereignty,* 13 Cornell L. Q. 1 (1927)

Coke, Edward, *Prohibitions del Roy,* 12 Co. Rep. 63 (London, 1608)

Cole, David, *Agon at Agora: Creative Misreadings of the First Amendment Tradition,* 95 Yale L.J. 857 (1986)

Collier, Charles W., *The Use and Abuse of Humanistic Theory in Law: Re-examining the Assumptions of Interdisciplinary Legal Scholarship,* 41 Duke L.J. 191 (1991)

Cooley, Thomas M., *Address,* in Address of Thomas M. Cooley and Poem of D. Bethune Duffield on the Dedication of the Law Lecture Hall (Ann Arbor, Mich., 1863)

_____, *Address of the President,* 17 A.B.A. Rep. 181 (1895)

_____, *The Administration of President Grant,* 4 Int'l. Rev. 145 (1877)

_____, *Arbitration in Labor Disputes,* 1 Forum 310 (1886)

_____, *Austria,* 16 W. Literary Messenger 65 (1851)

_____, Comparative Merits of Written and Prescriptive Constitutions, Proceedings of the 12th Annual Meeting of the New York State Bar Association 47 (New York, 1889)

_____, *Consider M. Stacy,* 14 Collections of the Pioneer Soc'y of the State of Michigan 268 (1907).

_____, The Elements of Torts (Boston, 1895)

_____, *The Founding of the Law Department of the University of Michigan,* in Senior Law Class Annual 93 (Ann Arbor, Mich., 1894)

_____, The General Principles of Constitutional Law in the United States of America (Boston, 1880)

_____, *Grave Obstacles to Hawaiian Annexation,* 15 The Forum 389 (1893)

_____, The Influence of Habits of Thought Upon Our Institutions, Second Annual Address before The South Carolina Bar Association, South Carolina Bar Proceedings (Columbia, 1887)

_____, *Labor and Capital Before the Law,* 139 N. Am. Rev. 503 (1884)

_____, Law as an Educating Force, Address before The Annual Commencement of the Law and Dental Schools of the University of Michigan March 26, 1884 (Ann Arbor, 1864)

_____, The Lawyer's Duty to the State, Proceedings of the Fourth Annual Meeting of the Bar Association of Tennessee (Nashville, 1886)

_____, *Lectures I–VIII: Equality in American Politics, Johns Hopkins University (1878),* unpublished manuscript in Box 1, Cooley Papers, Bentley Library, University of Michigan

_____, Letter to S. M. Collum, August 25, 1882 in Box 7 of the Cooley Papers, Bentley Library, University of Michigan

_____, *Liability of Public Officers to Private Actions for Neglect of Official Duty,* 3 Southern L. Rev. (N.S.) 531 (1877)

_____, *Limits to State Control of Private Business,* 1 Princeton Rev. 233 (1878)

_____, *The Method of Electing the President,* 5 Int'l Rev. 198 (1878)

_____, Michigan: A History of Governments (New York, 1885)

_____, *Popular and Legal Views of Traffic Pooling,* Railway Rev. 212 (April 26, 1884)

_____, *Sources of Inspiration in Legal Pursuits,* 9 W. Jurist 515 (1875)

_____, *State Regulation of Corporate Profits,* 137 N. Amer. Rev. 207 (1883)

_____, A Treatise on the Constitutional Limitations Which Rest upon the Legislative Power of the States of the American Union (Boston, 1868)

_____, A Treatise on the Law of Taxation Including the Law of Special Assessments (Chicago, 1876)

_____, A Treatise on the Law of Torts or the Wrongs Which Are Independent of Contracts (Chicago, 1879)

_____, *The Uncertainty of the Law*, 22 Am. L. Rev. 23 (1888)

_____, *What Can the Law Do for the Health of the People?*, in 1882 Annual Report of the Michigan State Board of Health 7

Cooper, James Fenimore, *A Letter to General Lafayette*, 2 Letters and Journals of James Fenimore Cooper 122 (Paris, 1831; 6 vols., 1960–1968)

_____, A Letter to His Countrymen (New York, 1834)

_____, Home As Found (New York, 1854)

_____, Homeward Bound (New York, 1838)

_____, Notions of Americans Picked Up by a Traveling Bachelor (New York, 1828)

Corwin, Edward S., Court Over Constitution: A Study of Judicial Review as an Instrument of Popular Government (1938)

_____, Liberty Against Government: The Rise, Flowering and Decline of a Famous Judicial Concept (1948)

Costonis, John J., *The MacCrate Report: Of Loaves, Fishes and the Future of American Legal Education*, 43 J. Leg. Educ. 157 (1993)

Cox, Archibald, The Role of the Supreme Court in American Government (1976)

Cramton, Roger C., *The Next Century: A Panel Discussion*, 73 Cornell L. Rev. 1270 (1988)

Croley, Steven P., *The Majoritarian Difficulty: Elective Judiciaries and the Rule of Law*, 62 U. Chi. L. Rev. 689 (1995)

Croly, Herbert, The Promise of American Life (1910)

Cross, Whitney N., The Burnt Over District: The Social and Intellectual History of Enthusiastic Religion in Western New York, 1800–1850 (1950)

Crowell, Charles, *Railway Receiverships in the United States: Their Origin and Development*, 7 Yale Rev. 319 (1898)

Culver, John H., and John T. Wold, *Judicial Reform in California*, in Judicial Reform in the States 156 (Anthony Champaign and Judith Haydel, eds., 1993)

Currie, Brainerd, *The Materials of Law Study*, 8 J. Leg. Educ. 1 (1955)

Currie, David P., The Constitution in the Supreme Court: The Second Century 1888–1986 (1990)

_____, The Constitution of the Federal Republic of Germany (1994)

Curti, Merle, The American Peace Crusade 1815–1860 (1929)

Curtis, James C., The Fox at Bay: Martin Van Buren and the Presidency, 1837–1841 (1970)

Curtis, Michael Kent, No State Shall Abridge: The Fourteenth Amendment and the Bill of Rights (1985)

Cushman, Barry, Rethinking the New Deal Court: The Structure of a Constitutional Revolution (1998)

Dahl, Robert A., Democracy and Its Critics (1989)

D'Alemberte, Talbot, *Searching for the Limits of Judicial Free Speech*, 61 Tul. L. Rev. 611 (1987)

Dallek, Robert, 1898: McKinley's Decision (1969)

Dane, Nathan, A General Abridgement and Digest of American Law (Boston 1823)

Daugherty, Michael, To Steal a Kingdom (1994)

Davis, Gawan, Shoal of Time: A History of the Hawaiian Islands (1974)

Dawson, John P., The Oracles of the Law (1968)

Deane, Eric T., *Reassessing Dred Scott: The Possibilities of Federal Power in the Antebellum Context*, 60 U. Cin. L. Rev. 713 (1992)

Degler, Carl, The Age of Economic Revolution, 1870–1910 (1977)

Delgado, Richard, *Coughlin's Complaint: How to Disparage Outsider Writing, One Year Later*, 82 Va. L. Rev. 82 (1996)

Destro, Robert A., *Law and the Politics of Marriage: Loving v. Virginia After 30 Years*, 47 Cath. U. L. Rev. 1207 (1998)

de Tocqueville, Alexis, Democracy in America (Paris, 1835; 2 vols., Henry Reeve, trans., New York, n.d.)

Dewey, Donald O., Marshall and Jefferson: The Political Background of Marbury v. Madison (1970)

Dewey, Ralph L., The Long and Short Haul Principle of Rate Regulation (1934)

Dillon, James Forrest, Removal of Causes from State Courts to Federal Courts (Chicago, 1876)

_____, Treatise on Municipal Corporations (Chicago, 1872)

Dixon, Robert G., *The "New" Substantive Due Process and the Democratic Elite: A Prolegomenon*, 1976 B.Y.U. L. Rev. 43

Donald, David H., Charles Sumner and the Rights of Man (1967)

Douglas, Davison M., *The Limits of Law in Accomplishing Racial Change: School Segregation in the Pre-Brown North*, 44 UCLA L. Rev. 677 (1997)

Drachman, Virginia C., Sisters in Law: Women Lawyers in Modern American History (1998)

Dragich, Martha J., *Justice Blackmun, Franz Kafka, and Capital Punishment*, 63 Mo. L. Rev. 853 (1998)

_____, *Once A Century: Time for Structural Overhaul of the Federal Courts*, 1996 Wis. L. Rev. 11

Driscoll, William Dennis, Benjamin F. Butler: Lawyer and Regency Politician (1987)

Duffy, Elizabeth A., and Idana Goldberg, Crafting A Class: College Admissions and Financial Aid (1998)

Dunscomb, S. Whitney, *The Police Power and Civil Liberty*, 6 Col. L. Rev. 95 (1906)

Dwight, Timothy, Travels in New England and New York (New Haven, 1822)

Dworkin, Andrea, and Catherine MacKinnon, Pornography in Civil Rights: A New Day for Women's Equality (1988)

Dworkin, Ronald, *Darwin's New Bulldog*, 111 Harv. L. Rev. 1718 (1998)

_____, Freedom's Law (1996)

_____, Taking Rights Seriously (1977)

Eaton, Amasa M., *The Right to Local Self-Government*, 13 Harv. L. Rev. 441, 470, 638 and 14 Harv. L. Rev. 19, 116 (1900)

Edwards, George, *Why Justice Cooley Left the Bench: A Missing Page of History*, 33 Wayne L. Rev. 1563 (1987)

Edwards, Harry T., *The Growing Disjunction Between Legal Education and the Legal Profession,* 91 Mich. L. Rev 34 (1992)

_____, *The Role of Legal Education in Shaping the Profession,* 38 J. Leg. Educ. 285 (1988)

Eggert, Gerard C., *Railroad Strikes in 1877,* in Labor Conflict in the United States: An Encyclopedia 15(Ronald L. Filipelli, ed., 1990)

Eisele, Thomas D., *Taking Our Actual Constitution Seriously,* 95 Mich. L. Rev. 1799 (1997)

Elhauge, Einer R., *Does Interest Group Theory Justify More Intrusive Judicial Review,* 101 Yale L. J. 31 (1991)

Elkins, James A., *Rites de Passage: Law Students "Telling Their Lives,"* 35 J. Leg. Educ. 26 (1985)

Elkins, Stanley, and Eric McKittrick, The Age of Federalism: The Early American Republic, 1788–1801 (1993)

Ellickson, Robert C., *Law and Economics Discovers Social Norms,* 27 J. Legal Stud. 537 (1998)

_____, *New Institutions for Old Neighborhoods,* 48 Duke L. J. 75 (1998)

Ellis, Richard E., The Jeffersonian Crisis: Courts and Politics in the Young Republic (New York 1971)

Ellsworth, Frank L., Law on The Midway: The Founding of the University of Chicago Law School (1977)

Ely, John Hart, *The Wages of Crying Wolf: A Comment on Roe v. Wade,* 82 Yale L. J. 920 (1973)

Ely, Richard T., *Past and Present of Political Economy,* in 2 Johns Hopkins University Studies in History and Political Science 143 (Baltimore, 1884)

England, Izhak, *Li v. Yellow Cab Co.: A Belated and Inglorious Centennial of the California Civil Code,* 65 Cal. L. Rev. 4 (1977)

Enrich, Peter, *Leaving Equity Behind: New Directions in School Finance Reform,* 48 Vand. L. Rev. 101 (1995)

Epstein, Richard A., *Substantive Due Process by Any Other Name: The Abortion Cases,* 1973 Sup. Ct. Rev. 159

Erickson, Nancy, *Muller v. Oregon Reconsidered: The Origins of a Sex-Based Doctrine of Liberty of Contract,* 30 J. Labor Hist. 228 (1989)

Erlanger, Howard S., *Law Student Idealism and Job Choice: Some New Data on An Old Question,* 30 Law & Soc'y Rev. 851 (1996)

Fairchild, William, *The Professorship of Law in Oberlin College,* Oberlin Rev. (November 8, 1884)

Fairman, Charles, *Does the Fourteenth Amendment Incorporate the Bill of Rights?,* 2 Stan. L. Rev. 5 (1949)

Farber, Daniel A., *The Case Against Brilliance,* 70 Minn. L. Rev. 917 (1986)

_____, *Reinventing Brandeis: Legal Pragmatism for the Twenty-First Century,* 1995 U. Ill. L. Rev. 163

Farber, Daniel A., and Philip P. Frickey, Law and Public Choice: A Critical Introduction (1991)

Farber, Daniel A., and Suzanna Sherry, A History of the American Constitution (1994)

_____, *The 200,000 Cards of Dimitri Yurasov: Further Reflections on Scholarship and Truth,* 46 Stan. L. Rev. 647 (1994)

Faulkner, Harold W., The Decline of Laissez-Faire 1897–1917 (1962)

Fehrenbacher, Don E., The Dred Scott Case: Its Significance in American Law and Politics (1978)

Ferguson, Robert A., Law and Letters in American Culture (1984)

Fessenden, Franklin G., *Rebirth of the Harvard Law School,* 33 Harv. L. Rev. 493 (1920)

Fine, Sidney, Laissez-Faire and the General Welfare State: A Study of Conflict in American Thought, 1865–1901 (1956)

Fineran, John Kingston, The Career of a Tinpot Napoleon: A Political Biography of Huey P. Long (1961)

Fink, Leon, Workingmen's Democracy: The Knights of Labor and American Politics (1983)

Fischel, William A., *How Serrano Caused Proposition 13,* 12 J. L. & Pol. 607 (1996)

_____, School Finance Litigation and Property Tax Revolts: How Undermining Local Control Turns Voters Away from Public Education (1998)

Fish, Stanley, *Mission Impossible: Settling the Just Bounds Between Church and State,* 97 Colum. L. Rev. 2255 (1997)

Fishlow, Albert, American Railroads and the Transformation of the Ante-Bellum Economy (1965)

Fiss, Owen, Liberalism Divided: Freedom of Speech and the Many Uses of State Power (1996)

_____, *Money and Politics,* 97 Colum. L. Rev. 2470 (1997)

Fiss, Owen, and Judith Resnik, Procedure (1988)

Fleming, Macklin, Lawyers, Money, and Success: The Consequences of Dollar Obsession (1997)

Fletcher, Robert Samuel, A History of Oberlin College: From Its Foundations through the Civil War (2 vols., 1943)

Foner, Eric, Reconstruction: America's Unfinished Revolution, 1863–1877 (1988)

Foner, Philip, History of the Labor Movement in the United States, Vol. 1: From Colonial Times to the Founding of the American Federation of Labor (1947); Vol. 2: From the Founding of the American Federation of Labor to the Emergence of American Imperialism (1955)

Forbath, William E., Law and the Shaping of the American Labor Movement (Cambridge, 1991)

Ford, Worthington Chaney, *Charles Francis Adams,* 1 Dictionary of American Biography 48 (Allen Johnson, ed., 1928)

Forres, Jacqueline Darroch, and Stanley K. Henshaw, *The Harassment of U. S. Abortion Providers,* 19 Fam. Planning Persp. 9 (1987)

Frank, John P, *Justice Black and The New Deal,* 9 Ariz. L. Rev. 26 (1967)

_____, Lincoln as a Lawyer (1961)

Frank, Robert H., and Philip J. Cook, The Winner-Take-All Society (1995)

Frankfurter, Felix, The Commerce Clause under Marshall, Taney and Waite (1937)

_____, The Ernst Freund Lecture: Some Observations on Supreme Court Litigation and Legal Education (1954)

_____, *The Task of Administrative Law,* 75 U. Pa. L. Rev. 614 (1927)

Frankfurter, Felix, and Nathan Greene, The Labor Injunction (1930)

Franklin, John Hope, Reconstruction After the Civil War (2d ed., 1994)

Freehling, William H., Prelude to Civil War: The Nullification Controversy in South Carolina 1816–1836 (1966)

Freidel, Frank, Francis Lieber: Nineteenth Century Liberal (1947)

Freund, Ernst, *The Debs Case and Freedom of Speech,* 19 New Republic 13 (May 3, 1919)

_____, *Interpretation of Statutes,* 65 U Pa L Rev 207 (1917)

_____, *Law School and University,* 18 Univ. Record 139 (1935)

_____, *Legislation,* 9 Encycl. Soc. Sci 347 (1930)

_____, Legislative Drafting (1916)

_____, Legislative Regulation: A Study of Ways and Means (1932)

_____, *Limitation of Hours of Labor and the Federal Supreme Court,* 17 Green Bag 411 (1905)

_____, The Police Power: Public Policy and Constitutional Rights (1904)

_____, *Private Claims Against the State,* 8 Pol. Sci. Q. 625 (1893)

_____, *The Problem of Intelligent Legislation,* 4 Proc. Am. Pol. Sci. Ass'n 69 (1908)

_____, *Some Inadequately Discussed Problems of the Law of City Planning and Zoning,* 29 Ill. L. Rev. 135 (1929)

_____, Standards of Legislation (Francis A. Allen, ed., 1965)

_____, *The Substitution of Rule for Discretion in Public Law,* 9 Am. Pol. Sci. Rev. 666 (1915)

Freyer, Tony, Harmony & Dissonance: The Swift and Erie Cases in American Federalism (1981)

_____, The Little Rock Crisis: A Constitutional Interpretation (1984)

Fried, Charles, *Philosophy Matters,* 111 Harv. L. Rev. 1739 (1998)

Friedman, Barry, *The History of the Countermajoritarian Difficulty: Part One,* 73 N.Y.U. L. Rev. 333 (1998)

_____, *The Turn to History,* 72 N.Y.U. L. Rev. 958 (1997)

_____, *Valuing Federalism,* 82 Minn. L. Rev. 317 (1997)

Friedman, Lawrence Meir, *Civil Wrongs: Personal Injury Law in the Late 19th Century,* 1987 Am. B. Found. Res. J. 351.

_____, A History of American Law (1973)

Friendly, Henry J., The Federal Administrative Agencies: The Need for Better Definition of Standards (1962)

Fuchs, Lawrence, Hawaii Pono: A Social History (1963)

Fuhrner, Mary O., Advocacy and Objectivity: A Crisis in the Professionalization of American Social Science, 1865–1905 (1975)

Fuller, Lon. The Morality of Law (1964)

Galanter, Marc, *The Portable Soc 21 or What to Do Until the Doctrine Comes,* in General Education in the Social Sciences: Centennial Reflections on the College of the University of Chicago 246 (John J. MacAloon, ed., 1992)

Gallo, Max, Mussolini's Italy: Twenty Years of the Fascist Era (Charles Lam Markmann, trans., 1973)

Gardbaum, Stephen A., *Why The Liberal State Can Promote Moral Ideals After All,* 104 Harv. L. Rev. 1350 (1991)

Gardner, James A., Legal Imperialism: American Lawyers and Foreign Aid in Latin America (1980)

Gardner, James M., *Southern Character, Confederate Nationalism, and the Interpretation of State Constitutions: A Case Study in Constitutional Argument,* 76 Tex. L. Rev. 1219 (1998)

Garrow, David J., *All Over But the Legislating: There Was a Genuine War Over Abortion, These Writers Think, But the Armistice Appears Durable,* N. Y. Times, Jan. 25, 1998, Book Review, 14

_____, Bearing the Cross: Martin Luther King and the Southern Christian Leadership Conference (1986)

Gawalt, Gerard W., Massachusetts Lawyers: A Historical Analysis of the Process of Professionalization, 1760–1840 (1976)

Gere, Edwin A., *Dillon's Rule and Cooley's Doctrine,* 8 J. Urb. Hist. 271 (1982)

Ghent, W. J., *Eugene Victor Debs,* 5 Dictionary of American Biography 183 (Allen Johnson and Dumas Malone, eds., 1930)

Gillman, Howard, The Constitution Besieged: The Rise and Demise of Lochner Era Police Powers Jurisprudence (1993)

Gilmore, Grant, The Ages of American Law (1977)

Gladden, Washington, Applied Christianity: Moral Aspects of Social Questions (Boston, 1887)

Glendon, Mary Ann, Abortion and Divorce in Western Law (1987)

_____, A Nation under Lawyers: How the Crisis in the Legal Profession Is Transforming American Society (1994)

Goebel, Julius, A History of the School of Law Columbia University (1955)

Gold, David M., The Shaping of Nineteenth Century Law: John Appleton and Responsible Individualism (1990)

Goldfarb, Ronald, The Contempt Power (1967)

Golding, Martin, *Holmes's Jurisprudence: Aspects of Its Development and Continuity,* 5 Soc. Theory and Prac. 183 (1979)

Goldston, Robert, The Civil War in Spain (1966)

Goodnow, Frank J., Comparative Administrative Law (New York, 1893)

_____, The Principles of Administrative Law in the United States (1905)

Goodrich, Frederick E., The Life and Public Service of Grover Cleveland (1888)

Goodspeed, Thomas W., William Rainey Harper, First President of the University of Chicago (1928)

Gordon, Robert, Comment, 70 N.Y.U. L. Rev. 569 (1995)

_____, *The Independence of Lawyers,* 68 Boston Univ. L. Rev. 1 (1988)

Gormley, Ken, Archibald Cox: Conscience of a Nation (1997)

Graglia, Lino A., *Constitutional Law: A Ruse for Government by an Intellectual Elite,* 14 Ga. St. U. L. Rev. 767(1998)

Graham, Fred P., The Self-Inflicted Wound (1970)

Graham, Howard J., *The Conspiracy Theory of the Fourteenth Amendment,* 47 Yale L. J. 371 (1938)

_____, Everyman's Constitution (1968)

Gray, John Chipman, The Natures and Sources of Law (2d ed., Roland Gray, ed., 1921)

Greenslet, Ferris, The Lowells and Their Seven Worlds (1946)

Greenstone, J. David, The Lincoln Persuasion: Remaking American Liberalism (1993)

Grey, Thomas C., *Do We Have an Unwritten Constitution?,* 27 Stan. L. Rev. 703 (1975)

_____, *Holmes and Legal Pragmatism,* 41 Stan. L. Rev. 787 (1989)

_____, *Langdell's Orthodoxy,* 45 U. Pitt. L. Rev. 1 (1983)

_____, *Molecular Motions: The Holmesian Judge in Theory and Practice,* 37 Wm. & Mary L. Rev. 19 (1995)

_____, *Thayer's Doctrine: Notes on Its Origin, Scope, and Present Implications,* 88 Nw. U. L. Rev. 28 (1993)

Grimke, Frederick, The Nature and Tendency of Free Institutions (2d ed. 1856; reprinted 1968); this work was first published in 1848, the second edition in 1856.

Grodin, Joseph R., *Developing A Consensus of Constraint: A Judge's Perspective on Judicial Retention Elections,* 61 S. Cal. L. Rev. 1969 (1988)

_____, In Pursuit of Justice (1990)

_____, *Rediscovering the State Constitutional Right to Happiness and Safety,* 25 Hastings Const. L. Q. 1 (1997)

Gross, Michael, Ethics and Activism: The Theory and Practice of Political Morality (1997)

Gulati, Mitu, and C. M. A. McCauliff, *On Not Making Law,* 61–63 L. & C. P. 157 (1998)

Gunther, Gerald, Learned Hand: The Man and the Judge (1994)

Gutmann, Amy, and Dennis Thompson, Democracy and Disagreement (1996)

Haar, Charles, Suburbs under Siege: Race, Space and Audacious Judges (1996)

Haber, Samuel, The Quest for Authority and Honor in the American Professions 1750–1900 (1991)

Haddow, Anna, Political Science in American Colleges and Universities, 1636–1900 (1939)

Hadley, Arthur T., *Railroad Business under the Interstate Commerce Act,* 3 Q. J. of Econ. 170 (1889)

Hain, Elwood, *Sealing Off the City: School Desegregation in Detroit,* in Limits of Justice : The Courts' Role in School Desegregation 223 (Howard Kalodner and James Fishman, eds., 1978)

Haines, Charles G., The Revival of Natural Law Concepts: A Study of the Limits on Legislatures with Special Reference to The Development of Certain Phases of American Constitutional Law (1930)

Hall, Kermit L., *Constitutional Machinery and Judicial Professionalism: The Careers of Midwestern State Appellate Court Judges, 1861–1899,* in The New High Priests: Lawyers in Post-Civil War America 29 (Gerard W. Gawalt, ed., 1984)

_____, The Magic Mirror: Law in American History (1989)

_____, *The "Route to Hell" Retraced: The Impact of Popular Election on the Southern Appellate Judiciary, 1832–1920,* in Ambivalent Legacy: A Legal History of the South 229 (David J. Bodenhamer and James W. Ely, eds., 1984)

Halperin, S. William, Germany Tried Democracy: A Political History of the Reich from 1918 to 1933 (1946)

Hamilton, Alexander, John Jay, and James Madison, The Federalist (1788) (George W. Carey and James McClellan, eds., 1990).

Hand, Learned, The Bill of Rights (1958)

_____, *Due Process of Law and the Eight-Hour Day,* 21 Harv. L. Rev. 495 (1908)

_____, *Mr. Justice Holmes,* 43 Harv. L. Rev. 857 (1950)

_____, *Sources of Tolerance,* 79 U. Pa. L. Rev. 1 (1930)

_____, *The Speech of Justice,* 29 Harv. L. Rev. 617 (1916).

_____, *To Yale Law Graduates, June 17, 1931,* in The Spirit of Liberty 65 (I. Dillard, ed., 1952)

Hanushek, Eric A., *When School Finance "Reform" May Not Be Good Policy,* 28 Harv. J. on Legis. 423 (1991)

Harlan, John Marshall, *Thoughts at a Dedication: Keeping the Judicial Function in Balance,* 49 A.B.A. J. 943 (1963).

Harley, Louis, Francis Lieber: His Life and Political Philosophy (New York, 1899)

Harper, Richard, and John Aldrich, T*he Political Economy of Sugar Legislation,* 70 Pub. Choice 299 (1991)

Harris, Michael H., *The Frontier Lawyer's Library: Southern Indiana, 1800–1850, As A Test Case,* 16 Am. J. Legis. Hist. 239 (1972)

Hartz, Louis, The Liberal Tradition in America (1955)

Haskell, Thomas L., The Emergence of Professional Social Science: The American Social Science Association and the Nineteenth Century Crisis of Authority (1977)

Haynes, Evan, The Selection and Tenure of Judges (1944).

Hazen, Richard L., *"High Court Wrongly Elected": A Public Choice Model of Judging and Its Implications for The Voting Rights Act,* 75 N.C. L. Rev. 1305 (1997)

Heck, Earl L. W., *Theodore Sedgwick,* 16 Dictionary of American Biography 551 (Dumas Malone, ed., 1935)

Helfer, Lawrence R., and Anne-Marie Slaughter, *Toward A Theory of Effective Supranational Adjudication,* 107 Yale L. J. 273 (1997)

Henderson, Edith Guild, *The Background of the Seventh Amendment,* 80 Harv. L. Rev. 289 (1966)

Henkin, Louis, International Law: Politics and Values (1995)

Hersch, Joni, *Teen Smoking Behavior and the Regulatory Environment,* 47 Duke L.J. 1143 (1998)

Hershkoff, Helen, *Rights and Freedoms under the State Constitutions: A New Deal for Welfare Rights,* 13 Touro L. Rev. 631 (1997)

Hershkoff, Helen, and Adam S. Cohen, *Begging to Differ: The First Amendment and the Right to Beg,* 104 Harv. L. Rev. 891 (1990)

Higginbotham, Leon, In the Matter of Color (1978)

Hirsch, Mark D., *Election of 1884,* in 2 History of American Presidential Elections 1789–1968, 1561 (Arthur M. Schlesinger, ed., 1971)

Hoeflich, Michael H., *Law and Geometry: Legal Science from Leibnitz to Langdell,* 30 Am. J. Legis. Hist. 95 (1986)

Hofstadter, Richard, Social Darwinism in American Thought (rev. ed., 1955)

_____*William Leggett, Spokesman of Jacksonian Democracy,* 58 Pol. Sci. Q. 581 (1943)

Holland, Randy J., *State Constitutions: Purpose and Functions,* 69 Temple L. Rev. 989 (1996)

Holmes, Oliver Wendell, Jr., Collected Legal Papers (1920)

_____, The Common Law (Boston, 1881)

_____, The Essential Holmes (Richard A. Posner, ed., 1991)

_____, *The Gas Stokers' Strike,* 7 Am. L. Rev. 582 (1873)

_____, Holmes-Pollock Letters (Mark DeWolfe Howe, ed., 1941)

_____, *Law in Science and Science in Law,* 12 Harv. L. Rev. 443 (1889)

_____, *The Path of the Law,* 10 Harv. L. Rev. 457 (1897)

_____, *Summary of Events, Great Britain,* 7 Am. L. Rev. 582 (1873)

_____, *Twenty Years in Retrospect,* in The Occasional Papers of Justice Oliver Wendell Holmes 154 (Mark DeWolfe Howe, ed., 1962)

Holmes, Stephen, Passions and Constraint: On the Theory of Liberal Democracy (1995)

Hook, Jay, *A Brief Life of James Bradley Thayer,* 88 Nw. U. L. Rev. 1, 7 (1993)

Hopkins, Charles H,. The Rise of the Social Gospel in American Protestantism, 1865–1915 (1940)

Horton, John T., James Kent: A Study in Conservatism 1763–1847 (1939)

Horowitz, Donald L., Courts and Social Policy (1977)

_____, Ethnic Groups in Conflict (1983)

Horwitz, Morton J., The Transformation of American Law, 1870–1960: The Crisis of Legal Orthodoxy (1992)

Hovenkamp, Herbert, *The Political Economy of Due Process,* 40 Stan. L. Rev. 379 (1988)

_____, *Regulatory Conflict in the Gilded Age: Federalism and the Railroad Problem,* 97 Yale L. J. 1017 (1988)

Howe, Mark DeWolfe, Justice Oliver Wendell Holmes: The Proving Years (1963)

Hurst, James Willard, The Growth of American Law: The Law Makers (1950)

Hutchins, Harry B., *The Cornell Law School,* 1 Green Bag 473 (1889)

Hutchins, Harry Burns, *Thomas McIntyre Cooley,* in 7 Great American Lawyers 431 (William D. Lewis, ed., 1909)

Hutchinson, Dennis J., The Man Who Was Whizzer White: A Portrait of Justice Byron R. White (1998)

Hyman, Harold M., A More Perfect Union (1973)

Inbau, Fred E., and John E. Reid, Criminal Interrogation and Confessions (2d ed., 1967)

Israel, Jerold H., Yale Kamisar, and Wayne R. LaFave, Criminal Procedure and the Constitution (1997)

Issacharoff, Samuel, and Richard H. Pildes, *Politics as Markets: Partisan Lockups of the Democratic Process,* 50 Stan. L. Rev. 643 (1998)

Issacharoff, Samuel, Pamela Kaplan, and Richard H. Pildes, The Law of Democracy: Legal Structure of the Political Process (1998)

Jack, Rand, and Dana C. Jack, Moral Vision and Professional Decisions: The Changing Values of Women and Men Lawyers (1989)

Jackson, Jeffrey, *Judicial Independence, Adequate Court Funding, and Inherent Judicial Power,* 43 Md. L. Rev. 217 (1993)

Jackson, Robert H., The Struggle for Judicial Supremacy: A Study of a Crisis in American Power Politics (1941)

_____, The Supreme Court in the American System of Government (1967)

Jacobs, Clyde E., Law Writers and the Courts: The Influence of Thomas M. Cooley, Christopher G. Tiedeman, and John F. Dillon upon American Constitutional Law (1954)

Jaffe, Louis L., Judicial Control of Administrative Action (1965)

_____, *Law Making by Private Groups,* 51 Harv. L. Rev. 212 (1937)

James, Fleming, Jr., and Geoffrey C. Hazard, Civil Procedure (3d ed., 1985)

Jamieson, Kathleen Hall, Dirty Politics (1992)

Jay, Stewart, *The Rehabilitation of Samuel Chase,* 41 Buff. L. Rev. 273 (1993)

Jefferson, Thomas, The Writings of Thomas Jefferson (H.A. Washington, ed., 1854)

_____, The Writings of Thomas Jefferson 391, 392 (Albert E. Bergh, ed., 1907)

Jencks, Christopher, and David Riesman, The Academic Revolution (1969)

Jensen, Robert M., *Advancing Education Through Education Clauses of State Constitutions,* 1997 B.Y.U. L. Rev. 1 (1997)

Jessup, Dwight W., Reaction and Accommodation: The United States Supreme Court and Political Conflict 1808–1835 (1987)

Jessup, Philip C., *The Doctrine of Erie Railroad v. Tompkins Applied to International Law,* 33 Am. J. Int'l L. 740 (1939)

Johansen, Robert W., The Frontier, The Union, and Stephen A. Douglas (1988)

Johnson, Orrin W., and Laura Johnson Uris, *Judicial Selection in Texas: A Gathering Storm?,* 23 Tex. Tech L. Rev. 525 (1992)

Jolls, Christine, Cass R. Sunstein, and Richard Thaler, *A Behavioral Approach to Law and Economics,* 50 Stan. L. Rev. 1471 (1998)

Jones, Alan R., The Constitutional Conservatism of Thomas McIntyre Cooley: A Study in the History of Ideas (1987)

_____, *Thomas M. Cooley and the Michigan Supreme Court: 1865–1885,* 10 Am. J. Legis. Hist. 97 (1966)

Jones, Theodore F., New York University 1832–1932 (1933)

Judson, Frederick N., The Law of Interstate Commerce and Its Federal Regulation (1905)

Kahn, Paul W., *State Constitutionalization and the Problems of Fairness,* 30 Val. U. L. Rev. 464 (1996)

Kaimen, James L., *Nineteenth Century Interpretations of the Federal Contract Clause: The Transformation of Vested to Substantive Rights Against the States,* 31 Buff. L. Rev. 381 (1982)

Kalman, Laura, Legal Realism at Yale, 1927–1960 (1986)

_____, The Strange Career of Legal Liberalism (1996)

_____, *To Hell with Langdell!*, 20 L. & Soc. Inq. 771 (1995)

Kalven, Harry, *Ernst Freund and the First Amendment Tradition,* 40 U. Chi. L. Rev. 235 (1972)

_____, The Negro and the First Amendment (1965)

_____, *The New York Times Case: A Note on the "Central Meaning" of the First Amendment,* 1964 Sup. Ct. Rev 191

_____, A Worthy Tradition: Freedom of Speech in America (Jamie Kalven, ed., 1988)

Kamisar, Yale, *On the Meaning and Impact of the Physician-Assisted Suicide Cases,* 82 Minn. L. Rev. 895 (1998)

Kant, Immanuel, Metaphysical Elements of Justice (John Ladd, trans., 1965)

Karst, Kenneth L., Belonging to America: Equal Citizenship and the Constitution (1989)

Kaufman, Rise E., Note, *The Cultural Meaning of the "Welfare Queen:" Using State Constitutions to Challenge Child Exclusion Provisions,* 23 N.Y.U. Rev. L. & Soc. Change 301 (1997)

Kaye, Judith S., *State Courts at the Dawn of a New Century: Common Law Courts Reading Statutes and Constitutions,* 70 N.Y.U. L. Rev. 1 (1995)

Keating, John M., History of the City of Memphis and Shelby County, Tennessee (Memphis, 1888)

Kennedy, Albert J., *Jane Addams,* 21 Dictionary of American Biography 10 (Harris E. Starr, ed., 1944)

Kennedy, Duncan, A Critique of Adjudication (1997)

_____, *Legal Education as Training for Hierarchy,* in The Politics of Law: A Progressive Critique (2d ed., David Kairys, ed., 1998)

Kennedy, Randall L., *Racial Critiques of Legal Academia,* 102 Harv. L. Rev. 1745 (1989)

Kens, Paul, Justice Stephen Field: Shaping Liberty from the Gold Rush to the Gilded Age (1997)

Kent, Arthur H., *Ernst Freund (1864–1932)—Jurist and Social Scientist,* 41 J. of Pol. Econ. 145 (1933)

Kent, Charles, *Municipal Subscription and in Aid of Railroads,* 9 Am. L. Reg., New Series 649 (1870)

Kent, James, Commentaries on American Law (4 vols., Boston, 1826–1832)

_____, Memoirs and Letters of James Kent (W. Kent, ed., New York, 1898)

Kimball, Bruce A., *"Warn Students That I Entertain Heretical Opinions, Which They Are Not to Take as Law": The Inception of Case Method Teaching in the Classrooms of the Early C. C. Langdell, 1870-1883,* 17 L. & Hist. Rev. 57 (1999)

Kirkland, Edward C., Business in the Gilded Age: The Conservative Balance Sheet (1952)

_____, A History of American Economic Life (1932)

Kirp, David, et al., Our Town: Race, Housing, and the Soul of Suburbia (1995)

Kissam, Philip C., *The Decline of Law School Professionalism,* 134 U. Pa. L. Rev. 251 (1986)

Klarman, Michael J., *Originalism and constitutional Theory: A Response to Professional McConnell,* 81 Va. L. Rev. 1881 (1995)

_____, *Rethinking the Civil Rights and Civil Liberties Revolution,* 82 Va. L. Rev. 1 (1996)

Kluger, Richard, Simple Justice: The History of Brown v. Board of Education and Black America's Struggle for Equality (1976)

Koh, Harold Hongju, *Is International Law Really State Law?,* 111 Harv. L. Rev. 1824 (1998)

_____, *Transnational Public Law Litigation,* 100 Yale L. J. 1547 (1991)

Kolko, Gabriel, Railroads and Regulation: 1877–1916 (1965)

Kolovos, Peter James, *Antitrust Law and Nonprofit Organizations: The Law School Accreditation Case,* 71 N.Y.U. L. Rev. 689 (1996)

Konefsky, Samuel J., The Legacy of Holmes and Brandeis: A Study in the Influence of Ideas (1961)

Kornhauser, Louis A., and Richard Revesz, *Legal Education and Entry into The Legal Profession: The Role of Race, Gender, and Educational Debt,* 70 N.Y.U. L. Rev. 829 (1995)

Kraines, Oscar, The World and Ideas of Ernst Freund (1974)

Kronman, Anthony T., The Lost Lawyer: Falling Ideals of the Legal Profession (1993)

Krotoszynski, Ronald J., Jr., *Constitutional Flares: On Judges, Legislatures, and Dialogue,* 83 Minn. L. Rev. 1 (1998)

Kyvig, David E., Explicit and Authentic Acts: Amending the U. S. Constitution 1776–1995 (1996)

Landis, James M., The Administrative Process (1938)

Langbein, John H., *Scholarly and Professional Objectives in Legal Education: American Trends and English Comparisons,* in 2 Pressing Problems in the Law: What Are Law Schools For? 1 (Peter Birks, ed., 1996)

Langston, John Mercer, From the Virginia Plantation to the National Capitol (Hartford, 1894)

LaPiana, William P., Logic and Experience: The Origin of Modern American Legal Education (1994)

Larson, Edward J., Summer for the Gods: The Scopes Trial and America's Continuing Debate Over Science and Religion (1997)

Larson, Magali S., The Rise of Professionalism (1977)

Lasch, Christopher, The Revolt of the Elites and the Betrayal of Democracy (1995)

Lathrop, John Hiram, Address Delivered on the Dedication of the College Building (Madison, 1843)

Lazarus, Edward, Closed Chambers: The First Eye Witness Account of the Epic Struggles Inside the Supreme Court (1998)

Leedes, Gary C., *Justice George Sutherland and the Status Quo: A Biographical and Review Essay,* 1995 J. Sup. Ct. Hist. Soc. 137 (1996)

Leff, Arthur A., *Law And,* 87 Yale L. J. 989 (1978)

Leggett, William, Democratick Editorials: Essays in Jacksonian Political Economy (Lawrence H. White, ed., 1984)

Leibmann, George W., The Gallows in the Groves: Civil Society in American Law (1997).

Lemann, Nicholas, The Promised Land: The Great Black Migration and How It Changed America (1991)

Lerner, Max, *The Supreme Court and American Capitalism,* 42 Yale L. J. 668 (1933)

Leuchtenburg, William E., The Supreme Court Reborn: The Constitutional Revolution in the Age of Roosevelt (1995)

Levinson, Sanford, *The Democratic Faith of Felix Frankfurter,* 25 Stan L. Rev. 430 (1973)

Levy, Leonard W., The Law of Commonwealth and Chief Justice Shaw (1957)

_____, Legacy of Suppression: Freedom of Speech and Press in Early American History (Cambridge, 1960)

Levy, Leonard W., and Douglas Jones. *Jim Crow Education: Origins of the "Separate but Equal" Doctrine,* in Judgments: Essays on American Constitutional History 316 (Leonard W. Levy, ed., 1972).

Lewis, Anthony, Make No Law: The Sullivan Case and the First Amendment (1991)

Lewis, Charles, The Buying of the Congress: How Special Interests Have Stolen Your Right to Life, Liberty and the Pursuit of Happiness (1998)

Lieber, Francis, *The Ancient and Modern Teacher of Politics,* in 1 Miscellaneous Writings of Francis Lieber 369 (Daniel Coit Gilman, ed., Philadelphia, 1880)

_____, Civil Liberty and Self-Government (1852; 3d ed., Theodore J. Woolsey, ed., Philadelphia, 1875)

_____, Legal and Political Hermeneutics (1838; 3d ed., William G. Hammond, ed., St. Louis, 1880)

_____, Manual of Political Ethics (2 vols., Boston, 1837; 2d ed, Theodore Woolsey, ed., Boston, 1875)

Lili'okalani, Hawaii's Story by Hawaii's Queen (1990 ed.)

Lincoln, Abraham, *The Perpetuation of Our Political Institutions, Address to the Young Men's Lyceum, Springfield, January, 1838,* in 1 Collected Works of Abraham Lincoln 108 (Roy Basler, ed., 1953)

Linde, Hans A., *First Things First: Rediscovering the States' Bills of Rights,* 9 U. Balt. L. Rev. 379 (1980)

Lindsay, Thomas K., *Defending Liberalism, Book Review of Stephen Holmes, Passions and Constraints: On the Theory of Liberal Democracy,* 82 Iowa L. Rev. 943 (1997)

Link, Arthur S., Wilson (2 vols., 1947).

Llewellyn, Karl N., The Common Law Tradition: Deciding Appeals (1960)

Locke, John, Of Civil Government (Dutton ed., 1947)

Logan, Rayford W., Howard University: The First Hundred Years, 1867–1967 (1969)

Lopez, Gerald, Rebellious Lawyering: One Chicano's Vision of Progressive Law Practice (1992)

Lusky, Louis, *Government by Judiciary: What Price Legitimacy?*, 6 Hastings Const. L. Q. 403 (1979)

Macey, Jonathan R., *Promoting Public-Regarding Legislation Through Statutory Interpretation: An Interest Group Model*, 86 Colum. L. Rev. 223 (1986)

MacKinnon, Katherine, Feminism Unmodified (1987)

_____, Sexual Harassment of Working Women: A Case of Sex Discrimination (1979)

Mahan: Alfred, *Hawaii and Our Future Sea Power*, 15 The Forum 1 (1893)

_____, The Influence of Sea Power upon History (3 vols., Boston, 1890–1905)

Maier, Harold G., *The Bases and Range of Federal Common Law in Private International Matters*, 5 Vand. J. Transnat'l L. 133 (1971)

_____, *The Role of Experts in Proving International Human Rights Law in Domestic Courts: A Commentary*, 25 Ga. J. Int'l & Comp. L. 205 (1996)

Malinowski, Bronislaw, Sex, Culture and Myth (1930)

Margulies, Peter, *The Citing of Law Reviews by the Supreme Court: An Empirical Study*, 34 UCLA L. Rev. 131 (1986)

Marion, David E., The Jurisprudence of Justice William J. Brennan: The Law and Politics of "Libertarian Dignity" (1997)

Martin, Albro, Enterprise Denied (1972)

Martineau, Harriet, Retrospect of Western Travels (1838)

_____, Society in America (1837)

Mason, Alpheus T., Brandeis: A Free Man's Life (1946)

McCullough, David, Truman (1992)

McCurdy, Charles, *Justice Field and the Jurisprudence of Government-Business Relations: Some Parameters of Laissez Faire Constitutionalism*, 61 J. Am. Hist. 970 (1975)

McIntyre, Alasdair, Whose Justice? Whose Rationality? (1988)

McKelvey, Blake, The Urbanization of America, 1860–1915 (1967).

McLaughlin, Andrew C., The Courts, the Constitution and Parties: Studies in Constitutional History and Politics (1912)

_____, *Thomas McIntyre Cooley*, 4 Dictionary of American Biography 392 (Alan Johnson and Dumas Malone, eds., 1930)

_____, *A Written Constitution in Some of Its Historical Aspects in the Courts*, 5 Mich. L. Rev. 605 (1907)

McLaurin, Melton Alonza, The Knights of Labor in the South (1978)

McLean, Joseph E., William Rufus Day, Supreme Court Justice from Ohio (1946)

McNeil, Genna Rae, Groundwork: Charles Hamilton Houston and the Struggle for Civil Rights (1983)

Mechem, Floyd, Elements of the Law of Partnership (Chicago, 1896)

_____, The Law of Public Offices and Officers (Chicago, 1890)

_____, A Treatise on the Law of Sales of Personal Property (1901)

Meese, Edwin, III, *Putting the Federal Judiciary Back on The Constitutional Track*, 14 Ga. St. U. L. Rev. 781 (1998)

Meikeljohn, Alexander, Free Speech and Its Relation to Self-Government in Political Freedom (1948)

Mendelson, Wallace, *The Influence of James B. Thayer Upon the Work of Holmes, Brandeis, and Frankfurter,* 31 Vand. L. Rev. 71 (1978)

_____, *Mr. Justice Holmes—Humility, Skepticism and Democracy,* 36 Minn. L. Rev. 343 (1952)

Meyer, Balthasar H., *Judge Cooley and the Interstate Commerce Commission,* 6 ICC Prac. J. 137 (1938)

Meyers, Marvin, The Jacksonian Persuasion (1957)

Michelman, Frank, *The Supreme Court 1985 Term—Traces of Self-Government,* 100 Harv. L. Rev. 4 (1986)

_____, *Law's Republic,* 97 Yale L. J. 1493 (1988)

_____, Brennan and Democracy, 86 Cal. L. Rev. 399 (1998)

Mill, John Stuart, *On Liberty (1859)* in John Stuart Mill Essays (Mary Warnock, ed., 1962)

Millon, David, *Objectivity and Democracy,* 67 N.Y U. L. Rev. 1 (1992)

Milton, John, *Aeropagitica: A Speech for the Liberty of Unlicensed Printing (London 1644),* in 32 Great Books of the Western World 406 (1952)

Monaghan, Henry Paul, Comment, *The Constitution Goes to Harvard,* 13 Harv. C.R.-C.L. L. Rev. 117 (1978)

Montgomery, David, Beyond Equality: Labor and the Radical Republicans, 1862–1872 (1967)

_____, The Fall of the House of Labor (1987)

Morgan, Martha I., *The Constitutional Right to Know Why,* 17 Harv. C.R.-C.L. L. Rev. 297 (1982)

Morgan, William, Illustrations of Masonry by One of The Fraternity Who Has Devoted Thirty Years to the Subject (New York, 1826)

Morison, Samuel Eliot, *Dissent in the War of 1812,* in Dissent in Three American Wars 18–26 (S. Morison, F. Merk, and D. Freidel, 1970)

_____, Three Centuries of Harvard, 1636–1936 (1936)

Morn, Frank, The Eye That Never Sleeps: A History of the Pinkerton National Detective Agency (1982)

Mosk, Stanley, *The Emerging Agenda in State Constitutional Rights Law,* 496 Annals Am. Acad. Pol. Soc. Sci. 54 (1988)

Mosteller, Robert P., *Essay: Victims' Rights and the United States Constitution: An Effort to Recast the Battle in Criminal Litigation,* 85 Geo. L. J. 1691 (1997)

Mullenix, Linda S., *God, Metaprocedure and Metarealism at Yale,* 87 Mich. L. Rev. 1139 (1989)

Murphy, Bruce Allen, The Brandeis-Frankfurter Connection: The Secret Political Activities of Two Supreme Court Justices (1982)

Myrdal, Gunnar, An American Dilemma: The Negro Problem and Modern Democracy (1944)

Nagel, Robert F., Judicial Power and American Character: Censoring Ourselves in an Anxious Age (1994)

_____, *Name-Calling and the Clear Error Rule,* 88 Nw. U.. L. Rev 193 (1993)

Navasky, Victor S., Kennedy Justice (1971)

Nedelsky, Jennifer, Private Property and the Limits of American Constitutionalism (1990)

Nelles, Walter, *A Strike and Its Consequences,* 40 Yale L. J. 507 (1931)

Nelson, Bruce C., Beyond the Martyrs: A Social History of Chicago's Anarchists (1988)

Nelson, Lars-Erik, *Democracy for Sale,* New York Review of Books (December 3, 1998)

Nelson, William E., The Fourteenth Amendment: From Political Principle to Judicial Doctrine (1988)

_____, *History and Neutral Principles in Constitutional Adjudication,* 72 Va. L. Rev. 1237 (1986)

_____, The Roots of American Bureaucracy (1982)

Newman, Roger K., Hugo Black: A Biography (1994)

Nichol, Gene R., Jr., *The Left, the Right, and Certainty in Constitutional Law,* 33 Wm. & Mary L. Rev. 1181 (1992)

Noonan, John T., Jr., Persons and Masks of the Law (1976)

_____, *Raw Judicial Power,* 22 Nat'l Rev. 260 (1973)

Novak, William J., *Public Economy and the Well-Ordered Market: Law and Economic Regulation in 19th Century America,* 18 L. & Soc. Inq. 1 (1993)

Oakes, James L., Comment, 70 N.Y.U. L. Rev. 562 (1995)

Oaks, Dallin H., *Studying the Exclusionary Rule in Search and Seizure,* 37 U. Chi. L Rev. 754 (1970)

O'Dea, Thomas F., The Mormons (1957)

Orfield, Gary, The Reconstruction of Southern Education: The Schools and the 1964 Civil Rights Act (1969)

Orfield, Gary, and Susan Eaton, Dismantling Desegregation: The Quiet Reversal of Brown v. Board of Education (1996)

Paludan, Phillip, A Covenant with Death (1975)

_____, *Law and the Failure of Reconstruction: The Case of Thomas Cooley,* 33 J. Hist. of Ideas 597 (1979)

Paris, Michael, *Legal Mobilization and Reform: School Finance Litigation in New Jersey,* in Leveraging the Law: Using the Courts to Achieve Social Change 83 (David A. Schultz, ed., 1998).

Parker, Richard D., "Here the People Rule": A Constitutional Populist Manifesto (1994)

_____, Statement re Flag-Burning, Hearings on Constitutional Amendment, 105th Congress (1998)

Parker, Robert M., and R. Chapman, *Accepting Reality: The Time for Accepting Discretionary Review in the Courts of Appeals Has Arrived,* 50 SMU L. Rev. 573 (1997)

Paschal, J. Francis, Mr. Justice Sutherland: A Man Against the State (1951)

Pasqualucci, Jo M., *Louis Sohn: Grandfather of International Human Rights Law in the United States,* 20 Hum. Rts. Q. 924 (1998)

Paul, Arnold M., Conservative Crisis and the Rule of Law: Attitudes of the Bar and Bench 1887–1895 (1969)

Payne, John M., *Lawyers, Judges, and the Public Interest,* 96 Mich. L. Rev. 1561 (1998)

Perry, Michael J., *The Authority of Text, Tradition and Reason: A Theory of Constitutional Interpretation,* 58 S. Cal. L. Rev. 551 (1985)

Perry, Thomas Sargent, The Life and Letters of Francis Lieber (Boston, 1882)

Peskin, Alan, Garfield: A Biography (1978)

Peters, Ellen A., *Getting Away from the Federal Paradigm: Separation of Powers in State Courts,* 81 Minn. L. Rev. 1542 (1997)

Peterson, Merrill D., The Great Triumvirate: Webster, Clay, and Calhoun (1987)

———, Thomas Jefferson and the New World Nation (1970)

Phillips, Harlan B., Felix Frankfurter Reminisces (1960)

Pierce, Bessie Louise, A History of Chicago 1871–1893 (1957)

Pinchot, Gifford, The Fight for Conservation (1910)

Pinello, Daniel R., The Impact of Judicial-Selection Method on State-Supreme-Court Policy: Innovation, Reaction and Atrophy (1995)

Posner, Richard A., Cardozo: A Study of Reputation (1990)

———, *An Economic Theory of Criminal Law,* 85 Colum. L. Rev. 1193 (1985)

———, *The Learned Hand Biography and the Question of Judicial Greatness,* 104 Yale L. J. 511 (1994)

———, *Legal Scholarship Today,* 45 Stan. L. Rev. 1647 (1993)

———, Overcoming Law (1995)

———, *The Problematics of Moral and Legal Theory,* 111 Harv. L. Rev. 1637 (1998)

Post, Robert C., *Community and the First Amendment,* 29 Ariz. St. L. J. 473 (1997)

———, *The Constitutional Concept of Public Discourse: Outrageous Opinion, Democratic Deliberation, and Hustler Magazine v. Falwell,* 103 Harv. L. Rev. 601 (1990)

———, *Democracy: Popular Sovereignty and Judicial Review,* 88 Cal. L. Rev. 429 (1998)

———, *Equality and Autonomy in First Amendment Jurisprudence,* 95 Mich. L. Rev. 1517 (1997)

———, *Lani Guinier, Joseph Biden, and the Vocation of Legal Scholarship,* 11 Const. Commentary 185 (1994)

———, *Popular Sovereignty and Judicial Review,* 86 Cal. L. Rev. 429 (1998)

Potter, Beatrice, The Cooperative Movement in Great Britain (London, 1893)

Pound, Roscoe, Administrative Law (1942)

———, *Do We Need a Philosophy of Law?,* 18 Yale L. J. 454 (1905)

———, The Formative Era of American Law (1938)

———, *Liberty of Contract,* 18 Yale L. J. 454 (1909)

———, *The Need of a Sociological Jurisprudence,* 19 Green Bag 607 (1907)

Powell, H. Jefferson, *Joseph Story's Commentaries on the Constitution: A Belated Review,* 94 Yale L. J. 1285 (1985)

———, *Loyalty to the Law: Politics and the Practice of Public Lawyering in the United States,* 72 Notre Dame L. Rev. 78 (1996)

———, The Moral Tradition of American Constitutionalism (1993)

Powell, Thomas Reed, *The Judiciality of Minimum Wage Legislation,* 37 Harv. L. Rev. 545 (1924)

Priest, George L., *The Increasing Division Between Legal Practice and Legal Education,* 37 Buff. L. Rev. 681 (1988)

Proctor, Lucien Brock, The Bench and Bar of New York (1870)

Purcell, Edward A., *Ideas and Interests: Businessmen and the Interstate Commerce Act*, 54 J. Am. Hist. 561 (1967)

_____, *Learned Hand: The Jurisprudential Trajectory of an Old Progressive*, 43 Buff. L. Rev. 873 (1995)

_____, Litigation and Inequality: Federal Diversity Jurisdiction in Industrial America, 1870–1958 (1992)

Quayle, Dan, *Agenda for Civil Justice Reform in America*, 60 U. Cin. L. Rev. 979 (1992)

Rabban, David M., *Can Academic Freedom Survive Postmodernism?*, 86 Cal. L. Rev. 1377 (1998)

_____, The First Amendment in Its Forgotten Years (1997)

Rabin, Robert L., *Federal Regulation in Historical Perspective*, 38 Stan. L. Rev. 1189 (1986)

Ranpersad, Arnold, Jackie Robinson: A Biography (1997)

Rawls, John, Political Liberalism (1993)

Redfield, Isaac F., *Regulation of Interstate Traffic in Railways by Congress*, 27 Am. L. Reg. 11 (n. s. 1874)

Reed, Alfred Z., Training for the Public Profession of Law: Historical Developments and Principal Contemporary Problems of Legal Education in the United States with Some Account of Conditions in England and Canada (1921)

Reske, Henry J., *ABA Settles Antitrust Suit on Accreditation*, 81 A.B.A. J. 24 (1995)

Rezneck, Samuel, *The Social History of an American Depression, 1837–1843*, 40 Am. Hist. Rev. 662 (1935)

Rhode, Deborah, *Ethical Perspectives on Legal Practice*, 37 Stan. L. Rev. 589 (1985)

Richberg, Donald, *The Industrial Liberalism of Mr. Justice Brandeis*, in Mr. Justice Brandeis 137 (Felix Frankfurter, ed., 1932).

Rifkin, Lester Harvey, *William Leggett: Journalist-Philosopher of Agrarian Democracy in New York*, 32 N.Y. Hist. 45 (1951)

Ripley, William Z., Railroads: Rates and Regulation (1912)

Ritchie, Donald A., *James McCawley Landis*, Dictionary of American Biography, Supplement 7, 453 (John A. Garraty, ed., 1965)

Robinson, Lelia, *Women Lawyers in the United States*, 2 Green Bag 10 (1890)

Roe, Mark J., *Backlash*, 98 Colum. L. Rev. 217 (1998)

Rogat, Yosal, *The Judge as Spectator*, 31 U. Chi. L. Rev. 213 (1964).

Rogers, Henry Wade, *The Constitution and the New Federalism*, 188 N. Am. Rev. 321 (1908)

_____, *Thomas McIntyre Cooley*, in Distinguished American Lawyers 205 (Henry W. Scott, ed., New York, 1891)

_____, Unpublished biography of Thomas McIntyre Cooley in Rogers Papers, Bentley Library, University of Michigan

Rosenberg, Charles E., The Trial of Assassin Guiteau: Psychiatry and Law in the Gilded Age (1968)

Rosenberg, Gerald N., The Hollow Hope: Can Courts Bring About Social Change? (1991)

Ross, Dorothy, The Origins of American Social Science (1991)

Ross, William G., A Muted Fury: Populists, Progressives, and Labor Unions Confront the Courts, 1890–1937 (1994)

Rostow, W. W., Theorists of Economic Growth from David Hume to the Present with a Perspective on the Next Century (1990)

Rubin, Edward L., *Law and the Methodology of Law*, 1997 Wis. L. Rev. 521 (1997)

———, *The Practice and Discourse of Legal Scholarship*, 86 Mich. L. Rev. 1835 (1988)

Rubin, Edward L., and Malcolm Feeley, *Creating Legal Doctrine*, 69 S. Cal. L. Rev. 1989 (1996)

Russ, William Adam, The Hawaiian Republic (1894–1898) and Its Struggle to Win Annexation (1961)

Sandalow, Terrance, *The Limits of Municipal Powers Under Home Rule: A Role for The Courts*, 48 Minn. L. Rev. 643 (1964)

Sandel, Michael J., Democracy's Discontent: America in Search of a Public Philosophy (1996)

Sarat, Austin, and Stuart Scheingold, Cause Lawyering: Political Commitments and Professional Responsibilities (1998)

Saxton, Alexander, The Indispensable Enemy: Labor and the Anti-Chinese Movement in California (1971)

Sayre, Paul L., *A Common Law of Administrative Powers*, 18 Iowa L. Rev. 242 (1933)

Scalia, Antonin, *Common-Law Courts in a Civil Law System: The Role of the United States Federal Courts in Interpreting the Constitution and Laws,* in A Matter of Interpretation: Federal Courts and the Law (1997)

———, *Originalism: The Lesser Evil*, 57 U. Cin. L. Rev. 849 (1989)

Schaefer, Matthew, *State Investment Attraction Subsidy Wars Resulting from a Prisoner's Dilemma: The Inadequacy of State Constitutional Solutions and the Appropriateness of a Federal Legislative Response*, 28 N.M. L. Rev. 303 (1998)

Scheiber, Harry N., *Instrumentalism and Property Rights: A Reconsideration of American Styles of Judicial Reasoning the 19th Century*, 1975 Wis. L. Rev. 1

Schick, Marvin, Learned Hand's Court (1978)

Schiltz, Patrick J., *Legal Ethics in Decline: The Elite Law Firm, the Elite Law School, and the Moral Formation of the Novice Attorney*, 82 Minn. L. Rev. 705 (1998)

Schlag, Pierre, *Normativity and Nowhere to Go*, 43 Stan. L. Rev. 167 (1990)

Schlegel, John Henry, *Langdell's Legacy or the Case of the Empty Envelope*, 36 Stan. L. Rev. 1517 (1984)

Schlesinger, Arthur, The Age of Jackson (1945)

Schmalbeck, Richard M., *The Justice of Economics: An Analysis of Wealth Maximization as a Normative Goal*, 83 Colum. L. Rev. 488 (1983)

Schoenberger, H. W., *Henry Philip Tappan*, 9 Dictionary of American Biography 302 (Dumas Malone, ed., 1935)

Scott, Daryl Michael, Contempt and Pity: Social Policy and the Image of the Damaged Black Psyche, 1880–1996 (1997)

Seagle, William, The Quest for Law (1946)

Searle, John R., The Construction of Social Reality (1995)

Sedgwick, Theodore, Jr., Public and Private Economy (3 vols., New York, 1836–1839)

_____, A Collection of Political Writings of William Leggett (New York, 1840)

Sedgwick, Theodore, III, A Treatise on the Rules Which Govern the Interpretation and Application of Statutory and Constitutional Law (New York, 1857)

Seligman, Joel, The High Citadel: The Influence of the Harvard Law School (1978)

Selinger, Carl M., *The Public's Interest in Preserving the Dignity and Unity of the Legal Profession*, 32 Wake Forest L. Rev. 861 (1997)

Sennett, Richard, The Corrosion of Character: The Personal Consequences of Work in the New Capitalism (1998)

_____, The Fall of Public Man (1972)

Shamir, Ronen, Managing Legal Uncertainty: Elite Lawyers in the New Deal (1995)

Sharfman, I. L., The Interstate Commerce Commission: A Study in Administrative Law and Procedure (4 vols., 1931)

Shepard, E. Lee, *George Wythe,* in Legal Education in Virginia 1779–1979 (W. Hamilton Bryson, ed., 1982)

Shepard, Randall T., *The Maturing Nature of State Constitutional Jurisprudence,* 30 Val. U. L. Rev. 421 (1996)

Sheppard, Steve, *Casebooks, Commentaries, and Curmudgeons: An Introductory History of Law in the Lecture Hall,* 82 Iowa L. Rev. 547 (1997)

Sherry, Suzanna, *Progressive Regression,* 47 Stan. L. Rev. 1097 (1995)

Shklar, Judith, Ordinary Vices (1984)

Siegel, Martin, The Taney Court, 1837–1864 (1987)

Siegel, Stephen A., *Historicism in Late Nineteenth Century Constitutional Thought,* 1990 Wis. L. Rev. 1431

Simpson, A. W. B., *The Rise and Fall of the Legal Treatise: Legal Principles and the Forms of Legal Literature,* 48 U. Chi. L. Rev. 632 (1981)

Singer, Joseph William, *The Player and the Cards: Nihilism and Legal Theory,* 94 Yale L. J. 1 (1984)

Sirico, Louis J., and Jeffrey B. Margulies, *The Citing of Law Reviews by the Supreme Court: An Empirical Study,* 34 UCLA L. Rev. 131 (1986)

Skillman, David B., The Biography of a College: Being The History of the First Century of the Life of Lafayette College (1932).

Smith, Adam, An Inquiry into the Nature and Causes of the Wealth of Nations (Edinburgh, 1776)

Smith, Carl, Urban Disorder and the Shape of Belief: The Great Chicago Fire, the Haymarket Bomb, and the Model Town of Pullman (1995)

Smith, Christopher E., Courts, Politics and the Judicial Process (1992)

Smith, J. Clay, Emancipation: The Making of the Black Lawyer (1993)

_____, *In Freedom's Birthplace: The Making of George Lewis Ruffin, The First Black Graduate of Harvard University,* 39 How. L. J. 201 (1996)

Smith, James M., Freedom's Fetters: The Alien and Sedition Laws and American Civil Liberties (1956)

Smith, Jean Edward, John Marshall: Definer of A Nation (1996)

Smith, Reginald Heber, Growth of Legal Aid Work in the United States: A Study of Our Administration of Justice Primarily As It Affects the Wage Earner (1936)

_____, Justice and the Poor: A Study of the Present Denial of Justice to the Poor and the Agencies Making More Equal Their Protection Before the Law (1919)

Smolla, Rodney A., Suing the Press (1986)

Spann, Girardeau A., Race Against the Court: The Supreme Court and Minorities in Contemporary America (1993)

Spencer, Herbert, Social Statics (London, 1892)

_____, Study of Sociology (London, 1870)

Starkman, Dean, *Ohio Effort to Cap Election Spending in Judicial Races Triggers Challenge,* Wall St. J., May 27, 1997

Starr, Harris Elwood, *Charles Grandison Finney,* 3 Dictionary of American Biography 394 (Allen Johnson and Dumas Malone, eds., 1935)

_____, William Graham Sumner (1925)

Starr, Paul, The Social Transformation of American Medicine: The Rise of a Sovereign Profession and the Making of a Vast Industry (1982)

Steffens, Joseph Lincoln, The Shame of the Cities (1904)

Steiker, Carol S., and Jordan M. Steiker, *Sober Second Thoughts: Reflection on Two Decades of Constitutional Regulation of Capital Punishment,* 109 Harv. L. Rev. 355 (1995)

Stevens, John Austin, Albert Gallatin (Boston, 1899)

Stevens, John Paul, *Reflections on the Removal of Sitting Judges,* 13 Stetson L. Rev. 215 (1984)

Stevens, Robert B., The Independence of the Judiciary: The View from the Lord Chancellor's Office (1993)

_____, Law School: Legal Education in America from the 1850s to the 1980s (1982)

Stick, John, *Can Nihilism Be Pragmatic?,* 100 Harv. L. Rev. 332 (1986)

Stolz, Preble, Judging Judges (1981)

Stone, Alan A., *Legal Education on the Couch,* 85 Harv. L. Rev. 392 (1971)

Stone, Irving, Clarence Darrow for the Defense (1977)

Stone, Richard D., The Interstate Commerce Commission and the Railroad Industry: A History of Regulatory Policy (1991)

Storr, Richard J., Harper's University: The Beginnings, a History of the University of Chicago (1966)

Story, Joseph, Commentaries on the Constitution of the United States (Boston, 1833)

_____, Commentaries on the Constitution of the United States (4th ed., T. Cooley, ed., Boston, 1872)

Strauss, David A., *Common Law Constitutional Interpretation,* 63 U. Chi. L. Rev. 877 (1996)

Strauss, Peter L., *One Hundred and Fifty Cases per Year: Some Implications of the Supreme Court's Limited Resources for Judicial Review of Agency Action,* 87 Colum. L. Rev. 1093 (1987)

Strong, Frank R., Judicial Function in Constitutional Limitation of Governmental Power (1997)

Strong, Theron, Landmarks of a Lawyer's Lifetime (1914)

Strum, Philippa, Brandeis: Beyond Progressivism (1993)

_____, Louis D. Brandeis: Justice for the People (1994)

Stumpf, Harry, and John Culver, The Politics of State Courts (1992)

Subrin, Stephen N., *How Equity Conquered Common Law: The Federal Rules of Civil Procedure in Historical Perspective*, 135 U. Pa. L. Rev. 409 (1987)

Sullivan, Kathleen M., *Epistemic Democracy and Minority Rights*, 86 Cal. L. Rev. 445 (1998)

Sumner, William Graham, Folkways: A Study of the Sociological Importance of Usages (1906)

_____, What Social Classes Owe to Each Other (1920).

Sunstein, Cass R., Free Markets and Social Justice (1997)

_____, *In Defense of Liberal Education*, 43 J. Leg. Educ. 22 (1993)

_____, Legal Reasoning and Political Conflict (1996)

_____, *Lochner's Legacy*, 87 Colum. L. Rev. 873 (1987)

_____, *The Right to Die*, 106 Yale L.J. 1123 (1997)

Sutherland, Arthur E., The Law at Harvard: A History of Ideas and Men 1817–1967 (1967)

Swisher, Carl Brent, Stephen J. Field, Craftsman of the Law (1930)

Syed, Anwar, The Political Theory of American Local Government (1966)

Tarr, G. Alan, *Robinson v. Cahill and the New Judicial Federalism*, 59 Alb. L. Rev. 1753 (1996)

Tarr,G. Alan, and Robert F. Williams, *Foreword: Western State Constitutions in the American Constitutional Tradition*, 28 N.M. L. Rev. 191 (1998)

Tate, Merze, The United States and the Hawaiian Kingdom (1965)

Taylor, Clifford, *Who Is In Charge Here? Some Thoughts on Judicial Review*, Mich. B. J. 32 (January 1998)

Taylor, George Rogers, The Transportation Revolution (1951)

ten Broek, Jacobus, Equal under Law (1965)

Thayer, James Bradley, *The Case of Gelpcke v. Dubuque*, 4 Harv. L. Rev. 311 (1891)

_____, *The Origin and Scope of the American Doctrine of Constitutional Law*, 7 Harv. L. Rev. 179 (1893)

_____, Our New Possessions, 12 Harv. L. Rev. 464 (1899)

Thomas, John L., The Liberator: William Lloyd Garrison, a Biography (1963)

Thompson, Robert S., *Judicial Independence, Judicial Accountability, Judicial Elections and the California Supreme Court: Defining the Terms of the Debate*, 59 S. Cal. L. Rev. 809 (1986)

Thucydides, A History of the Peloponnesian War (circa 400 B.C.) (P. J. Rhodes, trans., 1994)

Thurman, Edward, Charles Washburne, and Thomas Cooley, Constituting an Advisory Commission, Report on Differential Rates by Railroads Between the West and the Seaboard (New York, 1882)

Tiedeman, Christopher, A Treatise on the Limitations of Police Power in the United States (St. Louis, 1886)

Todd, A. L., Justice on Trial: The Case of Louis D. Brandeis (1964)

Toland, John, The Rising Sun: The Rise and Fall of the Japanese Empire (1970)

Tompkins, Leslie Jay, New York University Law School, Past and Present (1904)

Touster, Saul, *Holmes a Hundred Years Ago: The Common Law and Legal Theory*, 10 Hofstra L. Rev. 673 (1982)

Tribe, Laurence H., American Constitutional Law (2d ed., 1988)

Trubek, David M., and Marc Galanter, *Scholars in Self-Estrangement: Some Reflections on the Crisis in Law and Development Studies in the United States,* 1974 Wis. L. Rev. 1062

Tucker, John Randolph, *The History of the Federal Convention of 1787 and Its Work: An Address Delivered Before the Graduating Class on the Sixty Third Anniversary of the Yale Law School, June 28th, 1887* (New Haven , 1887)

Turkington, Richard C., *Constitutional Limitations on Tort Reform: Have the State Courts Placed Insurmountable Obstacles in the Path of Legislative Responses to the Perceived Liability Insurance Crisis?,* 32 Vill. L. Rev. 1299 (1987)

Tushnet, Mark, *Byron White: The Football Player as Supreme Court Justice,* 1 Green Bag 2d 418 (1998)

_____, *The Logic of Experience: Oliver Wendell Holmes on the Supreme Judicial Court,* 63 Va. L. Rev. 975 (1977)

_____, Making Civil Rights Law: Thurgood Marshall and the Supreme Court, 1936–1961 (1994)

_____, *Thayer's Target: Judicial Review or Democracy?,* 88 Nw. U. L. Rev. 9 (1993)

Twain, Mark, Life on the Mississippi (Heritage Press ed., 1944)

Twardy, Stewart A., Jr., *Justice Roger J. Traynor and the Development of Strict Liability in Products Liability Cases,* 53 Conn. Bus. J. 423 (1979)

Twining, William, Karl Llewellyn and the Realist Movement (1973)

Twiss, Benjamin, Lawyers and the Constitution: How Laissez-Faire Came to the Constitution (1942)

Tyack, David B., The One Best System: A History of Urban Education (1978)

Uelmen, Gerald F., *Review of Death Penalty Judgments by the Supreme Court of California: A Tale of Two Courts,* 23 Loy. L.A. L. Rev. 287 (1989)

Underkuffler-Freund, Laura, *The Perfidy of Property,* 70 Tex. L. Rev. 293 (1995)

Unger, Roberto, The Critical Legal Studies Movement (1986)

Urofsky, Melvin I., Felix Frankfurter: Judicial Restraint and Individual Liberties (1991)

_____, Louis D. Brandeis and the Progressive Tradition (1981)

_____, A Mind of One Piece: Brandeis and American Reform (1971)

_____, *Myth and Reality: The Supreme Court and Protective Legislation in the Progressive Era,* Y.B. of Supreme Court Hist. Soc'y 53 (1983)

VanAlstyne, William W., *Closing the Circle of Constitutional Review from Griswold v. Connecticut to Roe v. Wade: An Outline of a Decision Merely Overruling Roe,* 1989 Duke L. J. 1677 (1990)

Van Cleave, Rachel, *State Constitutional Interpretation and Methodology,* 28 N.M. L. Rev. 197 (1998)

Vander Velde, Lewis G., *Thomas McIntyre Cooley,* 15 ICC Prac. J. 857 (1948)

_____, *Thomas McIntyre Cooley,* in Michigan and the Cleveland Era 77 (E. Babst and L. Vander Velde, eds., 1948)

Van Dyk, Robert, *The Pro-Choice Mobilization and Decline of Clinic Blockades,* in Leveraging the Law: Using the Courts to Achieve Social Change 135 (David A. Schultz, ed., 1998)

Vernon, David H., *Educational Debt Burden: Law School Assistance Programs—A Review of Existing Programs and A Proposed Approach*, 39 J. Leg. Educ. 743 (1989)

Veysey, Laurence R., The Emergence of the American University (1965)

Viner, Jacob, *Adam Smith*, 14 International Encyclopedia of the Social Sciences 322 (David L. Sills, ed., 1968)

Viscusi, W. Kip, *Constructive Cigarette Regulation*, 47 Duke L. J. 1095 (1998)

Walker, Albert H., History of the Sherman Law of the United States of America (1910)

Walker, Timothy, Introduction to American Law (Boston, 1837)

Walters, Ronald, The Antislavery Appeal: American Abolitionism after 1830 (1976)

Ward, Kenneth D., *Free Speech and the Development of Liberal Virtues: An Examination of the Controversies Involving Flag-Burning and Hate Speech*, 52 U. Miami L. Rev. 733 (1998)

Warren, Charles, History of the Harvard Law School and of Early Legal Conditions in America (2 vols., 1908)

_____, The History of the Supreme Court (New York, 1928)

Washington, George, *Farewell Address of 1796*, in 12 The Writings of George Washington (Worthington Chauncey Ford, ed., 1892)

Watson, Andrew S., *The Quest for Professional Competence: Psychological Aspects of Legal Education*, 37 U. Cin. L. Rev. 93 (1968)

Webster, Daniel, The Works of Daniel Webster (6 vols., Boston, 1854)

_____, The Writings and Speeches of Daniel Webster (18 vols., James W. McIntyre, ed., 1903)

Weir, Robert E., Beyond Labor's Veil: The Culture of the Knights of Labor (1996)

Welke, Barbara Young, "All the Women are White; All the Blacks Are Men," Or Are They?: Law and Segregation on Common Carriers, 1855 to 1914 (1992)

Wellington, Harry H., Labor and the Legal Process (1968)

West, Robin, Progressive Constitutionalism: Reconstructing the Fourteenth Amendment (1994)

Wharton, Francis, Commentaries on Law Embracing Chapters on the Nature, the Sources, and the History of Law, On International Law, Public and Private, and on Constitutional and Statutory Law (Philadelphia, 1884)

White, Byron R., *Mr. Justice White Recalls to Students the Deftness of a Master Surgeon*, 18 U. Miami L. Rev. 1 (1963).

White, G. Edward, The American Legal Tradition: Profiles of Leading American Judges (1976)

_____, *The Canonization of Holmes and Brandeis: Epistemology and Judicial Reputations*, 70 N.Y.U. L. Rev. 576 (1995)

_____, Earl Warren: A Public Life (1982)

_____, Justice Oliver Wendell Holmes: Law and the Inner Self (1993)

_____, The Marshall Court and Cultural Change (1988)

_____, *Revisiting James Bradley Thayer*, 88 Nw. U. L. Rev 48 (1993)

White, James P., *The Impact of Law Student Debt Upon the Legal Profession*, 39 J. Leg. Educ. 923 (1989)

Whittington, Keith E., *Reconstructing the Federal Judiciary*, 9 Stud. Am. Pol. Dev. (1995)

Wiebe, Robert H., The Search for Order, 1877–1920 (1967)

———, Self-Rule: A Cultural History of American Democracy (1995)

Wiecek, William M., The Lost World of Classical Legal Thought: Law and Ideology in America, 1886–1937 (1998)

Wiggins, Jennifer, *Maine's Act to Protect Traditional Marriage and Prohibit Same-Sex Marriages: Questions of Constitutionality Under State and Federal Law*, 50 Me. L. Rev. 347 (1998)

Wilkins, David B., *Should a Black Lawyer Represent the Ku Klux Klan?*, 63 Geo. Wash. U. L. Rev. 1030 (1995)

Wilkinson, J. Harvie, III, From Brown to Bakke: The Supreme Court and School Integration, 1954–1978 (1979)

Williams, David R., Wilderness Lost: New England in the Jaws of an Angry God (1982)

Williams, Joan C., *The Constitutional Vulnerability of American Local Government: The Politics of City Status in American Law*, 1986 Wis. L. Rev. 83

Williams, Stephen F., *Book Review: Public Choice Theory and the Judiciary*, 73 N.D. L. Rev. 1599 (1998)

Williston, Samuel, *Joseph Henry Beale: A Biographical Sketch*, 56 Harv. L. Rev. 686 (1943)

———, Life and Law (1940)

Wilson, Woodrow, Mere Literature and Other Essays (Princeton, 1896)

Winters, Glenn R., *Selection of Judges—An Historical Introduction*, 44 Tex. L. Rev. 1081 (1966)

Wise, Edward M., *"The Ablest State Court": The Michigan Supreme Court Before 1885*, 33 Wayne L. Rev. 1509 (1987)

Wolfram, Charles W., *The Constitutional History of the Seventh Amendment*, 57 Minn. L. Rev. 639 (1973)

Woodburn, James Albert, History of Indiana University, 1820–1902 (1940)

Woodward, Frederic, *Ernst Freund*, 19 U. Rec. 143 (1932)

Woodward, Robert, and Scott Armstrong, The Brethren (1979)

Wright, Charles Alan, Federal Courts (5th ed., 1993)

Wyman, Bruce, The Principles of the Administrative Law Governing the Relations of Public Officers (1903)

Yarbrough, Tinsley, Mr. Justice Black and His Critics (1988)

Yeazell, Stephen C., *The Misunderstood Consequences of Modern Civil Process*, 1994 Wis. L. Rev. 631

Unauthored Works Listed by Title

"America's Third Party": A Study of Political Contributions by The Plaintiff's Lawyer Industry (American Tort Reform Association, 1994)

Anarchy as an End: Lives, Trial and Convictions of the Chicago Eight (Chicago, 1886)

Book Note, 14 Am. L. Rev. 233 (1880)

Book Note, 27 Alb. L. Rev. 300 (1883)

Book Notice, 3 Am. L. Rev. 141 (1868)

Book Notice, 3 Am. L. Rev. 757 (1869)

Book Notice, 6 Am. L. Rev. 354 (1872)

Book Notice, 6 Am. L. Rev. 558 (1872)

Book Notices, 14 Am. L. Rev. 14 (1880)

The Book of The States (The Council of State Governments, 1996)

Book Review, Michigan Reports, 4 S. L. Rev. 872 (1878)

The Burger Court: The Counter-Revolution That Wasn't (Vincent Blasi, ed., 1983)

Chambers's Information for the People: A Popular Encyclopedia (2 vols., Philadelphia, 1841).

Compilation of the Messages and Papers of the Presidents (J. D. Richardson, comp., 1908)

The Constitutions of the Countries of the World (Albert P. Blaustein and Gisbert H. Flanz. eds., 1997)

Created Equal? The Complete Lincoln-Douglas Debates of 1858 (Paul M. Angle, ed., 1958)

Death Row USA Reporter (NAACP Legal Defense and Education Fund, 1994)

Documentary History of Hamilton College (1922)

George Washington Rides Again, The Economist 18 (November 21, 1998)

Free Legal Services for the Poor (Comptroller General of the United States, 1978)

An Independent Judiciary: Report of the Commission on Separation of Powers and Judicial Independence, American Bar Association (1997)

Interstate Commerce Commission Annual Reports (1888–1891)

John Marshall's Defense of McCulloch v. Maryland (Gerald Gunther, ed., 1969)

Judicial Review and the Supreme Court (Leonard W. Levy, ed., 1967)

John Chipman Gray (R. Gray, ed., 1917)

Mr. Justice Brandeis (Felix Frankfurter, ed., 1932)

Mr. Justice Cooley, 32 Am. L. Rev. 916 (1898)

Legal Education and Professional Development—An Educational Continuum, Report of the Task Force on Law Schools and the Profession: Narrowing the Gap (American Bar Association Section on Legal Education and Admissions to the Bar, 1992)

Limits of Justice: The Courts' Role in School Desegregation (Howard I. Kalodner and James J. Fishman, eds., 1978)

Note, 2 Michigan Alumnus 7 (1895)

Note, 7 Am. L. Rev. 126 (1870)

Note, 22 Am. L. Rev. 477 (1888)

Note, *Cooley's Constitutional Law,* 21 Alb. L. J. 328 (1881)

Note, *Unfulfilled Promises: School Finance Remedies and State Courts,* 104 Harv. L. Rev. 1072 (1991)

A Record of Commemoration, November 5 to November 9, 1886, On the Two Hundred Fiftieth Anniversary of Harvard College (Cambridge, 1887)

Report of the Pennsylvania Special Commission to Limit Campaign Expenditures (1998)

Report of the President's Commission on Competitiveness (1992)

Report of the Special Committee on the Establishment of a Department of Law, Cornell University (1886)

The Responsible Judge: Readings in Judicial Ethics (John T. Noonan and Kenneth L. Winston, eds., 1993)

Speeches of Charles Sumner (Edward L. Pierce, ed., 1877)

Symposium: Milliken v. Bradley and the Future of Urban School Desegregation, 21 Wayne L. Rev. 751 (1975)

Symposium: National Power and State Autonomy: Calibrating the New "New Federalism," 32 Ind. L. Rev. 1 (Cynthia A. Baker and Jonathan D. Mattingly, eds, 1998)

Symposium, The Path of the Law After One Hundred Years, 110 Harv. L. Rev. 989 (1997)

When Lawsuits Make Policy, The Economist 17 (November 21, 1998)

Index

DATE DUE

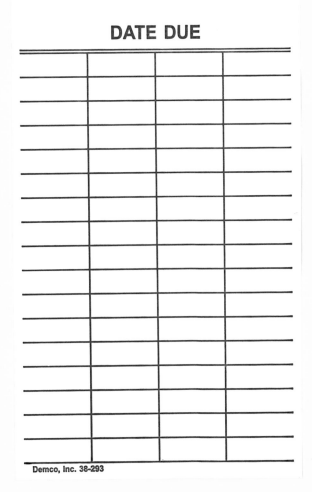

Demco, Inc. 38-293